Andersonville, A Story of Rebel Military Prisons
BY
John McElroy

INTRODUCTION.

The fifth part of a century almost has sped with the flight of time since the outbreak of the Slaveholder's Rebellion against the United States. The young men of to-day were then babes in their cradles, or, if more than that, too young to be appalled by the terror of the times. Those now graduating from our schools of learning to be teachers of youth and leaders of public thought, if they are ever prepared to teach the history of the war for the Union so as to render adequate honor to its martyrs and heroes, and at the same time impress the obvious moral to be drawn from it, must derive their knowledge from authors who can each one say of the thrilling story he is spared to tell: "All of which I saw, and part of which I was."

The writer is honored with the privilege of introducing to the reader a volume written by an author who was an actor and a sufferer in the scenes he has so vividly and faithfully described, and sent forth to the public by a publisher whose literary contributions in support of the loyal cause entitle him to the highest appreciation. Both author and publisher have had an honorable and efficient part in the great struggle, and are therefore worthy to hand down to the future a record of the perils encountered and the sufferings endured by patriotic soldiers in the prisons of the enemy. The publisher, at the beginning of the war, entered, with zeal and ardor upon the work of raising a company of men, intending to lead them to the field. Prevented from carrying out this design, his energies were directed to a more effective service. His famous "Nasby Letters" exposed the absurd and sophistical argumentations of rebels and their sympathisers, in such broad, attractive and admirable burlesque, as to direct against them the "loud, long laughter of a world!" The unique and telling satire of these papers became a power and inspiration to our armies in the field and to their anxious friends at home, more than equal to the might of whole battalions poured in upon the enemy. An athlete in logic may lay an error writhing at his feet, and after all it may recover to do great mischief. But the sharp wit of the humorist drives it before the world's derision into shame and everlasting contempt. These letters were read and shouted over gleefully at every camp-fire in the Union Army, and eagerly devoured by crowds of listeners when mails were opened at country post-offices. Other humorists were content when they simply amused the reader, but "Nasby's" jests were argumentsthey had a meaning—they were suggested by the necessities and emergencies of the Nation's peril, and written to support, with all earnestness, a most sacred cause.

The author, when very young, engaged in journalistic work, until the drum of the recruiting officer called him to join the ranks of his country's defenders. As the reader is told, he was made a prisoner. He took with him into the terrible prison enclosure not only a brave, vigorous, youthful spirit, but invaluable habits of mind and thought for storing up the incidents and experiences of his prison life. As a journalist he had acquired the habit of noticing and memorizing every striking or thrilling incident, and the experiences of his prison life were adapted to enstamp themselves indelibly on both feeling and memory. He speaks from personal experience and from the stand-paint of tender and complete sympathy with those of his comrades who suffered more than he did himself. Of his qualifications, the writer of these introductory words need not speak. The sketches themselves testify to his ability with such force that no commendation is required.

This work is needed. A generation is arising who do not know what the preservation of our free government cost in blood and suffering. Even the men of the passing generation begin to be forgetful, if we may judge from the recklessness or carelessness of their political action. The soldier is not always remembered nor honored as he should be. But, what to the future of the great Republic is more important, there is great danger of our people under-estimating the bitter animus and terrible malignity to the Union and its defenders cherished by those who made war upon it. This is a point we can not afford to be mistaken about. And yet, right at this point this volume will meet its severest criticism, and at this point its testimony is most vital and necessary. Many will be slow to believe all that is here told most truthfully of the tyranny and cruelty of the captors of our brave boys in blue. There are no parallels to the cruelties and malignities here described in Northern society. The system of slavery, maintained for over two hundred years at the South, had performed a most perverting, morally desolating, and we might say, demonizing work on the dominant race, which people bred under our free civilization can not at once understand, nor scarcely believe when it is declared unto them. This reluctance to believe unwelcome truths has been the snare of our national life. We have not been willing to believe how hardened, despotic, and cruel the wielders of irresponsible power may become.

When the anti-slavery reformers of thirty years ago set forth the cruelties of the slave system, they were met with a storm of indignant denial, villification and rebuke. When Theodore D. Weld issued his "Testimony of a Thousand Witnesses," to the cruelty of slavery, he introduced it with a few words, pregnant with sound philosophy, which can be applied to the work now introduced, and may help the reader better to accept and appreciate its statements. Mr. Weld said: "Suppose I should seize you, rob you of your liberty, drive you into the field, and make you work without pay as long as you lived. Would that be justice? Would it be kindness? Or would it be monstrous injustice and cruelty? Now, is the man who robs you every day too tender-hearted ever to cuff or kick you? He can empty your pockets without remorse, but if your stomach is empty, it cuts him to the quick. He can make you work a life-time without pay, but loves you too well to let you go hungry. He fleeces you of your rights with a relish, but is shocked if you work bare-headed in summer, or without warm stockings in winter. He can make you go without your liberty, but never without a shirt. He can crush in you all hope of bettering your condition by vowing that you shall die his slave, but though he can thus cruelly torture your feelings, he will never lacerate your back—he can break your heart, but is very tender of your skin. He can strip you of all protection of law, and all comfort in religion, and thus expose you to all outrages, but if you are exposed to the weather, half-clad and half-sheltered, how yearn his tender bowels! What! talk of a man treating you well while robbing you of all you get, and as fast as you get it? And robbing you of yourself, too, your hands and feet, your muscles, limbs and senses, your body and mind, your liberty and earnings, your free speech and rights of conscience, your right to acquire knowledge, property and reputation, and yet you are content to believe without question that men who do all this by their slaves have soft hearts oozing out so lovingly toward their human chattles that they always keep them well housed and well clad, never push them too hard in the field, never make their dear backs smart, nor let their dear stomachs get empty!"

In like manner we may ask, are not the cruelties and oppressions described in the following pages what we should legitimately expect from men who, all their lives, have used whip and thumb-screw, shot-gun and bloodhound, to keep human beings subservient to their will? Are we to expect nothing but chivalric tenderness and compassion from men who made war on a tolerant government to make more secure their barbaric system of oppression?

These things are written because they are true. Duty to the brave dead, to the heroic living, who have endured the pangs of a hundred deaths for their country's sake; duty to the government which depends on the wisdom and constancy of its good citizens for its support and perpetuity, calls for this "round, unvarnished tale" of suffering endured for freedom's sake.

The publisher of this work urged his friend and associate in journalism to write and send forth these sketches because the times demanded just such an expose of the inner hell of the Southern prisons. The tender mercies of oppressors are cruel. We must accept the truth and act in view of it. Acting wisely on the warnings of the past, we shall be able to prevent treason, with all its fearful concomitants, from being again the scourge and terror of our beloved land.

ROBERT McCUNE.

AUTHOR'S PREFACE

Fifteen months ago—and one month before it was begun—I had no more idea of writing this book than I have now of taking up my residence in China.

While I have always been deeply impressed with the idea that the public should know much more of the history of Andersonville and other Southern prisons than it does, it had never occurred to me that I was in any way charged with the duty of increasing that enlightenment. No affected deprecation of my own abilities had any part is this. I certainly knew enough of the matter, as did every other boy who had even a month's experience in those terrible places, but the very magnitude of that knowledge overpowered me, by showing me the vast requirements of the subject-requirements that seemed to make it presumption for any but the greatest pens in our literature to attempt the work. One day at Andersonville or Florence would be task enough for the genius of Carlyle or Hugo; lesser than they would fail preposterously to rise to the level of the theme. No writer ever described such a deluge of woes as swept over the unfortunates confined in Rebel prisons in the last year-and-a-half of the Confederacy's life. No man was ever called upon to describe the spectacle and the process of seventy thousand young, strong, able-bodied men, starving and rotting to death. Such a gigantic tragedy as this stuns the mind and benumbs the imagination.

I no more felt myself competent to the task than to accomplish one of Michael Angelo's grand creations in sculpture or painting.

Study of the subject since confirms me in this view, and my only claim for this book is that it is a contribution—a record of individual observation and experience—which will add something to the material which the historian of the future will find available for his work.

The work was begun at the suggestion of Mr. D. R. Locke, (Petroleum V. Nasby), the eminent political satirist. At first it was only intended to write a few short serial sketches of prison life for the columns of the TOLEDO BLADE. The exceeding favor with which the first of the series was received induced a great widening of their scope, until finally they took the range they now have.

I know that what is contained herein will be bitterly denied. I am prepared for this. In my boyhood I witnessed the savagery of the Slavery agitation—in my youth I felt the fierceness of the hatred directed against all those who stood by the Nation. I know that hell hath no fury like the vindictiveness of those who are hurt by the truth being told of them. I apprehend being assailed by a sirocco of contradiction and calumny. But I solemnly affirm in advance the entire and absolute truth of every material fact, statement and description. I assert that, so far from there being any exaggeration in any particular, that in no instance has the half of the truth been told, nor could it be, save by an inspired pen. I am ready to demonstrate this by any test that the deniers of this may require, and I am fortified in my position by unsolicited letters from over

3,000 surviving prisoners, warmly indorsing the account as thoroughly accurate in every respect. It has been charged that hatred of the South is the animus of this work. Nothing can be farther from the truth. No one has a deeper love for every part of our common country than I, and no one to-day will make more efforts and sacrifices to bring the South to the same plane of social and material development with the rest of the Nation than I will. If I could see that the sufferings at Andersonville and elsewhere contributed in any considerable degree to that end, and I should not regret that they had been. Blood and tears mark every step in the progress of the race, and human misery seems unavoidable in securing human advancement. But I am naturally embittered by the fruitlessness, as well as the uselessness of the misery of Andersonville. There was never the least military or other reason for inflicting all that wretchedness upon men, and, as far as mortal eye can discern, no earthly good resulted from the martyrdom of those tens of thousands. I wish I could see some hope that their wantonly shed blood has sown seeds that will one day blossom, and bear a rich fruitage of benefit to mankind, but it saddens me beyond expression that I can not.

The years 1864-5 were a season of desperate battles, but in that time many more Union soldiers were slain behind the Rebel armies, by starvation and exposure, than were killed in front of them by cannon and rifle. The country has heard much of the heroism and sacrifices of those loyal youths who fell on the field of battle; but it has heard little of the still greater number who died in prison pen. It knows full well how grandly her sons met death in front of the serried ranks of treason, and but little of the sublime firmness with which they endured unto the death, all that the ingenious cruelty of their foes could inflict upon them while in captivity.

It is to help supply this deficiency that this book is written. It is a mite contributed to the better remembrance by their countrymen of those who in this way endured and died that the Nation might live. It is an offering of testimony to future generations of the measureless cost of the expiation of a national sin, and of the preservation of our national unity.

This is all. I know I speak for all those still living comrades who went with me through the scenes that I have attempted to describe, when I say that we have no revenges to satisfy, no hatreds to appease. We do not ask that anyone shall be punished. We only desire that the Nation shall recognize and remember the grand fidelity of our dead comrades, and take abundant care that they shall not have died in vain.

For the great mass of Southern people we have only the kindliest feeling. We but hate a vicious social system, the lingering shadow of a darker age, to which they yield, and which, by elevating bad men to power, has proved their own and their country's bane.

The following story does not claim to be in any sense a history of Southern prisons. It is simply a record of the experience of one individual—one boy—who staid all the time with his comrades inside the prison, and had no better opportunities for gaining information than any other of his 60,000 companions.

The majority of the illustrations in this work are from the skilled pencil of Captain O. J. Hopkins, of Toledo, who served through the war in the ranks of the Forty-second Ohio. His army experience has been of peculiar value to the work, as it has enabled him to furnish a series of illustrations whose life-like fidelity of action, pose and detail are admirable.

Some thirty of the pictures, including the frontispiece, and the allegorical illustrations of War and Peace, are from the atelier of Mr. O. Reich, Cincinnati, O.

A word as to the spelling: Having always been an ardent believer in the reformation of our present preposterous system—or rather, no system—of orthography, I am anxious to do whatever lies in my power to promote it. In the following pages the spelling is simplified to the last degree allowed by Webster. I hope that the time is near when even that advanced spelling reformer will be left far in the rear by the progress of a people thoroughly weary of longer slavery to the orthographical absurdities handed down to us from a remote and grossly unlearned ancestry.

Toledo, O., Dec. 10, 1879.

JOHN McELROY.

We wait beneath the furnace blast
The pangs of transformation;
Not painlessly doth God recast
And mold anew the nation.
Hot burns the fire
Where wrongs expire;
Nor spares the hand
That from the land
Uproots the ancient evil.
The hand-breadth cloud the sages feared
Its bloody rain is dropping;
The poison plant the fathers spared
All else is overtopping.
East, West, South, North,
It curses the earth;
All justice dies,
And fraud and lies
Live only in its shadow.
Then let the selfish lip be dumb
And hushed the breath of sighing;
Before the joy of peace must come
The pains of purifying.
God give us grace
Each in his place
To bear his lot,
And, murmuring not,
Endure and wait and labor!
   WHITTIER

ANDERSONVILLE.A STORY OF REBEL MILITARY PRISONS

CHAPTER I.

A STRANGE LAND—THE HEART OF THE APPALACHIANS—THE GATEWAY OF AN EMPIRE —A SEQUESTERED VALE, AND A PRIMITIVE, ARCADIAN, NON-PROGRESSIVE PEOPLE.

A low, square, plainly-hewn stone, set near the summit of the eastern approach to the formidable natural fortress of Cumberland Gap, indicates the boundaries of—the three great States of Virginia, Kentucky and Tennessee. It is such a place as, remembering the old Greek and Roman myths and superstitions, one would recognize as fitting to mark the confines of the territories of great masses of strong, aggressive, and frequently conflicting peoples. There the god Terminus should have had one of his chief temples, where his shrine would be shadowed by barriers rising above the clouds, and his sacred solitude guarded from the rude invasion of armed hosts by range on range of battlemented rocks, crowning almost inaccessible mountains, interposed across every approach from the usual haunts of men.

Roundabout the land is full of strangeness and mystery. The throes of some great convulsion of Nature are written on the face of the four thousand square miles of territory, of which Cumberland Gap is the central point. Miles of granite mountains are thrust up like giant walls, hundreds of feet high, and as smooth and regular as the side of a monument.

Huge, fantastically-shaped rocks abound everywhere—sometimes rising into pinnacles on lofty summits—sometimes hanging over the verge of beetling cliffs, as if placed there in waiting for a time when they could be hurled down upon the path of an advancing army, and sweep it away. Large streams of water burst out in the most unexpected planes, frequently far up mountain sides, and fall in silver veils upon stones beaten round by the ceaseless dash for ages. Caves, rich in quaintly formed stalactites and stalagmites, and their recesses filled with metallic salts of the most powerful and diverse natures; break the mountain sides at frequent intervals. Everywhere one is met by surprises and anomalies. Even the rank vegetation is eccentric, and as prone to develop into bizarre forms as are the rocks and mountains.

The dreaded panther ranges through the primeval, rarely trodden forests; every crevice in the rocks has for tenants rattlesnakes or stealthy copperheads, while long, wonderfully swift "blue racers" haunt the edges of the woods, and linger around the fields to chill his blood who catches a glimpse of their upreared heads, with their great, balefully bright eyes, and "white-collar" encircled throats.

The human events happening here have been in harmony with the natural ones. It has always been a land of conflict. In 1540—339 years ago —De Soto, in that energetic but fruitless search for gold which occupied his later years, penetrated to this region, and found it the fastness of the Xualans, a bold, aggressive race, continually warring with its neighbors. When next the white man reached the country—a century and a half later—he found the Xualans had been swept away by the conquering Cherokees, and he witnessed there the most sanguinary contest between Indians of which our annals give any account—a pitched battle two days in duration, between the invading Shawnees, who lorded it over what is now Kentucky, Ohio and Indiana—and the Cherokees, who dominated the country the southeast of the Cumberland range. Again the Cherokees were victorious, and the discomfited Shawnees retired north of the Gap.

Then the white man delivered battle for the possession the land, and bought it with the lives of many gallant adventurers. Half a century later Boone and his hardy companion followed, and forced their way into Kentucky.

Another half century saw the Gap the favorite haunt of the greatest of American bandits—the noted John A. Murrell—and his gang. They infested the country for years, now waylaying the trader or drover threading his toilsome way over the lone mountains, now descending upon some little town, to plunder its stores and houses.

At length Murrell and his band were driven out, and sought a new field of operations on the Lower Mississippi. They left germs behind them, however, that developed into horse thieve counterfeiters, and later into guerrillas and bushwhackers.

When the Rebellion broke out the region at once became the theater of military operations. Twice Cumberland Gap was seized by the Rebels, and twice was it wrested away from them. In 1861 it was the point whence Zollicoffer launched out with his legions to "liberate Kentucky," and it was whither they fled, beaten and shattered, after the disasters of Wild Cat and Mill Springs. In 1862 Kirby Smith led his army through the Gap on his way to overrun Kentucky and invade the North. Three months later his beaten forces sought refuge from their pursuers behind its impregnable fortifications. Another year saw Burnside burst through the Gap with a conquering force and redeem loyal East Tennessee from its Rebel oppressors.

Had the South ever been able to separate from the North the boundary would have been established along this line.

Between the main ridge upon which Cumberland Gap is situated, and the next range on the southeast which runs parallel with it, is a narrow, long, very fruitful valley, walled in on either side for a hundred miles by tall mountains as a City street is by high buildings. It is called Powell's Valley. In it dwell a simple, primitive people, shut out from the world almost as much as if they lived in New Zealand, and with the speech, manners and ideas that their fathers brought into the Valley when they settled it a century ago. There has been but little change since then. The young men who have annually driven cattle to the distant markets in Kentucky, Tennessee and Virginia, have brought back occasional stray bits of finery for the "women folks," and the latest improved fire-arms for themselves, but this is about all the innovations the progress of the world has been allowed to make. Wheeled vehicles are almost unknown; men and women travel on horseback as they did a century ago, the clothing is the product of the farm and the busy looms of the women, and life is as rural and Arcadian as any ever described in a pastoral. The people are rich in cattle, hogs, horses, sheep and the products of the field. The fat soil brings forth the substantials of life in opulent plenty. Having this there seems to be little care for more. Ambition nor avarice, nor yet craving after luxury, disturb their contented souls or drag them away from the non-progressive round of simple life bequeathed them by their fathers.

CHAPTER II.

SCARCITY OF FOOD FOR THE ARMY—RAID FOR FORAGE—ENCOUNTER WIT THE REBELS —SHARP CAVALRY FIGHT—DEFEAT OF THE "JOHNNIES"—POWELL'S VALLEY OPENED UP.

As the Autumn of 1863 advanced towards Winter the difficulty of supplying the forces concentrated around Cumberland Gap—as well as the rest of Burnside's army in East Tennessee—became greater and greater. The base of supplies was at Camp Nelson, near Lexington, Ky., one hundred and eighty miles from the Gap, and all that the Army used had to be hauled that distance by mule teams over roads that, in their best state were wretched, and which the copious rains and heavy traffic had rendered well-nigh impassable. All the country to our possession had been drained of its stock of whatever would contribute to the support of man or beast. That portion of Powell's Valley extending from the Gap into Virginia was still in the hands of the Rebels; its stock of products was as yet almost exempt from military contributions. Consequently a raid was projected to reduce the Valley to our possession, and secure its much needed stores. It was guarded by the Sixty-fourth Virginia, a mounted regiment, made up of the young men of the locality, who had then been in the service about two years.

Maj. C. H. Beer's third Battalion, Sixteenth Illinois Cavalry—four companies, each about 75 strong—was sent on the errand of driving out the Rebels and opening up the Valley for our foraging teams. The writer was invited to attend the excursion. As he held the honorable, but not very lucrative position of "high, private" in Company L, of the Battalion, and the invitation came from his Captain, he did not feel at liberty to decline. He went, as private soldiers have been in the habit of doing ever since the days of the old Centurion, who said with the characteristic boastfulness of one of the lower grades of commissioned officers when he happens to be a snob: For I am also a man set under authority, having under me soldiers, and I say unto one, Go; and he goeth; and to another, Come, and he cometh; and to my servant, Do this, and he doeth it. Rather "airy" talk that for a man who nowadays would take rank with Captains of infantry.

Three hundred of us responded to the signal of "boots and saddles," buckled on three hundred more or less trusty sabers and revolvers, saddled three hundred more or less gallant steeds, came into line "as companies" with the automatic listlessness of the old soldiers, "counted off by fours" in that queer gamut-running style that makes a company of men "counting off"—each shouting a number in a different voice from his neighbor—sound like running the scales on some great organ badly out of tune; something like this:

One. Two. Three. Four. One. Two. Three. Four. One. Two. Three. Four.

Then, as the bugle sounded "Right forward! fours right!" we moved off at a walk through the melancholy mist that soaked through the very fiber of man and horse, and reduced the minds of both to a condition of limp indifference as to things past, present and future.

Whither we were going we knew not, nor cared. Such matters had long since ceased to excite any interest. A cavalryman soon recognizes as the least astonishing thing in his existence the signal to "Fall in!" and start somewhere. He feels that he is the "Poor Joe" of the Army—under perpetual orders to "move on."

Down we wound over the road that zig-tagged through the forts, batteries and rifle-pits covering the eastern ascent to the Flap-past the wonderful Murrell Spring—so-called because the robber chief had killed, as he stooped to drink of its crystal waters, a rich drover, whom he was pretending to pilot through the mountains—down to where the "Virginia road" turned off sharply to the left and entered Powell's Valley. The mist had become a chill, dreary rain, through, which we plodded silently, until night closed in around us some ten miles from the Gap. As we halted to go into camp, an indignant Virginian resented the invasion of the sacred soil by firing at one of the guards moving out to his place. The guard looked at the fellow contemptuously, as if he hated to waste powder on a man who had no better sense than to stay out in such a rain, when he could go in-doors, and the bushwhacker escaped, without even a return shot.

Fires were built, coffee made, horses rubbed, and we laid down with feet to the fire to get what sleep we could.

Before morning we were awakened by the bitter cold. It had cleared off during the night and turned so cold that everything was frozen stiff. This was better than the rain, at all events. A good fire and a hot cup of coffee would make the cold quite endurable.

At daylight the bugle sounded "Right forward! fours right!" again, and the 300 of us resumed our onward plod over the rocky, cedar-crowned hills.

In the meantime, other things were taking place elsewhere. Our esteemed friends of the Sixty-fourth Virginia, who were in camp at the little town of Jonesville, about 40 miles from the Gap, had learned of our starting up the Valley to drive them out, and they showed that warm reciprocity characteristic of the Southern soldier, by mounting and starting down the Valley to drive us out. Nothing could be more harmonious, it will be perceived. Barring the trifling divergence of yews as to who was to drive and who be driven, there was perfect accord in our ideas.

Our numbers were about equal. If I were to say that they considerably outnumbered us, I would be following the universal precedent. No soldier-high or low-ever admitted engaging an equal or inferior force of the enemy.

About 9 o'clock in the morning—Sunday—they rode through the streets of Jonesville on their way to give us battle. It was here that most of the members of the Regiment lived. Every man, woman and child in the town was related in some way to nearly every one of the soldiers.

The women turned out to wave their fathers, husbands, brothers and lovers on to victory. The old men gathered to give parting counsel and encouragement to their sons and kindred. The Sixty-fourth rode away to what hope told them would be a glorious victory.

At noon we are still straggling along without much attempt at soldierly order, over the rough, frozen hill-sides. It is yet bitterly cold, and men and horses draw themselves together, as if to expose as little surface as possible to the unkind elements. Not a word had been spoken by any one for hours.

The head of the column has just reached the top of the hill, and the rest of us are strung along for a quarter of a mile or so back.

Suddenly a few shots ring out upon the frosty air from the carbines of the advance. The general apathy is instantly, replaced by keen attention, and the boys instinctively range themselves into fours—the cavalry unit of action. The Major, who is riding about the middle of the first Company—I—dashes to the front. A glance seems to satisfy him, for he turns in his saddle and his voice rings out:

"Company I! FOURS LEFT INTO LINE!—MARCH!!"

The Company swings around on the hill-top like a great, jointed toy snake. As the fours come into line on a trot, we see every man draw his saber and revolver. The Company raises a mighty cheer and dashes forward.

Company K presses forward to the ground Company I has just left, the fours sweep around into line, the sabers and revolvers come out spontaneously, the men cheer and the Company flings itself forward.

All this time we of Company L can see nothing except what the companies ahead of us are doing. We are wrought up to the highest pitch. As Company K clears its ground, we press forward eagerly. Now we go into line just as we raise the hill, and as my four comes around, I catch a hurried glimpse through a rift in the smoke of a line of butternut and gray clad men a hundred yards or so away. Their guns are at their faces, and I see the smoke and fire spurt from the muzzles. At the same instant our sabers and revolvers are drawn. We shout in a frenzy of excitement, and the horses spring forward as if shot from a bow.

I see nothing more until I reach the place where the Rebel line stood. Then I find it is gone. Looking beyond toward the bottom of the hill, I see the woods filled with Rebels, flying in disorder and our men yelling in pursuit. This is the portion of the line which Companies I and K struck. Here and there are men in butternut clothing, prone on the frozen ground, wounded and dying. I have just time to notice closely one middle-aged man lying almost under my horse's feet. He has received a carbine bullet through his head and his blood colors a great space around him.

One brave man, riding a roan horse, attempts to rally his companions. He halts on a little knoll, wheels his horse to face us, and waves his hat to draw his companions to him. A tall, lank fellow in the next four to me—who goes by the nickname of "'Leven Yards"—aims his carbine at him, and, without checking his horse's pace, fires. The heavy Sharpe's bullet tears a gaping hole through the Rebel's heart. He drops from his saddle, his life-blood runs down in little rills on either side of the knoll, and his riderless horse dashes away in a panic.

At this instant comes an order for the Company to break up into fours and press on through the forest in pursuit. My four trots off to the road at the right. A Rebel bugler, who hag been cut off, leaps his horse into the road in front of us. We all fire at him on the impulse of the moment. He falls from his horse with a bullet through his back. Company M, which has remained in column as a reserve, is now thundering up close behind at a gallop. Its seventy-five powerful horses are spurning the solid earth with steel-clad hoofs. The man will be ground into a shapeless mass if left where he has fallen. We spring from our horses and drag him into a fence corner; then remount and join in the pursuit.

This happened on the summit of Chestnut Ridge, fifteen miles from Jonesville.

Late in the afternoon the anxious watchers at Jonesville saw a single fugitive urging his well-nigh spent horse down the slope of the hill toward town. In an agony of anxiety they hurried forward to meet him and learn his news.

The first messenger who rushed into Job's presence to announce the beginning of the series of misfortunes which were to afflict the upright man of Uz is a type of all the cowards who, before or since then, have been the first to speed away from the field of battle to spread the news of disaster. He said:

"And the Sabeans fell upon them, and took them away; yea, they have slain the servants with the edge of the sword; and I only am escaped alone to tell thee."

So this fleeing Virginian shouted to his expectant friends:

"The boys are all cut to pieces; I'm the only one that got away."

The terrible extent of his words was belied a little later, by the appearance on the distant summit of the hill of a considerable mob of fugitives, flying at the utmost speed of their nearly exhausted horses. As they came on down the hill as almost equally disorganized crowd of pursuers appeared on the summit, yelling in voices hoarse with continued shouting, and pouring an incessant fire of carbine and revolver bullets upon the hapless men of the Sixty-fourth Virginia. The two masses of men swept on through the town. Beyond it, the road branched in several directions, the pursued scattered on each of these, and the worn-out pursuers gave up the chase. Returning to Jonesville, we took an account of stock, and found that we were "ahead" one hundred and fifteen prisoners, nearly that many horses, and a considerable quantity of small arms. How many of the enemy had been killed and wounded could not be told, as they were scattered over the whole fifteen miles between where the fight occurred and the pursuit ended. Our loss was trifling.

Comparing notes around the camp-fires in the evening, we found that our success had been owing to the Major's instinct, his grasp of the situation, and the soldierly way in which he took advantage of it. When he reached the summit of the hill he found the Rebel line nearly formed and ready for action. A moment's hesitation might have been fatal to us. At his command Company I went into line with the thought-like celerity of trained cavalry, and instantly dashed through the right of the Rebel line. Company K followed and plunged through the Rebel center, and when we of Company L arrived on the ground, and charged the left, the last vestige of resistance was swept away. The whole affair did not probably occupy more than fifteen minutes. This was the way Powell's Valley was opened to our foragers.

CHAPTER III.

LIVING OFF THE ENEMY—REVELING IN THE FATNESS OF THE COUNTRY—SOLDIERLY PURVEYING AND CAMP COOKERY—SUSCEPTIBLE TEAMSTERS AND THEIR TENDENCY TO FLIGHTINESS—MAKING SOLDIER'S BED.

For weeks we rode up and down—hither and thither—along the length of the narrow, granite-walled Valley; between mountains so lofty that the sun labored slowly over them in the morning, occupying half the forenoon in getting to where his rays would reach the stream that ran through the Valley's center. Perpetual shadow reigned on the northern and western faces of these towering Nights—not enough warmth and sunshine reaching them in the cold months to check the growth of the ever-lengthening icicles hanging from the jutting cliffs, or melt the arabesque frost-forms with which the many dashing cascades decorated the adjacent rocks and shrubbery. Occasionally we would see where some little stream ran down over the face of the bare, black rocks for many hundred feet, and then its course would be a long band of sheeny white, like a great rich, spotless scarf of satin, festooning the war-grimed walls of some old castle.

Our duty now was to break up any nuclei of concentration that the Rebels might attempt to form, and to guard our foragers—that is, the teamsters and employee of the Quartermaster's Department—who were loading grain into wagons and hauling it away.

This last was an arduous task. There is no man in the world that needs as much protection as an Army teamster. He is worse in this respect than a New England manufacturer, or an old maid on her travels. He is given to sudden fears and causeless panics. Very innocent cedars have a fashion of assuming in his eyes the appearance of desperate Rebels armed with murderous guns, and there is no telling what moment a rock may take such a form as to freeze his young blood, and make each particular hair stand on end like quills upon the fretful porcupine. One has to be particular about snapping caps in his neighborhood, and give to him careful warning before discharging a carbine to clean it. His first impulse, when anything occurs to jar upon his delicate nerves, is to cut his wheel-mule loose and retire with the precipitation of a man having an appointment to keep and being behind time. There is no man who can get as much speed out of a mule as a teamster falling back from the neighborhood of heavy firing.

This nervous tremor was not peculiar to the engineers of our transportation department. It was noticeable in the gentry who carted the scanty provisions of the Rebels. One of Wheeler's cavalrymen told me that the brigade to which he belonged was one evening ordered to move at daybreak. The night was rainy, and it was thought best to discharge the guns and reload before starting. Unfortunately, it was neglected to inform the teamsters of this, and at the first discharge they varnished from the scene with such energy that it was over a week before the brigade succeeded in getting them back again.

Why association with the mule should thus demoralize a man, has always been a puzzle to me, for while the mule, as Col. Ingersoll has remarked, is an animal without pride of ancestry or hope of posterity, he is still not a coward by any means. It is beyond dispute that a full-grown and active lioness once attacked a mule in the grounds of the Cincinnati Zoological Garden, and was ignominiously beaten, receiving injuries from which she died shortly afterward.

The apparition of a badly-scared teamster urging one of his wheel mules at break-neck speed over the rough ground, yelling for protection against "them Johnnies," who had appeared on some hilltop in sight of where he was gathering corn, was an almost hourly occurrence. Of course the squad dispatched to his assistance found nobody.

Still, there were plenty of Rebels in the country, and they hung around our front, exchanging shots with us at long taw, and occasionally treating us to a volley at close range, from some favorable point. But we had the decided advantage of them at this game. Our Sharpe's carbines were much superior in every way to their Enfields. They would shoot much farther, and a great deal more rapidly, so that the Virginians were not long in discovering that they were losing more than they gained in this useless warfare.

Once they played a sharp practical joke upon us. Copper River is a deep, exceedingly rapid mountain stream, with a very slippery rocky bottom. The Rebels blockaded a ford in such a way that it was almost impossible for a horse to keep his feet. Then they tolled us off in pursuit of a small party to this ford. When we came to it there was a light line of skirmishers on the opposite bank, who popped away at us industriously. Our boys formed in line, gave the customary, cheer, and dashed in to carry the ford at a charge. As they did so at least one-half of the horses went down as if they were shot, and rolled over their riders in the swift running, ice-cold waters. The Rebels yelled a triumphant laugh, as they galloped away, and the laugh was re-echoed by our fellows, who were as quick to see the joke as the other side. We tried to get even with them by a sharp chase, but we gave it up after a few miles, without having taken any prisoners.

But, after all, there was much to make our sojourn in the Valley endurable. Though we did not wear fine linen, we fared sumptuously—for soldiers—every day. The cavalryman is always charged by the infantry and artillery with having a finer and surer scent for the good things in the country than any other man in the service. He is believed to have an instinct that will unfailingly lead him, in the dankest night, to the roosting place of the most desirable poultry, and after he has camped in a neighborhood for awhile it would require a close chemical analysis to find a trace of ham.

We did our best to sustain the reputation of our arm of the service. We found the most delicious hams packed away in the ash-houses. They were small, and had that; exquisite nutty flavor, peculiar to mast-fed bacon. Then there was an abundance of the delightful little apple known as "romanites." There were turnips, pumpkins, cabbages, potatoes, and the usual products of the field in plenty, even profusion. The corn in the fields furnished an ample supply of breadstuff. We carried it to and ground it in the quaintest, rudest little mills that can be imagined outside of the primitive affairs by which the women of Arabia coarsely powder the grain for the family meal. Sometimes the mill would consist only of four stout posts thrust into the ground at the edge of some stream. A line of boulders reaching diagonally across the stream answered for a dam, by diverting a portion of the volume of water to a channel at the side, where it moved a clumsily constructed wheel, that turned two small stones, not larger than good-sized grindstones. Over this would be a shed made by resting poles in forked posts stuck into the ground, and covering these with clapboards held in place by large flat stones. They resembled the mills of the gods—in grinding slowly. It used to seem that a healthy man could eat the meal faster than they ground it. But what savory meals we used to concoct around the campfires, out of the rich materials collected during the day's ride! Such stews, such soups, such broils, such wonderful commixtures of things diverse in nature and antagonistic in properties such daring culinary experiments in combining materials never before attempted to be combined. The French say of untasteful arrangement of hues in dress "that the colors swear at each other." I have often thought the same thing of the heterogeneities that go to make up a soldier's pot-a feu.

But for all that they never failed to taste deliciously after a long day's ride. They were washed down by a tincupful of coffee strong enough to tan leather, then came a brier-wood pipeful of fragrant kinnikinnic, and a seat by the ruddy, sparkling fire of aromatic cedar logs, that diffused at once warmth, and spicy, pleasing incense. A chat over the events of the day, and the prospect of the morrow, the wonderful merits of each man's horse, and the disgusting irregularities of the mails from home, lasted until the silver-voiced bugle rang out the sweet, mournful tattoo of the Regulations, to the flowing cadences of which the boys had arranged the absurdly incongruous words:

"S-a-y—D-e-u-t-c-h-e-r-will-you fight-mit Sigel!
Zwei-glass of lager-bier, ja! ja! JA!"

Words were fitted to all the calls, which generally bore some relativeness to the signal, but these were as, destitute of congruity as of sense.

Tattoo always produces an impression of extreme loneliness. As its weird, half-availing notes ring out and are answered back from the distant rocks shrouded in night, and perhaps concealing the lurking foe, the soldier remembers that he is far away from home and friends—deep in the enemy's country, encompassed on every hand by those in deadly hostility to him, who are perhaps even then maturing the preparations for his destruction.

As the tattoo sounds, the boys arise from around the fire, visit the horse line, see that their horses are securely tied, rub off from the fetlocks and legs such specks of mud as may have escaped the cleaning in the early evening, and if possible, smuggle their faithful four-footed friends a few ears of corn, or another bunch of hay.

If not too tired, and everything else is favorable, the cavalryman has prepared himself a comfortable couch for the night. He always sleeps with a chum. The two have gathered enough small tufts of pine or cedar to make a comfortable, springy, mattress-like foundation. On this is laid the poncho or rubber blanket. Next comes one of their overcoats, and upon this they lie, covering themselves with the two blankets and the other overcoat, their feet towards the fire, their boots at the foot, and their belts, with revolver, saber and carbine, at the sides of the bed. It is surprising what an amount of comfort a man can get out of such a couch, and how, at an alarm, he springs from it, almost instantly dressed and armed.

Half an hour after tattoo the bugle rings out another sadly sweet strain, that hath a dying sound.

CHAPTER IV.

A BITTER COLD MORNING AND A WARM AWAKENING—TROUBLE ALL ALONG THE LINE—FIERCE CONFLICTS, ASSAULTS AND DEFENSE—PROLONGED AND DESPERATE STRUGGLE ENDING WITH A SURRENDER.

The night had been the most intensely cold that the country had known for many years. Peach and other tender trees had been killed by the frosty rigor, and sentinels had been frozen to death in our neighborhood. The deep snow on which we made our beds, the icy covering of the streams near us, the limbs of the trees above us, had been cracking with loud noises all night, from the bitter cold.

We were camped around Jonesville, each of the four companies lying on one of the roads leading from the town. Company L lay about a mile from the Court House. On a knoll at the end of the village toward us, and at a point where two roads separated,—one of which led to us,—stood a three-inch Rodman rifle, belonging to the Twenty-second Ohio Battery. It and its squad of eighteen men, under command of Lieutenant Alger and Sergeant Davis, had been sent up to us a few days before from the Gap.

The comfortless gray dawn was crawling sluggishly over the mountain-tops, as if numb as the animal and vegetable life which had been shrinking all the long hours under the fierce chill. The Major's bugler had saluted the morn with the lively, ringing tarr-r-r-a-ta-ara of the Regulation reveille, and the company buglers, as fast as they could thaw out their mouth-pieces, were answering him.

I lay on my bed, dreading to get up, and yet not anxious to lie still. It was a question which would be the more uncomfortable. I turned over, to see if there was not another position in which it would be warmer, and began wishing for the thousandth time that the efforts for the amelioration of the horrors of warfare would progress to such a point as to put a stop to all Winter soldiering, so that a fellow could go home as soon as cold weather began, sit around a comfortable stove in a country store; and tell camp stories until the Spring was far enough advanced to let him go back to the front wearing a straw hat and a linen duster.

Then I began wondering how much longer I would dare lie there, before the Orderly Sergeant would draw me out by the heels, and accompany the operation with numerous unkind and sulphurous remarks.

This cogitation, was abruptly terminated by hearing an excited shout from the Captain:

"Turn Out!—COMPANY L!! TURNOUT ! ! !"

Almost at the same instant rose that shrill, piercing Rebel yell, which one who has once heard it rarely forgets, and this was followed by a crashing volley from apparently a regiment of rifles. I arose-promptly.

There was evidently something of more interest on hand than the weather.

Cap, overcoat, boots and revolver belt went on, and eyes opened at about the same instant.

As I snatched up my carbine, I looked out in front, and the whole woods appeared to be full of Rebels, rushing toward us, all yelling and some firing. My Captain and First Lieutenant had taken up position on the right front of the tents, and part of the boys were running up to form a line alongside them. The Second Lieutenant had stationed himself on a knoll on the left front, and about a third of the company was rallying around him.

My chum was a silent, sententious sort of a chap, and as we ran forward to the Captain's line, he remarked earnestly:

"Well: this beats hell!"

I thought he had a clear idea of the situation.

All this occupied an inappreciably short space of time. The Rebels had not stopped to reload, but were rushing impetuously toward us. We gave them a hot, rolling volley from our carbines. Many fell, more stopped to load and reply, but the mass surged straight forward at us. Then our fire grew so deadly that they showed a disposition to cover themselves behind the rocks and trees. Again they were urged forward; and a body of them headed by their Colonel, mounted on a white horse, pushed forward through the gap between us and the Second Lieutenant. The Rebel Colonel dashed up to the Second Lieutenant, and ordered him to surrender. The latter-a gallant old graybeard—cursed the Rebel bitterly and snapped his now empty revolver in his face. The Colonel fired and killed him, whereupon his squad, with two of its Sergeants killed and half its numbers on the ground, surrendered.

The Rebels in our front and flank pressed us with equal closeness. It seemed as if it was absolutely impossible to check their rush for an instant, and as we saw the fate of our companions the Captain gave the word for every man to look out for himself. We ran back a little distance, sprang over the fence into the fields, and rushed toward Town, the Rebels encouraging us to make good time by a sharp fire into our backs from the fence.

While we were vainly attempting to stem the onset of the column dashed against us, better success was secured elsewhere. Another column swept down the other road, upon which there was only an outlying picket. This had to come back on the run before the overwhelming numbers, and the Rebels galloped straight for the three-inch Rodman. Company M was the first to get saddled and mounted, and now came up at a steady, swinging gallop, in two platoons, saber and revolver in hand, and led by two Sergeants-Key and McWright,—printer boys from Bloomington, Illinois. They divined the object of the Rebel dash, and strained every nerve to reach the gun first. The Rebels were too near, and got the gun and turned it. Before they could fire it, Company M struck them headlong, but they took the terrible impact without flinching, and for a few minutes there was fierce hand-to-hand work, with sword and pistol. The Rebel leader sank under a half-dozen simultaneous wounds, and fell dead almost under the gun. Men dropped from their horses each instant, and the riderless steeds fled away. The scale of victory was turned by the Major dashing against the Rebel left flank at the head of Company I, and a portion of the artillery squad. The Rebels gave ground slowly, and were packed into a dense mass in the lane up which they had charged. After they had been crowded back, say fifty yards, word was passed through our men to open to the right and left on the sides of the road. The artillerymen had turned the gun and loaded it with a solid shot. Instantly a wide lane opened through our ranks; the man with the lanyard drew the fatal cord, fire burst from the primer and the muzzle, the long gun sprang up and recoiled, and there seemed to be a demoniac yell in its ear-splitting crash, as the heavy ball left the mouth, and tore its bloody way through the bodies of the struggling mass of men and horses.

This ended it. The Rebels gave way in disorder, and our men fell back to give the gun an opportunity to throw shell and canister.

The Rebels now saw that we were not to be run over like a field of cornstalks, and they fell back to devise further tactics, giving us a breathing spell to get ourselves in shape for defense.

The dullest could see that we were in a desperate situation. Critical positions were no new experience to us, as they never are to a cavalry command after a few months in the field, but, though the pitcher goes often to the well, it is broken at last, and our time was evidently at hand. The narrow throat of the Valley, through which lay the road back to the Gap, was held by a force of Rebels evidently much superior to our own, and strongly posted. The road was a slender, tortuous one, winding through rocks and gorges. Nowhere was there room enough to move with even a platoon front against the enemy, and this precluded all chances of cutting out. The best we could do was a slow, difficult movement, in column of fours, and this would have been suicide. On the other side of the Town the Rebels were massed stronger, while to the right and left rose the steep mountain sides. We were caught-trapped as surely as a rat ever was in a wire trap.

As we learned afterwards, a whole division of cavalry, under command of the noted Rebel, Major General Sam Jones, had been sent to effect our capture, to offset in a measure Longstreet's repulse at Knoxville. A gross overestimate of our numbers had caused the sending of so large a force on this errand, and the rough treatment we gave the two columns that attacked us first confirmed the Rebel General's ideas of our strength, and led him to adopt cautious tactics, instead of crushing us out speedily, by a determined advance of all parts of his encircling lines. The lull in the fight did not last long. A portion of the Rebel line on the east rushed forward to gain a more commanding position.

We concentrated in that direction and drove it back, the Rodman assisting with a couple of well-aimed shells.—This was followed by a similar but more successful attempt by another part of the Rebel line, and so it went on all day—the Rebels rushing up first on this side, and then on that, and we, hastily collecting at the exposed points, seeking to drive them back. We were frequently successful; we were on the inside, and had the advantage of the short interior lines, so that our few men and our breech-loaders told to a good purpose.

There were frequent crises in the struggle, that at some times gave encouragement, but never hope. Once a determined onset was made from the East, and was met by the equally determined resistance of nearly our whole force. Our fire was so galling that a large number of our foes crowded into a house on a knoll, and making loopholes in its walls, began replying to us pretty sharply. We sent word to our faithful artillerists, who trained the gun upon the house. The first shell screamed over the roof, and burst harmlessly beyond. We suspended fire to watch the next. It crashed through the side; for an instant all was deathly still; we thought it had gone on through. Then came a roar and a crash; the clapboards flew off the roof, and smoke poured out; panic-stricken Rebels rushed from the doors and sprang from the windows-like bees from a disturbed hive; the shell had burst among the confined mass of men inside! We afterwards heard that twenty-five were killed there.

At another time a considerable force of rebels gained the cover of a fence in easy range of our main force. Companies L and K were ordered to charge forward on foot and dislodge them. Away we went, under a fire that seemed to drop a man at every step. A hundred yards in front of the Rebels was a little cover, and behind this our men lay down as if by one impulse. Then came a close, desperate duel at short range. It was a question between Northern pluck and Southern courage, as to which could stand the most punishment. Lying as flat as possible on the crusted snow, only raising the head or body enough to load and aim, the men on both sides, with their teeth set, their glaring eyes fastened on the foe, their nerves as tense as tightly-drawn steel wires, rained shot on each other as fast as excited hands could crowd cartridges into the guns and discharge them.

Not a word was said.

The shallower enthusiasm that expresses itself in oaths and shouts had given way to the deep, voiceless rage of men in a death grapple. The Rebel line was a rolling torrent of flame, their bullets shrieked angrily as they flew past, they struck the snow in front of us, and threw its cold flakes in faces that were white with the fires of consuming hate; they buried themselves with a dull thud in the quivering bodies of the enraged combatants.

Minutes passed; they seemed hours.

Would the villains, scoundrels, hell-hounds, sons of vipers never go?
At length a few Rebels sprang up and tried to fly. They were shot down instantly.
Then the whole line rose and ran!

The relief was so great that we jumped to our feet and cheered wildly, forgetting in our excitement to make use of our victory by shooting down our flying enemies.

Nor was an element of fun lacking. A Second Lieutenant was ordered to take a party of skirmishers to the top of a hill and engage those of the Rebels stationed on another hill-top across a ravine. He had but lately joined us from the Regular Army, where he was a Drill Sergeant. Naturally, he was very methodical in his way, and scorned to do otherwise under fire than he would upon the parade ground. He moved his little command to the hill-top, in close order, and faced them to the front. The Johnnies received them with a yell and a volley, whereat the boys winced a little, much to the Lieutenant's disgust, who swore at them; then had them count off with great deliberation, and deployed them as coolly as if them was not an enemy within a hundred miles. After the line deployed, he "dressed" it, commanded "Front!" and "Begin, firing!" his attention was called another way for an instant, and when he looked back again, there was not a man of his nicely formed skirmish line visible. The logs and stones had evidently been put there for the use of skirmishers, the boys thought, and in an instant they availed themselves of their shelter.

Never was there an angrier man than that Second Lieutenant; he brandished his saber and swore; he seemed to feel that all his soldierly reputation was gone, but the boys stuck to their shelter for all that, informing him that when the Rebels would stand out in the open field and take their fire, they would likewise.

Despite all our efforts, the Rebel line crawled up closer an closer to us; we were driven back from knoll to knoll, and from one fence after another. We had maintained the unequal struggle for eight hours; over one-fourth of our number were stretched upon the snow, killed or badly wounded. Our cartridges were nearly all gone; the cannon had fired its last shot long ago, and having a blank cartridge left, had shot the rammer at a gathering party of the enemy.

Just as the Winter sun was going down upon a day of gloom the bugle called us all up on the hillside. Then the Rebels saw for the first time how few there were, and began an almost simultaneous charge all along the line. The Major raised piece of a shelter tent upon a pole. The line halted. An officer rode out from it, followed by two privates.

Approaching the Major, he said, "Who is in command this force?"

The Major replied: "I am."

"Then, Sir, I demand your sword."

"What is your rank, Sir!"

"I am Adjutant of the Sixty-fourth Virginia."

The punctillious soul of the old "Regular"—for such the Major was swelled up instantly, and he answered:

"By —-, sir, I will never surrender to my inferior in rank!"

The Adjutant reined his horse back. His two followers leveled their pieces at the Major and waited orders to fire. They were covered by a dozen carbines in the hands of our men. The

Adjutant ordered his men to "recover arms," and rode away with them. He presently returned with a Colonel, and to him the Major handed his saber.

As the men realized what was being done, the first thought of many of them was to snatch out the cylinder's of their revolvers, and the slides of their carbines, and throw them away, so as to make the arms useless.

We were overcome with rage and humiliation at being compelled to yield to an enemy whom we had hated so bitterly. As we stood there on the bleak mountain-side, the biting wind soughing through the leafless branches, the shadows of a gloomy winter night closing around us, the groans and shrieks of our wounded mingling with the triumphant yells of the Rebels plundering our tents, it seemed as if Fate could press to man's lips no cup with bitterer dregs in it than this.

CHAPTER V.

THE REACTION—DEPRESSION—BITTING COLD—SHARP HUNGER AND SAD REFLEXION.

"Of being taken by the Insolent foe."—Othello.

The night that followed was inexpressibly dreary: The high-wrought nervous tension, which had been protracted through the long hours that the fight lasted, was succeeded by a proportionate mental depression, such as naturally follows any strain upon the mind. This was intensified in our cases by the sharp sting of defeat, the humiliation of having to yield ourselves, our horses and our arms into the possession of the enemy, the uncertainty as to the future, and the sorrow we felt at the loss of so many of our comrades.

Company L had suffered very severely, but our chief regret was for the gallant Osgood, our Second Lieutenant. He, above all others, was our trusted leader. The Captain and First Lieutenant were brave men, and good enough soldiers, but Osgood was the one "whose adoption tried, we grappled to our souls with hooks of steel." There was never any difficulty in getting all the volunteers he wanted for a scouting party. A quiet, pleasant spoken gentleman, past middle age, he looked much better fitted for the office of Justice of the Peace, to which his fellow-citizens of Urbana, Illinois, had elected and reelected him, than to command a troop of rough riders in a great civil war. But none more gallant than he ever vaulted into saddle to do battle for the right. He went into the Army solely as a matter of principle, and did his duty with the unflagging zeal of an olden Puritan fighting for liberty and his soul's salvation. He was a superb horseman—as all the older Illinoisans are and, for all his two-score years and ten, he recognized few superiors for strength and activity in the Battalion. A radical, uncompromising Abolitionist, he had frequently asserted that he would rather die than yield to a Rebel, and he kept his word in this as in everything else.

As for him, it was probably the way he desired to die. No one believed more ardently than he that

Whether on the scaffold high,
Or in the battle's van;
The fittest place for man to die,
Is where he dies for man.

Among the many who had lost chums and friends was Ned Johnson, of Company K. Ned was a young Englishman, with much of the suggestiveness of the bull-dog common to the lower class of that nation. His fist was readier than his tongue. His chum, Walter Savage was of the same surly type. The two had come from England twelve years before, and had been together ever since. Savage was killed in the struggle for the fence described in the preceding chapter. Ned could not realize for a while that his friend was dead. It was only when the body rapidly stiffened on its icy bed, and the eyes which had been gleaming deadly hate when he was stricken down were glazed over with the dull film of death, that he believed he was gone from him forever. Then his rage was terrible. For the rest of the day he was at the head of every assault upon the enemy. His voice could ever be heard above the firing, cursing the Rebels bitterly, and urging the boys to "Stand up to 'em! Stand right up to 'em! Don't give a inch! Let them have the best you got in the shop! Shoot low, and don't waste a cartridge!"

When we surrendered, Ned seemed to yield sullenly to the inevitable. He threw his belt and apparently his revolver with it upon the snow. A guard was formed around us, and we gathered about the fires that were started. Ned sat apart, his arms folded, his head upon his breast, brooding bitterly upon Walter's death. A horseman, evidently a Colonel or General, clattered up to give some directions concerning us. At the sound of his voice Ned raised his head and gave him a swift glance; the gold stars upon the Rebel's collar led him to believe that he was the commander of the enemy. Ned sprang to his feet, made a long stride forward, snatched from the breast of his overcoat the revolver he had been hiding there, cocked it and leveled it at the Rebel's breast. Before he could pull the trigger Orderly Sergeant Charles Bentley, of his Company, who was watching him, leaped forward, caught his wrist and threw the revolver up. Others joined in, took the weapon away, and handed it over to the officer, who then ordered us all to be searched for arms, and rode away.

All our dejection could not make us forget that we were intensely hungry. We had eaten nothing all day. The fight began before we had time to get any breakfast, and of course there was no interval for refreshments during the engagement. The Rebels were no better off than we, having been marched rapidly all night in order to come upon us by daylight.

Late in the evening a few sacks of meal were given us, and we took the first lesson in an art that long and painful practice afterward was to make very familiar to us. We had nothing to mix the meal in, and it looked as if we would have to eat it dry, until a happy thought struck some one that our caps would do for kneading troughs. At once every cap was devoted to this. Getting water from an adjacent spring, each man made a little wad of dough—unsalted—and spreading it upon a flat stone or a chip, set it up in front of the fire to bake. As soon as it was browned on one side, it was pulled off the stone, and the other side turned to the fire. It was a very primitive way of cooking and I became thoroughly disgusted with it. It was fortunate for me that I little dreamed that this was the way I should have to get my meals for the next fifteen months. After somewhat of the edge had been taken off our hunger by this food, we crouched around the fires, talked over the events of the day, speculated as to what was to be done with us, and snatched such sleep as the biting cold would permit.

CHAPTER VI.

"ON TO RICHMOND!"—MARCHING ON FOOT OVER THE MOUNTAINS—MY HORSE HAS A NEW RIDER—UNSOPHISTICATED MOUNTAIN GIRLS—DISCUSSING THE ISSUES OF THE WAR—PARTING WITH "HIATOGA."

At dawn we were gathered together, more meal issued to us, which we cooked in the same way, and then were started under heavy guard to march on foot over the mountains to Bristol, a station at the point where the Virginia and Tennessee Railroad crosses the line between Virginia and Tennessee.

As we were preparing to set out a Sergeant of the First Virginia cavalry came galloping up to us on my horse! The sight of my faithful "Hiatoga" bestrid by a Rebel, wrung my heart. During the action I had forgotten him, but when it ceased I began to worry about his fate. As he and his rider came near I called out to him; he stopped and gave a whinny of recognition, which seemed also a plaintive appeal for an explanation of the changed condition of affairs.

The Sergeant was a pleasant, gentlemanly boy of about my own age. He rode up to me and inquired if it was my horse, to which I replied in the affirmative, and asked permission to take from the saddle pockets some letters, pictures and other trinkets. He granted this, and we became friends from thence on until we separated. He rode by my side as we plodded over the steep, slippery hills, and we beguiled the way by chatting of the thousand things that soldiers find to talk about, and exchanged reminiscences of the service on both sides. But the subject he was fondest of was that which I relished least: my—now his—horse. Into the open ulcer of my heart he poured the acid of all manner of questions concerning my lost steed's qualities and capabilities: would he swim? how was he in fording? did he jump well! how did he stand fire? I smothered my irritation, and answered as pleasantly as I could.

In the afternoon of the third day after the capture, we came up to where a party of rustic belles were collected at "quilting." The "Yankees" were instantly objects of greater interest than the parade of a menagerie would have been. The Sergeant told the girls we were going to camp for the night a mile or so ahead, and if they would be at a certain house, he would have a Yankee for them for close inspection. After halting, the Sergeant obtained leave to take me out with a guard, and I was presently ushered into a room in which the damsels were massed in force, —a carnation-checked, staring, open-mouthed, linsey-clad crowd, as ignorant of corsets and gloves as of Hebrew, and with a propensity to giggle that was chronic and irrepressible. When we entered the room there was a general giggle, and then a shower of comments upon my appearance,—each sentence punctuated with the chorus of feminine cachination. A remark was made about my hair and eyes, and their risibles gave way; judgment was passed on my nose, and then came a ripple of laughter. I got very red in the face, and uncomfortable generally. Attention was called to the size of my feet and hands, and the usual chorus followed. Those useful members of my body seemed to swell up as they do to a young man at his first party.

Then I saw that in the minds of these bucolic maidens I was scarcely, if at all, human; they did not understand that I belonged to the race; I was a "Yankee"—a something of the non-human class, as the gorilla or the chimpanzee. They felt as free to discuss my points before my face as they would to talk of a horse or a wild animal in a show. My equanimity was partially restored by this reflection, but I was still too young to escape embarrassment and irritation at being thus dissected and giggled at by a party of girls, even if they were ignorant Virginia mountaineers. I turned around to speak to the Sergeant, and in so doing showed my back to the ladies. The hum of comment deepened into surprise, that half stopped and then intensified the giggle.

I was puzzled for a minute, and then the direction of their glances, and their remarks explained it all. At the rear of the lower part of the cavalry jacket, about where the upper ornamental buttons are on the tail of a frock coat, are two funny tabs, about the size of small pin-cushions. They are fastened by the edge, and stick out straight behind. Their use is to support the heavy belt in the rear, as the buttons do in front. When the belt is off it would puzzle the Seven Wise Men to guess what they are for. The unsophisticated young ladies, with that swift intuition which is one of lovely woman's salient mental traits, immediately jumped at the conclusion that the projections covered some peculiar conformation of the Yankee anatomy—some incipient, dromedary-like humps, or perchance the horns of which they had heard so much.

This anatomical phenomena was discussed intently for a few minutes, during which I heard one of the girls inquire whether "it would hurt him to cut 'em off?" and another hazarded the opinion that "it would probably bleed him to death."

Then a new idea seized them, and they said to the Sergeant "Make him sing! Make him sing!" This was too much for the Sergeant, who had been intensely amused at the girls' wonderment. He turned to me, very red in the face, with:

"Sergeant: the girls want to hear you sing."

I replied that I could not sing a note. Said he:

"Oh, come now. I know better than that; I never seed or heerd of a Yankee that couldn't sing."

I nevertheless assured him that there really were some Yankees that did not have any musical accomplishments, and that I was one of that unfortunate number. I asked him to get the ladies to sing for me, and to this they acceded quite readily. One girl, with a fair soprano, who seemed to be the leader of the crowd, sang "The Homespun Dress," a song very popular in the South, and having the same tune as the "Bonnie Blue Flag." It began,

I envy not the Northern girl
Their silks and jewels fine,

and proceeded to compare the homespun habiliments of the Southern women to the finery and frippery of the ladies on the other side of Mason and Dixon's line in a manner very disadvantageous to the latter.

The rest of the girls made a fine exhibition of the lung-power acquired in climbing their precipitous mountains, when they came in on the chorus

Hurra! Hurra! for southern rights Hurra!
Hurra for the homespun dress,
The Southern ladies wear.

This ended the entertainment.

On our journey to Bristol we met many Rebel soldiers, of all ranks, and a small number of citizens. As the conscription had then been enforced pretty sharply for over a year the only able-bodied men seen in civil life were those who had some trade which exempted them from being forced into active service. It greatly astonished us at first to find that nearly all the mechanics were included among the exempts, or could be if they chose; but a very little reflection showed us the wisdom of such a policy. The South is as nearly a purely agricultural country as is Russia or South America. The people have, little inclination or capacity for anything else than pastoral pursuits. Consequently mechanics are very scarce, and manufactories much scarcer. The limited quantity of products of mechanical skill needed by the people was mostly imported from the North or Europe. Both these sources of supply were cutoff by the war, and the country was thrown upon its own slender manufacturing resources. To force its mechanics into the army would therefore be suicidal. The Army would gain a few thousand men, but its operations would be embarrassed, if not stopped altogether, by a want of supplies. This condition of affairs reminded one of the singular paucity of mechanical skill among the Bedouins of the desert, which renders the life of a blacksmith sacred. No matter how bitter the feud between tribes, no one will kill the other's workers of iron, and instances are told of warriors saving their lives at critical periods by falling on their knees and making with their garments an imitation of the action of a smith's bellows.

All whom we met were eager to discuss with us the causes, phases and progress of the war, and whenever opportunity offered or could be made, those of us who were inclined to talk were speedily involved in an argument with crowds of soldiers and citizens. But, owing to the polemic poverty of our opponents, the argument was more in name than in fact. Like all people of slender or untrained intellectual powers they labored under the hallucination that asserting was reasoning, and the emphatic reiteration of bald statements, logic. The narrow round which all from highest to lowest—traveled was sometimes comical, and sometimes irritating, according to one's mood! The dispute invariably began by their asking:

"Well, what are you 'uns down here a-fightin' we 'uns for?"

As this was replied to the newt one followed:

"Why are you'uns takin' our niggers away from we 'uns for?"

Then came:

"What do you 'uns put our niggers to fightin' we'uns for?" The windup always was: "Well, let me tell you, sir, you can never whip people that are fighting for liberty, sir."

Even General Giltner, who had achieved considerable military reputation as commander of a division of Kentucky cavalry, seemed to be as slenderly furnished with logical ammunition as the balance, for as he halted by us he opened the conversation with the well-worn formula:

"Well: what are you 'uns down here a-fighting we'uns for?"

The question had become raspingly monotonous to me, whom he addressed, and I replied with marked acerbity:

"Because we are the Northern mudsills whom you affect to despise, and we came down here to lick you into respecting us."

The answer seemed to tickle him, a pleasanter light came into his sinister gray eyes, he laughed lightly, and bade us a kindly good day.

Four days after our capture we arrived in Bristol. The guards who had brought us over the mountains were relieved by others, the Sergeant bade me good by, struck his spurs into "Hiatoga's" sides, and he and my faithful horse were soon lost to view in the darkness.

A new and keener sense of desolation came over me at the final separation from my tried and true four-footed friend, who had been my constant companion through so many perils and

hardships. We had endured together the Winter's cold, the dispiriting drench of the rain, the fatigue of the long march, the discomforts of the muddy camp, the gripings of hunger, the weariness of the drill and review, the perils of the vidette post, the courier service, the scout and the fight. We had shared in common
The whips and scorns of time,
The oppressor's wrong, the proud man's contumely,
The insolence of office, and the spurns
which a patient private and his horse of the unworthy take; we had had our frequently recurring rows with other fellows and their horses, over questions of precedence at watering places, and grass-plots, had had lively tilts with guards of forage piles in surreptitious attempts to get additional rations, sometimes coming off victorious and sometimes being driven off ingloriously. I had often gone hungry that he might have the only ear of corn obtainable. I am not skilled enough in horse lore to speak of his points or pedigree. I only know that his strong limbs never failed me, and that he was always ready for duty and ever willing.
Now at last our paths diverged. I was retired from actual service to a prison, and he bore his new master off to battle against his old friends.

....

Packed closely in old, dilapidated stock and box cars, as if cattle in shipment to market, we pounded along slowly, and apparently interminably, toward the Rebel capital.
The railroads of the South were already in very bad condition. They were never more than passably good, even in their best estate, but now, with a large part of the skilled men engaged upon them escaped back to the North, with all renewal, improvement, or any but the most necessary repairs stopped for three years, and with a marked absence of even ordinary skill and care in their management, they were as nearly ruined as they could well be and still run.
One of the severe embarrassments under which the roads labored was a lack of oil. There is very little fatty matter of any kind in the South. The climate and the food plants do not favor the accumulation of adipose tissue by animals, and there is no other source of supply. Lard oil and tallow were very scarce and held at exorbitant prices.
Attempts were made to obtain lubricants from the peanut and the cotton seed. The first yielded a fine bland oil, resembling the ordinary grade of olive oil, but it was entirely too expensive for use in the arts. The cotton seed oil could be produced much cheaper, but it had in it such a quantity of gummy matter as to render it worse than useless for employment on machinery.
This scarcity of oleaginous matter produced a corresponding scarcity of soap and similar detergents, but this was a deprivation which caused the Rebels, as a whole, as little inconvenience as any that they suffered from. I have seen many thousands of them who were obviously greatly in need of soap, but if they were rent with any suffering on that account they concealed it with marvelous self-control.
There seemed to be a scanty supply of oil provided for the locomotives, but the cars had to run with unlubricated axles, and the screaking and groaning of the grinding journals in the dry boxes was sometimes almost deafening, especially when we were going around a curve.
Our engine went off the wretched track several times, but as she was not running much faster than a man could walk, the worst consequence to us was a severe jolting. She was small, and was easily pried back upon the track, and sent again upon her wheezy, straining way.

The depression which had weighed us down for a night and a day after our capture had now been succeeded by a more cheerful feeling. We began to look upon our condition as the fortune of war. We were proud of our resistance to overwhelming numbers. We knew we had sold ourselves at a price which, if the Rebels had it to do over again, they would not pay for us. We believed that we had killed and seriously wounded as many of them as they had killed, wounded and captured of us. We had nothing to blame ourselves for. Moreover, we began to be buoyed up with the expectation that we would be exchanged immediately upon our arrival at Richmond, and the Rebel officers confidently assured us that this would be so. There was then a temporary hitch in the exchange, but it would all be straightened out in a few days, and it might not be a month until we were again marching out of Cumberland Gap, on an avenging foray against some of the force which had assisted in our capture.

Fortunately for this delusive hopefulness there was no weird and boding Cassandra to pierce the veil of the future for us, and reveal the length and the ghastly horror of the Valley of the Shadow of Death, through which we must pass for hundreds of sad days, stretching out into long months of suffering and death. Happily there was no one to tell us that of every five in that party four would never stand under the Stars and Stripes again, but succumbing to chronic starvation, long-continued exposure, the bullet of the brutal guard, the loathsome scurvy, the hideous gangrene, and the heartsickness of hope deferred, would find respite from pain low in the barren sands of that hungry Southern soil.

Were every doom foretokened by appropriate omens, the ravens along our route would have croaked themselves hoarse.

But, far from being oppressed by any presentiment of coming evil, we began to appreciate and enjoy the picturesque grandeur of the scenery through which we were moving. The rugged sternness of the Appalachian mountain range, in whose rock-ribbed heart we had fought our losing fight, was now softening into less strong, but more graceful outlines as we approached the pine-clad, sandy plains of the seaboard, upon which Richmond is built. We were skirting along the eastern base of the great Blue Ridge, about whose distant and lofty summits hung a perpetual veil of deep, dark, but translucent blue, which refracted the slanting rays of the morning and evening sun into masses of color more gorgeous than a dreamer's vision of an enchanted land. At Lynchburg we saw the famed Peaks of Otter—twenty miles away—lifting their proud heads far into the clouds, like giant watch-towers sentineling the gateway that the mighty waters of the James had forced through the barriers of solid adamant lying across their path to the far-off sea. What we had seen many miles back start from the mountain sides as slender rivulets, brawling over the worn boulders, were now great, rushing, full-tide streams, enough of them in any fifty miles of our journey to furnish water power for all the factories of New England. Their amazing opulence of mechanical energy has lain unutilized, almost unnoticed, in the two and one-half centuries that the white man has dwelt near them, while in Massachusetts and her near neighbors every rill that can turn a wheel has been put into harness and forced to do its share of labor for the benefit of the men who have made themselves its masters.

Here is one of the differences between the two sections: In the North man was set free, and the elements made to do his work. In the South man was the degraded slave, and the elements wantoned on in undisturbed freedom.

As we went on, the Valleys of the James and the Appomattox, down which our way lay, broadened into an expanse of arable acres, and the faces of those streams were frequently flecked by gem-like little islands.

CHAPTER VII.

ENTERING RICHMOND—DISAPPOINTMENT AT ITS APPEARANCE—EVERYBODY IN
UNIFORM—CURLED DARLINGS OF THE CAPITAL—THE REBEL FLAG—LIBBY
PRISON —DICK TURNER—SEARCHING THE NEW COMERS.

Early on the tenth morning after our capture we were told that we were about to enter Richmond.
Instantly all were keenly observant of every detail in the surroundings of a City that was then the
object of the hopes and fears of thirty-five millions of people—a City assailing which seventy-
five thousand brave men had already laid down their lives, defending which an equal number had
died, and which, before it fell, was to cost the life blood of another one hundred and fifty
thousand valiant assailants and defenders.

So much had been said and written about Richmond that our boyish minds had wrought up the
most extravagant expectations of it and its defenses. We anticipated seeing a City differing
widely from anything ever seen before; some anomaly of nature displayed in its site, itself
guarded by imposing and impregnable fortifications, with powerful forts and heavy guns,
perhaps even walls, castles, postern gates, moats and ditches, and all the other panoply of
defensive warfare, with which romantic history had made us familiar.

We were disappointed—badly disappointed—in seeing nothing of this as we slowly rolled along.
The spires and the tall chimneys of the factories rose in the distance very much as they had in
other Cities we had visited. We passed a single line of breastworks of bare yellow sand, but the
scrubby pines in front were not cut away, and there were no signs that there had ever been any
immediate expectation of use for the works. A redoubt or two—without guns—could be made
out, and this was all. Grim-visaged war had few wrinkles on his front in that neighborhood. They
were then seaming his brow on the Rappahannock, seventy miles away, where the Army of
Northern Virginia and the Army of the Potomac lay confronting each other.

At one of the stopping places I had been separated from my companions by entering a car in
which were a number of East Tennesseeans, captured in the operations around Knoxville, and
whom the Rebels, in accordance with their usual custom, were treating with studied contumely. I
had always had a very warm side for these simple rustics of the mountains and valleys. I knew
much of their unwavering fidelity to the Union, of the firm steadfastness with which they
endured persecution for their country's sake, and made sacrifices even unto death; and, as in
those days I estimated all men simply by their devotion to the great cause of National integrity,
(a habit that still clings to me) I rated these men very highly. I had gone into their car to do my
little to encourage them, and when I attempted to return to my own I was prevented by the guard.

Crossing the long bridge, our train came to a halt on the other side of the river with the usual
clamor of bell and whistle, the usual seemingly purposeless and vacillating, almost dizzying,
running backward and forward on a network of sidetracks and switches, that seemed unavoidably

necessary, a dozen years ago, in getting a train into a City.

Still unable to regain my comrades and share their fortunes, I was marched off with the Tennesseeans through the City to the office of some one who had charge of the prisoners of war. The streets we passed through were lined with retail stores, in which business was being carried on very much as in peaceful times. Many people were on the streets, but the greater part of the men wore some sort of a uniform. Though numbers of these were in active service, yet the wearing of a military garb did not necessarily imply this. Nearly every able-bodied man in Richmond was; enrolled in some sort of an organization, and armed, and drilled regularly. Even the members of the Confederate Congress were uniformed and attached, in theory at least, to the Home Guards.

It was obvious even to the casual glimpse of a passing prisoner of war, that the City did not lack its full share of the class which formed so large an element of the society of Washington and other Northern Cities during the war—the dainty carpet soldiers, heros of the promenade and the boudoir, who strutted in uniforms when the enemy was far off, and wore citizen's clothes when he was close at hand. There were many curled darlings displaying their fine forms in the nattiest of uniforms, whose gloss had never suffered from so much as a heavy dew, let alone a rainy day on the march. The Confederate gray could be made into a very dressy garb. With the sleeves lavishly embroidered with gold lace, and the collar decorated with stars indicating the wearer's rank—silver for the field officers, and gold for the higher grade,—the feet compressed into high-heeled, high-instepped boots, (no Virginian is himself without a fine pair of skin-tight boots) and the head covered with a fine, soft, broad-brimmed hat, trimmed with a gold cord, from which a bullion tassel dangled several inches down the wearer's back, you had a military swell, caparisoned for conquest—among the fair sex.

On our way we passed the noted Capitol of Virginia—a handsome marble building,—of the column-fronted Grecian temple style. It stands in the center of the City. Upon the grounds is Crawford's famous equestrian statue of Washington, surrounded by smaller statues of other Revolutionary patriots.

The Confederate Congress was then in session in the Capitol, and also the Legislature of Virginia, a fact indicated by the State flag of Virginia floating from the southern end of the building, and the new flag of the Confederacy from the northern end. This was the first time I had seen the latter, which had been recently adopted, and I examined it with some interest. The design was exceedingly plain. Simply a white banner, with a red field in the corner where the blue field with stars is in ours. The two blue stripes were drawn diagonally across this field in the shape of a letter X, and in these were thirteen white stars, corresponding to the number of States claimed to be in the Confederacy.

The battle-flag was simply the red field. My examination of all this was necessarily very brief. The guards felt that I was in Richmond for other purposes than to study architecture, statuary and heraldry, and besides they were in a hurry to be relieved of us and get their breakfast, so my art-education was abbreviated sharply.

We did not excite much attention on the streets. Prisoners had by that time become too common in Richmond to create any interest. Occasionally passers by would fling opprobrious epithets at "the East Tennessee traitors," but that was all.

The commandant of the prisons directed the Tennesseeans to be taken to Castle Lightning—a prison used to confine the Rebel deserters, among whom they also classed the East Tennesseeans, and sometimes the West Virginians, Kentuckians, Marylanders and Missourians found fighting against them. Such of our men as deserted to them were also lodged there, as the Rebels, very properly, did not place a high estimate upon this class of recruits to their army, and, as we shall see farther along, violated all obligations of good faith with them, by putting them among the regular prisoners of war, so as to exchange them for their own men.

Back we were all marched to a street which ran parallel to the river and canal, and but one square away from them. It was lined on both sides by plain brick warehouses and tobacco factories, four and five stories high, which were now used by the Rebel Government as prisons and military storehouses.

The first we passed was Castle Thunder, of bloody repute. This occupied the same place in Confederate history, that, the dungeons beneath the level of the water did in the annals of the Venetian Council of Ten. It was believed that if the bricks in its somber, dirt-grimed walls could speak, each could tell a separate story of a life deemed dangerous to the State that had gone down in night, at the behest of the ruthless Confederate authorities. It was confidently asserted that among the commoner occurrences within its confines was the stationing of a doomed prisoner against a certain bit of blood-stained, bullet-chipped wall, and relieving the Confederacy of all farther fear of him by the rifles of a firing party. How well this dark reputation was deserved, no one but those inside the inner circle of the Davis Government can say. It is safe to believe that more tragedies were enacted there than the archives of the Rebel civil or military judicature give any account of. The prison was employed for the detention of spies, and those charged with the convenient allegation of "treason against the Confederate States of America." It is probable that many of these were sent out of the world with as little respect for the formalities of law as was exhibited with regard to the 'suspects' during the French Revolution.

Next we came to Castle Lightning, and here I bade adieu to my Tennessee companions.

A few squares more and we arrived at a warehouse larger than any of the others. Over the door was a sign

THOMAS LIBBY & SON,
SHIP CHANDLERS AND GROCERS.

This was the notorious "Libby Prison," whose name was painfully familiar to every Union man in the land. Under the sign was a broad entrance way, large enough to admit a dray or a small wagon. On one side of this was the prison office, in which were a number of dapper, feeble-faced clerks at work on the prison records.

As I entered this space a squad of newly arrived prisoners were being searched for valuables, and having their names, rank and regiment recorded in the books. Presently a clerk addressed as "Majah Tunnah," the man who was superintending these operations, and I scanned him with increased interest, as I knew then that he was the ill-famed Dick Turner, hated all over the North for his brutality to our prisoners.

He looked as if he deserved his reputation. Seen upon the street he would be taken for a second or third class gambler, one in whom a certain amount of cunning is pieced out by a readiness to use brute force. His face, clean-shaved, except a "Bowery-b'hoy" goatee, was white, fat, and selfishly sensual. Small, pig-like eyes, set close together, glanced around continually. His legs were short, his body long, and made to appear longer, by his wearing no vest—a custom common them with Southerners.

His faculties were at that moment absorbed in seeing that no person concealed any money from him. His subordinates did not search closely enough to suit him, and he would run his fat, heavily-ringed fingers through the prisoner's hair, feel under their arms and elsewhere where he thought a stray five dollar greenback might be concealed. But with all his greedy care he was no match for Yankee cunning. The prisoners told me afterward that, suspecting they would be searched, they had taken off the caps of the large, hollow brass buttons of their coats, carefully folded a bill into each cavity, and replaced the cap. In this way they brought in several hundred dollars safely.

There was one dirty old Englishman in the party, who, Turner was convinced, had money concealed about his person. He compelled him to strip off everything, and stand shivering in the sharp cold, while he took up one filthy rag after another, felt over each carefully, and scrutinized each seam and fold. I was delighted to see that after all his nauseating work he did not find so much as a five cent piece.

It came my turn. I had no desire, in that frigid atmosphere, to strip down to what Artemus Ward called "the skanderlous costoom of the Greek Slave;" so I pulled out of my pocket my little store of wealth—ten dollars in greenbacks, sixty dollars in Confederate graybacks—and displayed it as Turner came up with, "There's all I have, sir." Turner pocketed it without a word, and did not search me. In after months, when I was nearly famished, my estimation of "Majah Tunnah" was hardly enhanced by the reflection that what would have purchased me many good meals was probably lost by him in betting on a pair of queens, when his opponent held a "king full."

I ventured to step into the office to inquire after my comrades. One of the whey-faced clerks said with the supercilious asperity characteristic of gnat-brained headquarters attaches:

"Get out of here!" as if I had been a stray cur wandering in in search of a bone lunch.

I wanted to feed the fellow to a pile-driver. The utmost I could hope for in the way of revenge was that the delicate creature might some day make a mistake in parting his hair, and catch his death of cold.

The guard conducted us across the street, and into the third story of a building standing on the next corner below. Here I found about four hundred men, mostly belonging to the Army of the Potomac, who crowded around me with the usual questions to new prisoners: What was my Regiment, where and when captured, and:

What were the prospects of exchange?

It makes me shudder now to recall how often, during the dreadful months that followed, this momentous question was eagerly propounded to every new comer: put with bated breath by men to whom exchange meant all that they asked of this world, and possibly of the next; meant life, home, wife or sweet-heart, friends, restoration to manhood, and self-respect —everything, everything that makes existence in this world worth having.

I answered as simply and discouragingly as did the tens of thousands that came after me: "I did not hear anything about exchange."

A soldier in the field had many other things of more immediate interest to think about than the exchange of prisoners. The question only became a living issue when he or some of his intimate friends fell into the enemy's hands.

Thus began my first day in prison.

CHAPTER VIII

INTRODUCTION TO PRISON LIFE—THE PEMBERTON BUILDING AND ITS OCCUPANTS —NEAT SAILORS—ROLL CALL—RATIONS AND CLOTHING— CHIVALRIC "CONFISCATION."

I began acquainting myself with my new situation and surroundings. The building into which I had been conducted was an old tobacco factory, called the "Pemberton building," possibly from an owner of that name, and standing on the corner of what I was told were Fifteenth and Carey streets. In front it was four stories high; behind but three, owing to the rapid rise of the hill, against which it was built.

It fronted towards the James River and Kanawha Canal, and the James River—both lying side by side, and only one hundred yards distant, with no intervening buildings. The front windows afforded a fine view. To the right front was Libby, with its guards pacing around it on the sidewalk, watching the fifteen hundred officers confined within its walls. At intervals during each day squads of fresh prisoners could be seen entering its dark mouth, to be registered, and searched, and then marched off to the prison assigned them. We could see up the James River for a mile or so, to where the long bridges crossing it bounded the view. Directly in front, across the river, was a flat, sandy plain, said to be General Winfield Scott's farm, and now used as a proving ground for the guns cast at the Tredegar Iron Works.

The view down the river was very fine. It extended about twelve miles, to where a gap in the woods seemed to indicate a fort, which we imagined to be Fort Darling, at that time the principal fortification defending the passage of the James.

Between that point and where we were lay the river, in a long, broad mirror-like expanse, like a pretty little inland lake. Occasionally a busy little tug would bustle up or down, a gunboat move along with noiseless dignity, suggestive of a reserved power, or a schooner beat lazily from one side to the other. But these were so few as to make even more pronounced the customary idleness that hung over the scene. The tug's activity seemed spasmodic and forced—a sort of protest against the gradually increasing lethargy that reigned upon the bosom of the waters —the gunboat floated along as if performing a perfunctory duty, and the schooners sailed about as if tired of remaining in one place. That little stretch of water was all that was left for a cruising ground. Beyond Fort Darling the Union gunboats lay, and the only vessel that passed the barrier was the occasional flag-of-truce steamer.

The basement of the building was occupied as a store-house for the taxes-in-kind which the Confederate Government collected. On the first floor were about five hundred men. On the second floor—where I was—were about four hundred men. These were principally from the First Division, First Corps distinguished by a round red patch on their caps; First Division, Second Corps, marked by a red clover leaf; and the First Division, Third Corps, who wore a red diamond. They were mainly captured at Gettysburg and Mine Run. Besides these there was a considerable number from the Eighth Corps, captured at Winchester, and a large infusion of

Cavalry-First, Second and Third West Virginia—taken in Averill's desperate raid up the Virginia Valley, with the Wytheville Salt Works as an objective.

On the third floor were about two hundred sailors and marines, taken in the gallant but luckless assault upon the ruins of Fort Sumter, in the September previous. They retained the discipline of the ship in their quarters, kept themselves trim and clean, and their floor as white as a ship's deck. They did not court the society of the "sojers" below, whose camp ideas of neatness differed from theirs. A few old barnacle-backs always sat on guard around the head of the steps leading from the lower rooms. They chewed tobacco enormously, and kept their mouths filled with the extracted juice. Any luckless "sojer" who attempted to ascend the stairs usually returned in haste, to avoid the deluge of the filthy liquid.

For convenience in issuing rations we were divided into messes of twenty, each mess electing a Sergeant as its head, and each floor electing a Sergeant-of-the-Floor, who drew rations and enforced what little discipline was observed.

Though we were not so neat as the sailors above us, we tried to keep our quarters reasonably clean, and we washed the floor every morning; getting down on our knees and rubbing it clean and dry with rags. Each mess detailed a man each day to wash up the part of the floor it occupied, and he had to do this properly or no ration would be given him. While the washing up was going on each man stripped himself and made close examination of his garments for the body-lice, which otherwise would have increased beyond control. Blankets were also carefully hunted over for these "small deer."

About eight o'clock a spruce little lisping rebel named Ross would appear with a book, and a body-guard, consisting of a big Irishman, who had the air of a Policeman, and carried a musket barrel made into a cane. Behind him were two or three armed guards. The Sergeant-of-the-Floor commanded:

"Fall in in four ranks for roll-call."

We formed along one side of the room; the guards halted at the head of the stairs; Ross walked down in front and counted the files, closely followed by his Irish aid, with his gun-barrel cane raised ready for use upon any one who should arouse his ruffianly ire. Breaking ranks we returned to our places, and sat around in moody silence for three hours. We had eaten nothing since the previous noon. Rising hungry, our hunger seemed to increase in arithmetical ratio with every quarter of an hour.

These times afforded an illustration of the thorough subjection of man to the tyrant Stomach. A more irritable lot of individuals could scarcely be found outside of a menagerie than these men during the hours waiting for rations. "Crosser than, two sticks" utterly failed as a comparison.

They were crosser than the lines of a check apron. Many could have given odds to the traditional bear with a sore head, and run out of the game fifty points ahead of him. It was astonishingly easy to get up a fight at these times. There was no need of going a step out of the way to search for it, as one could have a full fledged article of overwhelming size on his hands at any instant, by a trifling indiscretion of speech or manner. All the old irritating flings between the cavalry, the artillery and the infantry, the older "first-call" men, and the later or "Three-Hundred-Dollar-men," as they were derisively dubbed, between the different corps of the Army of the Potomac, between men of different States, and lastly between the adherents and opponents of McClellan, came to the lips and were answered by a blow with the fist, when a ring would be formed around the combatants by a crowd, which would encourage them with yells to do their best. In a few minutes one of the parties to the fistic debate, who found the point raised by him not well taken, would retire to the sink to wash the blood from his battered face, and the rest would resume their seats and glower at space until some fresh excitement roused them. For the last hour or so of these long waits hardly a word would be spoken. We were too ill-natured to talk for amusement, and there was nothing else to talk for.

This spell was broken about eleven o'clock by the appearance at the head of the stairway of the Irishman with the gun-barrel cane, and his singing out:

"Sargint uv the flure: fourtane min and a bread-box!"

Instantly every man sprang to his feet, and pressed forward to be one of the favored fourteen. One did not get any more gyrations or obtain them any sooner by this, but it was a relief, and a change to walk the half square outside the prison to the cookhouse, and help carry the rations back.

For a little while after our arrival in Richmond, the rations were tolerably good. There had been so much said about the privations of the prisoners that our Government had, after much quibbling and negotiation, succeeded in getting the privilege of sending food and clothing through the lines to us. Of course but a small part of that sent ever reached its destination. There were too many greedy Rebels along its line of passage to let much of it be received by those for whom it was intended. We could see from our windows Rebels strutting about in overcoats, in which the box wrinkles were still plainly visible, wearing new "U. S." blankets as cloaks, and walking in Government shoes, worth fabulous prices in Confederate money.

Fortunately for our Government the rebels decided to out themselves off from this profitable source of supply. We read one day in the Richmond papers that "President Davis and his Cabinet had come to the conclusion that it was incompatible with the dignity of a sovereign power to permit another power with which it was at war, to feed and clothe prisoners in its hands."

I will not stop to argue this point of honor, and show its absurdity by pointing out that it is not an unusual practice with nations at war. It is a sufficient commentary upon this assumption of punctiliousness that the paper went on to say that some five tons of clothing and fifteen tons of food, which had been sent under a flag of truce to City Point, would neither be returned nor delivered to us, but "converted to the use of the Confederate Government."

"And surely they are all honorable men!"

Heaven save the mark.

CHAPTER IX.

BRANS OR PEAS—INSUFFICIENCY OF DARKY TESTIMONY—A GUARD KILLS A
PRISONER—PRISONERS TEAZE THE GUARDS—DESPERATE OUTBREAK.

But, to return to the rations—a topic which, with escape or exchange, were to be the absorbing
ones for us for the next fifteen months. There was now issued to every two men a loaf of coarse
bread—made of a mixture of flour and meal—and about the size and shape of an ordinary brick.
This half loaf was accompanied, while our Government was allowed to furnish rations, with a
small piece of corned beef. Occasionally we got a sweet potato, or a half-pint or such a matter of
soup made from a coarse, but nutritious, bean or pea, called variously "nigger-pea," "stock-pea,"
or "cow-pea."

This, by the way, became a fruitful bone of contention during our stay in the South. One strong
party among us maintained that it was a bean, because it was shaped like one, and brown, which
they claimed no pea ever was. The other party held that it was a pea because its various names all
agreed in describing it as a pea, and because it was so full of bugs —none being entirely free
from insects, and some having as many as twelve by actual count—within its shell. This, they
declared, was a distinctive characteristic of the pea family. The contention began with our first
instalment of the leguminous ration, and was still raging between the survivors who passed into
our lines in 1865. It waxed hot occasionally, and each side continually sought evidence to
support its view of the case. Once an old darky, sent into the prison on some errand, was
summoned to decide a hot dispute that was raging in the crowd to which I belonged. The
champion of the pea side said, producing one of the objects of dispute:

"Now, boys, keep still, till I put the question fairly. Now, uncle, what do they call that there?"

The colored gentleman scrutinized the vegetable closely, and replied,

"Well, dey mos' generally calls 'em stock-peas, round hyar aways."

"There," said the pea-champion triumphantly.

"But," broke in the leader of the bean party, "Uncle, don't they also call them beans?"

"Well, yes, chile, I spec dat lots of 'em does."

And this was about the way the matter usually ended.

I will not attempt to bias the reader's judgment by saying which side I believed to be right. As the
historic British showman said, in reply to the question as to whether an animal in his collection
was a rhinoceros or an elephant, "You pays your money and you takes your choice."

The rations issued to us, as will be seen above, though they appear scanty, were still sufficient to
support life and health, and months afterward, in Andersonville, we used to look back to them as
sumptuous. We usually had them divided and eaten by noon, and, with the gnawings of hunger
appeased, we spent the afternoon and evening comfortably. We told stories, paced up and down,
the floor for exercise, played cards, sung, read what few books were available, stood at the
windows and studied the landscape, and watched the Rebels trying their guns and shells, and so
on as long as it was daylight. Occasionally it was dangerous to be about the windows. This
depended wholly on the temper of the guards. One day a member of a Virginia regiment, on
guard on the pavement in front, deliberately left his beat, walked out into the center of the street,
aimed his gun at a member of the Ninth West Virginia, who was standing at a window near, and
firing, shot him through the heart, the bullet passing through his body, and through the floor
above. The act was purely malicious, and was done, doubtless, in revenge for some injury which
our men had done the assassin or his family.

We were not altogether blameless, by any means. There were few opportunities to say bitterly
offensive things to the guards, let pass unimproved.

The prisoners in the third floor of the Smith building, adjoining us, had their own way of teasing them. Late at night, when everybody would be lying down, and out of the way of shots, a window in the third story would open, a broomstick, with a piece nailed across to represent arms, and clothed with a cap and blouse, would be protruded, and a voice coming from a man carefully protected by the wall, would inquire:

"S-a-y, g-uarr-d, what time is it?"

If the guard was of the long suffering kind he would answer:

"Take yo' head back in, up dah; you kno hits agin all odahs to do dat?"

Then the voice would say, aggravatingly, "Oh, well, go to —— you —— Rebel ——, if you can't answer a civil question."

Before the speech was ended the guard's rifle would be at his shoulder and he would fire. Back would come the blouse and hat in haste, only to go out again the next instant, with a derisive laugh, and,

"Thought you were going to hurt somebody, didn't you, you —— —— —— —— ——. But, Lord, you can't shoot for sour apples; if I couldn't shoot no better than you, Mr. Johnny Reb, I would ——"

By this time the guard, having his gun loaded again, would cut short the remarks with another shot, which, followed up with similar remarks, would provoke still another, when an alarm sounding, the guards at Libby and all the other buildings around us would turn out. An officer of the guard would go up with a squad into the third floor, only to find everybody up there snoring away as if they were the Seven Sleepers. After relieving his mind of a quantity of vigorous profanity, and threats to "buck and gag" and cut off the rations of the whole room, the officer would return to his quarters in the guard house, but before he was fairly ensconced there the cap and blouse would go out again, and the maddened guard be regaled with a spirited and vividly profane lecture on the depravity of Rebels in general, and his own unworthiness in particular.

One night in January things took a more serious turn. The boys on the lower floor of our building had long considered a plan of escape. There were then about fifteen thousand prisoners in Richmond—ten thousand on Belle Isle and five thousand in the buildings. Of these one thousand five hundred were officers in Libby. Besides there were the prisoners in Castles Thunder and Lightning. The essential features of the plan were that at a preconcerted signal we at the second and third floors should appear at the windows with bricks and irons from the tobacco presses, which a should shower down on the guards and drive them away, while the men of the first floor would pour out, chase the guards into the board house in the basement, seize their arms, drive those away from around Libby and the other prisons, release the officers, organize into regiments and brigades, seize the armory, set fire to the public buildings and retreat from the City, by the south side of the James, where there was but a scanty force of Rebels, and more could be prevented from coming over by burning the bridges behind us.

It was a magnificent scheme, and might have been carried out, but there was no one in the building who was generally believed to have the qualities of a leader.

But while it was being debated a few of the hot heads on the lower floor undertook to precipitate the crisis. They seized what they thought was a favorable opportunity, overpowered the guard who stood at the foot of the stairs, and poured into the street. The other guards fell back and opened fire on them; other troops hastened up, and soon drove them back into the building, after killing ten or fifteen. We of the second and third floors did not anticipate the break at that time, and were taken as much by surprise as were the Rebels. Nearly all were lying down and many were asleep. Some hastened to the windows, and dropped missiles out, but before any concerted action could be taken it was seen that the case was hopeless, and we remained quiet.

Among those who led in the assault was a drummer-boy of some New York Regiment, a recklessly brave little rascal. He had somehow smuggled a small four-shooter in with him, and when they rushed out he fired it off at the guards.

After the prisoners were driven back, the Rebel officers came in and vapored around considerably, but confined themselves to big words. They were particularly anxious to find the revolver, and ordered a general and rigorous search for it. The prisoners were all ranged on one side of the room and carefully examined by one party, while another hunted through the blankets and bundles. It was all in vain; no pistol could be found. The boy had a loaf of wheat bread, bought from a baker during the day. It was a round loaf, set together in two pieces like a biscuit. He pulled these apart, laid the fourshooter between them, pressed the two halves together, and went on calmly nibbling away at the loaf while the search was progressing.

Two gunboats were brought up the next morning, and anchored in the canal near us, with their heavy guns trained upon the building. It was thought that this would intimidate as from a repetition of the attack, but our sailors conceived that, as they laid against the shore next to us, they could be easily captured, and their artillery made to assist us. A scheme to accomplish this was being wrought out, when we received notice to move, and it came to naught.

CHAPTER X.

THE EXCHANGE AND THE CAUSE OF ITS INTERRUPTION—BRIEF RESUME OF THE DIFFERENT CARTELS, AND THE DIFFICULTIES THAT LED TO THEIR SUSPENSION.

Few questions intimately connected with the actual operations of the Rebellion have been enveloped with such a mass of conflicting statement as the responsibility for the interruption of the exchange. Southern writers and politicians, naturally anxious to diminish as much as possible the great odium resting upon their section for the treatment of prisoners of war during the last year and a half of the Confederacy's existence, have vehemently charged that the Government of the United States deliberately and pitilessly resigned to their fate such of its soldiers as fell into the hands of the enemy, and repelled all advances from the Rebel Government looking toward a resumption of exchange. It is alleged on our side, on the other hand, that our Government did all that was possible, consistent with National dignity and military prudence, to secure a release of its unfortunate men in the power of the Rebels.

Over this vexed question there has been waged an acrimonious war of words, which has apparently led to no decision, nor any convictions—the disputants, one and all, remaining on the sides of the controversy occupied by them when the debate began.

I may not be in possession of all the facts bearing upon the case, and may be warped in judgment by prejudices in favor of my own Government's wisdom and humanity, but, however this may be, the following is my firm belief as to the controlling facts in this lamentable affair:

1. For some time after the beginning of hostilities our Government refused to exchange prisoners

with the Rebels, on the ground that this might be held by the European powers who were seeking a pretext for acknowledging the Confederacy, to be admission by us that the war was no longer an insurrection but a revolution, which had resulted in the 'de facto' establishment of a new nation. This difficulty was finally gotten over by recognizing the Rebels as belligerents, which, while it placed them on a somewhat different plane from mere insurgents, did not elevate them to the position of soldiers of a foreign power.

2. Then the following cartel was agreed upon by Generals Dig on our side and Hill on that of the Rebels:

HAXALL'S LANDING, ON JAMES RIVER, July 22, 1882.

The undersigned, having been commissioned by the authorities they respectively represent to make arrangements for a general exchange of prisoners of war, have agreed to the following articles:

ARTICLE I.—It is hereby agreed and stipulated, that all prisoners of war, held by either party, including those taken on private armed vessels, known as privateers, shall be exchanged upon the conditions and terms following:

Prisoners to be exchanged man for man and officer for officer. Privateers to be placed upon the footing of officers and men of the navy.

Men and officers of lower grades may be exchanged for officers of a higher grade, and men and officers of different services may be exchanged according to the following scale of equivalents:

A General-commanding-in-chief, or an Admiral, shall be exchanged for officers of equal rank, or for sixty privates or common seamen.

A Commodore, carrying a broad pennant, or a Brigadier General, shall be exchanged for officers of equal rank, or twenty privates or common seamen.

A Captain in the Navy, or a Colonel, shall be exchanged for officers of equal rank, or for fifteen privates or common seamen.

A Lieutenant Colonel, or Commander in the Navy, shall be exchanged for officers of equal rank, or for ten privates or common seamen.

A Lieutenant, or a Master in the Navy, or a Captain in the Army or marines shall be exchanged for officers of equal rank, or six privates or common seamen.

Master's-mates in the Navy, or Lieutenants or Ensigns in the Army, shall be exchanged for officers of equal rank, or four privates or common seamen. Midshipmen, warrant officers in the Navy, masters of merchant vessels and commanders of privateers, shall be exchanged for officers of equal rank, or three privates or common seamen; Second Captains, Lieutenants or mates of merchant vessels or privateers, and all petty officers in the Navy, and all noncommissioned officers in the Army or marines, shall be severally exchanged for persons of equal rank, or for two privates or common seamen; and private soldiers or common seamen shall be exchanged for each other man for man.

ARTICLE II.—Local, State, civil and militia rank held by persons not in actual military service will not be recognized; the basis of exchange being the grade actually held in the naval and military service of the respective parties.

ARTICLE III.—If citizens held by either party on charges of disloyalty, or any alleged civil offense, are exchanged, it shall only be for citizens. Captured sutlers, teamsters, and all civilians in the actual service of either party, to be exchanged for persons in similar positions.

ARTICLE IV.—All prisoners of war to be discharged on parole in ten days after their capture; and the prisoners now held, and those hereafter taken, to be transported to the points mutually agreed upon, at the expense of the capturing party. The surplus prisoners not exchanged shall not be permitted to take up arms again, nor to serve as military police or constabulary force in any fort, garrison or field-work, held by either of the respective parties, nor as guards of prisoners, deposits or stores, nor to discharge any duty usually performed by soldiers, until exchanged under the provisions of this cartel. The exchange is not to be considered complete until the officer or soldier exchanged for has been actually restored to the lines to which he belongs.

ARTICLE V.—Each party upon the discharge of prisoners of the other party is authorized to discharge an equal number of their own officers or men from parole, furnishing, at the same time, to the other party a list of their prisoners discharged, and of their own officers and men relieved from parole; thus enabling each party to relieve from parole such of their officers and men as the party may choose. The lists thus mutually furnished, will keep both parties advised of the true condition of the exchange of prisoners.

ARTICLE VI.—The stipulations and provisions above mentioned to be of binding obligation during the continuance of the war, it matters not which party may have the surplus of prisoners; the great principles involved being, First, An equitable exchange of prisoners, man for man, or officer for officer, or officers of higher grade exchanged for officers of lower grade, or for privates, according to scale of equivalents. Second, That privates and officers and men of different services may be exchanged according to the same scale of equivalents. Third, That all prisoners, of whatever arm of service, are to be exchanged or paroled in ten days from the time of their capture, if it be practicable to transfer them to their own lines in that time; if not, so soon thereafter as practicable. Fourth, That no officer, or soldier, employed in the service of either party, is to be considered as exchanged and absolved from his parole until his equivalent has actually reached the lines of his friends. Fifth, That parole forbids the performance of field, garrison, police, or guard or constabulary duty.

JOHN A. DIX, Major General.

D. H. HILL, Major General, C. S. A.

SUPPLEMENTARY ARTICLES.

ARTICLE VII.—All prisoners of war now held on either side, and all prisoners hereafter taken, shall be sent with all reasonable dispatch to A. M. Aiken's, below Dutch Gap, on the James River, in Virginia, or to Vicksburg, on the Mississippi River, in the State of Mississippi, and there exchanged of paroled until such exchange can be effected, notice being previously given by each party of the number of prisoners it will send, and the time when they will be delivered at those points respectively; and in case the vicissitudes of war shall change the military relations of the places designated in this article to the contending parties, so as to render the same inconvenient for the delivery and exchange of prisoners, other places bearing as nearly as may be the present local relations of said places to the lines of said parties, shall be, by mutual agreement, substituted. But nothing in this article contained shall prevent the commanders of the two opposing armies from exchanging prisoners or releasing them on parole, at other points mutually agreed on by said commanders.

ARTICLE VIII.—For the purpose of carrying into effect the foregoing articles of agreement, each party will appoint two agents for the exchange of prisoners of war, whose duty it shall be to communicate with each other by correspondence and otherwise; to prepare the lists of prisoners; to attend to the delivery of the prisoners at the places agreed on, and to carry out promptly, effectually, and in good faith, all the details and provisions of the said articles of agreement.

ARTICLE IX.—And, in case any misunderstanding shall arise in regard to any clause or stipulation in the foregoing articles, it is mutually agreed that such misunderstanding shall not affect the release of prisoners on parole, as herein provided, but shall be made the subject of friendly explanation, in order that the object of this agreement may neither be defeated nor postponed.

JOHN A. DIX, Major General. D. H. HILL, Major General. C. S. A.

This plan did not work well. Men on both sides, who wanted a little rest from soldiering, could obtain it by so straggling in the vicinity of the enemy. Their parole—following close upon their capture, frequently upon the spot—allowed them to visit home, and sojourn awhile where were pleasanter pastures than at the front. Then the Rebels grew into the habit of paroling everybody that they could constrain into being a prisoner of war. Peaceable, unwarlike and decrepit citizens of Kentucky, East Tennessee, West Virginia, Missouri and Maryland were "captured" and paroled, and setoff against regular Rebel soldiers taken by us.

3. After some months of trial of this scheme, a modification of the cartel was agreed upon, the main feature of which was that all prisoners must be reduced to possession, and delivered to the exchange officers either at City Point, Va., or Vicksburg, Miss. This worked very well for some months, until our Government began organizing negro troops. The Rebels then issued an order that neither these troops nor their officers should be held as amenable to the laws of war, but that, when captured, the men should be returned to slavery, and the officers turned over to the Governors of the States in which they were taken, to be dealt with according to the stringent law punishing the incitement of servile insurrection. Our Government could not permit this for a day. It was bound by every consideration of National honor to protect those who wore its uniform and bore its flag. The Rebel Government was promptly informed that rebel officers and men would be held as hostages for the proper treatment of such members of colored regiments as might be taken.

4. This discussion did not put a stop to the exchange, but while it was going on Vicksburg was captured, and the battle of Gettysburg was fought. The first placed one of the exchange points in our hands. At the opening of the fight at Gettysburg Lee captured some six thousand Pennsylvania militia. He sent to Meade to have these exchanged on the field of battle. Meade declined to do so for two reasons: first, because it was against the cartel, which prescribed that prisoners must be reduced to possession; and second, because he was anxious to have Lee hampered with such a body of prisoners, since it was very doubtful if he could get his beaten army back across the Potomac, let alone his prisoners. Lee then sent a communication to General Couch, commanding the Pennsylvania militia, asking him to receive prisoners on parole, and Couch, not knowing what Meade had done, acceded to the request. Our Government disavowed Couch's action instantly, and ordered the paroles to be treated as of no force, whereupon the Rebel Government ordered back into the field twelve thousand of the prisoners captured by Grant's army at Vicksburg.

5. The paroling now stopped abruptly, leaving in the hands of both sides the prisoners captured at Gettysburg, except the militia above mentioned. The Rebels added considerably to those in their hands by their captures at Chickamauga, while we gained a great many at Mission Ridge, Cumberland Gap and elsewhere, so that at the time we arrived in Richmond the Rebels had about fifteen thousand prisoners in their hands and our Government had about twenty-five thousand.

6. The rebels now began demanding that the prisoners on both sides be exchanged—man for man—as far as they went, and the remainder paroled. Our Government offered to exchange man for man, but declined—on account of the previous bad faith of the Rebels—to release the balance on parole. The Rebels also refused to make any concessions in regard to the treatment of officers and men of colored regiments.

7. At this juncture General B. F. Butler was appointed to the command of the Department of the

Blackwater, which made him an ex-officio Commissioner of Exchange. The Rebels instantly refused to treat with him, on the ground that he was outlawed by the proclamation of Jefferson Davis. General Butler very pertinently replied that this only placed him nearer their level, as Jefferson Davis and all associated with him in the Rebel Government had been outlawed by the proclamation of President Lincoln. The Rebels scorned to notice this home thrust by the Union General.

8. On February 12, 1864, General Butler addressed a letter to the Rebel Commissioner Ould, in which be asked, for the sake of humanity, that the questions interrupting the exchange be left temporarily in abeyance while an informal exchange was put in operation. He would send five hundred prisoners to City Point; let them be met by a similar number of Union prisoners. This could go on from day to day until all in each other's hands should be transferred to their respective flags.

The five hundred sent with the General's letter were received, and five hundred Union prisoners returned for them. Another five hundred, sent the next day, were refused, and so this reasonable and humane proposition ended in nothing.

This was the condition of affairs in February, 1864, when the Rebel authorities concluded to send us to Andersonville. If the reader will fix these facts in his minds I will explain other phases as they develop.

CHAPTER XI.

PUTTING IN THE TIME—RATIONS—COOKING UTENSILS—"FIAT" SOUP— "SPOONING" —AFRICAN NEWSPAPER VENDERS—TRADING GREENBACKS FOR CONFEDERATE MONEY —VISIT FROM JOHN MORGAN.

The Winter days passed on, one by one, after the manner described in a former chapter,—the mornings in ill-nature hunger; the afternoons and evenings in tolerable comfort. The rations kept growing lighter and lighter; the quantity of bread remained the same, but the meat diminished, and occasional days would pass without any being issued. Then we receive a pint or less of soup made from the beans or peas before mentioned, but this, too, suffered continued change, in the gradually increasing proportion of James River water, and decreasing of that of the beans.

The water of the James River is doubtless excellent: it looks well—at a distance—and is said to serve the purposes of ablution and navigation admirably. There seems to be a limit however, to the extent of its advantageous combination with the bean (or pea) for nutritive purposes. This, though, was or view of the case, merely, and not shared in to any appreciably extent by the gentlemen who were managing our boarding house. We seemed to view the matter through allopathic spectacles, they through homoeopathic lenses. We thought that the atomic weight of peas (or beans) and the James River fluid were about equal, which would indicate that the proper combining proportions would be, say a bucket of beans (or peas) to a bucket of water. They held that the nutritive potency was increased by the dilution, and the best results were obtainable when the symptoms of hunger were combated by the trituration of a bucketful of the peas-beans with a barrel of 'aqua jamesiana.'

My first experience with this "flat" soup was very instructive, if not agreeable. I had come into prison, as did most other prisoners, absolutely destitute of dishes, or cooking utensils. The well-used, half-canteen frying-pan, the blackened quart cup, and the spoon, which formed the usual kitchen outfit of the cavalryman in the field, were in the haversack on my saddle, and were lost to me when I separated from my horse. Now, when we were told that we were to draw soup, I was in great danger of losing my ration from having no vessel in which to receive it. There were but few tin cups in the prison, and these were, of course, wanted by their owners. By great good fortune I found an empty fruit can, holding about a quart. I was also lucky enough to find a piece from which to make a bail. I next manufactured a spoon and knife combined from a bit of hoop-iron.

These two humble utensils at once placed myself and my immediate chums on another plane, as far as worldly goods were concerned. We were better off than the mass, and as well off as the most fortunate. It was a curious illustration of that law of political economy which teaches that so-called intrinsic value is largely adventitious. Their possession gave us infinitely more consideration among our fellows than would the possession of a brown-stone front in an eligible location, furnished with hot and cold water throughout, and all the modern improvements. It was a place where cooking utensils were in demand, and title-deeds to brown-stone fronts were not. We were in possession of something which every one needed every day, and, therefore, were persons of consequence and consideration to those around us who were present or prospective borrowers.

On our side we obeyed another law of political economy: We clung to our property with unrelaxing tenacity, made the best use of it in our intercourse with our fellows, and only gave it up after our release and entry into a land where the plenitude of cooking utensils of superior construction made ours valueless. Then we flung them into the sea, with little gratitude for the great benefit they had been to us. We were more anxious to get rid of the many hateful recollections clustering around them.

But, to return to the alleged soup: As I started to drink my first ration it seemed to me that there was a superfluity of bugs upon its surface. Much as I wanted animal food, I did not care for fresh meat in that form. I skimmed them off carefully, so as to lose as little soup as possible. But the top layer seemed to be underlaid with another equally dense. This was also skimmed off as deftly as possible. But beneath this appeared another layer, which, when removed, showed still another; and so on, until I had scraped to the bottom of the can, and the last of the bugs went with the last of my soup. I have before spoken of the remarkable bug fecundity of the beans (or peas). This was a demonstration of it. Every scouped out pea (or bean) which found its way into the soup bore inside of its shell from ten to twenty of these hard-crusted little weevil. Afterward I drank my soup without skimming. It was not that I hated the weevil less, but that I loved the soup more. It was only another step toward a closer conformity to that grand rule which I have made the guiding maxim of my life:

'When I must, I had better.'

I recommend this to other young men starting on their career.

The room in which we were was barely large enough for all of us to lie down at once. Even then it required pretty close "spooning" together —so close in fact that all sleeping along one side would have to turn at once. It was funny to watch this operation. All, for instance, would be lying on their right sides. They would begin to get tired, and one of the wearied ones would sing out to the Sergeant who was in command of the row—

"Sergeant: let's spoon the other way."

That individual would reply:

"All right. Attention! LEFT SPOON!!" and the whole line would at once flop over on their left sides.

The feet of the row that slept along the east wall on the floor below us were in a line with the edge of the outer door, and a chalk line drawn from the crack between the door and the frame to the opposite wall would touch, say 150 pairs of feet. They were a noisy crowd down there, and one night their noise so provoked the guard in front of the door that he called out to them to keep quiet or he would fire in upon them. They greeted this threat with a chorus profanely uncomplimentary to the purity of the guard's ancestry; they did not imply his descent a la Darwin, from the remote monkey, but more immediate generation by a common domestic animal. The incensed Rebel opened the door wide enough to thrust his gun in, and he fired directly down the line of toes. His piece was apparently loaded with buckshot, and the little balls must have struck the legs, nipped off the toes, pierced the feet, and otherwise slightly wounded the lower extremities of fifty men. The simultaneous shriek that went up was deafening. It was soon found out that nobody had been hurt seriously, and there was not a little fun over the occurrence.

One of the prisoners in Libby was Brigadier General Neal Dow, of Maine, who had then a National reputation as a Temperance advocate, and the author of the famous Maine Liquor Law. We, whose places were near the front window, used to see him frequently on the street, accompanied by a guard. He was allowed, we understood, to visit our sick in the hospital. His long, snowy beard and hair gave him a venerable and commanding appearance.

Newsboys seemed to be a thing unknown in Richmond. The papers were sold on the streets by negro men. The one who frequented our section with the morning journals had a mellow; rich baritone for which we would be glad to exchange the shrill cries of our street Arabs. We long remembered him as one of the peculiar features of Richmond. He had one unvarying formula for proclaiming his wares. It ran in this wise:

"Great Nooze in de papahs!

"Great Nooze from Orange Coaht House, Virginny!
"Great Nooze from Alexandry, Virginny!
"Great Nooze from Washington City!
"Great Nooze from Chattanoogy, Tennessee!
"Great Nooze from Chahlston, Sou' Cahlina!
"Great Nooze in depapahs!"

It did not matter to him that the Rebels had not been at some of these places for months. He would not change for such mere trifles as the entire evaporation of all possible interest connected with Chattanooga and Alexandria. He was a true Bourbon Southerner—he learned nothing and forgot nothing.

There was a considerable trade driven between the prisoners and the guard at the door. This was a very lucrative position for the latter, and men of a commercial turn of mind generally managed to get stationed there. The blockade had cut off the Confederacy's supplies from the outer world, and the many trinkets about a man's person were in good demand at high prices. The men of the Army of the Potomac, who were paid regularly, and were always near their supplies, had their pockets filled with combs, silk handkerchiefs, knives, neckties, gold pens, pencils, silver watches, playing cards, dice, etc. Such of these as escaped appropriation by their captors and Dick Turner, were eagerly bought by the guards, who paid fair prices in Confederate money, or traded wheat bread, tobacco, daily papers, etc., for them.

There was also considerable brokerage in money, and the manner of doing this was an admirable exemplification of the folly of the "fiat" money idea. The Rebels exhausted their ingenuity in framing laws to sustain the purchasing power of their paper money. It was made legal tender for all debts public and private; it was decreed that the man who refused to take it was a public enemy; all the considerations of patriotism were rallied to its support, and the law provided that any citizens found trafficking in the money of the enemy—i.e., greenbacks, should suffer imprisonment in the Penitentiary, and any soldier so offending should suffer death.

Notwithstanding all this, in Richmond, the head and heart of the Confederacy, in January, 1864—long before the Rebel cause began to look at all desperate—it took a dollar to buy such a loaf of bread as now sells for ten cents; a newspaper was a half dollar, and everything else in proportion. And still worse: There was not a day during our stay in Richmond but what one could go to the hole in the door before which the guard was pacing and call out in a loud whisper:

"Say, Guard: do you want to buy some greenbacks?"

And be sure that the reply would be, after a furtive glance around to see that no officer was watching:

"Yes; how much do you want for them?"

The reply was then: "Ten for one."

"All right; how much have you got?"

The Yankee would reply; the Rebel would walk to the farther end of his beat, count out the necessary amount, and, returning, put up one hand with it, while with the other he caught hold of one end of the Yankee's greenback. At the word, both would release their holds simultaneously, the exchange was complete, and the Rebel would pace industriously up and down his beat with the air of the school boy who "ain't been a-doin' nothing."

There was never any risk in approaching any guard with a proposition of this kind. I never heard of one refusing to trade for greenbacks, and if the men on guard could not be restrained by these stringent laws, what hope could there be of restraining anybody else?

One day we were favored with a visit from the redoubtable General John H. Morgan, next to J. E. B. Stuart the greatest of Rebel cavalry leaders. He had lately escaped from the Ohio Penitentiary. He was invited to Richmond to be made a Major General, and was given a grand ovation by the citizens and civic Government. He came into our building to visit a number of the First Kentucky Cavalry (loyal)—captured at New Philadelphia, East Tennessee—whom he was anxious to have exchanged for men of his own regiment—the First Kentucky Cavalry (Rebel)—who were captured at the same time he was. I happened to get very close to him while he was standing there talking to his old acquaintances, and I made a mental photograph of him, which still retains all its original distinctness. He was a tall, heavy man, with a full, coarse, and somewhat dull face, and lazy, sluggish gray eyes. His long black hair was carefully oiled, and turned under at the ends, as was the custom with the rural beaux some years ago. His face was clean shaved, except a large, sandy goatee. He wore a high silk hat, a black broadcloth coat, Kentucky jeans pantaloons, neatly fitting boots, and no vest. There was nothing remotely suggestive of unusual ability or force of character, and I thought as I studied him that the sting of George D. Prentice's bon mot about him was in its acrid truth. Said Mr. Prentice:

"Why don't somebody put a pistol to Basil Duke's head, and blow John Morgan's brains out!"

[Basil Duke was John Morgan's right hand man.]

CHAPTER XII.

REMARKS AS TO NOMENCLATURE—VACCINATION AND ITS EFFECTS—
"N'YAARKER'S" —THEIR CHARACTERISTICS AND THEIR METHODS OF
OPERATING.

Before going any further in this narrative it may be well to state that the nomenclature employed is not used in any odious or disparaging sense. It is simply the adoption of the usual terms employed by the soldiers of both sides in speaking to or of each other. We habitually spoke of them and to them, as "Rebels," and "Johnnies ;" they of and to us, as "Yanks," and "Yankees." To have said "Confederates," "Southerners," "Secessionists," or "Federalists," "Unionists," "Northerners" or "Nationalists," would have seemed useless euphemism. The plainer terms suited better, and it was a day when things were more important than names.

For some inscrutable reason the Rebels decided to vaccinate us all. Why they did this has been one of the unsolved problems of my life. It is true that there was small pox in the City, and among the prisoners at Danville; but that any consideration for our safety should have led them to order general inoculation is not among the reasonable inferences. But, be that as it may, vaccination was ordered, and performed. By great good luck I was absent from the building with the squad drawing rations, when our room was inoculated, so I escaped what was an infliction to all, and fatal to many. The direst consequences followed the operation. Foul ulcers appeared on various parts of the bodies of the vaccinated. In many instances the arms literally rotted off; and death followed from a corruption of the blood. Frequently the faces, and other parts of those who recovered, were disfigured by the ghastly cicatrices of healed ulcers. A special friend of mine, Sergeant Frank Beverstock—then a member of the Third Virginia Cavalry, (loyal), and after the war a banker in Bowling Green, O.,—bore upon his temple to his dying day, (which occurred a year ago), a fearful scar, where the flesh had sloughed off from the effects of the virus that had tainted his blood.

This I do not pretend to account for. We thought at the time that the Rebels had deliberately poisoned the vaccine matter with syphilitic virus, and it was so charged upon them. I do not now believe that this was so; I can hardly think that members of the humane profession of medicine would be guilty of such subtle diabolism—worse even than poisoning the wells from which an enemy must drink. The explanation with which I have satisfied myself is that some careless or stupid practitioner took the vaccinating lymph from diseased human bodies, and thus infected all with the blood venom, without any conception of what he was doing. The low standard of medical education in the South makes this theory quite plausible.

We now formed the acquaintance of a species of human vermin that united with the Rebels, cold, hunger, lice and the oppression of distraint, to leave nothing undone that could add to the miseries of our prison life.

These were the fledglings of the slums and dives of New York—graduates of that metropolitan sink of iniquity where the rogues and criminals of the whole world meet for mutual instruction in vice.

They were men who, as a rule, had never known, a day of honesty and cleanliness in their misspent lives; whose fathers, brothers and constant companions were roughs, malefactors and, felons; whose mothers, wives and sisters were prostitutes, procuresses and thieves; men who had from infancy lived in an atmosphere of sin, until it saturated every fiber of their being as a dweller in a jungle imbibes malaria by every one of his, millions of pores, until his very marrow is surcharged with it.

They included representatives from all nationalities, and their descendants, but the English and Irish elements predominated. They had an argot peculiar to themselves. It was partly made up of the "flash" language of the London thieves, amplified and enriched by the cant vocabulary and the jargon of crime of every European tongue. They spoke it with a peculiar accent and intonation that made them instantly recognizable from the roughs of all other Cities. They called themselves "N'Yaarkers;" we came to know them as "Raiders."

If everything in the animal world has its counterpart among men, then these were the wolves, jackals and hyenas of the race at once cowardly and fierce—audaciously bold when the power of numbers was on their side, and cowardly when confronted with resolution by anything like an equality of strength.

Like all other roughs and rascals of whatever degree, they were utterly worthless as soldiers. There may have been in the Army some habitual corner loafer, some fistic champion of the bar-room and brothel, some Terror of Plug Uglyville, who was worth the salt in the hard tack he consumed, but if there were, I did not form his acquaintance, and I never heard of any one else who did. It was the rule that the man who was the readiest in the use of fist and slungshot at home had the greatest diffidence about forming a close acquaintance with cold lead in the neighborhood of the front. Thousands of the so-called "dangerous classes" were recruited, from whom the Government did not receive so much service as would pay for the buttons on their uniforms. People expected that they would make themselves as troublesome to the Rebels as they were to good citizens and the Police, but they were only pugnacious to the provost guard, and terrible to the people in the rear of the Army who had anything that could be stolen.

The highest type of soldier which the world has yet produced is the intelligent, self-respecting American boy, with home, and father and mother and friends behind him, and duty in front beckoning him on. In the sixty centuries that war has been a profession no man has entered its ranks so calmly resolute in confronting danger, so shrewd and energetic in his aggressiveness, so tenacious of the defense and the assault, so certain to rise swiftly to the level of every emergency, as the boy who, in the good old phrase, had been "well-raised" in a Godfearing home, and went to the field in obedience to a conviction of duty. His unfailing courage and good sense won fights that the incompetency or cankering jealousy of commanders had lost. High officers were occasionally disloyal, or willing to sacrifice their country to personal pique; still more frequently they were ignorant and inefficient; but the enlisted man had more than enough innate soldiership to make amends for these deficiencies, and his superb conduct often brought honors and promotions to those only who deserved shame and disaster.

Our "N'Yaarkers," swift to see any opportunity for dishonest gain, had taken to bounty-jumping, or, as they termed it, "leppin' the bounty," for a livelihood. Those who were thrust in upon us had followed this until it had become dangerous, and then deserted to the Rebels. The latter kept them at Castle Lightning for awhile, and then, rightly estimating their character, and considering that it was best to trade them off for a genuine Rebel soldier, sent them in among us, to be exchanged regularly with us. There was not so much good faith as good policy shown by this. It was a matter of indifference to the Rebels how soon our Government shot these deserters after getting them in its hands again. They were only anxious to use them to get their own men back. The moment they came into contact with us our troubles began. They stole whenever opportunities offered, and they were indefatigable in making these offer; they robbed by actual force, whenever force would avail; and more obsequious lick-spittles to power never existed— they were perpetually on the look-out for a chance to curry favor by betraying some plan or scheme to those who guarded us.

I saw one day a queer illustration of the audacious side of these fellows' characters, and it shows at the same time how brazen effrontery will sometimes get the better of courage. In a room in an adjacent building were a number of these fellows, and a still greater number of East Tennesseeans. These latter were simple, ignorant folks, but reasonably courageous. About fifty of them were sitting in a group in one corner of the room, and near them a couple or three "N'Yaarkers." Suddenly one of the latter said with an oath:

"I was robbed last night; I lost two silver watches, a couple of rings, and about fifty dollars in greenbacks. I believe some of you fellers went through me."

This was all pure invention; he no more had the things mentioned than he had purity of heart and a Christian spirit, but the unsophisticated Tennesseeans did not dream of disputing his statement, and answered in chorus:

"Oh, no, mister; we didn't take your things; we ain't that kind."

This was like the reply of the lamb to the wolf, in the fable, and the N'Yaarker retorted with a simulated storm of passion, and a torrent of oaths:

"—— —— I know ye did; I know some uv yez has got them; stand up agin the wall there till I search yez!"

And that whole fifty men, any one of whom was physically equal to the N'Yaarker, and his superior in point of real courage, actually stood against the wall, and submitted to being searched and having taken from them the few Confederate bills they had, and such trinkets as the searcher took a fancy to.

I was thoroughly disgusted.

CHAPTER XIII.

BELLE ISLE—TERRIBLE SUFFERING FROM COLD AND HUNGER—FATE OF LIEUTENANT BOISSEUX'S DOG—OUR COMPANY MYSTERY—TERMINATION OF ALL HOPES OF ITS SOLUTION.

In February my chum—B. B. Andrews, now a physician in Astoria, Illinois —was brought into our building, greatly to my delight and astonishment, and from him I obtained the much desired news as to the fate of my comrades. He told me they had been sent to Belle Isle, whither he had gone, but succumbing to the rigors of that dreadful place, he had been taken to the hospital, and, upon his convalesence, placed in our prison.

Our men were suffering terribly on the island. It was low, damp, and swept by the bleak, piercing winds that howled up and down the surface of the James. The first prisoners placed on the island had been given tents that afforded them some shelter, but these were all occupied when our battalion came in, so that they were compelled to lie on the snow and frozen ground, without shelter, covering of any kind, or fire. During this time the cold had been so intense that the James had frozen over three times.

The rations had been much worse than ours. The so-called soup had been diluted to a ridiculous thinness, and meat had wholly disappeared. So intense became the craving for animal food, that one day when Lieutenant Boisseux—the Commandant—strolled into the camp with his beloved white bull-terrier, which was as fat as a Cheshire pig, the latter was decoyed into a tent, a blanket thrown over him, his throat cut within a rod of where his master was standing, and he was then skinned, cut up, cooked, and furnished a savory meal to many hungry men.

When Boisseux learned of the fate of his four-footed friend he was, of course, intensely enraged, but that was all the good it did him. The only revenge possible was to sentence more prisoners to ride the cruel wooden horse which he used as a means of punishment.

Four of our company were already dead. Jacob Lowry and John Beach were standing near the gate one day when some one snatched the guard's blanket from the post where he had hung it, and ran. The enraged sentry leveled his gun and fired into the crowd. The balls passed through Lowry's and Beach's breasts. Then Charley Osgood, son of our Lieutenant, a quiet, fair-haired, pleasant-spoken boy, but as brave and earnest as his gallant father, sank under the combination of hunger and cold. One stinging morning he was found stiff and stark, on the hard ground, his bright, frank blue eyes glazed over in death.

One of the mysteries of our company was a tall, slender, elderly Scotchman, who appeared on the rolls as William Bradford. What his past life had been, where he had lived, what his profession, whether married or single, no one ever knew. He came to us while in Camp of Instruction near Springfield, Illinois, and seemed to have left all his past behind him as he crossed the line of sentries around the camp. He never received any letters, and never wrote any; never asked for a furlough or pass, and never expressed a wish to be elsewhere than in camp. He was courteous and pleasant, but very reserved. He interfered with no one, obeyed orders promptly and without remark, and was always present for duty. Scrupulously neat in dress, always as clean-shaved as an old-fashioned gentleman of the world, with manners and conversation that showed him to have belonged to a refined and polished circle, he was evidently out of place as a private soldier in a company of reckless and none-too-refined young Illinois troopers, but he never availed himself of any of the numerous opportunities offered to change his associations. His elegant penmanship would have secured him an easy berth and better society at headquarters, but he declined to accept a detail. He became an exciting mystery to a knot of us imaginative young cubs, who sorted up out of the reminiscential rag-bag of high colors and strong contrasts with which the sensational literature that we most affected had plentifully stored our minds, a half-dozen intensely emotional careers for him. We spent much time in mentally trying these on, and discussing which fitted him best. We were always expecting a denouement that would come like a lightning flash and reveal his whole mysterious past, showing him to have been the disinherited scion of some noble house, a man of high station, who was expiating some fearful crime; an accomplished villain eluding his pursuers—in short, a Somebody who would be a fitting hero for Miss Braddon's or Wilkie Collins's literary purposes. We never got but two clues of his past, and they were faint ones. One day, he left lying near me a small copy of "Paradise Lost," that he always carried with him. Turning over its leaves I found all of Milton's bitter invectives against women heavily underscored. Another time, while on guard with him, he spent much of his time in writing some Latin verses in very elegant chirography upon the white painted boards of a fence along which his beat ran. We pressed in all the available knowledge of Latin about camp, and found that the tenor of the verses was very uncomplimentary to that charming sex which does us the honor of being our mothers and sweethearts. These evidences we accepted as sufficient demonstration that there was a woman at the bottom of the mystery, and made us more impatient for further developments. These were never to come. Bradford pined away an Belle Isle, and grew weaker, but no less reserved, each day. At length, one bitter cold night ended it all. He was found in the morning stone dead, with his iron-gray hair frozen fast to the ground, upon which he lay. Our mystery had to remain unsolved. There was nothing about his person to give any hint as to his past.

CHAPTER XIV.

HOPING FOR EXCHANGE—AN EXPOSITION OF THE DOCTRINE OF CHANCES —OFF FOR ANDERSONVILLE—UNCERTAINTY AS TO OUR DESTINATION—ARRIVAL AT ANDERSONVILLE.

As each lagging day closed, we confidently expected that the next would bring some news of the eagerly-desired exchange. We hopefully assured each other that the thing could not be delayed much longer; that the Spring was near, the campaign would soon open, and each government would make an effort to get all its men into the field, and this would bring about a transfer of prisoners. A Sergeant of the Seventh Indiana Infantry stated his theory to me this way:

"You know I'm just old lightnin' on chuck-a-luck. Now the way I bet is this: I lay down, say on the ace, an' it don't come up; I just double my bet on the ace, an' keep on doublin' every time it loses, until at last it comes up an' then I win a bushel o' money, and mebbe bust the bank. You see the thing's got to come up some time; an' every time it don't come up makes it more likely to come up the next time. It's just the same way with this 'ere exchange. The thing's got to happen some day, an' every day that it don't happen increases the chances that it will happen the next day."

Some months later I folded the sanguine Sergeant's stiffening hands together across his fleshless ribs, and helped carry his body out to the dead-house at Andersonville, in order to get a piece of wood to cook my ration of meal with.

On the evening of the 17th of February, 1864, we were ordered to get ready to move at daybreak the next morning. We were certain this could mean nothing else than exchange, and our exaltation was such that we did little sleeping that night. The morning was very cold, but we sang and joked as we marched over the creaking bridge, on our way to the cars. We were packed so tightly in these that it was impossible to even sit down, and we rolled slowly away after a wheezing engine to Petersburg, whence we expected to march to the exchange post. We reached Petersburg before noon, and the cars halted there along time, we momentarily expecting an order to get out. Then the train started up and moved out of the City toward the southeast. This was inexplicable, but after we had proceeded this way for several hours some one conceived the idea that the Rebels, to avoid treating with Butler, were taking us into the Department of some other commander to exchange us. This explanation satisfied us, and our spirits rose again.

Night found us at Gaston, N. C., where we received a few crackers for rations, and changed cars. It was dark, and we resorted to a little strategy to secure more room. About thirty of us got into a tight box car, and immediately announced that it was too full to admit any more. When an officer came along with another squad to stow away, we would yell out to him to take some of the men out, as we were crowded unbearably. In the mean time everybody in the car would pack closely around the door, so as to give the impression that the car was densely crowded. The Rebel would look convinced, and demand:

"Why, how many men have you got in de cah?"

Then one of us would order the imaginary host in the invisible recesses to—

"Stand still there, and be counted," while he would gravely count up to one hundred or one hundred and twenty, which was the utmost limit of the car, and the Rebel would hurry off to put his prisoners somewhere else. We managed to play this successfully during the whole journey, and not only obtained room to lie down in the car, but also drew three or four times as many rations as were intended for us, so that while we at no time had enough, we were farther from starvation than our less strategic companions.

The second afternoon we arrived at Raleigh, the capitol of North Carolina, and were camped in a piece of timber, and shortly after dark orders were issued to us all to lie flat on the ground and not rise up till daylight. About the middle of the night a man belonging to a New Jersey regiment, who had apparently forgotten the order, stood up, and was immediately shot dead by the guard.

For four or five days more the decrepit little locomotive strained along, dragging after it the rattling' old cars. The scenery was intensely monotonous. It was a flat, almost unending, stretch of pine barrens and the land so poor that a disgusted Illinoisan, used to the fertility of the great American Bottom, said rather strongly, that,

"By George, they'd have to manure this ground before they could even make brick out of it."

It was a surprise to all of us who had heard so much of the wealth of Virginia, North Carolina, South Carolina and Georgia, to find the soil a sterile sand bank, interspersed with swamps.

We had still no idea of where we were going. We only knew that our general course was southward, and that we had passed through the Carolinas, and were in Georgia. We furbished up our school knowledge of geography and endeavored to recall something of the location of Raleigh, Charlotte, Columbia and Augusta, through which we passed, but the attempt was not a success.

Late on the afternoon of the 25th of February the Seventh Indiana Sergeant approached me with the inquiry:

"Do you know where Macon is?"

The place had not then become as well known as it was afterward.

It seemed to me that I had read something of Macon in Revolutionary history, and that it was a fort on the sea coast. He said that the guard had told him that we were to be taken to a point near that place, and we agreed that it was probably a new place of exchange. A little later we passed through the town of Macon, Ga, and turned upon a road that led almost due south.

About midnight the train stopped, and we were ordered off. We were in the midst of a forest of tall trees that loaded the air with the heavy balsamic odor peculiar to pine trees. A few small rude houses were scattered around near.

Stretching out into the darkness was a double row of great heaps of burning pitch pine, that smoked and flamed fiercely, and lit up a little space around in the somber forest with a ruddy glare. Between these two rows lay a road, which we were ordered to take.

The scene was weird and uncanny. I had recently read the "Iliad," and the long lines of huge fires reminded me of that scene in the first book, where the Greeks burn on the sea shore the bodies of

those smitten by Apollo's pestilential-arrows
For nine long nights, through all the dusky air,
The pyres, thick flaming shot a dismal glare.
Five hundred weary men moved along slowly through double lines of guards. Five hundred men marched silently towards the gates that were to shut out life and hope from most of them forever. A quarter of a mile from the railroad we came to a massive palisade of great squared logs standing upright in the ground. The fires blazed up and showed us a section of these, and two massive wooden gates, with heavy iron hinges and bolts. They swung open as we stood there and we passed through into the space beyond.
We were in Andersonville.

CHAPTER XV.

GEORGIA—A LEAN AND HUNGRY LAND—DIFFERENCE BETWEEN UPPER AND LOWER GEORGIA—THE PILLAGE OF ANDERSONVILLE.

As the next nine months of the existence of those of us who survived were spent in intimate connection with the soil of Georgia, and, as it exercised a potential influence upon our comfort and well-being, or rather lack of these—a mention of some of its peculiar characteristics may help the reader to a fuller comprehension of the conditions surrounding us—our environment, as Darwin would say.

Georgia, which, next to Texas, is the largest State in the South, and has nearly twenty-five per cent. more area than the great State of New York, is divided into two distinct and widely differing sections, by a geological line extending directly across the State from Augusta, on the Savannah River, through Macon, on the Ocmulgee, to Columbus, on the Chattahoochie. That part lying to the north and west of this line is usually spoken of as "Upper Georgia;" while that lying to the south and east, extending to the Atlantic Ocean and the Florida line, is called "Lower Georgia." In this part of the State—though far removed from each other—were the prisons of Andersonville, Savannah, Millen and Blackshear, in which we were incarcerated one after the other.

Upper Georgia—the capital of which is Atlanta—is a fruitful, productive, metalliferous region, that will in time become quite wealthy. Lower Georgia, which has an extent about equal to that of Indiana, is not only poorer now than a worn-out province of Asia Minor, but in all probability will ever remain so.

It is a starved, sterile land, impressing one as a desert in the first stages of reclamation into productive soil, or a productive soil in the last steps of deterioration into a desert. It is a vast expanse of arid, yellow sand, broken at intervals by foul swamps, with a jungle-life growth of unwholesome vegetation, and teeming With venomous snakes, and all manner of hideous crawling thing.

The original forest still stands almost unbroken on this wide stretch of thirty thousand square miles, but it does not cover it as we say of forests in more favored lands. The tall, solemn pines, upright and symmetrical as huge masts, and wholly destitute of limbs, except the little, umbrella-like crest at the very top, stand far apart from each other in an unfriendly isolation. There is no fraternal interlacing of branches to form a kindly, umbrageous shadow. Between them is no genial undergrowth of vines, shrubs, and demi-trees, generous in fruits, berries and nuts, such as make one of the charms of Northern forests. On the ground is no rich, springing sod of emerald green, fragrant with the elusive sweetness of white clover, and dainty flowers, but a sparse, wiry, famished grass, scattered thinly over the surface in tufts and patches, like the hair on a mangy cur.

The giant pines seem to have sucked up into their immense boles all the nutriment in the earth, and starved out every minor growth. So wide and clean is the space between them, that one can look through the forest in any direction for miles, with almost as little interference with the view as on a prairie. In the swampier parts the trees are lower, and their limbs are hung with heavy festoons of the gloomy Spanish moss, or "death moss," as it is more frequently called, because where it grows rankest the malaria is the deadliest. Everywhere Nature seems sad, subdued and somber.

I have long entertained a peculiar theory to account for the decadence and ruin of countries. My reading of the world's history seems to teach me that when a strong people take possession of a fertile land, they reduce it to cultivation, thrive upon its bountifulness, multiply into millions the mouths to be fed from it, tax it to the last limit of production of the necessities of life, take from it continually, and give nothing back, starve and overwork it as cruel, grasping men do a servant or a beast, and when at last it breaks down under the strain, it revenges itself by starving many of them with great famines, while the others go off in search of new countries to put through the same process of exhaustion. We have seen one country after another undergo this process as the seat of empire took its westward way, from the cradle of the race on the banks of the Oxus to the fertile plains in the Valley of the Euphrates. Impoverishing these, men next sought the Valley of the Nile, then the Grecian Peninsula; next Syracuse and the Italian Peninsula, then the Iberian Peninsula, and the African shores of the Mediterranean. Exhausting all these, they were deserted for the French, German and English portions of Europe. The turn of the latter is now come; famines are becoming terribly frequent, and mankind is pouring into the virgin fields of America. Lower Georgia, the Carolinas and Eastern Virginia have all the characteristics of these starved and worn-out lands. It would seem as if, away back in the distance of ages, some numerous and civilized race had drained from the soil the last atom of food-producing constituents, and that it is now slowly gathering back, as the centuries pass, the elements that have been wrung from the land.

Lower Georgia is very thinly settled. Much of the land is still in the hands of the Government. The three or four railroads which pass through it have little reference to local traffic. There are no towns along them as a rule; stations are made every ten miles, and not named, but numbered, as "Station No. 4"—"No. 10", etc. The roads were built as through lines, to bring to the seaboard the rich products of the interior.

Andersonville is one of the few stations dignified with a same, probably because it contained some half dozen of shabby houses, whereas at the others there was usually nothing more than a mere open shed, to shelter goods and travelers. It is on a rudely constructed, rickety railroad, that runs from Macon to Albany, the head of navigation on the Flint River, which is, one hundred and six miles from Macon, and two hundred and fifty from the Gulf of Mexico. Andersonville is about sixty miles from Macon, and, consequently, about three hundred miles from the Gulf. The camp was merely a hole cut in the wilderness. It was as remote a point from, our armies, as they then lay, as the Southern Confederacy could give. The nearest was Sherman, at Chattanooga, four hundred miles away, and on the other side of a range of mountains hundreds of miles wide. To us it seemed beyond the last forlorn limits of civilization. We felt that we were more completely at the mercy of our foes than ever. While in Richmond we were in the heart of the Confederacy; we were in the midst of the Rebel military and, civil force, and were surrounded on every hand by visible evidences of the great magnitude of that power, but this, while it enforced our ready submission, did not overawe us depressingly, We knew that though the Rebels were all about us in great force, our own men were also near, and in still greater force—that while they were very strong our army was still stronger, and there was no telling what day this superiority of strength, might be demonstrated in such a way as to decisively benefit us.

But here we felt as did the Ancient Mariner:

Alone on a wide, wide sea,
So lonely 'twas that God himself
Scarce seemed there to be.

CHAPTER XVI.

WAKING UP IN ANDERSONVILLE—SOME DESCRIPTION OF THE PLACE—OUR FIRST MAIL—BUILDING SHELTER—GEN. WINDER—HIMSELF AND LINEAGE.

We roused up promptly with the dawn to take a survey of our new abiding place. We found ourselves in an immense pen, about one thousand feet long by eight hundred wide, as a young surveyor—a member of the Thirty-fourth Ohio—informed us after he had paced it off. He estimated that it contained about sixteen acres. The walls were formed by pine logs twenty-five feet long, from two to three feet in diameter, hewn square, set into the ground to a depth of five feet, and placed so close together as to leave no crack through which the country outside could be seen. There being five feet of the logs in the ground, the wall was, of course, twenty feet high. This manner of enclosure was in some respects superior to a wall of masonry. It was equally unscalable, and much more difficult to undermine or batter down.

The pen was longest due north and south. It was divided in the center by a creek about a yard wide and ten inches deep, running from west to east. On each side of this was a quaking bog of slimy ooze one hundred and fifty feet wide, and so yielding that one attempting to walk upon it would sink to the waist. From this swamp the sand-hills sloped north and south to the stockade. All the trees inside the stockade, save two, had been cut down and used in its construction. All the rank vegetation of the swamp had also been cut off.

There were two entrances to the stockade, one on each side of the creek, midway between it and the ends, and called respectively the "North Gate" and the "South Gate." These were constructed double, by building smaller stockades around them on the outside, with another set of gates. When prisoners or wagons with rations were brought in, they were first brought inside the outer gates, which were carefully secured, before the inner gates were opened. This was done to prevent the gates being carried by a rush by those confined inside.

At regular intervals along the palisades were little perches, upon which stood guards, who overlooked the whole inside of the prison.

The only view we had of the outside was that obtained by looking from the highest points of the North or South Sides across the depression where the stockade crossed the swamp. In this way we could see about forty acres at a time of the adjoining woodland, or say one hundred and sixty acres altogether, and this meager landscape had to content us for the next half year.

Before our inspection was finished, a wagon drove in with rations, and a quart of meal, a sweet potato and a few ounces of salt beef were issued to each one of us.

In a few minutes we were all hard at work preparing our first meal in Andersonville. The debris of the forest left a temporary abundance of fuel, and we had already a cheerful fire blazing for every little squad. There were a number of tobacco presses in the rooms we occupied in Richmond, and to each of these was a quantity of sheets of tin, evidently used to put between the layers of tobacco. The deft hands of the mechanics among us bent these up into square pans, which were real handy cooking utensils, holding about—a quart. Water was carried in them from the creek; the meal mixed in them to a dough, or else boiled as mush in the same vessels; the potatoes were boiled; and their final service was to hold a little meal to be carefully browned, and then water boiled upon it, so as to form a feeble imitation of coffee. I found my education at Jonesville in the art of baking a hoe-cake now came in good play, both for myself and companions. Taking one of the pieces of tin which had not yet been made into a pan, we spread upon it a layer of dough about a half-inch thick. Propping this up nearly upright before the fire, it was soon nicely browned over. This process made it sweat itself loose from the tin, when it was turned over and the bottom browned also. Save that it was destitute of salt, it was quite a toothsome bit of nutriment for a hungry man, and I recommend my readers to try making a "pone" of this kind once, just to see what it was like.

The supreme indifference with which the Rebels always treated the matter of cooking utensils for us, excited my wonder. It never seemed to occur to them that we could have any more need of vessels for our food than cattle or swine. Never, during my whole prison life, did I see so much as a tin cup or a bucket issued to a prisoner. Starving men were driven to all sorts of shifts for want of these. Pantaloons or coats were pulled off and their sleeves or legs used to draw a mess's meal in. Boots were common vessels for carrying water, and when the feet of these gave way the legs were ingeniously closed up with pine pegs, so as to form rude leathern buckets. Men whose pocket knives had escaped the search at the gates made very ingenious little tubs and buckets, and these devices enabled us to get along after a fashion.

After our meal was disposed of, we held a council on the situation. Though we had been sadly disappointed in not being exchanged, it seemed that on the whole our condition had been bettered. This first ration was a decided improvement on those of the Pemberton building; we had left the snow and ice behind at Richmond—or rather at some place between Raleigh, N. C., and Columbia, S. C.—and the air here, though chill, was not nipping, but bracing. It looked as if we would have a plenty of wood for shelter and fuel, it was certainly better to have sixteen acres to roam over than the stiffing confines of a building; and, still better, it seemed as if there would be plenty of opportunities to get beyond the stockade, and attempt a journey through the woods to that blissful land —"Our lines."

We settled down to make the best of things. A Rebel Sergeant came in presently and arranged us in hundreds. We subdivided these into messes of twenty-five, and began devising means for shelter. Nothing showed the inborn capacity of the Northern soldier to take care of himself better than the way in which we accomplished this with the rude materials at our command. No ax, spade nor mattock was allowed us by the Rebels, who treated us in regard to these the same as in respect to culinary vessels. The only tools were a few pocket-knives, and perhaps half-a-dozen hatchets which some infantrymen-principally members of the Third Michigan—were allowed to retain. Yet, despite all these drawbacks, we had quite a village of huts erected in a few days,— nearly enough, in fact, to afford tolerable shelter for the whole five hundred of us first-comers. The wither and poles that grew in the swamp were bent into the shape of the semi-circular bows that support the canvas covers of army wagons, and both ends thrust in the ground. These formed the timbers of our dwellings. They were held in place by weaving in, basket-wise, a network of briers and vines. Tufts of the long leaves which are the distinguishing characteristic of the Georgia pine (popularly known as the "long-leaved pine") were wrought into this network until a thatch was formed, that was a fair protection against the rain—it was like the Irishman's unglazed window-sash, which "kep' out the coarsest uv the cold."

The results accomplished were as astonishing to us as to the Rebels, who would have lain unsheltered upon the sand until bleached out like field-rotted flax, before thinking to protect themselves in this way. As our village was approaching completion, the Rebel Sergeant who called the roll entered. He was very odd-looking. The cervical muscles were distorted in such a way as to suggest to us the name of "Wry-necked Smith," by which we always designated him. Pete Bates, of the Third Michigan, who was the wag of our squad, accounted for Smith's condition by saying that while on dress parade once the Colonel of Smith's regiment had commanded "eyes right," and then forgot to give the order "front." Smith, being a good soldier, had kept his eyes in the position of gazing at the buttons of the third man to the right, waiting for the order to restore them to their natural direction, until they had become permanently fixed in their obliquity and he was compelled to go through life taking a biased view of all things.

Smith walked in, made a diagonal survey of the encampment, which, if he had ever seen "Mitchell's Geography," probably reminded him of the picture of a Kaffir village, in that instructive but awfully dull book, and then expressed the opinion that usually welled up to every Rebel's lips:

"Well, I'll be durned, if you Yanks don't just beat the devil."

Of course, we replied with the well-worn prison joke, that we supposed we did, as we beat the Rebels, who were worse than the devil.

There rode in among us, a few days after our arrival, an old man whose collar bore the wreathed stars of a Major General. Heavy white locks fell from beneath his slouched hat, nearly to his shoulders. Sunken gray eyes, too dull and cold to light up, marked a hard, stony face, the salient feature of which was a thin-upped, compressed mouth, with corners drawn down deeply—the mouth which seems the world over to be the index of selfish, cruel, sulky malignance. It is such a mouth as has the school-boy—the coward of the play ground, who delights in pulling off the wings of flies. It is such a mouth as we can imagine some remorseless inquisitor to have had—that is, not an inquisitor filled with holy zeal for what he mistakenly thought the cause of Christ demanded, but a spleeny, envious, rancorous shaveling, who tortured men from hatred of their superiority to him, and sheer love of inflicting pain.

The rider was John H. Winder, Commissary General of Prisoners, Baltimorean renegade and the malign genius to whose account should be charged the deaths of more gallant men than all the inquisitors of the world ever slew by the less dreadful rack and wheel. It was he who in August could point to the three thousand and eighty-one new made graves for that month, and exultingly tell his hearer that he was "doing more for the Confederacy than twenty regiments."

His lineage was in accordance with his character. His father was that General William H. Winder, whose poltroonery at Bladensburg, in 1814, nullified the resistance of the gallant Commodore Barney, and gave Washington to the British.

The father was a coward and an incompetent; the son, always cautiously distant from the scene of hostilities, was the tormentor of those whom the fortunes of war, and the arms of brave men threw into his hands.

Winder gazed at us stonily for a few minutes without speaking, and, turning, rode out again. Our troubles, from that hour, rapidly increased.

CHAPTER XVII.

THE PLANTATION NEGROS—NOT STUPID TO BE LOYAL—THEIR DITHYRAMBIC MUSIC —COPPERHEAD OPINION OF LONGFELLOW.

The stockade was not quite finished at the time of our arrival—a gap of several hundred feet appearing at the southwest corner. A gang of about two hundred negros were at work felling trees, hewing legs, and placing them upright in the trenches. We had an opportunity—soon to disappear forever—of studying the workings of the "peculiar institution" in its very home. The negros were of the lowest field-hand class, strong, dull, ox-like, but each having in our eyes an admixture of cunning and secretiveness that their masters pretended was not in them. Their demeanor toward us illustrated this. We were the objects of the most supreme interest to them, but when near us and in the presence of a white Rebel, this interest took the shape of stupid, open-eyed, open-mouthed wonder, something akin to the look on the face of the rustic lout, gazing for the first time upon a locomotive or a steam threshing machine. But if chance threw one of them near us when he thought himself unobserved by the Rebels, the blank, vacant face lighted up with an entirely different expression. He was no longer the credulous yokel who believed the Yankees were only slightly modified devils, ready at any instant to return to their original horn-and-tail condition and snatch him away to the bluest kind of perdition; he knew, apparently quite as well as his master, that they were in some way his friends and allies, and he lost no opportunity in communicating his appreciation of that fact, and of offering his services in any possible way. And these offers were sincere. It is the testimony of every Union prisoner in the South that he was never betrayed by or disappointed in a field-negro, but could always approach any one of them with perfect confidence in his extending all the aid in his power, whether as a guide to escape, as sentinel to signal danger, or a purveyor of food. These services were frequently attended with the greatest personal risk, but they were none the less readily undertaken. This applies only to the field-hands; the house servants were treacherous and wholly unreliable. Very many of our men who managed to get away from the prisons were recaptured through their betrayal by house servants, but none were retaken where a field hand could prevent it.

We were much interested in watching the negro work. They wove in a great deal of their peculiar, wild, mournful music, whenever the character of the labor permitted. They seemed to sing the music for the music's sake alone, and were as heedless of the fitness of the accompanying words, as the composer of a modern opera is of his libretto. One middle aged man, with a powerful, mellow baritone, like the round, full notes of a French horn, played by a virtuoso, was the musical leader of the party. He never seemed to bother himself about air, notes or words, but improvised all as he went along, and he sang as the spirit moved him. He would suddenly break out with—

"Oh, he's gone up dah, nevah to come back agin,"

At this every darkey within hearing would roll out, in admirable consonance with the pitch, air and time started by the leader—

"O-o-o-o-o-o-o-o-o-o-o-o-o-o!"

Then would ring out from the leader as from the throbbing lips of a silver trumpet:

"Lord bress him soul; I done hope he is happy now!"

And the antiphonal two hundred would chant back

"O-o-o-o-o-o-o-o-o-o-o-o-o-o!"

And so on for hours. They never seemed to weary of singing, and we certainly did not of listening to them. The absolute independence of the conventionalities of tune and sentiment, gave them freedom to wander through a kaleideoscopic variety of harmonic effects, as spontaneous and changeful as the song of a bird.

I sat one evening, long after the shadows of night had fallen upon the hillside, with one of my chums—a Frank Berkstresser, of the Ninth Maryland Infantry, who before enlisting was a mathematical tutor in college at Hancock, Maryland. As we listened to the unwearying flow of melody from the camp of the laborers, I thought of and repeated to him Longfellow's fine lines: THE SLAVE SINGING AT MIDNIGHT.

And the voice of his devotion
Filled my soul with strong emotion;
For its tones by turns were glad

Sweetly solemn, wildly sad.
Paul and Silas, in their prison,
Sang of Christ, the Lord arisen,
And an earthquake's arm of might
Broke their dungeon gates at night.
But, alas, what holy angel
Brings the slave this glad evangel
And what earthquake's arm of might.
Breaks his prison gags at night.
Said I: "Now, isn't that fine, Berkstresser?"
He was a Democrat, of fearfully pro-slavery ideas, and he replied, sententiously:
"O, the poetry's tolerable, but the sentiment's damnable."

CHAPTER XVIII.

SCHEMES AND PLANS TO ESCAPE—SCALING THE STOCKADE—ESTABLISHING THE DEAD LINE—THE FIRST MAN KILLED.

The official designation of our prison was "Camp Sumpter," but this was scarcely known outside of the Rebel documents, reports and orders. It was the same way with the prison five miles from Millen, to which we were afterward transferred. The Rebels styled it officially "Camp Lawton," but we called it always "Millen."

Having our huts finished, the next solicitude was about escape, and this was the burden of our thoughts, day and night. We held conferences, at which every man was required to contribute all the geographical knowledge of that section of Georgia that he might have left over from his schoolboy days, and also that gained by persistent questioning of such guards and other Rebels as he had come in contact with. When first landed in the prison we were as ignorant of our whereabouts as if we had been dropped into the center of Africa. But one of the prisoners was found to have a fragment of a school atlas, in which was an outline map of Georgia, that had Macon, Atlanta, Milledgeville, and Savannah laid down upon it. As we knew we had come southward from Macon, we felt pretty certain we were in the southwestern corner of the State. Conversations with guards and others gave us the information that the Chattahooche flowed some two score of miles to the westward, and that the Flint lay a little nearer on the east. Our map showed that these two united and flowed together into Appalachicola Bay, where, some of us remembered, a newspaper item had said that we had gunboats stationed. The creek that ran through the stockade flowed to the east, and we reasoned that if we followed its course we would be led to the Flint, down which we could float on a log or raft to the Appalachicola. This was the favorite scheme of the party with which I sided. Another party believed the most feasible plan was to go northward, and endeavor to gain the mountains, and thence get into East Tennessee. But the main thing was to get away from the stockade; this, as the French say of all first steps, was what would cost.

Our first attempt was made about a week after our arrival. We found two logs on the east side that were a couple of feet shorter than the rest, and it seemed as if they could be successfully scaled. About fifty of us resolved to make the attempt. We made a rope twenty-five or thirty feet long, and strong enough to bear a man, out of strings and strips of cloth. A stout stick was fastened to the end, so that it would catch on the logs on either side of the gap. On a night dark enough to favor our scheme, we gathered together, drew cuts to determine each boy's place in the line, fell in single rank, according to this arrangement, and marched to the place. The line was thrown skillfully, the stick caught fairly in the notch, and the boy who had drawn number one climbed up amid a suspense so keen that I could hear my heart beating. It seemed ages before he reached the top, and that the noise he made must certainly attract the attention of the guard. It did not. We saw our comrade's. figure outlined against the sky as he slid, over the top, and then heard the dull thump as he sprang to the ground on the other side. "Number two," was whispered by our leader, and he performed the feat as successfully as his predecessor. "Number, three," and he followed noiselessly and quickly. Thus it went on, until, just as we heard number fifteen drop, we also heard a Rebel voice say in a vicious undertone:

"Halt! halt, there, d—n you!"

This was enough. The game was up; we were discovered, and the remaining thirty-five of us left that locality with all the speed in our heels, getting away just in time to escape a volley which a squad of guards, posted in the lookouts, poured upon the spot where we had been standing.

The next morning the fifteen who had got over the Stockade were brought in, each chained to a sixty-four pound ball. Their story was that one of the N'Yaarkers, who had become cognizant of our scheme, had sought to obtain favor in the Rebel eyes by betraying us. The Rebels stationed a squad at the crossing place, and as each man dropped down from the Stockade he was caught by the shoulder, the muzzle of a revolver thrust into his face, and an order to surrender whispered into his ear. It was expected that the guards in the sentry-boxes would do such execution among those of us still inside as would prove a warning to other would-be escapes. They were defeated in this benevolent intention by the readiness with which we divined the meaning of that incautiously loud halt, and our alacrity in leaving the unhealthy locality.

The traitorous N'Yaarker was rewarded with a detail into the commissary department, where he fed and fattened like a rat that had secured undisturbed homestead rights in the center of a cheese. When the miserable remnant of us were leaving Andersonville months afterward, I saw him, sleek, rotund, and well-clothed, lounging leisurely in the door of a tent. He regarded us a moment contemptuously, and then went on conversing with a fellow N'Yaarker, in the foul slang that none but such as he were low enough to use.

I have always imagined that the fellow returned home, at the close of the war, and became a prominent member of Tweed's gang.

We protested against the barbarity of compelling men to wear irons for exercising their natural right of attempting to escape, but no attention was paid to our protest.

Another result of this abortive effort was the establishment of the notorious "Dead Line." A few days later a gang of negros came in and drove a line of stakes down at a distance of twenty feet from the stockade. They nailed upon this a strip of stuff four inches wide, and then an order was issued that if this was crossed, or even touched, the guards would fire upon the offender without warning.

Our surveyor figured up this new contraction of our space, and came to the conclusion that the Dead Line and the Swamp took up about three acres, and we were left now only thirteen acres. This was not of much consequence then, however, as we still had plenty of room.

The first man was killed the morning after the Dead-Line was put up. The victim was a German, wearing the white crescent of the Second Division of the Eleventh Corps, whom we had nicknamed "Sigel." Hardship and exposure had crazed him, and brought on a severe attack of St. Vitus's dance. As he went hobbling around with a vacuous grin upon his face, he spied an old piece of cloth lying on the ground inside the Dead Line. He stooped down and reached under for it. At that instant the guard fired. The charge of ball-and-buck entered the poor old fellow's shoulder and tore through his body. He fell dead, still clutching the dirty rag that had cost him his Life.

CHAPTER XIX.

CAPT. HENRI WIRZ—SOME DESCRIPTION OF A SMALL-MINDED PERSONAGE, WHO GAINED GREAT NOTORIETY—FIRST EXPERIENCE WITH HIS DISCIPLINARY METHOD.

The emptying of the prisons at Danville and Richmond into Andersonville went on slowly during the month of March. They came in by train loads of from five hundred to eight hundred, at intervals of two or three days. By the end of the month there were about five thousand in the stockade. There was a fair amount of space for this number, and as yet we suffered no inconvenience from our crowding, though most persons would fancy that thirteen acres of ground was a rather limited area for five thousand men to live, move and have their being a upon. Yet a few weeks later we were to see seven times that many packed into that space.

One morning a new Rebel officer came in to superintend calling the roll. He was an undersized, fidgety man, with an insignificant face, and a mouth that protruded like a rabbit's. His bright little eyes, like those of a squirrel or a rat, assisted in giving his countenance a look of kinship to the family of rodent animals—a genus which lives by stealth and cunning, subsisting on that which it can steal away from stronger and braver creatures. He was dressed in a pair of gray trousers, with the other part of his body covered with a calico garment, like that which small boys used to wear, called "waists." This was fastened to the pantaloons by buttons, precisely as was the custom with the garments of boys struggling with the orthography of words in two syllables. Upon his head was perched a little gray cap. Sticking in his belt, and fastened to his wrist by a strap two or three feet long, was one of those formidable looking, but harmless English revolvers, that have ten barrels around the edge of the cylinder, and fire a musket-bullet from the center. The wearer of this composite costume, and bearer of this amateur arsenal, stepped nervously about and sputtered volubly in very broken English. He said to Wry-Necked Smith:

"Py Gott, you don't vatch dem dam Yankees glose enough! Dey are schlippin' round, and peatin' you efery dimes."

This was Captain Henri Wirz, the new commandant of the interior of the prison. There has been a great deal of misapprehension of the character of Wirz. He is usually regarded as a villain of large mental caliber, and with a genius for cruelty. He was nothing of the kind. He was simply contemptible, from whatever point of view he was studied. Gnat-brained, cowardly, and feeble natured, he had not a quality that commanded respect from any one who knew him. His cruelty did not seem designed so much as the ebullitions of a peevish, snarling little temper, united to a mind incapable of conceiving the results of his acts, or understanding the pain he was Inflicting. I never heard anything of his profession or vocation before entering the army. I always believed, however, that he had been a cheap clerk in a small dry-goods store, a third or fourth rate book-keeper, or something similar. Imagine, if you please, one such, who never had brains or self-command sufficient to control himself, placed in command of thirty-five thousand men. Being a fool he could not help being an infliction to them, even with the best of intentions, and Wirz was not troubled with good intentions.

I mention the probability of his having been a dry-goods clerk or book-keeper, not with any disrespect to two honorable vocations, but because Wirz had had some training as an accountant, and this was what gave him the place over us. Rebels, as a rule, are astonishingly ignorant of arithmetic and accounting, generally. They are good shots, fine horsemen, ready speakers and ardent politicians, but, like all noncommercial people, they flounder hopelessly in what people of this section would consider simple mathematical processes. One of our constant amusements was in befogging and "beating" those charged with calling rolls and issuing rations. It was not at all difficult at times to make a hundred men count as a hundred and ten, and so on.

Wirz could count beyond one hundred, and this determined his selection for the place. His first move was a stupid change. We had been grouped in the natural way into hundreds and thousands. He re-arranged the men in "squads" of ninety, and three of these—two hundred and seventy men —into a "detachment." The detachments were numbered in order from the North Gate, and the squads were numbered "one, two, three." On the rolls this was stated after the man's name. For instance, a chum of mine, and in the same squad with me, was Charles L. Soule, of the Third Michigan Infantry. His name appeared on the rolls:

"Chas. L. Soule, priv. Co. E, 8d Mich. Inf., 1-2."

That is, he belonged to the Second Squad of the First Detachment.

Where Wirz got his, preposterous idea of organization from has always been a mystery to me. It was awkward in every way—in drawing rations, counting, dividing into messes, etc.

Wirz was not long in giving us a taste of his quality. The next morning after his first appearance he came in when roll-call was sounded, and ordered all the squads and detachments to form, and remain standing in ranks until all were counted. Any soldier will say that there is no duty more annoying and difficult than standing still in ranks for any considerable length of time, especially when there is nothing to do or to engage the attention. It took Wirz between two and three hours to count the whole camp, and by that time we of the first detachments were almost all out of ranks. Thereupon Wirz announced that no rations would be issued to the camp that day. The orders to stand in ranks were repeated the next morning, with a warning that a failure to obey would be punished as that of the previous day had been. Though we were so hungry, that, to use the words of a Thirty-Fifth Pennsylvanian standing next to me—his "big intestines were eating his little ones up," it was impossible to keep the rank formation during the long hours. One man after another straggled away, and again we lost our rations. That afternoon we became desperate. Plots were considered for a daring assault to force the gates or scale the stockade. The men were crazy enough to attempt anything rather than sit down and patiently starve. Many offered themselves as leaders in any attempt that it might be thought best to make. The hopelessness of any such venture was apparent, even to famished men, and the propositions went no farther than inflammatory talk.

The third morning the orders were again repeated. This time we succeeded in remaining in ranks in such a manner as to satisfy Wirz, and we were given our rations for that day, but those of the other days were permanently withheld.

That afternoon Wirz ventured into camp alone. He was assailed with a storm of curses and execrations, and a shower of clubs. He pulled out his revolver, as if to fire upon his assailants. A yell was raised to take his pistol away from him and a crowd rushed forward to do this. Without waiting to fire a shot, he turned and ran to the gate for dear life. He did not come in again for a long while, and never afterward without a retinue of guards.

CHAPTER XX.

PRIZE-FIGHT AMONG THE N'YAARKERS—A GREAT MANY FORMALITIES, AND LITTLE BLOOD SPILT—A FUTILE ATTEMPT TO RECOVER A WATCH—DEFEAT OF THE LAW AND ORDER PARTY.

One of the train-loads from Richmond was almost wholly made up of our old acquaintances—the N'Yaarkers. The number of these had swelled to four hundred or five hundred—all leagued together in the fellowship of crime.

We did not manifest any keen desire for intimate social relations with them, and they did not seem to hunger for our society, so they moved across the creek to the unoccupied South Side, and established their camp there, at a considerable distance from us.

One afternoon a number of us went across to their camp, to witness a fight according to the rules of the Prize Ring, which was to come off between two professional pugilists. These were a couple of bounty-jumpers who had some little reputation in New York sporting circles, under the names of the "Staleybridge Chicken" and the "Haarlem Infant."

On the way from Richmond a cast-iron skillet, or spider, had been stolen by the crowd from the Rebels. It was a small affair, holding a half gallon, and worth to-day about fifty cents. In Andersonville its worth was literally above rubies. Two men belonging to different messes each claimed the ownership of the utensil, on the ground of being most active in securing it. Their claims were strenuously supported by their respective messes, at the heads of which were the aforesaid Infant and Chicken. A great deal of strong talk, and several indecisive knock-downs resulted in an agreement to settle the matter by wager of battle between the Infant and Chicken. When we arrived a twenty-four foot ring had been prepared by drawing a deep mark in the sand. In diagonally opposite corners of these the seconds were kneeling on one knee and supporting their principals on the other by their sides they had little vessels of water, and bundles of rags to answer for sponges. Another corner was occupied by the umpire, a foul-mouthed, loud-tongued Tombs shyster, named Pete Bradley. A long-bodied, short-legged hoodlum, nick-named

"Heenan," armed with a club, acted as ring keeper, and "belted" back, remorselessly, any of the spectators who crowded over the line. Did he see a foot obtruding itself so much as an inch over the mark in the sand—and the pressure from the crowd behind was so great that it was difficult for the front fellows to keep off the line—his heavy club and a blasting curse would fall upon the offender simultaneously.

Every effort was made to have all things conform as nearly as possible to the recognized practices of the "London Prize Ring."

At Bradley's call of "Time!" the principals would rise from their seconds' knees, advance briskly to the scratch across the center of the ring, and spar away sharply for a little time, until one got in a blow that sent the other to the ground, where he would lie until his second picked him up, carried him back, washed his face off, and gave him a drink. He then rested until the next call of time.

This sort of performance went on for an hour or more, with the knockdowns and other casualties pretty evenly divided between the two. Then it became apparent that the Infant was getting more than he had storage room for. His interest in the skillet was evidently abating, the leering grin he wore upon his face during the early part of the engagement had disappeared long ago, as the successive "hot ones" which the Chicken had succeeded in planting upon his mouth, put it out of his power to "smile and smile," "e'en though he might still be a villain." He began coming up to the scratch as sluggishly as a hired man starting out for his day's work, and finally he did not come up at all. A bunch of blood soaked rags was tossed into the air from his corner, and Bradley declared the Chicken to be the victor, amid enthusiastic cheers from the crowd.

We voted the thing rather tame. In the whole hour and a-half there was not so much savage fighting, not so much damage done, as a couple of earnest, but unscientific men, who have no time to waste, will frequently crowd into an impromptu affair not exceeding five minutes in duration.

Our next visit to the N'Yaarkers was on a different errand. The moment they arrived in camp we began to be annoyed by their depredations. Blankets—the sole protection of men—would be snatched off as they slept at night. Articles of clothing and cooking utensils would go the same way, and occasionally a man would be robbed in open daylight. All these, it was believed, with good reason, were the work of the N'Yaarkers, and the stolen things were conveyed to their camp. Occasionally depredators would be caught and beaten, but they would give a signal which would bring to their assistance the whole body of N'Yaarkers, and turn the tables on their assailants.

We had in our squad a little watchmaker named Dan Martin, of the Eighth New York Infantry. Other boys let him take their watches to tinker up, so as to make a show of running, and be available for trading to the guards.

One day Martin was at the creek, when a N'Yaarker asked him to let him look at a watch. Martin incautiously did so, when the N'Yaarker snatched it and sped away to the camp of his crowd. Martin ran back to us and told his story. This was the last feather which was to break the camel's back of our patience. Peter Bates, of the Third Michigan, the Sergeant of our squad, had considerable confidence in his muscular ability. He flamed up into mighty wrath, and swore a sulphurous oath that we would get that watch back, whereupon about two hundred of us avowed our willingness to help reclaim it.

Each of us providing ourselves with a club, we started on our errand. The rest of the camp—about four thousand—gathered on the hillside to watch us. We thought they might have sent us some assistance, as it was about as much their fight as ours, but they did not, and we were too proud to ask it. The crossing of the swamp was quite difficult. Only one could go over at a time, and he very slowly. The N'Yaarkers understood that trouble was pending, and they began mustering to receive us. From the way they turned out it was evident that we should have come over with three hundred instead of two hundred, but it was too late then to alter the program. As we came up a stalwart Irishman stepped out and asked us what we wanted.

Bates replied: "We have come over to get a watch that one of your fellows took from one of ours, and by —— we're going to have it."

The Irishman's reply was equally explicit though not strictly logical in construction. Said he: "We havn't got your watch, and be ye can't have it."

This joined the issue just as fairly as if it had been done by all the documentary formula that passed between Turkey and Russia prior to the late war. Bates and the Irishman then exchanged very derogatory opinions of each other, and began striking with their clubs. The rest of us took this as our cue, and each, selecting as small a N'Yaarker as we could readily find, sailed in. There is a very expressive bit of slang coming into general use in the West, which speaks of a man "biting off more than he can chew."

That is what we had done. We had taken a contract that we should have divided, and sub-let the bigger half. Two minutes after the engagement became general there was no doubt that we would have been much better off if we had staid on our own side of the creek. The watch was a very poor one, anyhow. We thought we would just say good day to our N'Yaark friends, and return home hastily. But they declined to be left so precipitately. They wanted to stay with us awhile. It was lots of fun for them, and for the, four thousand yelling spectators on the opposite hill, who were greatly enjoying our discomfiture. There was hardly enough of the amusement to go clear around, however, and it all fell short just before it reached us. We earnestly wished that some of the boys would come over and help us let go of the N'Yaarkers, but they were enjoying the thing too much to interfere.

We were driven down the hill, pell-mell, with the N'Yaarkers pursuing hotly with yell and blow. At the swamp we tried to make a stand to secure our passage across, but it was only partially successful. Very few got back without some severe hurts, and many received blows that greatly hastened their deaths.

After this the N'Yaarkers became bolder in their robberies, and more arrogant in their demeanor than ever, and we had the poor revenge upon those who would not assist us, of seeing a reign of terror inaugurated over the whole camp.

CHAPTER XXI.

DIMINISHING RATIONS—A DEADLY COLD RAIN—HOVERING OVER PITCH PINE FIRES —INCREASE ON MORTALITY—A THEORY OF HEALTH.

The rations diminished perceptibly day by day. When we first entered we each received something over a quart of tolerably good meal, a sweet potato, a piece of meat about the size of one's two fingers, and occasionally a spoonful of salt. First the salt disappeared. Then the sweet potato took unto itself wings and flew away, never to return. An attempt was ostensibly made to issue us cow-peas instead, and the first issue was only a quart to a detachment of two hundred and seventy men. This has two-thirds of a pint to each squad of ninety, and made but a few spoonfuls for each of the four messes in the squad. When it came to dividing among the men, the beans had to be counted. Nobody received enough to pay for cooking, and we were at a loss what to do until somebody suggested that we play poker for them. This met general acceptance, and after that, as long as beans were drawn, a large portion of the day was spent in absorbing games of "bluff" and "draw," at a bean "ante," and no "limit."

After a number of hours' diligent playing, some lucky or skillful player would be in possession of all the beans in a mess, a squad, and sometimes a detachment, and have enough for a good meal. Next the meal began to diminish in quantity and deteriorate in quality. It became so exceedingly coarse that the common remark was that the next step would be to bring us the corn in the shock, and feed it to us like stock. Then meat followed suit with the rest. The rations decreased in size, and the number of days that we did not get any, kept constantly increasing in proportion to the days that we did, until eventually the meat bade us a final adieu, and joined the sweet potato in that undiscovered country from whose bourne no ration ever returned.

The fuel and building material in the stockade were speedily exhausted. The later comers had nothing whatever to build shelter with.

But, after the Spring rains had fairly set in, it seemed that we had not tasted misery until then. About the middle of March the windows of heaven opened, and it began a rain like that of the time of Noah. It was tropical in quantity and persistency, and arctic in temperature. For dreary hours that lengthened into weary days and nights, and these again into never-ending weeks, the driving, drenching flood poured down upon the sodden earth, searching the very marrow of the five thousand hapless men against whose chilled frames it beat with pitiless monotony, and soaked the sand bank upon which we lay until it was like a sponge filled with ice-water. It seems to me now that it must have been two or three weeks that the sun was wholly hidden behind the dripping clouds, not shining out once in all that time. The intervals when it did not rain were rare and short. An hour's respite would be followed by a day of steady, regular pelting of the great rain drops.

I find that the report of the Smithsonian Institute gives the average annual rainfall in the section around Andersonville, at fifty-six inches —nearly five feet—while that of foggy England is only thirty-two. Our experience would lead me to think that we got the five feet all at once.

We first comers, who had huts, were measurably better off than the later arrivals. It was much drier in our leaf-thatched tents, and we were spared much of the annoyance that comes from the steady dash of rain against the body for hours.

The condition of those who had no tents was truly pitiable.

They sat or lay on the hill-side the live-long day and night, and took the washing flow with such gloomy composure as they could muster.

All soldiers will agree with me that there is no campaigning hardship comparable to a cold rain. One can brace up against the extremes of heat and cold, and mitigate their inclemency in various ways. But there is no escaping a long-continued, chilling rain. It seems to penetrate to the heart, and leach away the very vital force.

The only relief attainable was found in huddling over little fires kept alive by small groups with their slender stocks of wood. As this wood was all pitch-pine, that burned with a very sooty flame, the effect upon the appearance of the hoverers was, startling. Face, neck and hands became covered with mixture of lampblack and turpentine, forming a coating as thick as heavy brown paper, and absolutely irremovable by water alone. The hair also became of midnight blackness, and gummed up into elflocks of fantastic shape and effect. Any one of us could have gone on the negro minstrel stage, without changing a hair, and put to blush the most elaborate make-up of the grotesque burnt-cork artists.

No wood was issued to us. The only way of getting it was to stand around the gate for hours until a guard off duty could be coaxed or hired to accompany a small party to the woods, to bring back a load of such knots and limbs as could be picked up. Our chief persuaders to the guards to do us this favor were rings, pencils, knives, combs, and such trifles as we might have in our pockets, and, more especially, the brass buttons on our uniforms. Rebel soldiers, like Indians, negros and other imperfectly civilized people, were passionately fond of bright and gaudy things. A handful of brass buttons would catch every one of them as swiftly and as surely as a piece of red flannel will a gudgeon. Our regular fee for an escort for three of us to the woods was six over-coat or dress-coat buttons, or ten or twelve jacket buttons. All in the mess contributed to this fund, and the fuel obtained was carefully guarded and husbanded.

This manner of conducting the wood business is a fair sample of the management, or rather the lack of it, of every other detail of prison administration. All the hardships we suffered from lack of fuel and shelter could have been prevented without the slightest expense or trouble to the Confederacy. Two hundred men allowed to go out on parole, and supplied with ages, would have brought in from the adjacent woods, in a week's time, enough material to make everybody comfortable tents, and to supply all the fuel needed.

The mortality caused by the storm was, of course, very great. The official report says the total number in the prison in March was four thousand six hundred and three, of whom two hundred and eighty-three died.

Among the first to die was the one whom we expected to live longest. He was by much the largest man in prison, and was called, because of this, "BIG JOE." He was a Sergeant in the Fifth Pennsylvania Cavalry, and seemed the picture of health. One morning the news ran through the prison that "Big Joe is dead," and a visit to his squad showed his stiff, lifeless form, occupying as much ground as Goliath's, after his encounter with David.

His early demise was an example of a general law, the workings of which few in the army failed to notice. It was always the large and strong who first succumbed to hardship. The stalwart, huge-limbed, toil-inured men sank down earliest on the march, yielded soonest to malarial influences, and fell first under the combined effects of home-sickness, exposure and the privations of army life. The slender, withy boys, as supple and weak as cats, had apparently the nine lives of those animals. There were few exceptions to this rule in the army—there were none in Andersonville. I can recall few or no instances where a large, strong, "hearty" man lived through a few months of imprisonment. The survivors were invariably youths, at the verge of manhood,—slender, quick, active, medium-statured fellows, of a cheerful temperament, in whom one would have expected comparatively little powers of endurance.

The theory which I constructed for my own private use in accounting for this phenomenon I offer with proper diffidence to others who may be in search of a hypothesis to explain facts that they have observed. It is this:

a. The circulation of the blood maintains health, and consequently life by carrying away from the various parts of the body the particles of worn-out and poisonous tissue, and replacing them with fresh, structure-building material.

b. The man is healthiest in whom this process goes on most freely and continuously.

c. Men of considerable muscular power are disposed to be sluggish; the exertion of great strength does not favor circulation. It rather retards it, and disturbs its equilibrium by congesting the blood in quantities in the sets of muscles called into action.

d. In light, active men, on the other hand, the circulation goes on perfectly and evenly, because all the parts are put in motion, and kept so in such a manner as to promote the movement of the blood to every extremity. They do not strain one set of muscles by long continued effort, as a strong man does, but call one into play after another.

There is no compulsion on the reader to accept this speculation at any valuation whatever. There is not even any charge for it. I will lay down this simple axiom:

No strong man, is a healthy man

from the athlete in the circus who lifts pieces of artillery and catches cannon balls, to the exhibition swell in a country gymnasium. If my theory is not a sufficient explanation of this, there is nothing to prevent the reader from building up one to suit him better.

CHAPTER XXII.

DIFFERENCE BETWEEN ALABAMIANS AND GEORGIANS—DEATH OF "POLL PARROTT" —A GOOD JOKE UPON THE GUARD—A BRUTAL RASCAL.

There were two regiments guarding us—the Twenty-Sixth Alabama and the Fifty-Fifth Georgia. Never were two regiments of the same army more different. The Alabamians were the superiors of the Georgians in every way that one set of men could be superior to another. They were manly, soldierly, and honorable, where the Georgians were treacherous and brutal. We had nothing to complain of at the hands of the Alabamians; we suffered from the Georgians everything that mean-spirited cruelty could devise. The Georgians were always on the look-out for something that they could torture into such apparent violation of orders, as would justify them in shooting men down; the Alabamians never fired until they were satisfied that a deliberate offense was intended. I can recall of my own seeing at least a dozen instances where men of the Fifty-Fifth Georgia Killed prisoners under the pretense that they were across the Dead Line, when the victims were a yard or more from the Dead Line, and had not the remotest idea of going any nearer.

The only man I ever knew to be killed by one of the Twenty-Sixth Alabama was named Hubbard, from Chicago, Ills., and a member of the Thirty-Eighth Illinois. He had lost one leg, and went hobbling about the camp on crutches, chattering continually in a loud, discordant voice, saying all manner of hateful and annoying things, wherever he saw an opportunity. This and his beak-like nose gained for him the name of "Poll Parrot." His misfortune caused him to be tolerated where another man would have been suppressed. By-and-by he gave still greater cause for offense by his obsequious attempts to curry favor with Captain Wirz, who took him outside several times for purposes that were not well explained. Finally, some hours after one of Poll

Parrot's visits outside, a Rebel officer came in with a guard, and, proceeding with suspicious directness to a tent which was the mouth of a large tunnel that a hundred men or more had been quietly pushing forward, broke the tunnel in, and took the occupants of the tent outside for punishment. The question that demanded immediate solution then was:

"Who is the traitor who has informed the Rebels?"

Suspicion pointed very strongly to "Poll Parrot." By the next morning the evidence collected seemed to amount to a certainty, and a crowd caught the Parrot with the intention of lynching him. He succeeded in breaking away from them and ran under the Dead Line, near where I was sitting in, my tent. At first it looked as if he had done this to secure the protection of the guard. The latter—a Twenty-Sixth Alabamian —ordered him out. Poll Parrot rose up on his one leg, put his back against the Dead Line, faced the guard, and said in his harsh, cackling voice:

"No; I won't go out. If I've lost the confidence of my comrades I want to die."

Part of the crowd were taken back by this move, and felt disposed to accept it as a demonstration of the Parrot's innocence. The rest thought it was a piece of bravado, because of his belief that the Rebels would not injure, him after he had served them. They renewed their yells, the guard again ordered the Parrot out, but the latter, tearing open his blouse, cackled out:

"No, I won't go; fire at me, guard. There's my heart shoot me right there."

There was no help for it. The Rebel leveled his gun and fired. The charge struck the Parrot's lower jaw, and carried it completely away, leaving his tongue and the roof of his mouth exposed. As he was carried back to die, he wagged his tongue rigorously, in attempting to speak, but it was of no use.

The guard set his gun down and buried his face in his hands. It was the only time that I saw a sentinel show anything but exultation at killing a Yankee.

A ludicrous contrast to this took place a few nights later. The rains had ceased, the weather had become warmer, and our spirits rising with this increase in the comfort of our surroundings, a number of us were sitting around "Nosey"—a boy with a superb tenor voice—who was singing patriotic songs. We were coming in strong on the chorus, in a way that spoke vastly more for our enthusiasm for the Union than our musical knowledge. "Nosey" sang the "Star Spangled Banner," "The Battle Cry of Freedom," "Brave Boys are They," etc., capitally, and we threw our whole lungs into the chorus. It was quite dark, and while our noise was going on the guards changed, new men coming on duty. Suddenly, bang! went the gun of the guard in the box about fifty feet away from us. We knew it was a Fifty-Fifth Georgian, and supposed that, irritated at our singing, he was trying to kill some of us for spite. At the sound of the gun we jumped up and scattered. As no one gave the usual agonized yell of a prisoner when shot, we supposed the ball had not taken effect. We could hear the sentinel ramming down another cartridge, hear him "return rammer," and cock his rifle. Again the gun cracked, and again there was no sound of anybody being hit. Again we could hear the sentry churning down another cartridge. The drums began beating the long roll in the camps, and officers could be heard turning the men out. The thing was becoming exciting, and one of us sang out to the guard:

"S-a-y! What the are you shooting at, any how?"

"I'm a shootin' at that —— —— Yank thar by the Dead Line, and by —- if you'uns don't take him in I'll blow the whole head offn him."

"What Yank? Where's any Yank?"

"Why, thar—right thar—a-standin' agin the Ded Line."

"Why, you Rebel fool, that's a chunk of wood. You can't get any furlough for shooting that!"

At this there was a general roar from the rest of the camp, which the other guards took up, and as the Reserves came double-quicking up, and learned the occasion of the alarm, they gave the rascal who had been so anxious to kill somebody a torrent of abuse for having disturbed them. A part of our crowd had been out after wood during the day, and secured a piece of a log as large as two of them could carry, and bringing it in, stood it up near the Dead Line. When the guard mounted to his post he was sure he saw a temerarious Yankee in front of him, and hastened to slay him.

It was an unusual good fortune that nobody was struck. It was very rare that the guards fired into the prison without hitting at least one person. The Georgia Reserves, who formed our guards later in the season, were armed with an old gun called a Queen Anne musket, altered to percussion. It carried a bullet as big as a large marble, and three or four buckshot. When fired into a group of men it was sure to bring several down.

I was standing one day in the line at the gate, waiting for a chance to go out after wood. A Fifty-Fifth Georgian was the gate guard, and he drew a line in the sand with his bayonet which we should not cross. The crowd behind pushed one man till he put his foot a few inches over the line, to save himself from falling; the guard sank a bayonet through the foot as quick as a flash.

CHAPTER XXIII

A NEW LOT OF PRISONERS—THE BATTLE OF OOLUSTEE—MEN SACRIFICED TO A GENERAL'S INCOMPETENCY—A HOODLUM REINFORCEMENT—A QUEER CROWD —MISTREATMENT OF AN OFFICER OF A COLORED REGIMENT—KILLING THE SERGEANT OF A NEGRO SQUAD.

So far only old prisoners—those taken at Gettysburg, Chicamauga and Mine Run—had been brought in. The armies had been very quiet during the Winter, preparing for the death grapple in the Spring. There had been nothing done, save a few cavalry raids, such as our own, and Averill's attempt to gain and break up the Rebel salt works at Wytheville, and Saltville. Consequently none but a few cavalry prisoners were added to the number already in the hands of the Rebels. The first lot of new ones came in about the middle of March. There were about seven hundred of them, who had been captured at the battle of Oolustee, Fla., on the 20th of February. About five hundred of them were white, and belonged to the Seventh Connecticut, the Seventh New Hampshire, Forty Seventh, Forty-Eighth and One Hundred and Fifteenth New York, and Sherman's regular battery. The rest were colored, and belonged to the Eighth United States, and Fifty-Fourth Massachusetts. The story they told of the battle was one which had many shameful reiterations during the war. It was the story told whenever Banks, Sturgis, Butler, or one of a host of similar smaller failures were trusted with commands. It was a senseless waste of the lives of private soldiers, and the property of the United States by pretentious blunderers, who, in some inscrutable manner, had attained to responsible commands. In this instance, a bungling Brigadier named Seymore had marched his forces across the State of Florida, to do he hardly knew what, and in the neighborhood of an enemy of whose numbers, disposition, location, and intentions he was profoundly ignorant. The Rebels, under General Finnegan, waited till he had strung his command along through swamps and cane brakes, scores of miles from his supports, and then fell unexpectedly upon his advance. The regiment was overpowered, and another regiment that hurried up to its support, suffered the same fate. The balance of the regiments were sent in in the same manner—each arriving on the field just after its predecessor had been thoroughly whipped by the concentrated force of the Rebels. The men fought gallantly, but the stupidity of a Commanding General is a thing that the gods themselves strive against in vain. We suffered a humiliating defeat, with a loss of two thousand men and a fine rifled battery, which was brought to Andersonville and placed in position to command the prison.

The majority of the Seventh New Hampshire were an unwelcome addition to our numbers. They were N'Yaarkers—old time colleagues of those already in with us—veteran bounty jumpers, that had been drawn to New Hampshire by the size of the bounty offered there, and had been assigned to fill up the wasted ranks of the veteran Seventh regiment. They had tried to desert as soon as they received their bounty, but the Government clung to them literally with hooks of steel, sending many of them to the regiment in irons. Thus foiled, they deserted to the Rebels during the retreat from the battlefield. They were quite an accession to the force of our N'Yaarkers, and helped much to establish the hoodlum reign which was shortly inaugurated over the whole prison.

The Forty-Eighth New Yorkers who came in were a set of chaps so odd in every way as to be a source of never-failing interest. The name of their regiment was 'L'Enfants Perdu' (the Lost Children), which we anglicized into "The Lost Ducks." It was believed that every nation in Europe was represented in their ranks, and it used to be said jocularly, that no two of them spoke the same language. As near as I could find out they were all or nearly all South Europeans, Italians, Spaniards; Portuguese, Levantines, with a predominance of the French element. They wore a little cap with an upturned brim, and a strap resting on the chin, a coat with funny little tales about two inches long, and a brass chain across the breast; and for pantaloons they had a sort of a petticoat reaching to the knees, and sewed together down the middle. They were just as singular otherwise as in their looks, speech and uniform. On one occasion the whole mob of us went over in a mass to their squad to see them cook and eat a large water snake, which two of them had succeeded in capturing in the swamps, and carried off to their mess, jabbering in high glee over their treasure trove. Any of us were ready to eat a piece of dog, cat, horse or mule, if we could get it, but, it was generally agreed, as Dawson, of my company expressed it, that "Nobody but one of them darned queer Lost Ducks would eat a varmint like a water snake."

Major Albert Bogle, of the Eighth United States, (colored) had fallen into the hands of the rebels by reason of a severe wound in the leg, which left him helpless upon the field at Oolustee. The Rebels treated him with studied indignity. They utterly refused to recognize him as an officer, or even as a man. Instead of being sent to Macon or Columbia, where the other officers were, he was sent to Andersonville, the same as an enlisted man. No care was given his wound, no surgeon would examine it or dress it. He was thrown into a stock car, without a bed or blanket, and hauled over the rough, jolting road to Andersonville. Once a Rebel officer rode up and fired several shots at him, as he lay helpless on the car floor. Fortunately the Rebel's marksmanship was as bad as his intentions, and none of the shots took effect. He was placed in a squad near me, and compelled to get up and hobble into line when the rest were mustered for roll-call. No opportunity to insult, "the nigger officer," was neglected, and the N'Yaarkers vied with the Rebels in heaping abuse upon him. He was a fine, intelligent young man, and bore it all with dignified self-possession, until after a lapse of some weeks the Rebels changed their policy and took him from the prison to send to where the other officers were.

The negro soldiers were also treated as badly as possible. The wounded were turned into the Stockade without having their hurts attended to. One stalwart, soldierly Sergeant had received a bullet which had forced its way under the scalp for some distance, and partially imbedded itself in the skull, where it still remained. He suffered intense agony, and would pass the whole night walking up and down the street in front of our tent, moaning distressingly. The bullet could be felt plainly with the fingers, and we were sure that it would not be a minute's work, with a sharp knife, to remove it and give the man relief. But we could not prevail upon the Rebel Surgeons even to see the man. Finally inflammation set in and he died.

The negros were made into a squad by themselves, and taken out every day to work around the prison. A white Sergeant was placed over them, who was the object of the contumely of the guards and other Rebels. One day as he was standing near the gate, waiting his orders to come out, the gate guard, without any provocation whatever, dropped his gun until the muzzle rested against the Sergeant's stomach, and fired, killing him instantly.

The Sergeantcy was then offered to me, but as I had no accident policy, I was constrained to decline the honor.

CHAPTER XXIV.

APRIL—LONGING TO GET OUT—THE DEATH RATE—THE PLAGUE OF LICE —THE SO-CALLED HOSPITAL.

April brought sunny skies and balmy weather. Existence became much more tolerable. With freedom it would have been enjoyable, even had we been no better fed, clothed and sheltered. But imprisonment had never seemed so hard to bear—even in the first few weeks—as now. It was easier to submit to confinement to a limited area, when cold and rain were aiding hunger to benumb the faculties and chill the energies than it was now, when Nature was rousing her slumbering forces to activity, and earth, and air and sky were filled with stimulus to man to imitate her example. The yearning to be up and doing something-to turn these golden hours to good account for self and country—pressed into heart and brain as the vivifying sap pressed into tree-duct and plant cell, awaking all vegetation to energetic life.

To be compelled, at such a time, to lie around in vacuous idleness —to spend days that should be crowded full of action in a monotonous, objectless routine of hunting lice, gathering at roll-call, and drawing and cooking our scanty rations, was torturing.

But to many of our number the aspirations for freedom were not, as with us, the desire for a wider, manlier field of action, so much as an intense longing to get where care and comforts would arrest their swift progress to the shadowy hereafter. The cruel rains had sapped away their stamina, and they could not recover it with the meager and innutritious diet of coarse meal, and an occasional scrap of salt meat. Quick consumption, bronchitis, pneumonia, low fever and diarrhea seized upon these ready victims for their ravages, and bore them off at the rate of nearly a score a day.

It now became a part of, the day's regular routine to take a walk past the gates in the morning, inspect and count the dead, and see if any friends were among them. Clothes having by this time become a very important consideration with the prisoners, it was the custom of the mess in which a man died to remove from his person all garments that were of any account, and so many bodies were carried out nearly naked. The hands were crossed upon the breast, the big toes tied together with a bit of string, and a slip of paper containing the man's name, rank, company and regiment was pinned on the breast of his shirt.

The appearance of the dead was indescribably ghastly. The unclosed eyes shone with a stony glitter—

An orphan's curse would drag to hell
A spirit from on high:
But, O, more terrible than that,
Is the curse in a dead man's eye.

The lips and nostrils were distorted with pain and hunger, the sallow, dirt-grimed skin drawn tensely over the facial bones, and the whole framed with the long, lank, matted hair and beard. Millions of lice swarmed over the wasted limbs and ridged ribs. These verminous pests had become so numerous—owing to our lack of changes of clothing, and of facilities for boiling what we had—that the most a healthy man could do was to keep the number feeding upon his person down to a reasonable limit—say a few tablespoonfuls. When a man became so sick as to be unable to help himself, the parasites speedily increased into millions, or, to speak more comprehensively, into pints and quarts. It did not even seem exaggeration when some one declared that he had seen a dead man with more than a gallon of lice on him.

There is no doubt that the irritation from the biting of these myriads materially the days of those who died.

Where a sick man had friends or comrades, of course part of their duty, in taking care of him, was to "louse" his clothing. One of the most effectual ways of doing this was to turn the garments wrong side out and hold the seams as close to the fire as possible, without burning the cloth. In a short time the lice would swell up and burst open, like pop-corn. This method was a favorite one for another reason than its efficacy: it gave one a keener sense of revenge upon his rascally little tormentors than he could get in any other way.

As the weather grew warmer and the number in the prison increased, the lice became more unendurable. They even filled the hot sand under our feet, and voracious troops would climb up on one like streams of ants swarming up a tree. We began to have a full comprehension of the third plague with which the Lord visited the Egyptians:

And the Lord said unto Moses, Say unto Aaron, Stretch out thy rod, and smite the dust of the land, that it may become lice through all the land of Egypt.

And they did so; for Aaron stretched out his hand with his rod, and smote the dust of the earth, and it became lice in man and in beast; all the dust of the land became lice throughout all the land of Egypt.

The total number of deaths in April, according to the official report, was five hundred and seventy-six, or an average of over nineteen a day. There was an average of five thousand prisoner's in the pen during all but the last few days of the month, when the number was increased by the arrival of the captured garrison of Plymouth. This would make the loss over eleven per cent., and so worse than decimation. At that rate we should all have died in about eight months. We could have gone through a sharp campaign lasting those thirty days and not lost so great a proportion of our forces. The British had about as many men as were in the Stockade at the battle of New Orleans, yet their loss in killed fell much short of the deaths in the pen in April.

A makeshift of a hospital was established in the northeastern corner of the Stockade. A portion of the ground was divided from the rest of the prison by a railing, a few tent flies were stretched, and in these the long leaves of the pine were made into apologies for beds of about the goodness of the straw on which a Northern farmer beds his stock. The sick taken there were no better off than if they had staid with their comrades.

What they needed to bring about their recovery was clean clothing, nutritious food, shelter and freedom from the tortures of the lice. They obtained none of these. Save a few decoctions of roots, there were no medicines; the sick were fed the same coarse corn meal that brought about the malignant dysentery from which they all suffered; they wore and slept in the same vermin-infested clothes, and there could be but one result: the official records show that seventy-six per cent. of those taken to the hospitals died there.

The establishment of the hospital was specially unfortunate for my little squad. The ground required for it compelled a general reduction of the space we all occupied. We had to tear down our huts and move. By this time the materials had become so dry that we could not rebuild with them, as the pine tufts fell to pieces. This reduced the tent and bedding material of our party— now numbering five—to a cavalry overcoat and a blanket. We scooped a hole a foot deep in the sand and stuck our tent-poles around it. By day we spread our blanket over the poles for a tent. At night we lay down upon the overcoat and covered ourselves with the blanket. It required considerable stretching to make it go over five; the two out side fellows used to get very chilly, and squeeze the three inside ones until they felt no thicker than a wafer. But it had to do, and we took turns sleeping on the outside. In the course of a few weeks three of my chums died and left myself and B. B. Andrews (now Dr. Andrews, of Astoria, Ill.) sole heirs to and occupants of, the overcoat and blanket.

CHAPTER XXV.

THE "PLYMOUTH PILGRIMS"—SAD TRANSITION FROM COMFORTABLE BARRACKS TO ANDERSONVILLE—A CRAZED PENNSYLVANIAN—DEVELOPMENT OF THE BUTLER BUSINESS.

We awoke one morning, in the last part of April, to find about two thousand freshly arrived prisoners lying asleep in the main streets running from the gates. They were attired in stylish new uniforms, with fancy hats and shoes; the Sergeants and Corporals wore patent leather or silk chevrons, and each man had a large, well-filled knapsack, of the kind new recruits usually carried on coming first to the front, and which the older soldiers spoke of humorously as "bureaus." They were the snuggest, nattiest lot of soldiers we had ever seen, outside of the "paper collar" fellows forming the headquarter guard of some General in a large City. As one of my companions surveyed them, he said:

"Hulloa! I'm blanked if the Johnnies haven't caught a regiment of Brigadier Generals, somewhere."

By-and-by the "fresh fish," as all new arrivals were termed, began to wake up, and then we learned that they belonged to a brigade consisting of the Eighty-Fifth New York, One Hundred and First and One Hundred and Third Pennsylvania, Sixteenth Connecticut, Twenty-Fourth New York Battery, two companies of Massachusetts heavy artillery, and a company of the Twelfth New York Cavalry.

They had been garrisoning Plymouth, N. C., an important seaport on the Roanoke River. Three small gunboats assisted them in their duty. The Rebels constructed a powerful iron clad called the "Albemarle," at a point further up the Roanoke, and on the afternoon of the 17th, with her and three brigades of infantry, made an attack upon the post. The "Albemarle" ran past the forts unharmed, sank one of the gunboats, and drove the others away. She then turned her attention to the garrison, which she took in the rear, while the infantry attacked in front. Our men held out until the 20th, when they capitulated. They were allowed to retain their personal effects, of all kinds, and, as is the case with all men in garrison, these were considerable.

The One Hundred and First and One Hundred and Third Pennsylvania and Eighty-Fifth New York had just "veteranized," and received their first instalment of veteran bounty. Had they not been attacked they would have sailed for home in a day or two, on their veteran furlough, and this accounted for their fine raiment. They were made up of boys from good New York and Pennsylvania families, and were, as a rule, intelligent and fairly educated.

Their horror at the appearance of their place of incarceration was beyond expression. At one moment they could not comprehend that we dirty and haggard tatterdemalions had once been clean, self-respecting, well-fed soldiers like themselves; at the next they would affirm that they knew they could not stand it a month, in here we had then endured it from four to nine months. They took it, in every way, the hardest of any prisoners that came in, except some of the 'Hundred-Days' men, who were brought in in August, from the Valley of Virginia. They had served nearly all their time in various garrisons along the seacoast—from Fortress Monroe to Beaufort—where they had had comparatively little of the actual hardships of soldiering in the field. They had nearly always had comfortable quarters, an abundance of food, few hard marches or other severe service. Consequently they were not so well hardened for Andersonville as the majority who came in. In other respects they were better prepared, as they had an abundance of clothing, blankets and cooking utensils, and each man had some of his veteran bounty still in possession.

It was painful to see how rapidly many of them sank under the miseries of the situation. They gave up the moment the gates were closed upon them, and began pining away. We older prisoners buoyed ourselves up continually with hopes of escape or exchange. We dug tunnels with the persistence of beavers, and we watched every possible opportunity to get outside the accursed walls of the pen. But we could not enlist the interest of these discouraged ones in any of our schemes, or talk. They resigned themselves to Death, and waited despondingly till he came.

A middle-aged One Hundred and First Pennsylvanian, who had taken up his quarters near me, was an object of peculiar interest. Reasonably intelligent and fairly read, I presume that he was a respectable mechanic before entering the Army. He was evidently a very domestic man, whose whole happiness centered in his family.

When he first came in he was thoroughly dazed by the greatness of his misfortune. He would sit for hours with his face in his hands and his elbows on his knees, gazing out upon the mass of men and huts, with vacant, lack-luster eyes. We could not interest him in anything. We tried to show him how to fix his blanket up to give him some shelter, but he went at the work in a disheartened way, and finally smiled feebly and stopped. He had some letters from his family and a melaineotype of a plain-faced woman—his wife—and her children, and spent much time in looking at them. At first he ate his rations when he drew them, but finally began to reject, them. In a few days he was delirious with hunger and homesick ness. He would sit on the sand for hours imagining that he was at his family table, dispensing his frugal hospitalities to his wife and children.

Making a motion, as if presenting a dish, he would say:

"Janie, have another biscuit, do!"

Or,

"Eddie, son, won't you have another piece of this nice steak?"

Or,

"Maggie, have some more potatos," and so on, through a whole family of six, or more. It was a relief to us when he died in about a month after he came in.

As stated above, the Plymouth men brought in a large amount of money —variously estimated at from ten thousand to one hundred thousand dollars. The presence of this quantity of circulating medium immediately started a lively commerce. All sorts of devices were resorted to by the other prisoners to get a little of this wealth. Rude chuck-a-luck boards were constructed out of such material as was attainable, and put in operation. Dice and cards were brought out by those skilled in such matters. As those of us already in the Stockade occupied all the ground, there was no disposition on the part of many to surrender a portion of their space without exacting a pecuniary compensation. Messes having ground in a good location would frequently demand and get ten dollars for permission for two or three to quarter with them. Then there was a great demand for poles to stretch blankets over to make tents; the Rebels, with their usual stupid cruelty, would not supply these, nor allow the prisoners to go out and get them themselves. Many of the older prisoners had poles to spare which they were saying up for fuel. They sold these to the Plymouth folks at the rate of ten dollars for three—enough to put up a blanket.

The most considerable trading was done through the gates. The Rebel guards were found quite as keen to barter as they had been in Richmond. Though the laws against their dealing in the money of the enemy were still as stringent as ever, their thirst for greenbacks was not abated one whit, and they were ready to sell anything they had for the coveted currency. The rate of exchange was seven or eight dollars in Confederate money for one dollar in greenbacks. Wood, tobacco, meat, flour, beans, molasses, onions and a villainous kind of whisky made from sorghum, were the staple articles of trade. A whole race of little traffickers in these articles sprang up, and finally Selden, the Rebel Quartermaster, established a sutler shop in the center of the North Side, which he put in charge of Ira Beverly, of the One Hundredth Ohio, and Charlie Huckleby, of the Eighth

Tennessee. It was a fine illustration of the development of the commercial instinct in some men. No more unlikely place for making money could be imagined, yet starting in without a cent, they contrived to turn and twist and trade, until they had transferred to their pockets a portion of the funds which were in some one else's. The Rebels, of course, got nine out of every ten dollars there was in the prison, but these middle men contrived to have a little of it stick to their fingers. It was only the very few who were able to do this. Nine hundred and ninety-nine out of every thousand were, like myself, either wholly destitute of money and unable to get it from anybody else, or they paid out what money they had to the middlemen, in exorbitant prices for articles of food.

The N'Yaarkers had still another method for getting food, money, blankets and clothing. They formed little bands called "Raiders," under the leadership of a chief villain. One of these bands would select as their victim a man who had good blankets, clothes, a watch, or greenbacks. Frequently he would be one of the little traders, with a sack of beans, a piece of meat, or something of that kind. Pouncing upon him at night they would snatch away his possessions, knock down his friends who came to his assistance, and scurry away into the darkness.

CHAPTER XXVI

LONGINGS FOR GOD'S COUNTRY—CONSIDERATIONS OF THE METHODS OF GETTING THERE—EXCHANGE AND ESCAPE—DIGGING TUNNELS, AND THE DIFFICULTIES CONNECTED THEREWITH—PUNISHMENT OF A TRAITOR.

To our minds the world now contained but two grand divisions, as widely different from each other as happiness and misery. The first—that portion over which our flag floated was usually spoken of as "God's Country;" the other—that under the baneful shadow of the banner of rebellion—was designated by the most opprobrious epithets at the speaker's command.

To get from the latter to the former was to attain, at one bound, the highest good. Better to be a doorkeeper in the House of the Lord, under the Stars and Stripes, than to dwell in the tents of wickedness, under the hateful Southern Cross.

To take even the humblest and hardest of service in the field now would be a delightsome change. We did not ask to go home—we would be content with anything, so long as it was in that blest place "within our lines." Only let us get back once, and there would be no more grumbling at rations or guard duty—we would willingly endure all the hardships and privations that soldier flesh is heir to.

There were two ways of getting back—escape and exchange. Exchange was like the ever receding mirage of the desert, that lures the thirsty traveler on over the parched sands, with illusions of refreshing springs, only to leave his bones at last to whiten by the side of those of his unremembered predecessors. Every day there came something to build up the hopes that exchange was near at hand—every day brought something to extinguish the hopes of the preceding one. We took these varying phases according to our several temperaments. The sanguine built themselves up on the encouraging reports; the desponding sank down and died under the discouraging ones.

Escape was a perpetual allurement. To the actively inclined among us it seemed always possible, and daring, busy brains were indefatigable in concocting schemes for it. The only bit of Rebel brain work that I ever saw for which I did not feel contempt was the perfect precautions taken to prevent our escape. This is shown by the fact that, although, from first to last, there were nearly fifty thousand prisoners in Andersonville, and three out of every five of these were ever on the alert to take French leave of their captors, only three hundred and twenty-eight succeeded in getting so far away from Andersonville as to leave it to be presumed that they had reached our lines.

The first, and almost superhuman difficulty was to get outside the Stockade. It was simply impossible to scale it. The guards were too close together to allow an instant's hope to the most sanguine, that he could even pass the Dead Line without being shot by some one of them. This same closeness prevented any hope of bribing them. To be successful half those on post would have to be bribed, as every part of the Stockade was clearly visible from every other part, and there was no night so dark as not to allow a plain view to a number of guards of the dark figure outlined against the light colored logs of any Yankee who should essay to clamber towards the top of the palisades.

The gates were so carefully guarded every time they were opened as to preclude hope of slipping out through theme. They were only unclosed twice or thrice a day—once to admit, the men to call the roll, once to let them out again, once to let the wagons come in with rations, and once, perhaps, to admit, new prisoners. At all these times every precaution was taken to prevent any one getting out surreptitiously.

This narrowed down the possibilities of passing the limits of the pen alive, to tunneling. This was also surrounded by almost insuperable difficulties. First, it required not less than fifty feet of subterranean excavation to get out, which was an enormous work with our limited means. Then the logs forming the Stockade were set in the ground to a depth of five feet, and the tunnel had to go down beneath them. They had an unpleasant habit of dropping down into the burrow under them. It added much to the discouragements of tunneling to think of one of these massive timbers dropping upon a fellow as he worked his mole-like way under it, and either crushing him to death outright, or pinning him there to die of suffocation or hunger.

In one instance, in a tunnel near me, but in which I was not interested, the log slipped down after the digger had got out beyond it. He immediately began digging for the surface, for life, and was fortunately able to break through before he suffocated. He got his head above the ground, and then fainted. The guard outside saw him, pulled him out of the hole, and when he recovered sensibility hurried him back into the Stockade.

In another tunnel, also near us, a broad-shouldered German, of the Second Minnesota, went in to take his turn at digging. He was so much larger than any of his predecessors that he stuck fast in a narrow part, and despite all the efforts of himself and comrades, it was found impossible to move him one way or the other. The comrades were at last reduced to the humiliation of informing the Officer of the Guard of their tunnel and the condition of their friend, and of asking assistance to release him, which was given.

The great tunneling tool was the indispensable half-canteen. The inventive genius of our people, stimulated by the war, produced nothing for the comfort and effectiveness of the soldier equal in usefulness to this humble and unrecognized utensil. It will be remembered that a canteen was composed of two pieces of tin struck up into the shape of saucers, and soldered together at the edges. After a soldier had been in the field a little while, and thrown away or lost the curious and complicated kitchen furniture he started out with, he found that by melting the halves of his canteen apart, he had a vessel much handier in every way than any he had parted with. It could be used for anything —to make soup or coffee in, bake bread, brown coffee, stew vegetables, etc., etc. A sufficient handle was made with a split stick. When the cooking was done, the handle was thrown away, and the half canteen slipped out of the road into the haversack. There seemed to be no end of the uses to which this ever-ready disk of blackened sheet iron could be turned. Several instances are on record where infantry regiments, with no other tools than this, covered themselves on the field with quite respectable rifle pits.

The starting point of a tunnel was always some tent close to the Dead Line, and sufficiently well closed to screen the operations from the sight of the guards near by. The party engaged in the work organized by giving every man a number to secure the proper apportionment of the labor. Number One began digging with his half canteen. After he had worked until tired, he came out, and Number Two took his place, and so on. The tunnel was simply a round, rat-like burrow, a little larger than a man's body. The digger lay on his stomach, dug ahead of him, threw the dirt under him, and worked it back with his feet till the man behind him, also lying on his stomach, could catch it and work it back to the next. As the tunnel lengthened the number of men behind each other in this way had to be increased, so that in a tunnel seventy-five feet long there would be from eight to ten men lying one behind the other. When the dirt was pushed back to the mouth of the tunnel it was taken up in improvised bags, made by tying up the bottoms of pantaloon legs, carried to the Swamp, and emptied. The work in the tunnel was very exhausting, and the digger had to be relieved every half-hour.

The greatest trouble was to carry the tunnel forward in a straight line. As nearly everybody dug most of the time with the right hand, there was an almost irresistible tendency to make the course veer to the left. The first tunnel I was connected with was a ludicrous illustration of this. About twenty of us had devoted our nights for over a week to the prolongation of a burrow. We had not yet reached the Stockade, which astonished us, as measurement with a string showed that we had gone nearly twice the distance necessary for the purpose. The thing was inexplicable, and we ceased operations to consider the matter. The next day a man walking by a tent some little distance from the one in which the hole began, was badly startled by the ground giving way under his feet, and his sinking nearly to his waist in a hole. It was very singular, but after wondering over the matter for some hours, there came a glimmer of suspicion that it might be, in some way, connected with the missing end of our tunnel. One of us started through on an exploring expedition, and confirmed the suspicions by coming out where the man had broken through. Our tunnel was shaped like a horse shoe, and the beginning and end were not fifteen feet apart. After that we practised digging with our left hand, and made certain compensations for the tendency to the sinister side.

Another trouble connected with tunneling was the number of traitors and spies among us. There were many—principally among the N'Yaarker crowd who were always zealous to betray a tunnel, in order to curry favor with the Rebel officers. Then, again, the Rebels had numbers of their own men in the pen at night, as spies. It was hardly even necessary to dress these in our uniform, because a great many of our own men came into the prison in Rebel clothes, having been compelled to trade garments with their captors.

One day in May, quite an excitement was raised by the detection of one of these "tunnel traitors" in such a way as left no doubt of his guilt. At first everybody was in favor of killing him, and they actually started to beat him to death. This was arrested by a proposition to "have Captain Jack tattoo him," and the suggestion was immediately acted upon.

"Captain Jack" was a sailor who had been with us in the Pemberton building at Richmond. He was a very skilful tattoo artist, but, I am sure, could make the process nastier than any other that I ever saw attempt it. He chewed tobacco enormously. After pricking away for a few minutes at the design on the arm or some portion of the body, he would deluge it with a flood of tobacco spit, which, he claimed, acted as a kind of mordant. Piping this off with a filthy rag, he would study the effect for an instant, and then go ahead with another series of prickings and tobacco juice drenchings.

The tunnel-traitor was taken to Captain Jack. That worthy decided to brand him with a great "T," the top part to extend across his forehead and the stem to run down his nose. Captain Jack got his tattooing kit ready, and the fellow was thrown upon the ground and held there. The Captain took his head between his legs, and began operations. After an instant's work with the needles, he opened his mouth, and filled the wretch's face and eyes full of the disgusting saliva. The crowd round about yelled with delight at this new process. For an hour, that was doubtless an eternity to the rascal undergoing branding, Captain Jack continued his alternate pickings and drenchings. At the end of that time the traitor's face was disfigured with a hideous mark that he would bear to his grave. We learned afterwards that he was not one of our men, but a Rebel spy. This added much to our satisfaction with the manner of his treatment. He disappeared shortly after the operation was finished, being, I suppose, taken outside. I hardly think Captain Jack would be pleased to meet him again.

CHAPTER XXVII.

THE HOUNDS, AND THE DIFFICULTIES THEY PUT IN THE WAY OF ESCAPE —THE WHOLE SOUTH PATROLLED BY THEM.

Those who succeeded, one way or another, in passing the Stockade limits, found still more difficulties lying between them and freedom than would discourage ordinarily resolute men. The first was to get away from the immediate vicinity of the prison. All around were Rebel patrols, pickets and guards, watching every avenue of egress. Several packs of hounds formed efficient coadjutors of these, and were more dreaded by possible "escapes," than any other means at the command of our jailors. Guards and patrols could be evaded, or circumvented, but the hounds could not. Nearly every man brought back from a futile attempt at escape told the same story: he had been able to escape the human Rebels, but not their canine colleagues. Three of our detachment—members of the Twentieth Indiana—had an experience of this kind that will serve to illustrate hundreds of others. They had been taken outside to do some work upon the cook-house that was being built. A guard was sent with the three a little distance into the woods to get a piece of timber. The boys sauntered, along carelessly with the guard, and managed to get pretty near him. As soon as they were fairly out of sight of the rest, the strongest of them—Tom Williams—snatched the Rebel's gun away from him, and the other two springing upon him as swift as wild cats, throttled him, so that he could not give the alarm.

Still keeping a hand on his throat, they led him off some distance, and tied him to a sapling with strings made by tearing up one of their blouses. He was also securely gagged, and the boys, bidding him a hasty, but not specially tender, farewell, struck out, as they fondly hoped, for freedom. It was not long until they were missed, and the parties sent in search found and released the guard, who gave all the information he possessed as to what had become of his charges. All the packs of hounds, the squads of cavalry, and the foot patrols were sent out to scour the adjacent country. The Yankees kept in the swamps and creeks, and no trace of them was found that afternoon or evening. By this time they were ten or fifteen miles away, and thought that they could safely leave the creeks for better walking on the solid ground. They had gone but a few miles, when the pack of hounds Captain Wirz was with took their trail, and came after them in full cry. The boys tried to ran, but, exhausted as they were, they could make no headway. Two of them were soon caught, but Tom Williams, who was so desperate that he preferred death to recapture, jumped into a mill-pond near by. When he came up, it was in a lot of saw logs and drift wood that hid him from being seen from the shore. The dogs stopped at the shore, and bayed after the disappearing prey. The Rebels with them, who had seen Tom spring in, came up and made a pretty thorough search for him. As they did not think to probe around the drift wood this was unsuccessful, and they came to the conclusion that Tom had been drowned. Wirz marched the other two back and, for a wonder, did not punish them, probably because he was so rejoiced at his success in capturing them. He was beaming with delight when he returned them to our squad, and said, with a chuckle:

"Brisoners, I pring you pack two of dem tam Yankees wat got away yesterday, unt I run de oder raskal into a mill-pont and trownted him."

What was our astonishment, about three weeks later, to see Tom, fat and healthy, and dressed in a full suit of butternut, come stalking into the pen. He had nearly reached the mountains, when a pack of hounds, patrolling for deserters or negros, took his trail, where he had crossed the road from one field to another, and speedily ran him down. He had been put in a little country jail, and well fed till an opportunity occurred to send him back. This patrolling for negros and deserters was another of the great obstacles to a successful passage through the country. The rebels had put, every able-bodied white man in the ranks, and were bending every energy to keep him there. The whole country was carefully policed by Provost Marshals to bring out those who were shirking military duty, or had deserted their colors, and to check any movement by the negros. One could not go anywhere without a pass, as every road was continually watched by men and hounds. It was the policy of our men, when escaping, to avoid roads as much as possible by traveling through the woods and fields.

From what I saw of the hounds, and what I could learn from others, I believe that each pack was made up of two bloodhounds and from twenty-five to fifty other dogs, The bloodhounds were debased descendants of the strong and fierce hounds imported from Cuba—many of them by the United States Government—for hunting Indians, during the Seminole war. The other dogs were the mongrels that are found in such plentifulness about every Southern house—increasing, as a rule, in numbers as the inhabitant of the house is lower down and poorer. They are like wolves, sneaking and cowardly when alone, fierce and bold when in packs. Each pack was managed by a well-armed man, who rode a mule; and carried, slung over his shoulders by a cord, a cow horn, scraped very thin, with which he controlled the band by signals.

What always puzzled me much was why the hounds took only Yankee trails, in the vicinity of the prison. There was about the Stockade from six thousand to ten thousand Rebels and negros, including guards, officers, servants, workmen, etc. These were, of course, continually in motion and must have daily made trails leading in every direction. It was the custom of the Rebels to send a pack of hounds around the prison every morning, to examine if any Yankees had escaped during the night. It was believed that they rarely failed to find a prisoner's tracks, and still more rarely ran off upon a Rebel's. If those outside the Stockade had been confined to certain path and roads we could have understood this, but, as I understand, they were not. It was part of the interest of the day, for us, to watch the packs go yelping around the pen searching for tracks. We got information in this way whether any tunnel had been successfully opened during the night.

The use of hounds furnished us a crushing reply to the ever recurring Rebel question:
"Why are you-uns puttin' niggers in the field to fight we-uns for?"
The questioner was always silenced by the return interrogatory:
"Is that as bad as running white men down with blood hounds?"

CHAPTER XXVIII

MAY—INFLUX OF NEW PRISONERS—DISPARITY IN NUMBERS BETWEEN THE EASTERN AND WESTERN ARMIES—TERRIBLE CROWDING—SLAUGHTER OF MEN AT THE CREEK.

In May the long gathering storm of war burst with angry violence all along the line held by the contending armies. The campaign began which was to terminate eleven months later in the obliteration of the Southern Confederacy. May 1, Sigel moved up the Shenandoah Valley with thirty thousand men; May 3, Butler began his blundering movement against Petersburg; May 3, the Army of the Potomac left Culpeper, and on the 5th began its deadly grapple with Lee, in the Wilderness; May 6, Sherman moved from Chattanooga, and engaged Joe Johnston at Rocky Face Ridge and Tunnel Hill.

Each of these columns lost heavily in prisoners. It could not be otherwise; it was a consequence of the aggressive movements. An army acting offensively usually suffers more from capture than one on the defensive. Our armies were penetrating the enemy's country in close proximity to a determined and vigilant foe. Every scout, every skirmish line, every picket, every foraging party ran the risk of falling into a Rebel trap. This was in addition to the risk of capture in action. The bulk of the prisoners were taken from the Army of the Potomac. For this there were two reasons: First, that there were many more men in that Army than in any other; and second, that the entanglement in the dense thickets and shrubbery of the Wilderness enabled both sides to capture great numbers of the other's men. Grant lost in prisoners from May 5 to May 31, seven thousand four hundred and fifty; he probably captured two-thirds of that number from the Johnnies.

Wirz's headquarters were established in a large log house which had been built in the fort a little distant from the southeast corner of the prison. Every day—and sometimes twice or thrice a day—we would see great squads of prisoners marched up to these headquarters, where they would be searched, their names entered upon the prison records, by clerks (detailed prisoners; few Rebels had the requisite clerical skill) and then be marched into the prison. As they entered, the Rebel guards would stand to arms. The infantry would be in line of battle, the cavalry mounted, and the artillerymen standing by their guns, ready to open at the instant with grape and canister.

The disparity between the number coming in from the Army of the Potomac and Western armies was so great, that we Westerners began to take some advantage of it. If we saw a squad of one hundred and fifty or thereabouts at the headquarters, we felt pretty certain they were from Sherman, and gathered to meet them, and learn the news from our friends. If there were from five hundred to two thousand we knew they were from the Army of the Potomac, and there were none of our comrades among them. There were three exceptions to this rule while we were in Andersonville. The first was in June, when the drunken and incompetent Sturgis (now Colonel of the Seventh United States Cavalry) shamefully sacrificed a superb division at Guntown, Miss. The next was after Hood made his desperate attack on Sherman, on the 22d of July, and the third was when Stoneman was captured at Macon. At each of these times about two thousand prisoners were brought in.

By the end of May there were eighteen thousand four hundred and fifty-four prisoners in the Stockade. Before the reader dismisses this statement from his mind let him reflect how great a number this is. It is more active, able-bodied young men than there are in any of our leading Cities, save New York and Philadelphia. It is more than the average population of an Ohio County. It is four times as many troops as Taylor won the victory of Buena Vista with, and about twice as many as Scott went into battle with at any time in his march to the City of Mexico. These eighteen thousand four hundred and fifty-four men were cooped up on less than thirteen acres of ground, making about fifteen hundred to the acre. No room could be given up for streets, or for the usual arrangements of a camp, and most kinds of exercise were wholly precluded. The men crowded together like pigs nesting in the woods on cold nights. The ground, despite all our efforts, became indescribably filthy, and this condition grew rapidly worse as the season advanced and the sun's rays gained fervency. As it is impossible to describe this adequately, I must again ask the reader to assist with a few comparisons. He has an idea of how much filth is produced, on an ordinary City lot, in a week, by its occupation by a family say of six persons. Now let him imagine what would be the result if that lot, instead of having upon it six persons, with every appliance for keeping themselves clean, and for removing and concealing filth, was the home of one hundred and eight men, with none of these appliances.

That he may figure out these proportions for himself, I will repeat some of the elements of the problem: We will say that an average City lot is thirty feet front by one hundred deep. This is more front than most of them have, but we will be liberal. This gives us a surface of three thousand square feet. An acre contains forty-three thousand five hundred and sixty square feet. Upon thirteen of these acres, we had eighteen thousand four hundred and fifty-four men. After he has found the number of square feet that each man had for sleeping apartment, dining room, kitchen, exercise grounds and outhouses, and decided that nobody could live for any length of time in such contracted space, I will tell him that a few weeks later double that many men were crowded upon that space that over thirty-five thousand were packed upon those twelve and a-half or thirteen acres.

But I will not anticipate. With the warm weather the condition of the swamp in the center of the prison became simply horrible. We hear so much now-a-days of blood poisoning from the effluvia of sinks and sewers, that reading it, I wonder how a man inside the Stockade, and into whose nostrils came a breath of that noisomeness, escaped being carried off by a malignant typhus. In the slimy ooze were billions of white maggots. They would crawl out by thousands on the warm sand, and, lying there a few minutes, sprout a wing or a pair of them. With these they would essay a clumsy flight, ending by dropping down upon some exposed portion of a man's body, and stinging him like a gad-fly. Still worse, they would drop into what he was cooking, and the utmost care could not prevent a mess of food from being contaminated with them.

All the water that we had to use was that in the creek which flowed through this seething mass of corruption, and received its sewerage. How pure the water was when it came into the Stockade was a question. We always believed that it received the drainage from the camps of the guards, a half-a-mile away.

A road was made across the swamp, along the Dead Line at the west side, where the creek entered the pen. Those getting water would go to this spot, and reach as far up the stream as possible, to get the water that was least filthy. As they could reach nearly to the Dead Line this furnished an excuse to such of the guards as were murderously inclined to fire upon them. I think I hazard nothing in saying that for weeks at least one man a day was killed at this place. The murders became monotonous; there was a dreadful sameness to them. A gun would crack; looking up we would see, still smoking, the muzzle of the musket of one of the guards on either side of the creek. At the same instant would rise a piercing shriek from the man struck, now floundering in the creek in his death agony. Then thousands of throats would yell out curses and denunciations, and—

"O, give the Rebel —— —— —— —— a furlough!"

It was our belief that every guard who killed a Yankee was rewarded with a thirty-day furlough. Mr. Frederick Holliger, now of Toledo, formerly a member of the Seventy-Second Ohio, and captured at Guntown, tells me, as his introduction to Andersonville life, that a few hours after his entry he went to the brook to get a drink, reached out too far, and was fired upon by the guard, who missed him, but killed another man and wounded a second. The other prisoners standing near then attacked him, and beat him nearly to death, for having drawn the fire of the guard. Nothing could be more inexcusable than these murders. Whatever defense there might be for firing on men who touched the Dead Line in other parts of the prison, there could be none here. The men had no intention of escaping; they had no designs upon the Stockade; they were not leading any party to assail it. They were in every instance killed in the act of reaching out with their cups to dip up a little water.

CHAPTER XXIX

SOME DISTINCTION BETWEEN SOLDIERLY DUTY AND MURDER—A PLOT TO ESCAPE —IT IS REVEALED AND FRUSTRATED.

Let the reader understand that in any strictures I make I do not complain of the necessary hardships of war. I understood fully and accepted the conditions of a soldier's career. My going into the field uniformed and armed implied an intention, at least, of killing, wounding, or capturing, some of the enemy. There was consequently no ground of complaint if I was, myself killed, wounded, or captured. If I did not want to take these chances I ought to stay at home. In the same way, I recognized the right of our captors or guards to take proper precautions to prevent our escape. I never questioned for an instant the right of a guard to fire upon those attempting to escape, and to kill them. Had I been posted over prisoners I should have had no compunction about shooting at those trying to get away, and consequently I could not blame the Rebels for doing the same thing. It was a matter of soldierly duty.

But not one of the men assassinated by the guards at Andersonville were trying to escape, nor could they have got away if not arrested by a bullet. In a majority of instances there was not even a transgression of a prison rule, and when there was such a transgression it was a mere harmless inadvertence. The slaying of every man there was a foul crime.

The most of this was done by very young boys; some of it by old men. The Twenty-Sixth Alabama and Fifty-Fifth Georgia, had guarded us since the opening of the prison, but now they were ordered to the field, and their places filled by the Georgia "Reserves," an organization of boys under, and men over the military age. As General Grant aptly-phrased it, "They had robbed the cradle and the grave," in forming these regiments. The boys, who had grown up from children since the war began, could not comprehend that a Yankee was a human being, or that it was any more wrongful to shoot one than to kill a mad dog. Their young imaginations had been inflamed with stories of the total depravity of the Unionists until they believed it was a meritorious thing to seize every opportunity to exterminate them.

Early one morning I overheard a conversation between two of these youthful guards:

"Say, Bill, I heerd that you shot a Yank last night?"

"Now, you just bet I did. God! you jest ought to've heerd him holler."

Evidently the juvenile murderer had no more conception that he had committed crime than if he had killed a rattlesnake.

Among those who came in about the last of the month were two thousand men from Butler's command, lost in the disastrous action of May 15, by which Butler was "bottled up" at Bermuda Hundreds. At that time the Rebel hatred for Butler verged on insanity, and they vented this upon these men who were so luckless—in every sense—as to be in his command. Every pains was taken to mistreat them. Stripped of every article of clothing, equipment, and cooking utensils—everything, except a shirt and a pair of pantaloons, they were turned bareheaded and barefooted into the prison, and the worst possible place in the pen hunted out to locate them upon. This was under the bank, at the edge of the Swamp and at the eastern side of the prison, where the sinks were, and all filth from the upper part of the camp flowed down to them. The sand upon which they lay was dry and burning as that of a tropical desert; they were without the slightest shelter of any kind, the maggot flies swarmed over them, and the stench was frightful. If one of them survived the germ theory of disease is a hallucination.

The increasing number of prisoners made it necessary for the Rebels to improve their means of guarding and holding us in check. They threw up a line of rifle pits around the Stockade for the infantry guards. At intervals along this were piles of hand grenades, which could be used with fearful effect in case of an outbreak. A strong star fort was thrown up at a little distance from the southwest corner. Eleven field pieces were mounted in this in such a way as to rake the Stockade diagonally. A smaller fort, mounting five guns, was built at the northwest corner, and at the northeast and southeast corners were small lunettes, with a couple of howitzers each. Packed as we were we had reason to dread a single round from any of these works, which could not fail to produce fearful havoc.

Still a plot was concocted for a break, and it seemed to the sanguine portions of us that it must prove successful. First a secret society was organized, bound by the most stringent oaths that could be devised. The members of this were divided into companies of fifty men each; under officers regularly elected. The secrecy was assumed in order to shut out Rebel spies and the traitors from a knowledge of the contemplated outbreak. A man named Baker—belonging, I think, to some New York regiment—was the grand organizer of the scheme. We were careful in each of our companies to admit none to membership except such as long acquaintance gave us entire confidence in.

The plan was to dig large tunnels to the Stockade at various places, and then hollow out the ground at the foot of the timbers, so that a half dozen or so could be pushed over with a little effort, and make a gap ten or twelve feet wide. All these were to be thrown down at a preconcerted signal, the companies were to rush out and seize the eleven guns of the headquarters fort. The Plymouth Brigade was then to man these and turn them on the camp of the Reserves who, it was imagined, would drop their arms and take to their heels after receiving a round or so of shell. We would gather what arms we could, and place them in the hands of the most active and determined. This would give us frown eight to ten thousand fairly armed, resolute men, with which we thought we could march to Appalachicola Bay, or to Sherman.

We worked energetically at our tunnels, which soon began to assume such shape as to give assurance that they would answer our expectations in opening the prison walls.

Then came the usual blight to all such enterprises: a spy or a traitor revealed everything to Wirz. One day a guard came in, seized Baker and took him out. What was done with him I know not; we never heard of him after he passed the inner gate.

Immediately afterward all the Sergeants of detachments were summoned outside. There they met Wirz, who made a speech informing them that he knew all the details of the plot, and had made sufficient preparations to defeat it. The guard had been strongly reinforced, and disposed in such a manner as to protect the guns from capture. The Stockade had been secured to prevent its falling, even if undermined. He said, in addition, that Sherman had been badly defeated by Johnston, and driven back across the river, so that any hopes of co-operation by him would be ill-founded.

When the Sergeants returned, he caused the following notice to be posted on the gates NOTICE.

Not wishing to shed the blood of hundreds, not connected with those who concocted a mad plan to force the Stockade, and make in this way their escape, I hereby warn the leaders and those who formed themselves into a band to carry out this, that I am in possession of all the facts, and have made my dispositions accordingly, so as to frustrate it. No choice would be left me but to open with grape and canister on the Stockade, and what effect this would have, in this densely crowded place, need not be told.

May 25, 1864.

H. Wirz.

The next day a line of tall poles, bearing white flags, were put up at some little distance from the Dead Line, and a notice was read to us at roll call that if, except at roll call, any gathering exceeding one hundred was observed, closer the Stockade than these poles, the guns would open with grape and canister without warning.

The number of deaths in the Stockade in May was seven hundred and eight, about as many as had been killed in Sherman's army during the same time.

CHAPTER XXX.

JUNE—POSSIBILITIES OF A MURDEROUS CANNONADE—WHAT WAS PROPOSED TO BE DONE IN THAT EVENT—A FALSE ALARM—DETERIORATION OF THE RATIONS —FEARFUL INCREASE OF MORTALITY.

After Wirz's threat of grape and canister upon the slightest provocation, we lived in daily apprehension of some pretext being found for opening the guns upon us for a general massacre. Bitter experience had long since taught us that the Rebels rarely threatened in vain. Wirz, especially, was much more likely to kill without warning, than to warn without killing. This was because of the essential weakness of his nature. He knew no art of government, no method of discipline save "kill them!" His petty little mind's scope reached no further. He could conceive of no other way of managing men than the punishment of every offense, or seeming offense, with death. Men who have any talent for governing find little occasion for the death penalty. The stronger they are in themselves—the more fitted for controlling others—the less their need of enforcing their authority by harsh measures.

There was a general expression of determination among the prisoners to answer any cannonade with a desperate attempt to force the Stockade. It was agreed that anything was better than dying like rats in a pit or wild animals in a battue. It was believed that if anything would occur which would rouse half those in the pen to make a headlong effort in concert, the palisade could be scaled, and the gates carried, and, though it would be at a fearful loss of life, the majority of those making the attempt would get out. If the Rebels would discharge grape and canister, or throw a shell into the prison, it would lash everybody to such a pitch that they would see that the sole forlorn hope of safety lay in wresting the arms away from our tormentors. The great element in our favor was the shortness of the distance between us and the cannon. We could hope to traverse this before the guns could be reloaded more than once.

Whether it would have been possible to succeed I am unable to say. It would have depended wholly upon the spirit and unanimity with which the effort was made. Had ten thousand rushed forward at once, each with a determination to do or die, I think it would have been successful without a loss of a tenth of the number. But the insuperable trouble—in our disorganized state—was want of concert of action. I am quite sure, however, that the attempt would have been made had the guns opened.

One day, while the agitation of this matter was feverish, I was cooking my dinner—that is, boiling my pitiful little ration of unsalted meal, in my fruit can, with the aid of a handful of splinters that I had been able to pick up by a half day's diligent search. Suddenly the long rifle in the headquarters fort rang out angrily. A fuse shell shrieked across the prison—close to the tops of the logs, and burst in the woods beyond. It was answered with a yell of defiance from ten thousand throats.

I sprang up-my heart in my mouth. The long dreaded time had arrived; the Rebels had opened the massacre in which they must exterminate us, or we them.

I looked across to the opposite bank, on which were standing twelve thousand men—erect, excited, defiant. I was sure that at the next shot they would surge straight against the Stockade like a mighty human billow, and then a carnage would begin the like of which modern times had never seen.

The excitement and suspense were terrible. We waited for what seemed ages for the next gun. It was not fired. Old Winder was merely showing the prisoners how he could rally the guards to oppose an outbreak. Though the gun had a shell in it, it was merely a signal, and the guards came double-quicking up by regiments, going into position in the rifle pits and the hand-grenade piles. As we realized what the whole affair meant, we relieved our surcharged feelings with a few general yells of execration upon Rebels generally, and upon those around us particularly, and resumed our occupation of cooking rations, killing lice, and discussing the prospects of exchange and escape.

The rations, like everything else about us, had steadily grown worse. A bakery was built outside of the Stockade in May and our meal was baked there into loaves about the size of brick. Each of us got a half of one of these for a day's ration. This, and occasionally a small slice of salt pork, was call that I received. I wish the reader would prepare himself an object lesson as to how little life can be supported on for any length of time, by procuring a piece of corn bread the size of an ordinary brickbat, and a thin slice of pork, and then imagine how he would fare, with that as his sole daily ration, for long hungry weeks and months. Dio Lewis satisfied himself that he could sustain life on sixty cents, a week. I am sure that the food furnished us by the Rebels would not, at present prices cost one-third that. They pretended to give us one-third of pound of bacon and one and one-fourth pounds of corn meal. A week's rations then would be two and one-third pounds of bacon—worth ten cents, and eight and three-fourths pounds of meal, worth, say, ten cents more. As a matter of fact, I do not presume that at any time we got this full ration. It would surprise me to learn that we averaged two-thirds of it.

The meal was ground very coarse and produced great irrition in the bowels. We used to have the most frightful cramps that men ever suffered from. Those who were predisposed intestinal affections were speedily carried off by incurable diarrhea and dysentery. Of the twelve thousand and twelve men who died, four thousand died of chronic diarrhea; eight hundred and seventeen died of acute diarrhea, and one thousand three hundred and eighty-four died of dysenteria, making total of six thousand two hundred and one victims to enteric disorders.

Let the reader reflect a moment upon this number, till comprehends fully how many six thousand two hundred and men are, and how much force, energy, training, and rich possibilities for the good of the community and country died with those six thousand two hundred and one young, active men. It may help his perception of the magnitude of this number to remember that the total loss of the British, during the Crimean war, by death in all shapes, was four thousand five hundred and ninety-five, or one thousand seven hundred and six less than the deaths in Andersonville from dysenteric diseases alone.

The loathsome maggot flies swarmed about the bakery, and dropped into the trough where the dough was being mixed, so that it was rare to get a ration of bread not contaminated with a few of them.

It was not long until the bakery became inadequate to supply bread for all the prisoners. Then great iron kettles were set, and mush was issued to a number of detachments, instead of bread. There was not so much cleanliness and care in preparing this as a farmer shows in cooking food for stock. A deep wagon-bed would be shoveled full of the smoking paste, which was then hailed inside and issued out to the detachments, the latter receiving it on blankets, pieces of shelter tents, or, lacking even these, upon the bare sand.

As still more prisoners came in, neither bread nor mush could be furnished them, and a part of the detachments received their rations in meal. Earnest solicitation at length resulted in having occasional scanty issues of wood to cook this with. My detachment was allowed to choose which it would take—bread, mush or meal. It took the latter.

Cooking the meal was the topic of daily interest. There were three ways of doing it: Bread, mush and "dumplings." In the latter the meal was dampened until it would hold together, and was rolled into little balls, the size of marbles, which were then boiled. The bread was the most satisfactory and nourishing; the mush the bulkiest—it made a bigger show, but did not stay with one so long. The dumplings held an intermediate position—the water in which they were boiled becoming a sort of a broth that helped to stay the stomach. We received no salt, as a rule. No one knows the intense longing for this, when one goes without it for a while. When, after a privation of weeks we would get a teaspoonful of salt apiece, it seemed as if every muscle in our bodies was invigorated. We traded buttons to the guards for red peppers, and made our mush, or bread, or dumplings, hot with the fiery-pods, in hopes that this would make up for the lack of salt, but it was a failure. One pinch of salt was worth all the pepper pods in the Southern Confederacy. My little squad—now diminished by death from five to three—cooked our rations together to economize wood and waste of meal, and quarreled among ourselves daily as to whether the joint stock should be converted into bread, mush or dumplings. The decision depended upon the state of the stomach. If very hungry, we made mush; if less famished, dumplings; if disposed to weigh matters, bread.

This may seem a trifling matter, but it was far from it. We all remember the man who was very fond of white beans, but after having fifty or sixty meals of them in succession, began to find a suspicion of monotony in the provender. We had now six months of unvarying diet of corn meal and water, and even so slight a change as a variation in the way of combining the two was an agreeable novelty.

At the end of June there were twenty-six thousand three hundred and sixty-seven prisoners in the Stockade, and one thousand two hundred—just forty per day—had died during the month.

CHAPTER XXXI

DYING BY INCHES—SEITZ, THE SLOW, AND HIS DEATH—STIGGALL AND EMERSON —RAVAGES ON THE SCURVY.

May and June made sad havoc in the already thin ranks of our battalion. Nearly a score died in my company—L—and the other companies suffered proportionately. Among the first to die of my company comrades, was a genial little Corporal, "Billy" Phillips—who was a favorite with us all. Everything was done for him that kindness could suggest, but it was of little avail. Then "Bruno" Weeks—a young boy, the son of a preacher, who had run away from his home in Fulton County, Ohio, to join us, succumbed to hardship and privation.

The next to go was good-natured, harmless Victor Seitz, a Detroit cigar maker, a German, and one of the slowest of created mortals. How he ever came to go into the cavalry was beyond the wildest surmises of his comrades. Why his supernatural slowness and clumsiness did not result in his being killed at least once a day, while in the service, was even still farther beyond the power of conjecture. No accident ever happened in the company that Seitz did not have some share in. Did a horse fall on a slippery road, it was almost sure to be Seitz's, and that imported son of the Fatherland was equally sure to be caught under him. Did somebody tumble over a bank of a dark night, it was Seitz that we soon heard making his way back, swearing in deep German gutterals, with frequent allusion to 'tausend teuflin.' Did a shanty blow down, we ran over and pulled Seitz out of the debris, when he would exclaim:

"Zo! dot vos pretty vunny now, ain't it?"

And as he surveyed the scene of his trouble with true German phlegm, he would fish a brier-wood pipe from the recesses of his pockets, fill it with tobacco, and go plodding off in a cloud of smoke in search of some fresh way to narrowly escape destruction. He did not know enough about horses to put a snaffle-bit in one's mouth, and yet he would draw the friskiest, most mettlesome animal in the corral, upon whose back he was scarcely more at home than he would be upon a slack rope. It was no uncommon thing to see a horse break out of ranks, and go past the battalion like the wind, with poor Seitz clinging to his mane like the traditional grim Death to a deceased African. We then knew that Seitz had thoughtlessly sunk the keen spurs he would persist in wearing; deep into the flanks of his high-mettled animal.

These accidents became so much a matter-of-course that when anything unusual occurred in the company our first impulse was to go and help Seitz out.

When the bugle sounded "boots and saddles," the rest of us would pack up, mount, "count off by fours from the right," and be ready to move out before the last notes of the call had fairly died away. Just then we would notice an unsaddled horse still tied to the hitching place. It was Seitz's, and that worthy would be seen approaching, pipe in mouth, and bridle in hand, with calm, equable steps, as if any time before the expiration of his enlistment would be soon enough to accomplish the saddling of his steed. A chorus of impatient and derisive remarks would go up from his impatient comrades:

"For heaven's sake, Seitz, hurry up!"

"Seitz! you are like a cow's tail—always behind!"

"Seitz, you are slower than the second coming of the Savior!"

"Christmas is a railroad train alongside of you, Seitz!"

"If you ain't on that horse in half a second, Seitz, we'll go off and leave you, and the Johnnies will skin you alive!" etc., etc.

Not a ripple of emotion would roll over Seitz's placid features under the sharpest of these objurgations. At last, losing all patience, two or three boys would dismount, run to Seitz's horse, pack, saddle and bridle him, as if he were struck with a whirlwind. Then Seitz would mount, and we would move 'off.

For all this, we liked him. His good nature was boundless, and his disposition to oblige equal to the severest test. He did not lack a grain of his full share of the calm, steadfast courage of his race, and would stay where he was put, though Erebus yawned and bade him fly. He was very useful, despite his unfitness for many of the duties of a cavalryman. He was a good guard, and always ready to take charge of prisoners, or be sentry around wagons or a forage pile-duties that most of the boys cordially hated.

But he came into the last trouble at Andersonville. He stood up pretty well under the hardships of Belle Isle, but lost his cheerfulness—his unrepining calmness—after a few weeks in the Stockade. One day we remembered that none of us had seen him for several days, and we started in search of him. We found him in a distant part of the camp, lying near the Dead Line. His long fair hair was matted together, his blue eyes had the flush of fever. Every part of his clothing was gray with the lice that were hastening his death with their torments. He uttered the first complaint I ever heard him make, as I came up to him:

"My Gott, M——, dis is worse dun a dog's det!"

In a few days we gave him all the funeral in our power; tied his big toes together, folded his hands across his breast, pinned to his shirt a slip of paper, upon which was written:

VICTOR E. SEITZ,

Co. L, Sixteenth Illinois Cavalry.

And laid his body at the South Gate, beside some scores of others that were awaiting the arrival of the six-mule wagon that hauled them to the Potter's Field, which was to be their last resting-place.

John Emerson and John Stiggall, of my company, were two Norwegian boys, and fine specimens of their race—intelligent, faithful, and always ready for duty. They had an affection for each other that reminded one of the stories told of the sworn attachment and the unfailing devotion that were common between two Gothic warrior youths. Coming into Andersonville some little time after the rest of us, they found all the desirable ground taken up, and they established their quarters at the base of the hill, near the Swamp. There they dug a little hole to lie in, and put in a layer of pine leaves. Between them they had an overcoat and a blanket. At night they lay upon the coat and covered themselves with the blanket. By day the blanket served as a tent. The hardships and annoyances that we endured made everybody else cross and irritable. At times it seemed impossible to say or listen to pleasant words, and nobody was ever allowed to go any length of time spoiling for a fight. He could usually be accommodated upon the spot to any extent he desired, by simply making his wishes known. Even the best of chums would have sharp quarrels and brisk fights, and this disposition increased as disease made greater inroads upon them. I saw in one instance two brothers-both of whom died the next day of scurvy—and who were so helpless as to be unable to rise, pull themselves up on their knees by clenching the poles of their tents —in order to strike each other with clubs, and they kept striking until the bystanders interfered and took their weapons away from them.

But Stiggall and Emerson never quarreled with each other. Their tenderness and affection were remarkable to witness. They began to go the way that so many were going; diarrhea and scurvy set in; they wasted away till their muscles and tissues almost disappeared, leaving the skin lying flat upon the bones; but their principal solicitude was for each other, and each seemed actually jealous of any person else doing anything for the other. I met Emerson one day, with one leg drawn clear out of shape, and rendered almost useless by the scurvy. He was very weak, but was hobbling down towards the Creek with a bucket made from a boot leg. I said:

"Johnny, just give me your bucket. I'll fill it for you, and bring it up to your tent."

"No; much obliged, M ——" he wheezed out; "my pardner wants a cool drink, and I guess I'd better get it for him."

Stiggall died in June. He was one of the first victims of scurvy, which, in the succeeding few weeks, carried off so many. All of us who had read sea-stories had read much of this disease and its horrors, but we had little conception of the dreadful reality. It usually manifested itself first in the mouth. The breath became unbearably fetid; the gums swelled until they protruded, livid and disgusting, beyond the lips. The teeth became so loose that they frequently fell out, and the sufferer would pick them up and set them back in their sockets. In attempting to bite the hard corn bread furnished by the bakery the teeth often stuck fast and were pulled out. The gums had a fashion of breaking away, in large chunks, which would be swallowed or spit out. All the time one was eating his mouth would be filled with blood, fragments of gums and loosened teeth. Frightful, malignant ulcers appeared in other parts of the body; the ever-present maggot flies laid eggs in these, and soon worms swarmed therein. The sufferer looked and felt as if, though he yet lived and moved, his body was anticipating the rotting it would undergo a little later in the grave. The last change was ushered in by the lower parts of the legs swelling. When this appeared, we considered the man doomed. We all had scurvy, more or less, but as long as it kept out of our legs we were hopeful. First, the ankle joints swelled, then the foot became useless. The swelling increased until the knees became stiff, and the skin from these down was distended until it looked pale, colorless and transparent as a tightly blown bladder. The leg was so much larger at the bottom than at the thigh, that the sufferers used to make grim jokes about being modeled like a churn, "with the biggest end down." The man then became utterly helpless and usually died in a short time.

The official report puts down the number of deaths from scurvy at three thousand five hundred and seventy-four, but Dr. Jones, the Rebel surgeon, reported to the Rebel Government his belief that nine-tenths of the great mortality of the prison was due, either directly or indirectly, to this cause.

The only effort made by the Rebel doctors to check its ravages was occasionally to give a handful of sumach berries to some particularly bad case.

When Stiggall died we thought Emerson would certainly follow him in a day or two, but, to our surprise, he lingered along until August before dying.

CHAPTER XXXII

"OLE BOO," AND "OLE SOL, THE HAYMAKER"—A FETID, BURNING DESERT—
NOISOME WATER, AND THE EFFECTS OF DRINKING IT—STEALING SOFT SOAP.

The gradually lengthening Summer days were insufferably long and wearisome. Each was hotter, longer and more tedious than its predecessors. In my company was a none-too-bright fellow, named Dawson. During the chilly rains or the nipping, winds of our first days in prison, Dawson would, as he rose in, the morning, survey the forbidding skies with lack-luster eyes and remark, oracularly:

"Well, Ole Boo gits us agin, to-day."

He was so unvarying in this salutation to the morn that his designation of disagreeable weather as "Ole Boo" became generally adopted by us. When the hot weather came on, Dawson's remark, upon rising and seeing excellent prospects for a scorcher, changed to: "Well, Ole Sol, the Haymaker, is going to git in his work on us agin to-day."

As long as he lived and was able to talk, this was Dawson's invariable observation at the break of day.

He was quite right. The Ole Haymaker would do some famous work before he descended in the West, sending his level rays through the wide interstices between the somber pines.

By nine o'clock in the morning his beams would begin to fairly singe everything in the crowded pen. The hot sand would glow as one sees it in the center of the unshaded highway some scorching noon in August. The high walls of the prison prevented the circulation inside of any breeze that might be in motion, while the foul stench rising from the putrid Swamp and the rotting ground seemed to reach the skies.

One can readily comprehend the horrors of death on the burning sands of a desert. But the desert sand is at least clean; there is nothing worse about it than heat and intense dryness. It is not, as that was at Andersonville, poisoned with the excretions of thousands of sick and dying men, filled with disgusting vermin, and loading the air with the germs of death. The difference is as that between a brick-kiln and a sewer. Should the fates ever decide that I shall be flung out upon sands to perish, I beg that the hottest place in the Sahara may be selected, rather than such a spot as the interior of the Andersonville Stockade.

It may be said that we had an abundance of water, which made a decided improvement on a desert. Doubtless—had that water been pure. But every mouthful of it was a blood poison, and helped promote disease and death. Even before reaching the Stockade it was so polluted by the drainage of the Rebel camps as to be utterly unfit for human use. In our part of the prison we sank several wells—some as deep as forty feet—to procure water. We had no other tools for this than our ever-faithful half canteens, and nothing wherewith to wall the wells. But a firm clay was reached a few feet below the surface, which afforded tolerable strong sides for the lower part, ana furnished material to make adobe bricks for curbs to keep out the sand of the upper part. The sides were continually giving away, however, and fellows were perpetually falling down the holes, to the great damage of their legs and arms. The water, which was drawn up in little cans, or boot leg buckets, by strings made of strips of cloth, was much better than that of the creek, but was still far from pure, as it contained the seepage from the filthy ground.

The intense heat led men to drink great quantities of water, and this superinduced malignant dropsical complaints, which, next to diarrhea, scurvy and gangrene, were the ailments most active in carrying men off. Those affected in this way swelled up frightfully from day to day. Their clothes speedily became too small for them, and were ripped off, leaving them entirely naked, and they suffered intensely until death at last came to their relief. Among those of my squad who died in this way, was a young man named Baxter, of the Fifth Indiana Cavalry, taken at Chicamauga. He was very fine looking—tall, slender, with regular features and intensely black hair and eyes; he sang nicely, and was generally liked. A more pitiable object than he, when last I saw him, just before his death, can not be imagined. His body had swollen until it seemed marvelous that the human skin could bear so much distention without disruption, All the old look of bright intelligence had been. driven from his face by the distortion of his features. His swarthy hair and beard, grown long and ragged, had that peculiar repulsive look which the black hair of the sick is prone to assume.

I attributed much of my freedom from the diseases to which others succumbed to abstention from water drinking. Long before I entered the army, I had constructed a theory—on premises that were doubtless as insufficient as those that boyish theories are usually based upon—that drinking water was a habit, and a pernicious one, which sapped away the energy. I took some trouble to curb my appetite for water, and soon found that I got along very comfortably without drinking anything beyond that which was contained in my food. I followed this up after entering the army, drinking nothing at any time but a little coffee, and finding no need, even on the dustiest marches, for anything more. I do not presume that in a year I drank a quart of cold water. Experience seemed to confirm my views, for I noticed that the first to sink under a fatigue, or to yield to sickness, were those who were always on the lookout for drinking water, springing from their horses and struggling around every well or spring on the line of march for an opportunity to fill their canteens.

I made liberal use of the Creek for bathing purposes, however, visiting it four or five times a day during the hot days, to wash myself all over. This did not cool one off much, for the shallow stream was nearly as hot as the sand, but it seemed to do some good, and it helped pass away the tedious hours. The stream was nearly all the time filled as full of bathers as they could stand, and the water could do little towards cleansing so many. The occasional rain storms that swept across the prison were welcomed, not only because they cooled the air temporarily, but because they gave us a shower-bath. As they came up, nearly every one stripped naked and got out where he could enjoy the full benefit of the falling water. Fancy, if possible, the spectacle of twenty-five thousand or thirty thousand men without a stitch of clothing upon them. The like has not been seen, I imagine, since the naked followers of Boadicea gathered in force to do battle to the Roman invaders.

It was impossible to get really clean. Our bodies seemed covered with a varnish-like, gummy matter that defied removal by water alone. I imagined that it came from the rosin or turpentine, arising from the little pitch pine fires over which we hovered when cooking our rations. It would yield to nothing except strong soap-and soap, as I have before stated—was nearly as scarce in the Southern Confederacy as salt. We in prison saw even less of it, or rather, none at all. The scarcity of it, and our desire for it, recalls a bit of personal experience.

I had steadfastly refused all offers of positions outside the prison on parole, as, like the great majority of the prisoners, my hatred of the Rebels grew more bitter, day by day; I felt as if I would rather die than accept the smallest favor at their hands, and I shared the common contempt for those who did. But, when the movement for a grand attack on the Stockade—mentioned in a previous chapter—was apparently rapidly coming to a head, I was offered a temporary detail outside to, assist in making up some rolls. I resolved to accept; first because I thought I might get some information that would be of use in our enterprise; and, next, because I foresaw that the rush through the gaps in the Stockade would be bloody business, and by going out in advance I would avoid that much of the danger, and still be able to give effective assistance.

I was taken up to Wirz's office. He was writing at a desk at one end of a large room when the Sergeant brought me in. He turned around, told the Sergeant to leave me, and ordered me to sit down upon a box at the other end of the room.

Turning his back and resuming his writing, in a few minutes he had forgotten me. I sat quietly, taking in the details for a half-hour, and then, having exhausted everything else in the room, I began wondering what was in the box I was sitting upon. The lid was loose; I hitched it forward a little without attracting Wirz's attention, and slipped my left hand down of a voyage of discovery. It seemed very likely that there was something there that a loyal Yankee deserved better than a Rebel. I found that it was a fine article of soft soap. A handful was scooped up and speedily shoved into my left pantaloon pocket. Expecting every instant that Wirz would turn around and order me to come to the desk to show my handwriting, hastily and furtively wiped my hand on the back of my shirt and watched Wirz with as innocent an expression as a school boy assumes when he has just flipped a chewed paper wad across the room. Wirz was still engrossed in his writing, and did not look around. I was emboldened to reach down for another handful. This was also successfully transferred, the hand wiped off on the back of the shirt, and the face wore its expression of infantile ingenuousness. Still Wirz did not look up. I kept dipping up handful after handful, until I had gotten about a quart in the left hand pocket. After each handful I rubbed my hand off on the back of my shirt and waited an instant for a summons to the desk. Then the process was repeated with the other hand, and a quart of the saponaceous mush was packed in the right hand pocket.

Shortly after Wirz rose and ordered a guard to take me away and keep me, until he decided what to do with me. The day was intensely hot, and soon the soap in my pockets and on the back of my shirt began burning like double strength Spanish fly blisters. There was nothing to do but grin and bear it. I set my teeth, squatted down under the shade of the parapet of the fort, and stood it silently and sullenly. For the first time in my life I thoroughly appreciated the story of the Spartan boy, who stole the fox and suffered the animal to tear his bowels out rather than give a sign which would lead to the exposure of his theft.

Between four and five o'clock-after I had endured the thing for five or six hours, a guard came with orders from Wirz that I should be returned to the Stockade. Upon hastily removing my clothes, after coming inside, I found I had a blister on each thigh, and one down my back, that would have delighted an old practitioner of the heroic school. But I also had a half gallon of excellent soft soap. My chums and I took a magnificent wash, and gave our clothes the same, and we still had soap enough left to barter for some onions that we had long coveted, and which tasted as sweet to us as manna to the Israelites.

CHAPTER XXXIII

"POUR PASSER LE TEMPS"—A SET OF CHESSMEN PROCURED UNDER DIFFICULTIES —RELIGIOUS SERVICES—THE DEVOTED PRIEST—WAR SONG.

The time moved with leaden feet. Do the best we could, there were very many tiresome hours for which no occupation whatever could be found. All that was necessary to be done during the day—attending roll call, drawing and cooking rations, killing lice and washing—could be disposed of in an hour's time, and we were left with fifteen or sixteen waking hours, for which there was absolutely no employment. Very many tried to escape both the heat and ennui by sleeping as much as possible through the day, but I noticed that those who did this soon died, and consequently I did not do it. Card playing had sufficed to pass away the hours at first, but our cards soon wore out, and deprived us of this resource. My chum, Andrews, and I constructed a set of chessmen with an infinite deal of trouble. We found a soft, white root in the swamp which answered our purpose. A boy near us had a tolerably sharp pocket-knife, for the use of which a couple of hours each day, we gave a few spoonfuls of meal. The knife was the only one among a large number of prisoners, as the Rebel guards had an affection for that style of cutlery, which led them to search incoming prisoners, very closely. The fortunate owner of this derived quite a little income of meal by shrewdly loaning it to his knifeless comrades. The shapes that we made for pieces and pawns were necessarily very rude, but they were sufficiently distinct for identification. We blackened one set with pitch pine soot, found a piece of plank that would answer for a board and purchased it from its possessor for part of a ration of meal, and so were fitted out with what served until our release to distract our attention from much of the surrounding misery.

Every one else procured such amusement as they could. Newcomers, who still had money and cards, gambled as long as their means lasted. Those who had books read them until the leaves fell apart. Those who had paper and pen and ink tried to write descriptions and keep journals, but this was usually given up after being in prison a few weeks. I was fortunate enough to know a boy who had brought a copy of "Gray's Anatomy" into prison with him. I was not specially interested in the subject, but it was Hobson's choice; I could read anatomy or nothing, and so I tackled it with such good will that before my friend became sick and was taken outside, and his book with him, I had obtained a very fair knowledge of the rudiments of physiology.

There was a little band of devoted Christian workers, among whom were Orderly Sergeant Thomas J. Sheppard, Ninety-Seventh O. Y. L, now a leading Baptist minister in Eastern Ohio; Boston Corbett, who afterward slew John Wilkes Booth, and Frank Smith, now at the head of the Railroad Bethel work at Toledo. They were indefatigable in trying to evangelize the prison. A few of them would take their station in some part of the Stockade (a different one every time), and begin singing some old familiar hymn like:

"Come, Thou fount of every blessing,"

and in a few minutes they would have an attentive audience of as many thousand as could get within hearing. The singing would be followed by regular services, during which Sheppard, Smith, Corbett, and some others would make short, spirited, practical addresses, which no doubt did much good to all who heard them, though the grains of leaven were entirely too small to leaven such an immense measure of meal. They conducted several funerals, as nearly like the way it was done at home as possible. Their ministrations were not confined to mere lip service, but they labored assiduously in caring for the sick, and made many a poor fellow's way to the grave much smoother for him.

This was about all the religious services that we were favored with. The Rebel preachers did not make that effort to save our misguided souls which one would have imagined they would having us where we could not choose but hear they might have taken advantage of our situation to rake us fore and aft with their theological artillery. They only attempted it in one instance. While in Richmond a preacher came into our room and announced in an authoritative way that he would address us on religious subjects. We uncovered respectfully, and gathered around him. He was a loud-tongued, brawling Boanerges, who addressed the Lord as if drilling a brigade.

He spoke but a few moments before making apparent his belief that the worst of crimes was that of being a Yankee, and that a man must not only be saved through Christ's blood, but also serve in the Rebel army before he could attain to heaven.

Of course we raised such a yell of derision that the sermon was brought to an abrupt conclusion. The only minister who came into the Stockade was a Catholic priest, middle-aged, tall, slender, and unmistakably devout. He was unwearied in his attention to the sick, and the whole day could be seen moving around through the prison, attending to those who needed spiritual consolation. It was interesting to see him administer the extreme unction to a dying man. Placing a long purple scarf about his own neck and a small brazen crucifix in the hands of the dying one, he would kneel by the latter's side and anoint him upon the eyes, ears, nostrils; lips, hands, feet and breast, with sacred oil; from a little brass vessel, repeating the while, in an impressive voice, the solemn offices of the Church.

His unwearying devotion gained the admiration of all, no matter how little inclined one might be to view priestliness generally with favor. He was evidently of such stuff as Christian heros have ever been made of, and would have faced stake and fagot, at the call of duty, with unquailing eye. His name was Father Hamilton, and he was stationed at Macon. The world should know more of a man whose services were so creditable to humanity and his Church:

The good father had the wisdom of the serpent, with the harmlessness of the dove. Though full of commiseration for the unhappy lot of the prisoners, nothing could betray him into the slightest expression of opinion regarding the war or those who were the authors of all this misery. In our impatience at our treatment, and hunger for news, we forgot his sacerdotal character, and importuned him for tidings of the exchange. His invariable reply was that he lived apart from these things and kept himself ignorant of them.

"But, father," said I one day, with an impatience that I could not wholly repress, "you must certainly hear or read something of this, while you are outside among the Rebel officers." Like many other people, I supposed that the whole world was excited over that in which I felt a deep interest.

"No, my son," replied he, in his usual calm, measured tones. "I go not among them, nor do I hear anything from them. When I leave the prison in the evening, full of sorrow at what I have seen here, I find that the best use I can make of my time is in studying the Word of God, and especially the Psalms of David."

We were not any longer good company for each other. We had heard over and over again all each other's stories and jokes, and each knew as much about the other's previous history as we chose to communicate. The story of every individual's past life, relations, friends, regiment, and soldier experience had been told again and again, until the repetition was wearisome. The cool nights following the hot days were favorable to little gossiping seances like the yarn-spinning watches of sailors on pleasant nights. Our squad, though its stock of stories was worn threadbare, was fortunate enough to have a sweet singer in Israel "Nosey" Payne—of whose tunefulness we never tired. He had a large repertoire of patriotic songs, which he sang with feeling and correctness, and which helped much to make the calm Summer nights pass agreeably. Among the best of these was "Brave Boys are They," which I always thought was the finest ballad, both in poetry and music, produced by the War.

CHAPTER XXXIV.

MAGGOTS, LICE AND RAIDERS—PRACTICES OF THESE HUMAN VERMIN—
PLUNDERING THE SICK AND DYING—NIGHT ATTACKS, AND BATTLES BY DAY—
HARD TIMES FOR THE SMALL TRADERS.

With each long, hot Summer hour the lice, the maggot-flies and the N'Yaarkers increased in numbers and venomous activity. They were ever-present annoyances and troubles; no time was free from them. The lice worried us by day and tormented us by night; the maggot-flies fouled our food, and laid in sores and wounds larvae that speedily became masses of wriggling worms. The N'Yaarkers were human vermin that preyed upon and harried us unceasingly.

They formed themselves into bands numbering from five to twenty-five, each led by a bold, unscrupulous, energetic scoundrel. We now called them "Raiders," and the most prominent and best known of the bands were called by the names of their ruffian leaders, as "Mosby's Raiders," "Curtis's Raiders," "Delaney's Raiders," "Sarsfield's Raiders," "Collins's Raiders," etc.

As long as we old prisoners formed the bulk of those inside the Stockade, the Raiders had slender picking. They would occasionally snatch a blanket from the tent poles, or knock a boy down at the Creek and take his silver watch from him; but this was all. Abundant opportunities for securing richer swag came to them with the advent of the Plymouth Pilgrims. As had been before stated, these boys brought in with them a large portion of their first instalment of veteran bounty—aggregating in amount, according to varying estimates, between twenty-five thousand and one hundred thousand dollars. The Pilgrims were likewise well clothed, had an abundance of blankets and camp equipage, and a plentiful supply of personal trinkets, that could be readily traded off to the Rebels. An average one of them—even if his money were all gone—was a bonanza to any band which could succeed in plundering him. His watch and chain, shoes, knife, ring, handkerchief, combs and similar trifles, would net several hundred dollars in Confederate money. The blockade, which cut off the Rebel communication with the outer world, made these in great demand. Many of the prisoners that came in from the Army of the Potomac repaid robbing equally well. As a rule those from that Army were not searched so closely as those from the West, and not unfrequently they came in with all their belongings untouched, where Sherman's men, arriving the same day, would be stripped nearly to the buff.

The methods of the Raiders were various, ranging all the way from sneak thievery to highway robbery. All the arts learned in the prisons and purlieus of New York were put into exercise. Decoys, "bunko-steerers" at home, would be on the look-out for promising subjects as each crowd of fresh prisoners entered the gate, and by kindly offers to find them a sleeping place, lure them to where they could be easily despoiled during the night. If the victim resisted there was always sufficient force at hand to conquer him, and not seldom his life paid the penalty of his contumacy. I have known as many as three of these to be killed in a night, and their bodies—with throats cut, or skulls crushed in—be found in the morning among the dead at the gates.

All men having money or valuables were under continual espionage, and when found in places convenient for attack, a rush was made for them. They were knocked down and their persons rifled with such swift dexterity that it was done before they realized what had happened.

At first these depredations were only perpetrated at night. The quarry was selected during the day, and arrangements made for a descent. After the victim was asleep the band dashed down upon him, and sheared him of his goods with incredible swiftness. Those near would raise the cry of "Raiders!" and attack the robbers. If the latter had secured their booty they retreated with all possible speed, and were soon lost in the crowd. If not, they would offer battle, and signal for assistance from the other bands. Severe engagements of this kind were of continual occurrence, in which men were so badly beaten as to die from the effects. The weapons used were fists, clubs, axes, tent-poles, etc. The Raiders were plentifully provided with the usual weapons of their class—slung-shots and brass-knuckles. Several of them had succeeded in smuggling bowie-knives into prison.

They had the great advantage in these rows of being well acquainted with each other, while, except the Plymouth Pilgrims, the rest of the prisoners were made up of small squads of men from each regiment in the service, and total strangers to all outside of their own little band. The Raiders could concentrate, if necessary, four hundred or five hundred men upon any point of attack, and each member of the gangs had become so familiarized with all the rest by long association in New York, and elsewhere, that he never dealt a blow amiss, while their opponents were nearly as likely to attack friends as enemies.

By the middle of June the continual success of the Raiders emboldened them so that they no longer confined their depredations to the night, but made their forays in broad daylight, and there was hardly an hour in the twenty-four that the cry of "Raiders! Raiders!" did, not go up from some part of the pen, and on looking in the direction of the cry, one would see a surging commotion, men struggling, and clubs being plied vigorously. This was even more common than the guards shooting men at the Creek crossing.

One day I saw "Dick Allen's Raiders," eleven in number, attack a man wearing the uniform of Ellett's Marine Brigade. He was a recent comer, and alone, but he was brave. He had come into possession of a spade, by some means or another, and he used this with delightful vigor and effect. Two or three times he struck one of his assailants so fairly on the head and with such good will that I congratulated myself that he had killed him. Finally, Dick Allen managed to slip around behind him unnoticed, and striking him on the head with a slung-shot, knocked him down, when the whole crowd pounced upon him to kill him, but were driven off by others rallying to his assistance.

The proceeds of these forays enabled the Raiders to wax fat and lusty, while others were dying from starvation. They all had good tents, constructed of stolen blankets, and their headquarters was a large, roomy tent, with a circular top, situated on the street leading to the South Gate, and capable of accommodating from seventy-five to one hundred men. All the material for this had been wrested away from others. While hundreds were dying of scurvy and diarrhea, from the miserable, insufficient food, and lack of vegetables, these fellows had flour, fresh meat, onions, potatoes, green beans, and other things, the very looks of which were a torture to hungry, scorbutic, dysenteric men. They were on the best possible terms with the Rebels, whom they fawned upon and groveled before, and were in return allowed many favors, in the way of trading, going out upon detail, and making purchases.

Among their special objects of attack were the small traders in the prison. We had quite a number of these whose genius for barter was so strong that it took root and flourished even in that unpropitious soil, and during the time when new prisoners were constantly coming in with money, they managed to accumulate small sums—from ten dollars upward, by trading between the guards and the prisoners. In the period immediately following a prisoner's entrance he was likely to spend all his money and trade off all his possessions for food, trusting to fortune to get him out of there when these were gone. Then was when he was profitable to these go-betweens, who managed to make him pay handsomely for what he got. The Raiders kept watch of these traders, and plundered them whenever occasion served. It reminded one of the habits of the fishing eagle, which hovers around until some other bird catches a fish, and then takes it away.

CHAPTER XXXV

A COMMUNITY WITHOUT GOVERNMENT—FORMATION OF THE REGULATORS—RAIDERS ATTACK KEY BUT ARE BLUFFED OFF—ASSAULT OF THE REGULATORS ON THE RAIDERS —DESPERATE BATTLE—OVERTHROW OF THE RAIDERS.

To fully appreciate the condition of affairs let it be remembered that we were a community of twenty-five thousand boys and young men—none too regardful of control at best—and now wholly destitute of government. The Rebels never made the slightest attempt to maintain order in the prison. Their whole energies were concentrated in preventing our escape. So long as we staid inside the Stockade, they cared as little what we did there as for the performances of savages in the interior of Africa. I doubt if they would have interfered had one-half of us killed and eaten the other half. They rather took a delight in such atrocities as came to their notice. It was an ocular demonstration of the total depravity of the Yankees.

Among ourselves there was no one in position to lay down law and enforce it. Being all enlisted men we were on a dead level as far as rank was concerned—the highest being only Sergeants, whose stripes carried no weight of authority. The time of our stay was—it was hoped—too transient to make it worth while bothering about organizing any form of government. The great bulk of the boys were recent comers, who hoped that in another week or so they would be out again. There were no fat salaries to tempt any one to take upon himself the duty of ruling the masses, and all were left to their own devices, to do good or evil, according to their several bents, and as fear of consequences swayed them. Each little squad of men was a law unto themselves, and made and enforced their own regulations on their own territory. The administration of justice was reduced to its simplest terms. If a fellow did wrong he was pounded—if there was anybody capable of doing it. If not he went free.

The almost unvarying success of the Raiders in—their forays gave the general impression that they were invincible—that is, that not enough men could be concentrated against them to whip them. Our ill-success in the attack we made on them in April helped us to the same belief. If we could not beat them then, we could not now, after we had been enfeebled by months of starvation and disease. It seemed to us that the Plymouth Pilgrims, whose organization was yet very strong, should undertake the task; but, as is usually the case in this world, where we think somebody else ought to undertake the performance of a disagreeable public duty, they did not see it in the light that we wished them to. They established guards around their squads, and helped beat off the Raiders when their own territory was invaded, but this was all they would do. The rest of us formed similar guards. In the southwest corner of the Stockade—where I was—we formed ourselves into a company of fifty active boys—mostly belonging to my own battalion and to other Illinois regiments—of which I was elected Captain. My First Lieutenant was a tall, taciturn, long-armed member of the One Hundred and Eleventh Illinois, whom we called "Egypt," as he came from that section of the State. He was wonderfully handy with his fists. I think he could knock a fellow down so that he would fall-harder, and lie longer than any person I ever saw. We made a tacit division of duties: I did the talking, and "Egypt" went through the manual labor of knocking our opponents down. In the numerous little encounters in which our company was engaged, "Egypt" would stand by my side, silent, grim and patient, while I pursued the dialogue with the leader of the other crowd. As soon as he thought the conversation had reached the proper point, his long left arm stretched out like a flash, and the other fellow dropped as if he had suddenly come in range of a mule that was feeling well. That unexpected left-hander never failed. It would have made Charles Reade's heart leap for joy to see it.

In spite of our company and our watchfulness, the Raiders beat us badly on one occasion. Marion Friend, of Company I of our battalion, was one of the small traders, and had accumulated forty dollars by his bartering. One evening at dusk Delaney's Raiders, about twenty-five strong, took advantage of the absence of most of us drawing rations, to make a rush for Marion. They knocked him down, cut him across the wrist and neck with a razor, and robbed him of his forty dollars. By the time we could rally Delaney and his attendant scoundrels were safe from pursuit in the midst of their friends.

This state of things had become unendurable. Sergeant Leroy L. Key, of Company M, our battalion, resolved to make an effort to crush the Raiders. He was a printer, from Bloomington, Illinois, tall, dark, intelligent and strong-willed, and one of the bravest men I ever knew. He was ably seconded by "Limber Jim," of the Sixty-Seventh Illinois, whose lithe, sinewy form, and striking features reminded one of a young Sioux brave. He had all of Key's desperate courage, but not his brains or his talent for leadership. Though fearfully reduced in numbers, our battalion had still about one hundred well men in it, and these formed the nucleus for Key's band of "Regulators," as they were styled. Among them were several who had no equals in physical strength and courage in any of the Raider chiefs. Our best man was Ned Carrigan, Corporal of Company I, from Chicago—who was so confessedly the best man in the whole prison that he was never called upon to demonstrate it. He was a big-hearted, genial Irish boy, who was never known to get into trouble on his own account, but only used his fists when some of his comrades were imposed upon. He had fought in the ring, and on one occasion had killed a man with a single blow of his fist, in a prize fight near St. Louis. We were all very proud of him, and it was as good as an entertainment to us to see the noisiest roughs subside into deferential silence as Ned would come among them, like some grand mastiff in the midst of a pack of yelping curs. Ned entered into the regulating scheme heartily. Other stalwart specimens of physical manhood in our battalion were Sergeant Goody, Ned Johnson, Tom Larkin, and others, who, while not approaching Carrigan's perfect manhood, were still more than a match for the best of the Raiders.

Key proceeded with the greatest secrecy in the organization of his forces. He accepted none but Western men, and preferred Illinoisans, Iowans, Kansans, Indianians and Ohioans. The boys from those States seemed to naturally go together, and be moved by the same motives. He informed Wirz what he proposed doing, so that any unusual commotion within the prison might not be mistaken for an attempt upon the Stockade, and made the excuse for opening with the artillery. Wirz, who happened to be in a complaisant humor, approved of the design, and allowed him the use of the enclosure of the North Gate to confine his prisoners in.

In spite of Key's efforts at secrecy, information as to his scheme reached the Raiders. It was debated at their headquarters, and decided there that Key must be killed. Three men were selected to do this work. They called on Key, a dusk, on the evening of the 2d of July. In response to their inquiries, he came out of the blanket-covered hole on the hillside that he called his tent. They told him what they had heard, and asked if it was true. He said it was. One of them then drew a knife, and the other two, "billies" to attack him. But, anticipating trouble, Key had procured a revolver which one of the Pilgrims had brought in in his knapsack and drawing this he drove them off, but without firing a shot.

The occurrence caused the greatest excitement. To us of the Regulators it showed that the Raiders had penetrated our designs, and were prepared for them. To the great majority of the prisoners it was the first intimation that such a thing was contemplated; the news spread from squad to squad with the greatest rapidity, and soon everybody was discussing the chances of the movement. For awhile men ceased their interminable discussion of escape and exchange—let those over worked words and themes have a rare spell of repose—and debated whether the Raiders would whip the regulators, or the Regulators conquer the Raiders. The reasons which I have previously enumerated, induced a general disbelief in the probability of our success. The Raiders were in good health well fed, used to operating together, and had the confidence begotten by a long series of successes. The Regulators lacked in all these respects.

Whether Key had originally fixed on the next day for making the attack, or whether this affair precipitated the crisis, I know not, but later in the evening he sent us all order: to be on our guard all night, and ready for action the next morning.

There was very little sleep anywhere that night. The Rebels learned through their spies that something unusual was going on inside, and as their only interpretation of anything unusual there was a design upon the Stockade, they strengthened the guards, took additional precautions in every way, and spent the hours in anxious anticipation.

We, fearing that the Raiders might attempt to frustrate the scheme by an attack in overpowering force on Key's squad, which would be accompanied by the assassination of him and Limber Jim, held ourselves in readiness to offer any assistance that might be needed.

The Raiders, though confident of success, were no less exercised. They threw out pickets to all the approaches to their headquarters, and provided otherwise against surprise. They had smuggled in some canteens of a cheap, vile whisky made from sorghum—and they grew quite hilarious in their Big Tent over their potations. Two songs had long ago been accepted by us as peculiarly the Raiders' own—as some one in their crowd sang them nearly every evening, and we never heard them anywhere else. The first began:

In Athol lived a man named Jerry Lanagan;
He battered away till he hadn't a pound.
His father he died, and he made him a man agin;
Left him a farm of ten acres of ground.

The other related the exploits of an Irish highwayman named Brennan, whose chief virtue was that

What he rob-bed from the rich he gave unto the poor.

And this was the villainous chorus in which they all joined, and sang in such a way as suggested highway robbery, murder, mayhem and arson:

Brennan on the moor!
Brennan on the moor!
Proud and undaunted stood
John Brennan on the moor.

They howled these two nearly the live-long night. They became eventually quite monotonous to us, who were waiting and watching. It would have been quite a relief if they had thrown in a new one every hour or so, by way of variety.

Morning at last came. Our companies mustered on their grounds, and then marched to the space on the South Side where the rations were issued. Each man was armed with a small club, secured to his wrist by a string.

The Rebels—with their chronic fear of an outbreak animating them—had all the infantry in line of battle with loaded guns. The cannon in the works were shotted, the fuses thrust into the touch-holes and the men stood with lanyards in hand ready to mow down everybody, at any instant.

The sun rose rapidly through the clear sky, which soon glowed down on us like a brazen oven. The whole camp gathered where it could best view the encounter. This was upon the North Side. As I have before explained the two sides sloped toward each other like those of a great trough. The Raiders' headquarters stood upon the center of the southern slope, and consequently those standing on the northern slope saw everything as if upon the stage of a theater.

While standing in ranks waiting the orders to move, one of my comrades touched me on the arm, and said:

"My God! just look over there!"

I turned from watching the Rebel artillerists, whose intentions gave me more uneasiness than anything else, and looked in the direction indicated by the speaker. The sight was the strangest one my eyes ever encountered. There were at least fifteen thousand perhaps twenty thousand—men packed together on the bank, and every eye was turned on us. The slope was such that each man's face showed over the shoulders of the one in front of him, making acres on acres of faces. It was as if the whole broad hillside was paved or thatched with human countenances.

When all was ready we moved down upon the Big Tent, in as good order as we could preserve while passing through the narrow tortuous paths between the tents. Key, Limber Jim, Ned Carigan, Goody, Tom Larkin, and Ned Johnson led the advance with their companies. The prison was as silent as a graveyard. As we approached, the Raiders massed themselves in a strong, heavy line, with the center, against which our advance was moving, held by the most redoubtable of their leaders. How many there were of them could not be told, as it was impossible to say where their line ended and the mass of spectators began. They could not themselves tell, as the attitude of a large portion of the spectators would be determined by which way the battle went. Not a blow was struck until the lines came close together. Then the Raider center launched itself forward against ours, and grappled savagely with the leading Regulators. For an instant—it seemed an hour—the struggle was desperate.

Strong, fierce men clenched and strove to throttle each other; great muscles strained almost to bursting, and blows with fist and club-dealt with all the energy of mortal hate—fell like hail. One—perhaps two endless minutes the lines surged—throbbed—backward and forward a step or two, and then, as if by a concentration of mighty effort, our men flung the Raider line back from it—broken—shattered. The next instant our leaders were striding through the mass like raging lions. Carrigan, Limber Jim, Larkin, Johnson and Goody each smote down a swath of men before them, as they moved resistlessly forward.

We light weights had been sent around on the flanks to separate the spectators from the combatants, strike the Raiders 'en revers,' and, as far as possible, keep the crowd from reinforcing them.

In five minutes after the first blow—was struck the overthrow of the Raiders was complete. Resistance ceased, and they sought safety in flight.

As the result became apparent to the—watchers on the opposite hillside, they vented their pent-up excitement in a yell that made the very ground tremble, and we answered them with a shout that expressed not only our exultation over our victory, but our great relief from the intense strain we had long borne.

We picked up a few prisoners on the battle field, and retired without making any special effort to get any more then, as we knew, that they could not escape us.

We were very tired, and very hungry. The time for drawing rations had arrived. Wagons containing bread and mush had driven to the gates, but Wirz would not allow these to be opened, lest in the excited condition of the men an attempt might be made to carry them. Key ordered operations to cease, that Wirz might be re-assured and let the rations enter. It was in vain. Wirz was thoroughly scared. The wagons stood out in the hot sun until the mush fermented and soured, and had to be thrown away, while we event rationless to bed, and rose the next day with more than usually empty stomachs to goad us on to our work.

CHAPTER XXXVI.

WHY THE REGULATORS WERE NOT ASSISTED BY THE ENTIRE CAMP—PECULIARITIES OF BOYS FROM DIFFERENT SECTIONS—HUNTING THE RAIDERS DOWN—EXPLOITS OF MY LEFT-HANDED LIEUTENANT—RUNNING THE GAUNTLET.

I may not have made it wholly clear to the reader why we did not have the active assistance of the whole prison in the struggle with the Raiders. There were many reasons for this. First, the great bulk of the prisoners were new comers, having been, at the farthest, but three or four weeks in the Stockade. They did not comprehend the situation of affairs as we older prisoners did. They did not understand that all the outrages—or very nearly all—were the work of—a relatively small crowd of graduates from the metropolitan school of vice. The activity and audacity of the Raiders gave them the impression that at least half the able-bodied men in the Stockade were engaged in these depredations. This is always the case. A half dozen burglars or other active criminals in a town will produce the impression that a large portion of the population are law breakers. We never estimated that the raiding N'Yaarkers, with their spies and other accomplices, exceeded five hundred, but it would have been difficult to convince a new prisoner that there were not thousands of them. Secondly, the prisoners were made up of small squads from every regiment at the front along the whole line from the Mississippi to the Atlantic. These were strangers to and distrustful of all out side their own little circles. The Eastern men were especially so. The Pennsylvanians and New Yorkers each formed groups, and did not fraternize readily with those outside their State lines. The New Jerseyans held aloof from all the rest, while the Massachusetts soldiers had very little in Common with anybody—even their fellow New Englanders. The Michigan men were modified New Englanders. They had the same tricks of speech; they said "I be" for "I am," and "haag" for "hog;" "Let me look at your knife half a second," or "Give me just a sup of that water," where we said simply "Lend me your knife," or "hand me a drink." They were less reserved than the true Yankees, more disposed to be social, and, with all their eccentricities, were as manly, honorable a set of fellows as it was my fortune to meet with in the army. I could ask no better comrades than the boys of the Third Michigan Infantry, who belonged to the same "Ninety" with me. The boys from Minnesota and Wisconsin were very much like those from Michigan. Those from Ohio, Indiana, Illinois, Iowa and Kansas all seemed cut off the same piece. To all intents and purposes they might have come from the same County. They spoke the same dialect, read the same newspapers, had studied McGuffey's Readers, Mitchell's Geography, and Ray's Arithmetics at school, admired the same great men, and held generally the same opinions on any given subject. It was never difficult to get them to act in unison—they did it spontaneously; while it required an effort to bring about harmony of action with those from other sections. Had the Western boys in prison been thoroughly advised of the nature of our enterprise, we could, doubtless, have commanded their cordial assistance, but they were not, and there was no way in which it could be done readily, until after the decisive blow was struck.

The work of arresting the leading Raiders went on actively all day on the Fourth of July. They made occasional shows of fierce resistance, but the events of the day before had destroyed their prestige, broken their confidence, and driven away from their support very many who followed their lead when they were considered all-powerful. They scattered from their former haunts, and mingled with the crowds in other parts of the prison, but were recognized, and reported to Key, who sent parties to arrest them. Several times they managed to collect enough adherents to drive off the squads sent after them, but this only gave them a short respite, for the squad would return reinforced, and make short work of them. Besides, the prisoners generally were beginning to understand and approve of the Regulators' movement, and were disposed to give all the assistance needed.

Myself and "Egypt," my taciturn Lieutenant of the sinewy left arm, were sent with our company to arrest Pete Donnelly, a notorious character, and leader of, a bad crowd. He was more "knocker" than Raider, however. He was an old Pemberton building acquaintance, and as we marched up to where he was standing at the head of his gathering clan, he recognized me and said:

"Hello, Illinoy," (the name by which I was generally known in prison) "what do you want here?"

I replied, "Pete, Key has sent me for you. I want you to go to headquarters."

"What the —— does Key want with me?"

"I don't know, I'm sure; he only said to bring you."

"But I haven't had anything to do with them other snoozers you have been a-having trouble with."

"I don't know anything about that; you can talk to Key as to that. I only know that we are sent for you."

"Well, you don't think you can take me unless I choose to go? You haint got anybody in that crowd big enough to make it worth while for him to waste his time trying it."

I replied diffidently that one never knew what—he could do till he tried; that while none of us were very big, we were as willing a lot of little fellows as he ever saw, and if it were all the same to him, we would undertake to waste a little time getting him to headquarters.

The conversation seemed unnecessarily long to "Egypt," who stood by my side; about a half step in advance. Pete was becoming angrier and more defiant every minute. His followers were crowding up to us, club in hand. Finally Pete thrust his fist in my face, and roared out:

"By ——, I ain't a going with ye, and ye can't take me, you —— —— —— "

This was "Egypt's" cue. His long left arm uncoupled like the loosening of the weight of a pile-driver. It caught Mr. Donnelly under the chin, fairly lifted him from his feet, and dropped him on his back among his followers. It seemed to me that the predominating expression in his face as he went, over was that of profound wonder as to where that blow could have come from, and why he did not see it in time to dodge or ward it off.

As Pete dropped, the rest of us stepped forward with our clubs, to engage his followers, while "Egypt" and one or two others tied his hands and otherwise secured him. But his henchmen made no effort to rescue him, and we carried him over to headquarters without molestation.

The work of arresting increased in interest and excitement until it developed into the furore of a hunt, with thousands eagerly engaged in it. The Raiders' tents were torn down and pillaged. Blankets, tent poles, and cooking utensils were carried off as spoils, and the ground was dug over for secreted property. A large quantity of watches, chains, knives, rings, gold pens, etc., etc.—the booty of many a raid—was found, and helped to give impetus to the hunt. Even the Rebel Quartermaster, with the characteristic keen scent of the Rebels for spoils, smelled from the outside the opportunity for gaining plunder, and came in with a squad of Rebels equipped with spades, to dig for buried treasures. How successful he was I know not, as I took no part in any of the operations of that nature.

It was claimed that several skeletons of victims of the Raiders were found buried beneath the tent. I cannot speak with any certainty as to this, though my impression is that at least one was found.

By evening Key had perhaps one hundred and twenty-five of the most noted Raiders in his hands. Wirz had allowed him the use of the small stockade forming the entrance to the North Gate to confine them in.

The next thing was the judgment and punishment of the arrested ones. For this purpose Key organized a court martial composed of thirteen Sergeants, chosen from the latest arrivals of prisoners, that they might have no prejudice against the Raiders. I believe that a man named Dick McCullough, belonging to the Third Missouri Cavalry, was the President of the Court. The trial was carefully conducted, with all the formality of a legal procedure that the Court and those managing the matter could remember as applicable to the crimes with which the accused were charged. Each of these confronted by the witnesses who testified against him, and allowed to cross-examine them to any extent he desired. The defense was managed by one of their crowd, the foul-tongued Tombs shyster, Pete Bradley, of whom I have before spoken. Such was the fear of the vengeance of the Raiders and their friends that many who had been badly abused dared not testify against them, dreading midnight assassination if they did. Others would not go before the Court except at night. But for all this there was no lack of evidence; there were thousands who had been robbed and maltreated, or who had seen these outrages committed on others, and the boldness of the leaders in their bight of power rendered their identification a matter of no difficulty whatever.

The trial lasted several days, and concluded with sentencing quite a large number to run the gauntlet, a smaller number to wear balls and chains, and the following six to be hanged:

John Sarsfield, One Hundred and Forty-Fourth New York.

William Collins, alias "Mosby," Company D, Eighty-Eighth Pennsylvania,

Charles Curtis, Company A, Fifth Rhode Island Artillery.

Patrick Delaney, Company E, Eighty-Third Pennsylvania.

A. Muir, United States Navy.

Terence Sullivan, Seventy-Second New York.

These names and regiments are of little consequence, however, as I believe all the rascals were professional bounty-jumpers, and did not belong to any regiment longer than they could find an opportunity to desert and join another.

Those sentenced to ball-and-chain were brought in immediately, and had the irons fitted to them that had been worn by some of our men as a punishment for trying to escape.

It was not yet determined how punishment should be meted out to the remainder, but circumstances themselves decided the matter. Wirz became tired of guarding so large a number as Key had arrested, and he informed Key that he should turn them back into the Stockade immediately. Key begged for little farther time to consider the disposition of the cases, but Wirz refused it, and ordered the Officer of the Guard to return all arrested, save those sentenced to death, to the Stockade. In the meantime the news had spread through the prison that the Raiders were to be sent in again unpunished, and an angry mob, numbering some thousands, and mostly composed of men who had suffered injuries at the hands of the marauders, gathered at the South Gate, clubs in hand, to get such satisfaction as they could out of the rascals. They formed in two long, parallel lines, facing inward, and grimly awaited the incoming of the objects of their vengeance.

The Officer of the Guard opened the wicket in the gate, and began forcing the Raiders through it—one at a time—at the point of the bayonet, and each as he entered was told what he already realized well—that he must run for his life. They did this with all the energy that they possessed, and as they ran blows rained on their heads, arms and backs. If they could succeed in breaking through the line at any place they were generally let go without any further punishment. Three of the number were beaten to death. I saw one of these killed. I had no liking for the gauntlet performance, and refused to have anything to do with it, as did most, if not all, of my crowd.

While the gauntlet was in operation, I was standing by my tent at the head of a little street, about two hundred feet from the line, watching what was being done. A sailor was let in. He had a large bowie knife concealed about his person somewhere, which he drew, and struck savagely with at his tormentors on either side. They fell back from before him, but closed in behind and pounded him terribly. He broke through the line, and ran up the street towards me. About midway of the distance stood a boy who had helped carry a dead man out during the day, and while out had secured a large pine rail which he had brought in with him. He was holding this straight up in the air, as if at a "present arms." He seemed to have known from the first that the Raider would run that way. Just as he came squarely under it, the boy dropped the rail like the bar of a toll gate. It struck the Raider across the head, felled him as if by a shot, and his pursuers then beat him to death.

CHAPTER XXXVII.

THE EXECUTION—BUILDING THE SCAFFOLD—DOUBTS OF THE CAMP-CAPTAIN WIRZ THINKS IT IS PROBABLY A RUSE TO FORCE THE STOCKADE—HIS PREPARATIONS AGAINST SUCH AN ATTEMPT—ENTRANCE OF THE DOOMED ONES—THEY REALIZE THEIR FATE—ONE MAKES A DESPERATE ATTEMPT TO ESCAPE—HIS RECAPTURE—INTENSE EXCITEMENT—WIRZ ORDERS THE GUNS TO OPEN—FORTUNATELY THEY DO NOT—THE SIX ARE HANGED—ONE BREAKS HIS ROPE—SCENE WHEN THE RAIDERS ARE CUT DOWN.

It began to be pretty generally understood through the prison that six men had been sentenced to be hanged, though no authoritative announcement of the fact had been made. There was much canvassing as to where they should be executed, and whether an attempt to hang them inside of the Stockade would not rouse their friends to make a desperate effort to rescue them, which would precipitate a general engagement of even larger proportions than that of the 3d. Despite the result of the affairs of that and the succeeding days, the camp was not yet convinced that the Raiders were really conquered, and the Regulators themselves were not thoroughly at ease on that score. Some five thousand or six thousand new prisoners had come in since the first of the month, and it was claimed that the Raiders had received large reinforcements from those,—a claim rendered probable by most of the new-comers being from the Army of the Potomac.

Key and those immediately about him kept their own counsel in the matter, and suffered no secret of their intentions to leak out, until on the morning of the 11th, when it became generally known that the sentences were too be carried into effect that day, and inside the prison.

My first direct information as to this was by a messenger from Key with an order to assemble my company and stand guard over the carpenters who were to erect the scaffold. He informed me that all the Regulators would be held in readiness to come to our relief if we were attacked in force. I had hoped that if the men were to be hanged I would be spared the unpleasant duty of assisting, for, though I believed they richly deserved that punishment, I had much rather some one else administered it upon them. There was no way out of it, however, that I could see, and so "Egypt" and I got the boys together, and marched down to the designated place, which was an open space near the end of the street running from the South Gate, and kept vacant for the purpose of issuing rations. It was quite near the spot where the Raiders' Big Tent had stood, and afforded as good a view to the rest of the camp as could be found.

Key had secured the loan of a few beams and rough planks, sufficient to build a rude scaffold with. Our first duty was to care for these as they came in, for such was the need of wood, and plank for tent purposes, that they would scarcely have fallen to the ground before they were spirited away, had we not stood over them all the time with clubs.

The carpenters sent by Key came over and set to work. The N'Yaarkers gathered around in considerable numbers, sullen and abusive. They cursed us with all their rich vocabulary of foul epithets, vowed that we should never carry out the execution, and swore that they had marked each one for vengeance. We returned the compliments in kind, and occasionally it seemed as if a general collision was imminent; but we succeeded in avoiding this, and by noon the scaffold was finished. It was a very simple affair. A stout beam was fastened on the top of two posts, about fifteen feet high. At about the height of a man's head a couple of boards stretched across the space between the posts, and met in the center. The ends at the posts laid on cleats; the ends in the center rested upon a couple of boards, standing upright, and each having a piece of rope fastened through a hole in it in such a manner, that a man could snatch it from under the planks serving as the floor of the scaffold, and let the whole thing drop. A rude ladder to ascend by completed the preparations.

As the arrangements neared completion the excitement in and around the prison grew intense. Key came over with the balance of the Regulators, and we formed a hollow square around the scaffold, our company marking the line on the East Side. There were now thirty thousand in the prison. Of these about one-third packed themselves as tightly about our square as they could stand. The remaining twenty thousand were wedged together in a solid mass on the North Side. Again I contemplated the wonderful, startling, spectacle of a mosaic pavement of human faces covering the whole broad hillside.

Outside, the Rebel, infantry was standing in the rifle pits, the artillerymen were in place about their loaded and trained pieces, the No. 4 of each gun holding the lanyard cord in his hand, ready to fire the piece at the instant of command. The small squad of cavalry was drawn up on the hill near the Star Fort, and near it were the masters of the hounds, with their yelping packs.

All the hangers-on of the Rebel camp—clerks, teamsters, employer, negros, hundreds of white and colored women, in all forming a motley crowd of between one and two thousand, were gathered together in a group between the end of the rifle pits and the Star Fort. They had a good view from there, but a still better one could be had, a little farther to the right, and in front of the guns. They kept edging up in that direction, as crowds will, though they knew the danger they would incur if the artillery opened.

The day was broiling hot. The sun shot his perpendicular rays down with blistering fierceness, and the densely packed, motionless crowds made the heat almost insupportable.

Key took up his position inside the square to direct matters. With him were Limber Jim, Dick McCullough, and one or two others. Also, Ned Johnson, Tom Larkin, Sergeant Goody, and three others who were to act as hangmen. Each of these six was provided with a white sack, such as the Rebels brought in meal in. Two Corporals of my company—"Stag" Harris and Wat Payne— were appointed to pull the stays from under the platform at the signal.

A little after noon the South Gate opened, and Wirz rode in, dressed in a suit of white duck, and mounted on his white horse—a conjunction which had gained for him the appellation of "Death on a Pale Horse." Behind him walked the faithful old priest, wearing his Church's purple insignia of the deepest sorrow, and reading the service for the condemned. The six doomed men followed, walking between double ranks of Rebel guards.

All came inside the hollow square and halted. Wirz then said:

"Brizners, I return to you dose men so Boot as I got dem. You haf tried dem yourselves, and found dem guilty—I haf had notting to do wit it. I vash my hands of eferyting connected wit dem. Do wit dem as you like, and may Gott haf mercy on you and on dem. Garts, about face! Voryvarts, march!"

With this he marched out and left us.

For a moment the condemned looked stunned. They seemed to comprehend for the first time that it was really the determination of the Regulators to hang them. Before that they had evidently thought that the talk of hanging was merely bluff. One of them gasped out:

"My God, men, you don't really mean to hang us up there!"

Key answered grimly and laconically:

"That seems to be about the size of it."

At this they burst out in a passionate storm of intercessions and imprecations, which lasted for a minute or so, when it was stopped by one of them saying imperatively:

"All of you stop now, and let the priest talk for us."

At this the priest closed the book upon which he had kept his eyes bent since his entrance, and facing the multitude on the North Side began a plea for mercy.

The condemned faced in the same direction, to read their fate in the countenances of those whom he was addressing. This movement brought Curtis—a low-statured, massively built man—on the right of their line, and about ten or fifteen steps from my company.

The whole camp had been as still as death since Wirz's exit. The silence seemed to become even more profound as the priest began his appeal. For a minute every ear was strained to catch what he said. Then, as the nearest of the thousands comprehended what he was saying they raised a shout of "No! no!! NO!!" "Hang them! hang them!" "Don't let them go! Never!"

"Hang the rascals! hang the villains!"

"Hang,'em! hang 'em! hang 'em!"

This was taken up all over the prison, and tens of thousands throats yelled it in a fearful chorus. Curtis turned from the crowd with desperation convulsing his features. Tearing off the broad-brimmed hat which he wore, he flung it on the ground with the exclamation!

"By God, I'll die this way first!" and, drawing his head down and folding his arms about it, he dashed forward for the center of my company, like a great stone hurled from a catapult.

"Egypt" and I saw where he was going to strike, and ran down the line to help stop him. As he came up we rained blows on his head with our clubs, but so many of us struck at him at once that we broke each other's clubs to pieces, and only knocked him on his knees. He rose with an almost superhuman effort, and plunged into the mass beyond.

The excitement almost became delirium. For an instant I feared that everything was gone to ruin. "Egypt" and I strained every energy to restore our lines, before the break could be taken advantage of by the others. Our boys behaved splendidly, standing firm, and in a few seconds the line was restored.

As Curtis broke through, Delaney, a brawny Irishman standing next to him, started to follow. He took one step. At the same instant Limber Jim's long legs took three great strides, and placed him directly in front of Delaney. Jim's right hand held an enormous bowie-knife, and as he raised it above Delaney he hissed out:

"If you dare move another step, I'll open you —— —— ——, I'll open you from one end to the other.

Delaney stopped. This checked the others till our lines reformed.

When Wirz saw the commotion he was panic-stricken with fear that the long-dreaded assault on the Stockade had begun. He ran down from the headquarter steps to the Captain of the battery, shrieking:

"Fire! fire! fire!"

The Captain, not being a fool, could see that the rush was not towards the Stockade, but away from it, and he refrained from giving the order.

But the spectators who had gotten before the guns, heard Wirz's excited yell, and remembering the consequences to themselves should the artillery be discharged, became frenzied with fear, and screamed, and fell down over and trampled upon each other in endeavoring to get away. The guards on that side of the Stockade ran down in a panic, and the ten thousand prisoners immediately around us, expecting no less than that the next instant we would be swept with grape and canister, stampeded tumultuously. There were quite a number of wells right around us, and all of these were filled full of men that fell into them as the crowd rushed away. Many had legs and arms broken, and I have no doubt that several were killed.

It was the stormiest five minutes that I ever saw.

While this was going on two of my company, belonging to the Fifth Iowa Cavalry, were in hot pursuit of Curtis. I had seen them start and shouted to them to come back, as I feared they would be set upon by the Raiders and murdered. But the din was so overpowering that they could not hear me, and doubtless would not have come back if they had heard.

Curtis ran diagonally down the hill, jumping over the tents and knocking down the men who happened in his way. Arriving at the swamp he plunged in, sinking nearly to his hips in the fetid, filthy ooze. He forged his way through with terrible effort. His pursuers followed his example, and caught up to him just as he emerged on the other side. They struck him on the back of the head with their clubs, and knocked him down.

By this time order had been restored about us. The guns remained silent, and the crowd massed around us again. From where we were we could see the successful end of the chase after Curtis, and could see his captors start back with him. Their success was announced with a roar of applause from the North Side. Both captors and captured were greatly exhausted, and they were coming back very slowly. Key ordered the balance up on to the scaffold. They obeyed promptly. The priest resumed his reading of the service for the condemned. The excitement seemed to make the doomed ones exceedingly thirsty. I never saw men drink such inordinate quantities of water. They called for it continually, gulped down a quart or more at a time, and kept two men going nearly all the time carrying it to them.

When Curtis finally arrived, he sat on the ground for a minute or so, to rest, and then, reeking with filth, slowly and painfully climbed the steps. Delaney seemed to think he was suffering as much from fright as anything else, and said to him:

"Come on up, now, show yourself a man, and die game."

Again the priest resumed his reading, but it had no interest to Delaney, who kept calling out directions to Pete Donelly, who was standing in the crowd, as to dispositions to be made of certain bits of stolen property: to give a watch to this one, a ring to another, and so on. Once the priest stopped and said:

"My son, let the things of this earth go, and turn your attention toward those of heaven."

Delaney paid no attention to this admonition. The whole six then began delivering farewell messages to those in the crowd. Key pulled a watch from his pocket and said:

"Two minutes more to talk."

Delaney said cheerfully:

"Well, good by, b'ys; if I've hurted any of y ez, I hope ye'll forgive me. Shpake up, now, any of yez that I've hurted, and say yell forgive me."

We called upon Marion Friend, whose throat Delaney had tried to cut three weeks before while robbing him of forty dollars, to come forward, but Friend was not in a forgiving mood, and refused with an oath.

Key said:

"Time's up!" put the watch back in his pocket and raised his hand like an officer commanding a gun. Harris and Payne laid hold of the ropes to the supports of the planks. Each of the six hangmen tied a condemned man's hands, pulled a meal sack down over his head, placed the noose around his neck, drew it up tolerably close, and sprang to the ground. The priest began praying aloud.

Key dropped his hand. Payne and Harris snatched the supports out with a single jerk. The planks fell with a clatter. Five of the bodies swung around dizzily in the air. The sixth that of "Mosby," a large, powerful, raw-boned man, one of the worst in the lot, and who, among other crimes, had killed Limber Jim's brother-broke the rope, and fell with a thud to the ground. Some of the men ran forward, examined the body, and decided that he still lived. The rope was cut off his neck, the meal sack removed, and water thrown in his face until consciousness returned. At the first instant he thought he was in eternity. He gasped out:

"Where am I? Am I in the other world?"

Limber Jim muttered that they would soon show him where he was, and went on grimly fixing up the scaffold anew. "Mosby" soon realized what had happened, and the unrelenting purpose of the Regulator Chiefs. Then he began to beg piteously for his life, saying:

"O for God's sake, do not put me up there again! God has spared my life once. He meant that you should be merciful to me."

Limber Jim deigned him no reply. When the scaffold was rearranged, and a stout rope had replaced the broken one, he pulled the meal sack once more over "Mosby's" head, who never ceased his pleadings. Then picking up the large man as if he were a baby, he carried him to the scaffold and handed him up to Tom Larkin, who fitted the noose around his neck and sprang down. The supports had not been set with the same delicacy as at first, and Limber Jim had to set his heel and wrench desperately at them before he could force them out. Then "Mosby" passed away without a struggle.

After hanging till life was extinct, the bodies were cut down, the meal-sacks pulled off their faces, and the Regulators formal two parallel lines, through which all the prisoners passed and took a look at the bodies. Pete Donnelly and Dick Allen knelt down and wiped the froth off

Delaney's lips, and swore vengeance against those who had done him to death.

CHAPTER XXXVIII.

AFTER THE EXECUTION—FORMATION OF A POLICE FORCE—ITS FIRST CHIEF — "SPANKING" AN OFFENDER.

After the executions Key, knowing that he, and all those prominently connected with the hanging, would be in hourly danger of assassination if they remained inside, secured details as nurses and ward-masters in the hospital, and went outside. In this crowd were Key, Ned Carrigan, Limber Jim, Dick McCullough, the six hangmen, the two Corporals who pulled the props from under the scaffold, and perhaps some others whom I do not now remember.

In the meanwhile provision had been made for the future maintenance of order in the prison by the organization of a regular police force, which in time came to number twelve hundred men. These were divided into companies, under appropriate officers. Guards were detailed for certain locations, patrols passed through the camp in all directions continually, and signals with whistles could summon sufficient assistance to suppress any disturbance, or carry out any orders from the chief.

The chieftainship was first held by Key, but when he went outside he appointed Sergeant A. R. Hill, of the One Hundredth O. V. I.—now a resident of Wauseon, Ohio,—his successor. Hill was one of the notabilities of that immense throng. A great, broad-shouldered, giant, in the prime of his manhood—the beginning of his thirtieth year—he was as good-natured as big, and as mild-mannered as brave. He spoke slowly, softly, and with a slightly rustic twang, that was very tempting to a certain class of sharps to take him up for a "luberly greeny." The man who did so usually repented his error in sack-cloth and ashes.

Hill first came into prominence as the victor in the most stubbornly contested fight in the prison history of Belle Isle. When the squad of the One Hundredth Ohio—captured at Limestone Station, East Tennessee, in September,1863—arrived on Belle Isle, a certain Jack Oliver, of the Nineteenth Indiana, was the undisputed fistic monarch of the Island. He did not bear his blushing honors modestly; few of a right arm that indefinite locality known as "the middle of next week," is something that the possessor can as little resist showing as can a girl her first solitaire ring. To know that one can certainly strike a disagreeable fellow out of time is pretty sure to breed a desire to do that thing whenever occasion serves. Jack Oliver was one who did not let his biceps rust in inaction, but thrashed everybody on the Island whom he thought needed it, and his ideas as to those who should be included in this class widened daily, until it began to appear that he would soon feel it his duty to let no unwhipped man escape, but pound everybody on the Island.

One day his evil genius led him to abuse a rather elderly man belonging to Hill's mess. As he fired off his tirade of contumely, Hill said with more than his usual "soft" rusticity:

"Mister—I—don't—think—it—just—right—for—a—young—man—to—call—an—old—one—such—bad names."

Jack Oliver turned on him savagely.

"Well! may be you want to take it up?"

The grin on Hill's face looked still more verdant, as he answered with gentle deliberation: "Well—mister—I—don't—go—around—a—hunting—things—but—I —ginerally—take—care—of—all—that's—sent—me!"

Jack foamed, but his fiercest bluster could not drive that infantile smile from Hill's face, nor provoke a change in the calm slowness of his speech.

It was evident that nothing would do but a battle-royal, and Jack had sense enough to see that the imperturbable rustic was likely to give him a job of some difficulty. He went off and came back with his clan, while Hill's comrades of the One Hundredth gathered around to insure him fair play. Jack pulled off his coat and vest, rolled up his sleeves, and made other elaborate preparations for the affray. Hill, without removing a garment, said, as he surveyed him with a mocking smile:

"Mister—you—seem—to—be—one—of—them—partick-e-ler—fellers."

Jack roared out,

"By —-, I'll make you partickeler before I get through with you. Now, how shall we settle this? Regular stand-up-and knock-down, or rough and tumble?"

If anything Hill's face was more vacantly serene, and his tones blander than ever, as he answered: "Strike—any—gait—that—suits—you,—Mister;—I—guess—I—will—be —able—to—keep—up—with—you."

They closed. Hill feinted with his left, and as Jack uncovered to guard, he caught him fairly on the lower left ribs, by a blow from his mighty right fist, that sounded—as one of the by-standers expressed it—"like striking a hollow log with a maul."

The color in Jack's face paled. He did not seem to understand how he had laid himself open to such a pass, and made the same mistake, receiving again a sounding blow in the short ribs. This taught him nothing, either, for again he opened his guard in response to a feint, and again caught a blow on his luckless left, ribs, that drove the blood from his face and the breath from his body. He reeled back among his supporters for an instant to breathe. Recovering his wind, be dashed at Hill feinted strongly with his right, but delivered a terrible kick against the lower part of the latter's abdomen. Both closed and fought savagely at half-arm's length for an instant; during which Hill struck Jack so fairly in the mouth as to break out three front teeth, which the latter swallowed. Then they clenched and struggled to throw each other. Hill's superior strength and skill crushed his opponent to the ground, and he fell upon him. As they grappled there, one of Jack's followers sought to aid his leader by catching Hill by the hair, intending to kick him in the face. In an instant he was knocked down by a stalwart member of the One Hundredth, and then literally lifted out of the ring by kicks.

Jack was soon so badly beaten as to be unable to cry "enough!" One of his friends did that service for him, the fight ceased, and thenceforth Mr. Oliver resigned his pugilistic crown, and retired to the shades of private life. He died of scurvy and diarrhea, some months afterward, in Andersonville.

The almost hourly scenes of violence and crime that marked the days and nights before the Regulators began operations were now succeeded by the greatest order. The prison was freer from crime than the best governed City. There were frequent squabbles and fights, of course, and many petty larcenies. Rations of bread and of wood, articles of clothing, and the wretched little cans and half canteens that formed our cooking utensils, were still stolen, but all these were in a sneak-thief way. There was an entire absence of the audacious open-day robbery and murder — the "raiding" of the previous few weeks. The summary punishment inflicted on the condemned was sufficient to cow even bolder men than the Raiders, and they were frightened into at least quiescence.

Sergeant Hill's administration was vigorous, and secured the best results. He became a judge of all infractions of morals and law, and sat at the door of his tent to dispense justice to all comers, like the Cadi of a Mahometan Village. His judicial methods and punishments also reminded one strongly of the primitive judicature of Oriental lands. The wronged one came before him and told his tale: he had his blouse, or his quart cup, or his shoes, or his watch, or his money stolen during the night. The suspected one was also summoned, confronted with his accuser, and sharply interrogated. Hill would revolve the stories in his mind, decide the innocence or guilt of the accused, and if he thought the accusation sustained, order the culprit to punishment. He did not imitate his Mussulman prototypes to the extent of bowstringing or decapitating the condemned, nor did he cut any thief's hands off, nor yet nail his ears to a doorpost, but he introduced a modification of the bastinado that made those who were punished by it even wish they were dead. The instrument used was what is called in the South a "shake" —a split shingle, a yard or more long, and with one end whittled down to form a handle. The culprit was made to bend down until he could catch around his ankles with his hands. The part of the body thus brought into most prominence was denuded of clothing and "spanked" from one to twenty times, as Hill ordered, by the "shake" in same strong and willing hand. It was very amusing—to the bystanders. The "spankee" never seemed to enter very heartily into the mirth of the occasion. As a rule he slept on his face for a week or so after, and took his meals standing.

The fear of the spanking, and Hill's skill in detecting the guilty ones, had a very salutary effect upon the smaller criminals.

The Raiders who had been put into irons were very restive under the infliction, and begged Hill daily to release them. They professed the greatest penitence, and promised the most exemplary behavior for the future. Hill refused to release them, declaring that they should wear the irons until delivered up to our Government.

One of the Raiders—named Heffron—had, shortly after his arrest, turned State's evidence, and given testimony that assisted materially in the conviction of his companions. One morning, a week or so after the hanging, his body was found lying among the other dead at the South Gate. The impression made by the fingers of the hand that had strangled him, were still plainly visible about the throat. There was no doubt as to why he had been killed, or that the Raiders were his murderers, but the actual perpetrators were never discovered.

CHAPTER XXXIX.

JULY—THE PRISON BECOMES MORE CROWDED, THE WEATHER HOTTER, NATIONS POORER, AND MORTALITY GREATER—SOME OF THE PHENOMENA OF SUFFERING AND DEATH.

All during July the prisoners came streaming in by hundreds and thousands from every portion of the long line of battle, stretching from the Eastern bank of the Mississippi to the shores of the Atlantic. Over one thousand squandered by Sturgis at Guntown came in; two thousand of those captured in the desperate blow dealt by Hood against the Army of the Tennessee on the 22d of the month before Atlanta; hundreds from Hunter's luckless column in the Shenandoah Valley, thousands from Grant's lines in front of Petersburg. In all, seven thousand one hundred and twenty-eight were, during the month, turned into that seething mass of corrupting humanity to be polluted and tainted by it, and to assist in turn to make it fouler and deadlier. Over seventy hecatombs of chosen victims —of fair youths in the first flush of hopeful manhood, at the threshold of a life of honor to themselves and of usefulness to the community; beardless boys, rich in the priceless affections of homes, fathers, mothers, sisters and sweethearts, with minds thrilling with high aspirations for the bright future, were sent in as the monthly sacrifice to this Minotaur of the Rebellion, who, couched in his foul lair, slew them, not with the merciful delivery of speedy death, as his Cretan prototype did the annual tribute of Athenian youths and maidens, but, gloating over his prey, doomed them to lingering destruction. He rotted their flesh with the scurvy, racked their minds with intolerable suspense, burned their bodies with the slow fire of famine, and delighted in each separate pang, until they sank beneath the fearful accumulation. Theseus [Sherman. D.W.]—the deliverer—was coming. His terrible sword could be seen gleaming as it rose and fell on the banks of the James, and in the mountains beyond Atlanta, where he was hewing his way towards them and the heart of the Southern Confederacy. But he came too late to save them. Strike as swiftly and as heavily as he would, he could not strike so hard nor so sure at his foes with saber blow and musket shot, as they could at the hapless youths with the dreadful armament of starvation and disease.

Though the deaths were one thousand eight hundred and seventeen more than were killed at the battle of Shiloh—this left the number in the prison at the end of the month thirty-one thousand six hundred and seventy-eight. Let me assist the reader's comprehension of the magnitude of this number by giving the population of a few important Cities, according to the census of 1870:

Cambridge, Mass	89,639
Charleston, S. C.	48,958
Columbus, O.	31,274
Dayton, O.	30,473
Fall River, Mass	26,766
Kansas City, Mo	32,260

The number of prisoners exceeded the whole number of men between the ages of eighteen and forty-five in several of the States and Territories in the Union. Here, for instance, are the returns for 1870, of men of military age in some portions of the country:

Arizona	5,157

Colorado   15,166
Dakota 5,301
Idaho   9,431
Montana   12,418
Nebraska   35,677
Nevada   24,762
New Hampshire   60,684
Oregon23,959
Rhode Island 44,377
Vermont   62,450
West Virginia 6,832

It was more soldiers than could be raised to-day, under strong pressure, in either Alabama, Arizona, Arkansas, California, Colorado, Connecticut, Dakota, Delaware, District of Columbia, Florida, Idaho, Louisiana, Maine, Minnesota, Montana, Nebraska, Nevada, New Hampshire, New Medico, Oregon, Rhode Island, South Carolina, Utah, Vermont or West Virginia. These thirty-one thousand six hundred and seventy-eight active young men, who were likely to find the confines of a State too narrow for them, were cooped up on thirteen acres of ground— less than a farmer gives for play-ground for a half dozen colts or a small flock of sheep. There was hardly room for all to lie down at night, and to walk a few hundred feet in any direction would require an hour's patient threading of the mass of men and tents. The weather became hotter and hotter; at midday the sand would burn the hand. The thin skins of fair and auburn-haired men blistered under the sun's rays, and swelled up in great watery puffs, which soon became the breeding grounds of the hideous maggots, or the still more deadly gangrene. The loathsome swamp grew in rank offensiveness with every burning hour. The pestilence literally stalked at noon-day, and struck his victims down on every hand. One could not look a rod in any direction without seeing at least a dozen men in the last frightful stages of rotting Death.
Let me describe the scene immediately around my own tent during the last two weeks of July, as a sample of the condition of the whole prison: I will take a space not larger than a good sized parlor or sitting room. On this were at least fifty of us. Directly in front of me lay two brothers— named Sherwood—belonging to Company I, of my battalion, who came originally from Missouri. They were now in the last stages of scurvy and diarrhea. Every particle of muscle and fat about their limbs and bodies had apparently wasted away, leaving the skin clinging close to the bone of the face, arms, hands, ribs and thighs—everywhere except the feet and legs, where it was swollen tense and transparent, distended with gallons of purulent matter. Their livid gums, from which most of their teeth had already fallen, protruded far beyond their lips. To their left lay a Sergeant and two others of their company, all three slowly dying from diarrhea, and beyond was a fair-haired German, young and intelligent looking, whose life was ebbing tediously away. To my right was a handsome young Sergeant of an Illinois Infantry Regiment, captured at Kenesaw. His left arm had been amputated between the shoulder and elbow, and he was turned into the Stockade with the stump all undressed, save the ligating of the arteries. Of course, he had not been inside an hour until the maggot flies had laid eggs in the open wound, and before the day was gone the worms were hatched out, and rioting amid the inflamed and super-sensitive nerves, where their every motion was agony. Accustomed as we were to misery, we found a still

lower depth in his misfortune, and I would be happier could I forget his pale, drawn face, as he wandered uncomplainingly to and fro, holding his maimed limb with his right hand, occasionally stopping to squeeze it, as one does a boil, and press from it a stream of maggots and pus. I do not think he ate or slept for a week before he died. Next to him staid an Irish Sergeant of a New York Regiment, a fine soldierly man, who, with pardonable pride, wore, conspicuously on his left breast, a medal gained by gallantry while a British soldier in the Crimea. He was wasting away with diarrhea, and died before the month was out.

This was what one could see on every square rod of the prison. Where I was was not only no worse than the rest of the prison, but was probably much better and healthier, as it was the highest ground inside, farthest from the Swamp, and having the dead line on two sides, had a ventilation that those nearer the center could not possibly have. Yet, with all these conditions in our favor, the mortality was as I have described.

Near us an exasperating idiot, who played the flute, had established himself. Like all poor players, he affected the low, mournful notes, as plaintive as the distant cooing of the dove in lowering, weather. He played or rather tooted away in his "blues"-inducing strain hour after hour, despite our energetic protests, and occasionally flinging a club at him. There was no more stop to him than to a man with a hand-organ, and to this day the low, sad notes of a flute are the swiftest reminder to me of those sorrowful, death-laden days.

I had an illustration one morning of how far decomposition would progress in a man's body before he died. My chum and I found a treasure-trove in the streets, in the shape of the body of a man who died during the night. The value of this "find" was that if we took it to the gate, we would be allowed to carry it outside to the deadhouse, and on our way back have an opportunity to pick up a chunk of wood, to use in cooking. While discussing our good luck another party came up and claimed the body. A verbal dispute led to one of blows, in which we came off victorious, and I hastily caught hold of the arm near the elbow to help bear the body away. The skin gave way under my hand, and slipped with it down to the wrist, like a torn sleeve. It was sickening, but I clung to my prize, and secured a very good chunk of wood while outside with it. The wood was very much needed by my mess, as our squad had then had none for more than a week.

CHAPTER XL.

THE BATTLE OF THE 22D OF JULY—THE ARMS OF THE TENNESSEE ASSAULTED FRONT AND REAR—DEATH OF GENERAL MCPHERSON—ASSUMPTION OF COMMAND BY GENERAL LOGAN—RESULT OF THE BATTLE.

Naturally, we had a consuming hunger for news of what was being accomplished by our armies toward crushing the Rebellion. Now, more than ever, had we reason to ardently wish for the destruction of the Rebel power. Before capture we had love of country and a natural desire for the triumph of her flag to animate us. Now we had a hatred of the Rebels that passed expression, and a fierce longing to see those who daily tortured and insulted us trampled down in the dust of humiliation.

The daily arrival of prisoners kept us tolerably well informed as to the general progress of the campaign, and we added to the information thus obtained by getting—almost daily—in some manner or another—a copy of a Rebel paper. Most frequently these were Atlanta papers, or an issue of the "Memphis-Corinth-Jackson-Grenada-Chattanooga-Resacca-Marietta-Atlanta Appeal," as they used to facetiously term a Memphis paper that left that City when it was taken in 1862, and for two years fell back from place to place, as Sherman's Army advanced, until at last it gave up the struggle in September, 1864, in a little Town south of Atlanta, after about two thousand miles of weary retreat from an indefatigable pursuer. The papers were brought in by "fresh fish," purchased from the guards at from fifty cents to one dollar apiece, or occasionally thrown in to us when they had some specially disagreeable intelligence, like the defeat of Banks, or Sturgis, or Bunter, to exult over. I was particularly fortunate in getting hold of these.

Becoming installed as general reader for a neighborhood of several thousand men, everything of this kind was immediately brought to me, to be read aloud for the benefit of everybody. All the older prisoners knew me by the nick-name of "Illinoy"—a designation arising from my wearing on my cap, when I entered prison, a neat little white metal badge of "ILLS." When any reading matter was brought into our neighborhood, there would be a general cry of:

"Take it up to 'Illinoy,'" and then hundreds would mass around my quarters to hear the news read.

The Rebel papers usually had very meager reports of the operations of the armies, and these were greatly distorted, but they were still very interesting, and as we always started in to read with the expectation that the whole statement was a mass of perversions and lies, where truth was an infrequent accident, we were not likely to be much impressed with it.

There was a marled difference in the tone of the reports brought in from the different armies. Sherman's men were always sanguine. They had no doubt that they were pushing the enemy straight to the wall, and that every day brought the Southern Confederacy much nearer its downfall. Those from the Army of the Potomac were never so hopeful. They would admit that Grant was pounding Lee terribly, but the shadow of the frequent defeats of the Army of the Potomac seemed to hang depressingly over them.

There came a day, however, when our sanguine hopes as to Sherman were checked by a possibility that he had failed; that his long campaign towards Atlanta had culminated in such a reverse under the very walls of the City as would compel an abandonment of the enterprise, and possibly a humiliating retreat. We knew that Jeff. Davis and his Government were strongly dissatisfied with the Fabian policy of Joe Johnston. The papers had told us of the Rebel President's visit to Atlanta, of his bitter comments on Johnston's tactics; of his going so far as to sneer about the necessity of providing pontoons at Key West, so that Johnston might continue his retreat even to Cuba. Then came the news of Johnston's Supersession by Hood, and the papers were full of the exulting predictions of what would now be accomplished "when that gallant young soldier is once fairly in the saddle."

All this meant one supreme effort to arrest the onward course of Sherman. It indicated a resolve to stake the fate of Atlanta, and the fortunes of the Confederacy in the West, upon the hazard of one desperate fight. We watched the summoning up of every Rebel energy for the blow with apprehension. We dreaded another Chickamauga.

The blow fell on the 22d of July. It was well planned. The Army of the Tennessee, the left of Sherman's forces, was the part struck. On the night of the 21st Hood marched a heavy force around its left flank and gained its rear. On the 22d this force fell on the rear with the impetuous violence of a cyclone, while the Rebels in the works immediately around Atlanta attacked furiously in front.

It was an ordeal that no other army ever passed through successfully. The steadiest troops in Europe would think it foolhardiness to attempt to withstand an assault in force in front and rear at the same time. The finest legions that follow any flag to-day must almost inevitably succumb to such a mode of attack. But the seasoned veterans of the Army of the Tennessee encountered the shock with an obstinacy which showed that the finest material for soldiery this planet holds was that in which undaunted hearts beat beneath blue blouses. Springing over the front of their breastworks, they drove back with a withering fire the force assailing them in the rear. This beaten off, they jumped back to their proper places, and repulsed the assault in front. This was the way the battle was waged until night compelled a cessation of operations. Our boys were alternately behind the breastworks firing at Rebels advancing upon the front, and in front of the works firing upon those coming up in the rear. Sometimes part of our line would be on one side of the works, and part on the other.

In the prison we were greatly excited over the result of the engagement, of which we were uncertain for many days. A host of new prisoners perhaps two thousand—was brought in from there, but as they were captured during the progress of the fight, they could not speak definitely as to its issue. The Rebel papers exulted without stint over what they termed "a glorious victory." They were particularly jubilant over the death of McPherson, who, they claimed, was the brain and guiding hand of Sherman's army. One paper likened him to the pilot-fish, which guides the shark to his prey. Now that he was gone, said the paper, Sherman's army becomes a great lumbering hulk, with no one in it capable of directing it, and it must soon fall to utter ruin under the skilfully delivered strokes of the gallant Hood.

We also knew that great numbers of wounded had been brought to the prison hospital, and this seemed to confirm the Rebel claim of a victory, as it showed they retained possession of the battle field.

About the 1st of August a large squad of Sherman's men, captured in one of the engagements subsequent to the 22d, came in. We gathered around them eagerly. Among them I noticed a bright, curly-haired, blue-eyed infantryman—or boy, rather, as he was yet beardless. His cap was marked "68th O. Y. Y. L," his sleeves were garnished with re-enlistment stripes, and on the breast of his blouse was a silver arrow. To the eye of the soldier this said that he was a veteran member of the Sixty-Eighth Regiment of Ohio Infantry (that is, having already served three years, he had re-enlisted for the war), and that he belonged to the Third Division of the Seventeenth Army Corps. He was so young and fresh looking that one could hardly believe him to be a veteran, but if his stripes had not said this, the soldierly arrangement of clothing and accouterments, and the graceful, self-possessed pose of limbs and body would have told the observer that he was one of those "Old Reliables" with whom Sherman and Grant had already subdued a third of the Confederacy. His blanket, which, for a wonder, the Rebels had neglected to take from him, was tightly rolled, its ends tied together, and thrown over his shoulder scarf-fashion. His pantaloons were tucked inside his stocking tops, that were pulled up as far as possible, and tied tightly around his ankle with a string. A none-too-clean haversack, containing the inevitable sooty quart cup, and even blacker half-canteen, waft slung easily from the shoulder opposite to that on which the blanket rested. Hand him his faithful Springfield rifle, put three days' rations in his haversack, and forty rounds in his cartridge bog, and he would be ready, without an instant's demur or question, to march to the ends of the earth, and fight anything that crossed his path. He was a type of the honest, honorable, self respecting American boy, who, as a soldier, the world has not equaled in the sixty centuries that war has been a profession. I suggested to him that he was rather a youngster to be wearing veteran chevrons. "Yes," said he, "I am not so old as some of the rest of the boys, but I have seen about as much service and been in the business about as long as any of them. They call me 'Old Dad,' I suppose because I was the youngest boy in the Regiment, when we first entered the service, though our whole Company, officers and all, were only a lot of boys, and the Regiment to day, what's left of 'em, are about as young a lot of officers and men as there are in the service. Why, our old Colonel ain't only twenty-four years old now, and he has been in command ever since we went into Vicksburg. I have heard it said by our boys that since we veteranized the whole Regiment, officers, and men, average less than twenty-four years old. But they are gray-hounds to march and stayers in a fight, you bet. Why, the rest of the troops over in West Tennessee used to call our Brigade 'Leggett's Cavalry,' for they always had us chasing Old Forrest, and we kept him skedaddling, too, pretty lively. But I tell you we did get into a red hot scrimmage on the 22d. It just laid over Champion Hills, or any of the big fights around Vicksburg, and they were lively enough to amuse any one." "So you were in the affair on the 22d, were you! We are awful anxious to hear all about it. Come over here to my quarters and tell us all you know. All we know is that there has been a big fight, with McPherson killed, and a heavy loss of life besides, and the Rebels claim a great victory." "O, they be ——. It was the sickest victory they ever got. About one more victory of that kind would make their infernal old Confederacy ready for a coroner's inquest. Well, I can tell you pretty much all about that fight, for I reckon if the truth was known, our regiment fired about the first and last shot that opened and closed the fighting on that day. Well, you see the whole Army got across the river, and were closing in around the City of Atlanta. Our Corps, the Seventeenth, was the extreme left of the army, and were moving up toward the City from the East. The Fifteenth (Logan's) Corps joined us on the right, then the Army of the Cumberland further to the right. We run onto the Rebs about sundown the 21st. They had some breastworks on a ridge in front of us, and we had a pretty sharp fight before we drove them off. We went right to work, and kept at it all night in changing and strengthening the old Rebel barricades, fronting them towards Atlanta, and by morning had some good solid works along our whole line. During the night we fancied we could hear wagons or artillery moving away in front of us, apparently going South, or towards our left. About three or four o'clock in the morning, while I was shoveling dirt like a beaver out on the works, the Lieutenant came to me and said the Colonel wanted to see me, pointing to a large tree in the rear, where I could find him. I reported and found him with General

Leggett, who commanded our Division, talking mighty serious, and Bob Wheeler, of F Company, standing there with his Springfield at a parade rest. As soon as I came up, the Colonel says:
"Boys, the General wants two level-headed chaps to go out beyond the pickets to the front and toward the left. I have selected you for the duty. Go as quietly as possible and as fast as you can; keep your eyes and ears open; don't fire a shot if you can help it, and come back and tell us exactly what you have seen and heard, and not what you imagine or suspect. I have selected you for the duty.'
"He gave us the countersign, and off we started over the breastworks and through the thick woods. We soon came to our skirmish or pickets, only a few rods in front of our works, and cautioned them not to fire on us in going or returning. We went out as much as half a mile or more, until we could plainly hear the sound of wagons and artillery. We then cautiously crept forward until we could see the main road leading south from the City filled with marching men, artillery and teams. We could hear the commands of the officers and see the flags and banners of regiment after regiment as they passed us. We got back quietly and quickly, passed through our picket line all right, and found the General and our Colonel sitting on a log where we had left them, waiting for us. We reported what we had seen and heard, and gave it as our opinion that the Johnnies were evacuating Atlanta. The General shook his head, and the Colonel says: 'You may re turn to your company.' Bob says to me:
"'The old General shakes his head as though he thought them d——-d Rebs ain't evacuating Atlanta so mighty sudden, but are up to some devilment again. I ain't sure but he's right. They ain't going to keep falling back and falling back to all eternity, but are just agoin' to give us a rip-roaring great big fight one o' these days—when they get a good ready. You hear me!'

"Saying which we both went to our companies, and laid down to get a little sleep. It was about daylight then, and I must have snoozed away until near noon, when I heard the order 'fall in!' and found the regiment getting into line, and the boys all tallying about going right into Atlanta; that the Rebels had evacuated the City during the night, and that we were going to have a race with the Fifteenth Corps as to which would get into the City first. We could look away out across a large field in front of our works, and see the skirmish line advancing steadily towards the main works around the City. Not a shot was being, fired on either side.
"To our surprise, instead of marching to the front and toward the City, we filed off into a small road cut through the woods and marched rapidly to the rear. We could not understand what it meant. We marched at quick time, feeling pretty mad that we had to go to the rear, when the rest of our Division were going into Atlanta.
"We passed the Sixteenth Corps lying on their arms, back in some open fields, and the wagon trains of our Corps all comfortably corralled, and finally found ourselves out by the Seventeenth Corps headquarters. Two or three companies were sent out to picket several roads that seemed to cross at that point, as it was reported 'Rebel Cavalry' had been seen on these roads but a short time before, and this accounted for our being rushed out in such a great hurry.
"We had just stacked arms and were going to take a little rest after our rapid march, when several Rebel prisoners were brought in by some of the boys who had straggled a little. They found the

Rebels on the road we had just marched out on. Up to this time not a shot had been fired. All was quiet back at the main works we had just left, when suddenly we saw several staff officers come tearing up to the Colonel, who ordered us to 'fall in!' 'Take aims!' 'about, face!' The Lieutenant Colonel dashed down one of the roads where one of the companies had gone out on picket. The Major and Adjutant galloped down the others. We did not wait for them to come back, though, but moved right back on the road we had just come out, in line of battle, our colors in the road, and our flanks in open timber. We soon reached a fence enclosing a large field, and there could see a line of Rebels moving by the flank, and forming, facing toward Atlanta, but to the left and in the rear of the position occupied by our Corps. As soon as we reached the fence we fired a round or two into the backs of these gray coats, who broke into confusion.

"Just then the other companies joined us, and we moved off on 'double quick by the right flank,' for you see we were completely cut off from the troops up at the front, and we had to get well over to the right to get around the flank of the Rebels. Just about the time we fired on the rebels the Sixteenth Corps opened up a hot fire of musketry and artillery on them, some of their shot coming over mighty close to where we were. We marched pretty fast, and finally turned in through some open fields to the left, and came out just in the rear of the Sixteenth Corps, who were fighting like devils along their whole line.

"Just as we came out into the open field we saw General R. K. Scott, who used to be our Colonel, and who commanded our brigade, come tearing toward us with one or two aids or orderlies. He was on his big clay-bank horse, 'Old Hatchie,' as we called him, as we captured him on the battlefield at the battle of 'Matamora,' or 'Hell on the Hatchie,' as our boys always called it. He rode up to the Colonel, said something hastily, when all at once we heard the all-firedest crash of musketry and artillery way up at the front where we had built the works the night before and left the rest of our brigade and Division getting ready to prance into Atlanta when we were sent off to the rear. Scott put spurs to his old horse, who was one of the fastest runners in our Division, and away he went back towards the position where his brigade and the troops immediately to their left were now hotly engaged. He rode right along in rear of the Sixteenth Corps, paying no attention apparently to the shot and shell and bullets that were tearing up the earth and exploding and striking all around him. His aids and orderlies vainly tried to keep up with him. We could plainly see the Rebel lines as they came out of the woods into the open grounds to attack the Sixteenth Corps, which had hastily formed in the open field, without any signs of works, and were standing up like men, having a hand-to-hand fight. We were just far enough in the rear so that every blasted shot or shell that was fired too high to hit the ranks of the Sixteenth Corps came rattling over amongst us. All this time we were marching fast, following in the direction General Scott had taken, who evidently had ordered the Colonel to join his brigade up at the front. We were down under the crest of a little hill, following along the bank of a little creek, keeping under cover of the bank as much as possible to protect us from the shots of the enemy. We suddenly saw General Logan and one or two of his staff upon the right bank of the ravine riding rapidly toward us. As he neared the head of the regiment he shouted:

"'Halt! What regiment is that, and where are you going?'" The Colonel, in a loud voice, that all could hear, told him: "The Sixty-Eighth Ohio; going to join our brigade of the Third Division— your old Division, General, of the Seventeenth Corps."

"Logan says, 'you had better go right in here on the left of Dodge. The Third Division have hardly ground enough left now to bury their dead. God knows they need you. But try it on, if you think you can get to them.'

"Just at this moment a staff officer came riding up on the opposite side of the ravine from where

Logan was and interrupted Logan, who was about telling the Colonel not to try to go to the position held by the Third Division by the road cut through the woods whence we had come out, but to keep off to the right towards the Fifteenth Corps, as the woods referred to were full of Rebels. The officer saluted Logan, and shouted across:

"General Sherman directs me to inform you of the death of General McPherson, and orders you to take command of the Army of the Tennessee; have Dodge close well up to the Seventeenth Corps, and Sherman will reinforce you to the extent of the whole army.'

"Logan, standing in his stirrups, on his beautiful black horse, formed a picture against the blue sky as we looked up the ravine at him, his black eyes fairly blazing and his long black hair waving in the wind. He replied in a ringing, clear tone that we all could hear:

"Say to General Sherman I have heard of McPherson's death, and have assumed the command of the Army of the Tennessee, and have already anticipated his orders in regard to closing the gap between Dodge and the Seventeenth Corps.'

"This, of course, all happened in one quarter of the time I have been telling you. Logan put spurs to his horse and rode in one direction, the staff officer of General Sherman in another, and we started on a rapid step toward the front. This was the first we had heard of McPherson's death, and it made us feel very bad. Some of the officers and men cried as though they had lost a brother; others pressed their lips, gritted their teeth, and swore to avenge his death. He was a great favorite with all his Army, particularly of our Corps, which he commanded for a long while. Our company, especially, knew him well, and loved him dearly, for we had been his Headquarters Guard for over a year. As we marched along, toward the front, we could see brigades, and regiments, and batteries of artillery; coming over from the right of the Army, and taking position in new lines in rear of the Sixteenth and Seventeenth Corps. Major Generals and their staffs, Brigadier Generals and their staffs, were mighty thick along the banks of the little ravine we were following; stragglers and wounded men by the hundred were pouring in to the safe shelter formed by the broken ground along which we were rapidly marching; stories were heard of divisions, brigades and regiments that these wounded or stragglers belonged, having been all cut to pieces; officers all killed; and the speaker, the only one of his command not killed, wounded or captured. But you boys have heard and seen the same cowardly sneaks, probably, in fights that you were in. The battle raged furiously all this time; part of the time the Sixteenth Corps seemed to be in the worst; then it would let up on them and the Seventeenth Corps would be hotly engaged along their whole front.

"We had probably marched half an hour since leaving Logan, and were getting pretty near back to our main line of works, when the Colonel ordered a halt and knapsacks to be unslung and piled up. I tell you it was a relief to get them off, for it was a fearful hot day, and we had been marching almost double quick. We knew that this meant business though, and that we were stripping for the fight, which we would soon be in. Just at this moment we saw an ambulance, with the horses on a dead run, followed by two or three mounted officers and men, coming right towards us out of the very woods Logan had cautioned the Colonel to avoid. When the ambulance got to where we were it halted. It was pretty well out of danger from the bullets and shell of the enemy. They stopped, and we recognized Major Strong, of McPherson's Staff, whom the all knew, as he was the Chief Inspector of our Corps, and in the ambulance he had the body of General McPherson. Major Strong, it appears, during a slight lull in the fighting at that part of the line, having taken an ambulance and driven into the very jaws of death to recover the remains of his loved commander. It seems he found the body right by the side of the little road that we had gone out on when we went to the rear. He was dead when he found him, having been shot off his horse, the bullet striking him in the back, just below his heart, probably killing him instantly. There was a young fellow with him who was wounded also, when Strong found them. He belonged to our First Division, and recognized General McPherson, and stood by him until Major Strong came up. He was in the ambulance with the body of McPherson when they stopped by us.

"It seems that when the fight opened away back in the rear where we had been, and at the left of the Sixteenth Corps which was almost directly in the rear of the Seventeenth Corps, McPherson sent his staff and orderlies with various orders to different parts of the line, and started himself to ride over from the Seventeenth Corps to the Sixteenth Corps, taking exactly the same course our Regiment had, perhaps an hour before, but the Rebels had discovered there was a gap between the Sixteenth and Seventeenth Corps, and meeting no opposition to their advances in this strip of woods, where they were hidden from view, they had marched right along down in the rear, and with their line at right angles with the line of works occupied by the left of the Seventeenth Corps; they were thus parallel and close to the little road McPherson had taken, and probably he rode right into them and was killed before he realized the true situation.

"Having piled our knapsacks, and left a couple of our older men, who were played out with the heat and most ready to drop with sunstroke, to guard them, we started on again. The ambulance with the corpse of Gen. McPherson moved off towards the right of the Army, which was the last we ever saw of that brave and handsome soldier.

"We bore off a little to the right of a large open field on top of a high hill where one of our batteries was pounding away at a tremendous rate. We came up to the main line of works just about at the left of the Fifteenth Corps. They seemed to be having an easy time of it just then — no fighting going on in their front, except occasional shots from some heavy guns on the main line of Rebel works around the City. We crossed right over the Fifteenth Corps' works and filed to the left, keeping along on the outside of our works. We had not gone far before the Rebel gunners in the main works around the City discovered us; and the way they did tear loose at us was a caution. Their aim was rather bad, however, and most of their shots went over us. We saw one of them—I think it was a shell—strike an artillery caisson belonging to one of our-batteries. It exploded as it struck, and then the caisson, which was full of ammunition, exploded with an awful noise, throwing pieces of wood and iron and its own load of shot and shell high into the air, scattering death and destruction to the men and horses attached to it. We thought we saw arms and legs and parts of bodies of men flying in every direction; but we were glad to learn afterwards that it was the contents of the knapsacks of the Battery boys, who had strapped them on the caissons for transportation.

"Just after passing the hill where our battery was making things so lively, they stopped firing to let us pass. We saw General Leggett, our Division Commander, come riding toward us. He was outside of our line of works, too. You know how we build breastworks—sort of zigzag like, you know, so they cannot be enfiladed. Well, that's just the way the works were along there, and you never saw such a curious shape as we formed our Division in. Why, part of them were on one side of the works, and go along a little further and here was a regiment, or part of a regiment on the other side, both sets firing in opposite directions.

"No sir'ee, they were not demoralized or in confusion, they were cool and as steady as on parade. But the old Division had, you know, never been driven from any position they had once taken, in all their long service, and they did not propose to leave that ridge until they got orders from some one beside the Rebs.

"There were times when a fellow did not know which side of the works was the safest, for the Johnnies were in front of us and in rear of us. You see, our Fourth Division, which had been to the left of us, had been forced to quit their works, when the Rebs got into the works in their rear, so that our Division was now at the point where our line turned sharply to the left, and rear—in the direction of the Sixteenth Corps.

"We got into business before we had been there over three minutes. A line of the Rebs tried to charge across the open fields in front of us, but by the help of the old twenty-four pounders (which proved to be part of Cooper's Illinois Battery, that we had been alongside of in many a hard fight before), we drove them back a-flying, only to have to jump over on the outside of our works the next minute to tackle a heavy force that came for our rear through that blasted strip of woods. We soon drove them off, and the firing on both sides seemed to have pretty much stopped.

"'Our Brigade,' which we discovered, was now commanded by 'Old Whiskers' (Colonel Piles, of the Seventy-Eighth Ohio. I'll bet he's got the longest whiskers of any man in the Army.) You see General Scott had not been seen or heard of since he had started to the rear after our regiment when the fighting first commenced. We all believed that he was either killed or captured, or he would have been with his command. He was a splendid soldier, and a bull-dog of a fighter. His absence was a great loss, but we had not much time to think of such things, for our brigade was then ordered to leave the works and to move to the right about twenty or thirty rods across a large ravine, where we were placed in position in an open corn-field, forming a new line at quite an angle from the line of works we had just left, extending to the left, and getting us back nearer onto a line with the Sixteenth Corps. The battery of howitzers, now reinforced by a part of the Third Ohio heavy guns, still occupied the old works on the highest part of the hill, just to the right of our new line. We took our position just on the brow of a hill, and were ordered to lie down, and the rear rank to go for rails, which we discovered a few rods behind us in the shape of a good ten-rail fence. Every rear-rank chap came back with all the rails he could lug, and we barely had time to lay them down in front of us, forming a little barricade of six to eight or ten inches high, when we heard the most unearthly Rebel yell directly in front of us. It grew louder and came nearer and nearer, until we could see a solid line of the gray coats coming out of the woods and down the opposite slope, their battle flags flying, officers in front with drawn swords, arms at right shoulder, and every one of them yelling like so many Sioux Indians. The line seemed to be massed six or eight ranks deep, followed closely by the second line, and that by the third, each, if possible, yelling louder and appearing more desperately reckless than the one ahead. At their first appearance we opened on them, and so did the bully old twenty-four-pounders, with canister.

"On they came; the first line staggered and wavered back on to the second, which was coming on the double quick. Such a raking as we did give them. Oh, Lordy, how we did wish that we had the breech loading Spencers or Winchesters. But we had the old reliable Springfields, and we poured it in hot and heavy. By the time the charging column got down the opposite slope, and were struggling through the thicket of undergrowth in the ravine, they were one confused mass of officers and men, the three lines now forming one solid column, which made several desperate efforts to rush up to the top of the hill where we were punishing them so. One of their first surges came mighty near going right over the left of our Regiment, as they were lying down behind their little rail piles. But the boys clubbed their guns and the officers used their revolvers and swords and drove them back down the hill.

"The Seventy-Eighth and Twentieth Ohio, our right and left bowers, who had been brigaded with us ever since 'Shiloh,' were into it as hot and heavy as we had been, and had lost numbers of their officers and men, but were hanging on to their little rail piles when the fight was over. At one time the Rebs were right in on top of the Seventy-Eighth. One big Reb grabbed their colors, and tried to pull them out of the hands of the color-bearer. But old Captain Orr, a little, short, dried-up fellow, about sixty years old, struck him with his sword across the back of the neck, and killed him deader than a mackerel, right in his tracks.

"It was now getting dark, and the Johnnies concluded they had taken a bigger contract in trying to drive us off that hill in one day than they had counted on, so they quit charging on us, but drew back under cover of the woods and along the old line of works that we had left, and kept up a pecking away and sharp-shooting at us all night long. They opened fire on us from a number of pieces of artillery from the front, from the left, and from some heavy guns away over to the right of us, in the main works around Atlanta.

"We did not fool away much time that night, either. We got our shovels and picks, and while part of us were sharpshooting and trying to keep the Rebels from working up too close to us, the rest of the boys were putting up some good solid earthworks right where our rail piles had been, and by morning we were in splendid shape to have received our friends, no matter which way they had come at us, for they kept up such an all-fired shelling of us from so many different directions; that the boys had built traverses and bomb-proofs at all sorts of angles and in all directions.

"There was one point off to our right, a few rods up along our old line of works where there was a crowd of Rebel sharpshooters that annoyed us more than all the rest, by their constant firing at us through the night. They killed one of Company H's boys, and wounded several others. Finally Captain Williams, of D Company, came along and said he wanted a couple of good shots out of our company to go with him, so I went for one. He took about ten of us, and we crawled down into the ravine in front of where we were building the works, and got behind a large fallen tree, and we laid there and could just fire right up into the rear of those fellows as they lay behind a traverse extending back from our old line of works. It was so dark we could only see where to fire by the flash of guns, but every time they would shoot, some of us would let them have one. They staid there until almost daylight, when they, concluded as things looked, since we were going to stay, they had better be going.

"It was an awful night. Down in the ravine below us lay hundreds of killed and wounded Rebels, groaning and crying aloud for water and for help. We did do what we could for those right around us—but it was so dark, and so many shell bursting and bullets flying around that a fellow could not get about much. I tell you it was pretty tough next morning to go along to the different companies of our regiment and hear who were among the killed and wounded, and to see the long row of graves that were being dug to bury our comrades and our officers. There was the Captain of Company E, Nelson Skeeles, of Fulton County, O., one of—the bravest and best officers in the regiment. By his side lay First Sergeant Lesnit, and next were the two great, powerful Shepherds—cousins but more like brothers. One, it seems, was killed while supporting the head of the other, who had just received a death wound, thus dying in each other's arms.

"But I can't begin to think or tell you the names of all the poor boys that we laid away to rest in their last, long sleep on that gloomy day. Our Major was severely wounded, and several other officers had been hit more or less badly.

"It was a frightful sight, though, to go over the field in front of our works on that morning. The Rebel dead and badly wounded laid where they had fallen. The bottom and opposite side of the ravine showed how destructive our fire and that of the canister from the howitzers had been. The underbrush was cut, slashed, and torn into shreds, and the larger trees were scarred, bruised and broken by the thousands of bullets and other missiles that had been poured into them from almost every conceivable direction during the day before.

"A lot of us boys went way over to the left into Fuller's Division of the Sixteenth Corps, to see how some of our boys over there had got through the scrimmage, for they had about as nasty a fight as any part of the Army, and if it had not been for their being just where they were, I am not sure but what the old Seventeenth Corps would have had a different story to tell now. We found our friends had been way out by Decatur, where their brigade had got into a pretty lively fight on their own hook.

"We got back to camp, and the first thing I knew I was detailed for picket duty, and we were posted over a few rods across the ravine in our front. We had not been out but a short time when we saw a flag of truce, borne by an officer, coming towards us. We halted him, and made him wait until a report was sent back to Corps headquarters. The Rebel officer was quite chatty and talkative with our picket officer, while waiting. He said he was on General Cleburne's staff, and that the troops that charged us so fiercely the evening before was Cleburne's whole Division, and that after their last repulse, knowing the hill where we were posted was the most important position along our line, he felt that if they would keep close to us during the night, and keep up a show of fight, that we would pull out and abandon the hill before morning. He said that he, with about fifty of their best men, had volunteered to keep up the demonstration, and it was his party that had occupied the traverse in our old works the night before and had annoyed us and the Battery men by their constant sharpshooting, which we fellows behind the old tree had finally tired out. He said they staid until almost daylight, and that he lost more than half his men before he left. He also told us that General Scott was captured by their Division, at about the time and almost the same spot as where General McPherson was killed, and that he was not hurt or wounded, and was now a prisoner in their hands.

"Quite a lot of our staff officers soon came out, and as near as we could learn the Rebels wanted a truce to bury their dead. Our folks tried to get up an exchange of prisoners that had been taken by both sides the day before, but for some reason they could not bring it about. But the truce for burying the dead was agreed to. Along about dusk some of the boys on my post got to telling about a lot of silver and brass instruments that belonged to one of the bands of the Fourth Division, which had been hung up in some small trees a little way over in front of where we were when the fight was going on the day before, and that when, a bullet would strike one of the horns they could hear it go 'pin-g' and in a few minutes 'pan-g' would go another bullet through one of them.

"A new picket was just coming' on, and I had picked up my blanket and haversack, and was about ready to start back to camp, when, thinks I, 'I'll just go out there and see about them horns.' I told the boys what I was going to do. They all seemed to think it was safe enough, so out I started. I had not gone more than a hundred yards, I should think, when here I found the horns all hanging around on the trees just as the boys had described. Some of them had lots of bullet holes in them. But I saw a beautiful, nice looking silver bugle hanging off to one side a little. 'I Thinks,' says I, 'I'll just take that little toot horn in out of the wet, and take it back to camp.' I was just reaching up after it when I heard some one say,

"'Halt!' and I'll be dog-Boned if there wasn't two of the meanest looking Rebels, standing not ten feet from me, with their guns cocked and pointed at me, and, of course, I knew I was a goner; they walked me back about one hundred and fifty yards, where their picket line was. From there I was kept going for an hour or two until we got over to a place on the railroad called East Point. There I got in with a big crowd of our prisoners, who were taken the day before, and we have been fooling along in a lot of old cattle cars getting down here ever since.

"So this is 'Andersonville,' is it! Well, by—!"

CHAPTER XLI.

CLOTHING: ITS RAPID DETERIORATION, AND DEVICES TO REPLENISH IT—
DESPERATE EFFORTS TO COVER NAKEDNESS—"LITTLE RED CAP" AND HIS
LETTER.

Clothing had now become an object of real solicitude to us older prisoners. The veterans of our crowd—the surviving remnant of those captured at Gettysburg—had been prisoners over a year. The next in seniority—the Chickamauga boys—had been in ten months. The Mine Run fellows were eight months old, and my battalion had had seven months' incarceration. None of us were models of well-dressed gentlemen when captured. Our garments told the whole story of the hard campaigning we had undergone. Now, with months of the wear and tear of prison life, sleeping on the sand, working in tunnels, digging wells, etc., we were tattered and torn to an extent that a second-class tramp would have considered disgraceful.

This is no reflection upon the quality of the clothes furnished by the Government. We simply reached the limit of the wear of textile fabrics. I am particular to say this, because I want to contribute my little mite towards doing justice to a badly abused part of our Army organization —the Quartermaster's Department. It is fashionable to speak of "shoddy," and utter some stereotyped sneers about "brown paper shoes," and "musketo-netting overcoats," when any discussion of the Quartermaster service is the subject of conversation, but I have no hesitation in asking the indorsement of my comrades to the statement that we have never found anywhere else as durable garments as those furnished us by the Government during our service in the Army. The clothes were not as fine in texture, nor so stylish in cut as those we wore before or since, but when it came to wear they could be relied on to the last thread. It was always marvelous to me that they lasted so well, with the rough usage a soldier in the field must necessarily give them.

But to return to my subject. I can best illustrate the way our clothes dropped off us, piece by piece, like the petals from the last rose of Summer, by taking my own case as an example: When I entered prison I was clad in the ordinary garb of an enlisted man of the cavalry—stout, comfortable boots, woolen pocks, drawers, pantaloons, with a "reenforcement," or "ready-made patches," as the infantry called them; vest, warm, snug-fitting jacket, under and over shirts, heavy overcoat, and a forage-cap. First my boots fell into cureless ruin, but this was no special hardship, as the weather had become quite warm, and it was more pleasant than otherwise to go barefooted. Then part of the underclothing retired from service. The jacket and vest followed, their end being hastened by having their best portions taken to patch up the pantaloons, which kept giving out at the most embarrassing places. Then the cape of the overcoat was called upon to assist in repairing these continually-recurring breaches in the nether garments. The same insatiate demand finally consumed the whole coat, in a vain attempt to prevent an exposure of person greater than consistent with the usages of society. The pantaloons—or what, by courtesy, I called such, were a monument of careful and ingenious, but hopeless, patching, that should have called forth the admiration of a Florentine artist in mosaic. I have been shown—in later years—many table tops, ornamented in marquetry, inlaid with thousands of little bits of wood, cunningly arranged, and patiently joined together. I always look at them with interest, for I know the work spent upon them: I remember my Andersonville pantaloons.

The clothing upon the upper part of my body had been reduced to the remains of a knit undershirt. It had fallen into so many holes that it looked like the coarse "riddles" through which ashes and gravel are sifted. Wherever these holes were the sun had burned my back, breast and shoulders deeply black. The parts covered by the threads and fragments forming the boundaries of the holes, were still white. When I pulled my alleged shirt off, to wash or to free it from some of its teeming population, my skin showed a fine lace pattern in black and white, that was very interesting to my comrades, and the subject of countless jokes by them.

They used to descant loudly on the chaste elegance of the design, the richness of the tracing, etc., and beg me to furnish them with a copy of it when I got home, for their sisters to work window curtains or tidies by. They were sure that so striking a novelty in patterns would be very acceptable. I would reply to their witticisms in the language of Portia's Prince of Morocco:

Mislike me not for my complexion—
The shadowed livery of the burning sun.

One of the stories told me in my childhood by an old negro nurse, was of a poverty stricken little girl "who slept on the floor and was covered with the door," and she once asked—

"Mamma how do poor folks get along who haven't any door?"

In the same spirit I used to wonder how poor fellows got along who hadn't any shirt.

One common way of keeping up one's clothing was by stealing mealsacks. The meal furnished as rations was brought in in white cotton sacks. Sergeants of detachments were required to return these when the rations were issued the next day. I have before alluded to the general incapacity of the Rebels to deal accurately with even simple numbers. It was never very difficult for a shrewd Sergeant to make nine sacks count as ten. After awhile the Rebels began to see through this sleight of hand manipulation, and to check it. Then the Sergeants resorted to the device of tearing the sacks in two, and turning each half in as a whole one. The cotton cloth gained in this way was used for patching, or, if a boy could succeed in beating the Rebels out of enough of it, he would fabricate himself a shirt or a pair of pantaloons. We obtained all our thread in the same way. A half of a sack, carefully raveled out, would furnish a couple of handfuls of thread. Had it not been for this resource all our sewing and mending would have come to a standstill.

Most of our needles were manufactured by ourselves from bones. A piece of bone, split as near as possible to the required size, was carefully rubbed down upon a brick, and then had an eye laboriously worked through it with a bit of wire or something else available for the purpose. The needles were about the size of ordinary darning needles, and answered the purpose very well. These devices gave one some conception of the way savages provide for the wants of their lives. Time was with them, as with us, of little importance. It was no loss of time to them, nor to us, to spend a large portion of the waking hours of a week in fabricating a needle out of a bone, where a civilized man could purchase a much better one with the product of three minutes' labor. I do not think any red Indian of the plains exceeded us in the patience with which we worked away at these minutia of life's needs.

Of course the most common source of clothing was the dead, and no body was carried out with any clothing on it that could be of service to the survivors. The Plymouth Pilgrims, who were so well clothed on coming in, and were now dying off very rapidly, furnished many good suits to cover the nakedness of older, prisoners. Most of the prisoners from the Army of the Potomac were well dressed, and as very many died within a month or six weeks after their entrance, they left their clothes in pretty good condition for those who constituted themselves their heirs, administrators and assigns.

For my own part, I had the greatest aversion to wearing dead men's clothes, and could only bring myself to it after I had been a year in prison, and it became a question between doing that and freezing to death.

Every new batch of prisoners was besieged with anxious inquiries on the subject which lay closest to all our hearts:

"What are they doing about exchange!"

Nothing in human experience—save the anxious expectancy of a sail by castaways on a desert island—could equal the intense eagerness with which this question was asked, and the answer awaited. To thousands now hanging on the verge of eternity it meant life or death. Between the first day of July and the first of November over twelve thousand men died, who would doubtless have lived had they been able to reach our lines—"get to God's country," as we expressed it.

The new comers brought little reliable news of contemplated exchange. There was none to bring in the first place, and in the next, soldiers in active service in the field had other things to busy themselves with than reading up the details of the negotiations between the Commissioners of Exchange. They had all heard rumors, however, and by the time they reached Andersonville, they had crystallized these into actual statements of fact. A half hour after they entered the Stockade, a report like this would spread like wildfire:

"An Army of the Potomac man has just come in, who was captured in front of Petersburg. He says that he read in the New York Herald, the day before he was taken, that an exchange had been agreed upon, and that our ships had already started for Savannah to take us home."

Then our hopes would soar up like balloons. We fed ourselves on such stuff from day to day, and doubtless many lives were greatly prolonged by the continual encouragement. There was hardly a day when I did not say to myself that I would much rather die than endure imprisonment another month, and had I believed that another month would see me still there, I am pretty certain that I should have ended the matter by crossing the Dead Line. I was firmly resolved not to die the disgusting, agonizing death that so many around me were dying.

One of our best purveyors of information was a bright, blue-eyed, fair-haired little drummer boy, as handsome as a girl, well-bred as a lady, and evidently the darling of some refined loving mother. He belonged, I think, to some loyal Virginia regiment, was captured in one of the actions in the Shenandoa Valley, and had been with us in Richmond. We called him "Red Cap," from his wearing a jaunty, gold-laced, crimson cap. Ordinarily, the smaller a drummer boy is the harder he is, but no amount of attrition with rough men could coarse the ingrained refinement of Red Cap's manners. He was between thirteen and fourteen, and it seemed utterly shameful that men, calling themselves soldier should make war on such a tender boy and drag him off to prison. But no six-footer had a more soldierly heart than little Red Cap, and none were more loyal to the cause. It was a pleasure to hear him tell the story of the fights and movements his regiment had been engaged in. He was a good observer and told his tale with boyish fervor. Shortly after Wirz assumed command he took Red Cap into his office as an Orderly. His bright face and winning manner; fascinated the women visitors at headquarters, and numbers of them tried to adopt him, but with poor success. Like the rest of us, he could see few charms in an existence under the Rebel flag, and turned a deaf ear to their blandishments. He kept his ears open to the conversation of the Rebel officers around him, and frequently secured permission to visit the interior of the Stockade, when he would communicate to us all that he has heard. He received a flattering reception every time he cams in, and no orator ever secured a more attentive audience than would gather around him to listen to what he had to say. He was, beyond a doubt, the best known and most popular person in the prison, and I know all the survivors of his old admirer; share my great interest in him, and my curiosity as to whether he yet lives, and whether his subsequent career has justified the sanguine hopes we all had as to his future. I hope that if he sees this, or any one who knows anything about him, he will communicate with me. There are thousands who will be glad to hear from him.

A most remarkable coincidence occurred in regard to this comrade. Several days after the above had been written, and "set up," but before it had yet appeared in the paper, I received the following letter:

ECKHART MINES,

Alleghany County, Md., March 24.

To the Editor of the BLADE:

Last evening I saw a copy of your paper, in which was a chapter or two of a prison life of a soldier during the late war. I was forcibly struck with the correctness of what he wrote, and the names of several of my old comrades which he quoted: Hill, Limber Jim, etc., etc. I was a drummer boy of Company I, Tenth West Virginia Infantry, and was fifteen years of age a day or two after arriving in Andersonville, which was in the last of February, 1884. Nineteen of my comrades were there with me, and, poor fellows, they are there yet. I have no doubt that I would have remained there, too, had I not been more fortunate.

I do not know who your soldier correspondent is, but assume to say that from the following description he will remember having seen me in Andersonville: I was the little boy that for three or four months officiated as orderly for Captain Wirz. I wore a red cap, and every day could be seen riding Wirz's gray mare, either at headquarters, or about the Stockade. I was acting in this capacity when the six raiders —"Mosby," (proper name Collins) Delaney, Curtis, and—I forget the other names—were executed. I believe that I was the first that conveyed the intelligence to them that Confederate General Winder had approved their sentence. As soon as Wirz received the dispatch to that effect, I ran down to the stocks and told them.

I visited Hill, of Wauseon, Fulton County, O., since the war, and found him hale and hearty. I have not heard from him for a number of years until reading your correspondent's letter last evening. It is the only letter of the series that I have seen, but after reading that one, I feel called upon to certify that I have no doubts of the truthfulness of your correspondent's story. The world will never know or believe the horrors of Andersonville and other prisons in the South. No living, human being, in my judgment, will ever be able to properly paint the horrors of those infernal dens.

I formed the acquaintance of several Ohio soldiers whilst in prison. Among these were O. D. Streeter, of Cleveland, who went to Andersonville about the same time that I did, and escaped, and was the only man that I ever knew that escaped and reached our lines. After an absence of several months he was retaken in one of Sherman's battles before Atlanta, and brought back. I also knew John L. Richards, of Fostoria, Seneca County, O. or Eaglesville, Wood County. Also, a man by the name of Beverly, who was a partner of Charley Aucklebv, of Tennessee. I would like to hear from all of these parties. They all know me.

Mr. Editor, I will close by wishing all my comrades who shared in the sufferings and dangers of Confederate prisons, a long and useful life.

Yours truly,

RANSOM T. POWELL

CHAPTER XLII

SOME FEATURES OF THE MORTALITY—PERCENTAGE OF DEATHS TO THOSE LIVING —AN AVERAGE MEAN ONLY STANDS THE MISERY THREE MONTHS— DESCRIPTION OF THE PRISON AND THE CONDITION OF THE MEN THEREIN, BY A LEADING SCIENTIFIC MAN OF THE SOUTH.

Speaking of the manner in which the Plymouth Pilgrims were now dying, I am reminded of my theory that the ordinary man's endurance of this prison life did not average over three months. The Plymouth boys arrived in May; the bulk of those who died passed away in July and August. The great increase of prisoners from all sources was in May, June and July. The greatest mortality among these was in August, September and October.

Many came in who had been in good health during their service in the field, but who seemed utterly overwhelmed by the appalling misery they saw on every hand, and giving way to despondency, died in a few days or weeks. I do not mean to include them in the above class, as their sickness was more mental than physical. My idea is that, taking one hundred ordinarily healthful young soldiers from a regiment in active service, and putting them into Andersonville, by the end of the third month at least thirty-three of those weakest and most vulnerable to disease would have succumbed to the exposure, the pollution of ground and air, and the insufficiency of the ration of coarse corn meal. After this the mortality would be somewhat less, say at the end of six months fifty of them would be dead. The remainder would hang on still more tenaciously, and at the end of a year there would be fifteen or twenty still alive. There were sixty-three of my company taken; thirteen lived through. I believe this was about the usual proportion for those who were in as long as we. In all there were forty-five thousand six hundred and thirteen prisoners brought into Andersonville. Of these twelve thousand nine hundred and twelve died there, to say nothing of thousands that died in other prisons in Georgia and the Carolinas, immediately after their removal from Andersonville. One of every three and a-half men upon whom the gates of the Stockade closed never repassed them alive. Twenty-nine per cent. of the boys who so much as set foot in Andersonville died there. Let it be kept in mind all the time, that the average stay of a prisoner there was not four months. The great majority came in after the 1st of May, and left before the middle of September. May 1, 1864, there were ten thousand four hundred and twenty-seven in the Stockade. August 8 there were thirty-three thousand one hundred and fourteen; September 30 all these were dead or gone, except eight thousand two hundred and eighteen, of whom four thousand five hundred and ninety died inside of the next thirty days. The records of the world can shove no parallel to this astounding mortality.

Since the above matter was first published in the BLADE, a friend has sent me a transcript of the evidence at the Wirz trial, of Professor Joseph Jones, a Surgeon of high rank in the Rebel Army, and who stood at the head of the medical profession in Georgia. He visited Andersonville at the instance of the Surgeon-General of the Confederate States' Army, to make a study, for the benefit of science, of the phenomena of disease occurring there. His capacity and opportunities for observation, and for clearly estimating the value of the facts coming under his notice were, of course, vastly superior to mine, and as he states the case stronger than I dare to, for fear of being accused of exaggeration and downright untruth, I reproduce the major part of his testimony—embodying also his official report to medical headquarters at Richmond—that my readers may know how the prison appeared to the eyes of one who, though a bitter Rebel, was still a humane man and a conscientious observer, striving to learn the truth:

MEDICAL TESTIMONY.

[Transcript from the printed testimony at the Wirz Trial, pages 618 to 639, inclusive.]
OCTOBER 7, 1885.
Dr. Joseph Jones, for the prosecution:
By the Judge Advocate:
Question. Where do you reside
Answer. In Augusta, Georgia.
Q. Are you a graduate of any medical college?
A. Of the University of Pennsylvania.
Q. How long have you been engaged in the practice of medicine?
A. Eight years.
Q. Has your experience been as a practitioner, or rather as an investigator of medicine as a science?
A. Both.
Q. What position do you hold now?
A. That of Medical Chemist in the Medical College of Georgia, at Augusta.
Q. How long have you held your position in that college?
A. Since 1858.
Q. How were you employed during the Rebellion?
A. I served six months in the early part of it as a private in the ranks, and the rest of the time in the medical department.
Q. Under the direction of whom?
A. Under the direction of Dr. Moore, Surgeon General.
Q. Did you, while acting under his direction, visit Andersonville, professionally?
A. Yes, Sir.
Q. For the purpose of making investigations there?

A. For the purpose of prosecuting investigations ordered by the Surgeon General.

Q. You went there in obedience to a letter of instructions?

A. In obedience to orders which I received.

Q. Did you reduce the results of your investigations to the shape of a report?

A. I was engaged at that work when General Johnston surrendered his army.

(A document being handed to witness.)

Q. Have you examined this extract from your report and compared it with the original?

A. Yes, Sir; I have.

Q. Is it accurate?

A. So far as my examination extended, it is accurate.'

The document just examined by witness was offered in evidence, and is as follows:

Observations upon the diseases of the Federal prisoners, confined to Camp Sumter, Andersonville, in Sumter County, Georgia, instituted with a view to illustrate chiefly the origin and causes of hospital gangrene, the relations of continued and malarial fevers, and the pathology of camp diarrhea and dysentery, by Joseph Jones; Surgeon P. A. C. S., Professor of Medical Chemistry in the Medical College of Georgia, at Augusta, Georgia.

Hearing of the unusual mortality among the Federal prisoners confined at Andersonville; Georgia, in the month of August, 1864, during a visit to Richmond, Va., I expressed to the Surgeon General, S. P. Moore, Confederate States of America, a desire to visit Camp Sumter, with the design of instituting a series of inquiries upon the nature and causes of the prevailing diseases. Smallpox had appeared among the prisoners, and I believed that this would prove an admirable field for the establishment of its characteristic lesions. The condition of Peyer's glands in this disease was considered as worthy of minute investigation. It was believed that a large body of men from the Northern portion of the United States, suddenly transported to a warm Southern climate, and confined upon a small portion of land, would furnish an excellent field for the investigation of the relations of typhus, typhoid, and malarial fevers.

The Surgeon General of the Confederate States of America furnished me with the following letter of introduction to the Surgeon in charge of the Confederate States Military Prison at Andersonville, Ga.:

CONFEDERATE STATES OF AMERICA,
SURGEON GENERAL'S OFFICE, RICHMOND, VA.,
August 6, 1864.

SIR:—The field of pathological investigations afforded by the large collection of Federal prisoners in Georgia, is of great extant and importance, and it is believed that results of value to the profession may be obtained by careful investigation of the effects of disease upon the large body of men subjected to a decided change of climate and those circumstances peculiar to prison life. The Surgeon in charge of the hospital for Federal prisoners, together with his assistants, will afford every facility to Surgeon Joseph Jones, in the prosecution of the labors ordered by the Surgeon General. Efficient assistance must be rendered Surgeon Jones by the medical officers, not only in his examinations into the causes and symptoms of the various diseases, but especially in the arduous labors of post mortem examinations.

The medical officers will assist in the performance of such post-mortems as Surgeon Jones may indicate, in order that this great field for pathological investigation may be explored for the benefit of the Medical Department of the Confederate Army.

S. P. MOORE, Surgeon General.
Surgeon ISAIAH H. WHITE,
In charge of Hospital for Federal prisoners, Andersonville, Ga.

In compliance with this letter of the Surgeon General, Isaiah H. White, Chief Surgeon of the post, and R. R. Stevenson, Surgeon in charge of the Prison Hospital, afforded the necessary facilities for the prosecution of my investigations among the sick outside of the Stockade. After the completion of my labors in the military prison hospital, the following communication was addressed to Brigadier General John H. Winder, in consequence of the refusal on the part of the commandant of the interior of the Confederate States Military Prison to admit me within the Stockade upon the order of the Surgeon General:

CAMP SUMTER, ANDERSONVILLE GA.,
September 16, 1864.
GENERAL:—I respectfully request the commandant of the post of Andersonville to grant me permission and to furnish the necessary pass to visit the sick and medical officers within the Stockade of the Confederate States Prison. I desire to institute certain inquiries ordered by the Surgeon General. Surgeon Isaiah H. White, Chief Surgeon of the post, and Surgeon R. R. Stevenson, in charge of the Prison Hospital, have afforded me every facility for the prosecution of my labors among the sick outside of the Stockade.
Very respectfully, your obedient servant,
JOSEPH JONES, Surgeon P. A. C. S.
Brigadier General JOHN H. WINDER,
Commandant, Post Andersonville.

In the absence of General Winder from the post, Captain Winder furnished the following order:
CAMP SUMTER, ANDERSONVILLE;
September 17, 1864.

CAPTAIN:—You will permit Surgeon Joseph Jones, who has orders from the Surgeon General, to visit the sick within the Stockade that are under medical treatment. Surgeon Jones is ordered to make certain investigations which may prove useful to his profession. By direction of General Winder. Very respectfully, W. S. WINDER, A. A. G.
Captain H. WIRZ, Commanding Prison.

Description of the Confederate States Military Prison Hospital at Andersonville. Number of prisoners, physical condition, food, clothing, habits, moral condition, diseases.

The Confederate Military Prison at Andersonville, Ga., consists of a strong Stockade, twenty feet in height, enclosing twenty-seven acres. The Stockade is formed of strong pine logs, firmly planted in the ground. The main Stockade is surrounded by two other similar rows of pine logs, the middle Stockade being sixteen feet high, and the outer twelve feet. These are intended for offense and defense. If the inner Stockade should at any time be forced by the prisoners, the second forms another line of defense; while in case of an attempt to deliver the prisoners by a force operating upon the exterior, the outer line forms an admirable protection to the Confederate troops, and a most formidable obstacle to cavalry or infantry. The four angles of the outer line are strengthened by earthworks upon commanding eminences, from which the cannon, in case of an outbreak among the prisoners, may sweep the entire enclosure; and it was designed to connect these works by a line of rifle pits, running zig-zag, around the outer Stockade; those rifle pits have never been completed. The ground enclosed by the innermost Stockade lies in the form of a parallelogram, the larger diameter running almost due north and south. This space includes the northern and southern opposing sides of two hills, between which a stream of water runs from west to east. The surface soil of these hills is composed chiefly of sand with varying admixtures of clay and oxide of iron. The clay is sufficiently tenacious to give a considerable degree of consistency to the soil. The internal structure of the hills, as revealed by the deep wells, is similar to that already described. The alternate layers of clay and sand, as well as the oxide of iron, which forms in its various combinations a cement to the sand, allow of extensive tunneling. The prisoners not only constructed numerous dirt huts with balls of clay and sand, taken from the wells which they have excavated all over those hills, but they have also, in some cases, tunneled extensively from these wells. The lower portions of these hills, bordering on the stream, are wet and boggy from the constant oozing of water. The Stockade was built originally to accommodate only ten thousand prisoners, and included at first seventeen acres. Near the close of the month of June the area was enlarged by the addition of ten acres. The ground added was situated on the northern slope of the largest hill.

The average number of square feet of ground to each prisoner in August 1864: 35.7

Within the circumscribed area of the Stockade the Federal prisoners were compelled to perform all the offices of life—cooking, washing, the calls of nature, exercise, and sleeping. During the month of March the prison was less crowded than at any subsequent time, and then the average space of ground to each prisoner was only 98.7 feet, or less than seven square yards. The Federal prisoners were gathered from all parts of the Confederate States east of the Mississippi, and crowded into the confined space, until in the month of June the average number of square feet of ground to each prisoner was only 33.2 or less than four square yards. These figures represent the condition of the Stockade in a better light even than it really was; for a considerable breadth of land along the stream, flowing from west to east between the hills, was low and boggy, and was covered with the excrement of the men, and thus rendered wholly uninhabitable, and in fact useless for every purpose except that of defecation. The pines and other small trees and shrubs, which originally were scattered sparsely over these hills, were in a short time cut down and consumed by the prisoners for firewood, and no shade tree was left in the entire enclosure of the stockade. With their characteristic industry and ingenuity, the Federals constructed for themselves small huts and caves, and attempted to shield themselves from the rain and sun and night damps and dew. But few tents were distributed to the prisoners, and those were in most cases torn and rotten. In the location and arrangement of these tents and huts no order appears to have been followed; in fact, regular streets appear to be out of the question in so crowded an area; especially too, as large bodies of prisoners were from time to time added suddenly without any previous preparations. The irregular arrangement of the huts and imperfect shelters was very unfavorable for the maintenance of a proper system of police.

The police and internal economy of the prison was left almost entirely in the hands of the prisoners themselves; the duties of the Confederate soldiers acting as guards being limited to the occupation of the boxes or lookouts ranged around the stockade at regular intervals, and to the manning of the batteries at the angles of the prison. Even judicial matters pertaining to themselves, as the detection and punishment of such crimes as theft and murder appear to have been in a great measure abandoned to the prisoners. A striking instance of this occurred in the month of July, when the Federal prisoners within the Stockade tried, condemned, and hanged six (6) of their own number, who had been convicted of stealing and of robbing and murdering their fellow-prisoners. They were all hung upon the same day, and thousands of the prisoners gathered around to witness the execution. The Confederate authorities are said not to have interfered with these proceedings. In this collection of men from all parts of the world, every phase of human character was represented; the stronger preyed upon the weaker, and even the sick who were unable to defend themselves were robbed of their scanty supplies of food and clothing. Dark stories were afloat, of men, both sick and well, who were murdered at night, strangled to death by their comrades for scant supplies of clothing or money. I heard a sick and wounded Federal prisoner accuse his nurse, a fellow-prisoner of the United States Army, of having stealthily, during his sleep inoculated his wounded arm with gangrene, that he might destroy his life and fall heir to his clothing.

....

The large number of men confined within the Stockade soon, under a defective system of police, and with imperfect arrangements, covered the surface of the low grounds with excrements. The sinks over the lower portions of the stream were imperfect in their plan and structure, and the excrements were in large measure deposited so near the borders of the stream as not to be washed away, or else accumulated upon the low boggy ground. The volume of water was not sufficient to wash away the feces, and they accumulated in such quantities in the lower portion of the stream as to form a mass of liquid excrement heavy rains caused the water of the stream to rise, and as the arrangements for the passage of the increased amounts of water out of the Stockade were insufficient, the liquid feces overflowed the low grounds and covered them several inches, after the subsidence of the waters. The action of the sun upon this putrefying mass of excrements and fragments of bread and meat and bones excited most rapid fermentation and developed a horrible stench. Improvements were projected for the removal of the filth and for the prevention of its accumulation, but they were only partially and imperfectly carried out. As the forces of the prisoners were reduced by confinement, want of exercise, improper diet, and by scurvy, diarrhea, and dysentery, they were unable to evacuate their bowels within the stream or along its banks, and the excrements were deposited at the very doors of their tents. The vast majority appeared to lose all repulsion to filth, and both sick and well disregarded all the laws of hygiene and personal cleanliness. The accommodations for the sick were imperfect and insufficient. From the organization of the prison, February 24, 1864, to May 22, the sick were treated within the Stockade. In the crowded condition of the Stockade, and with the tents and huts clustered thickly around the hospital, it was impossible to secure proper ventilation or to maintain the necessary police. The Federal prisoners also made frequent forays upon the hospital stores and carried off the food and clothing of the sick. The hospital was, on the 22d of May, removed to its present site without the Stockade, and five acres of ground covered with oaks and pines appropriated to the use of the sick.

The supply of medical officers has been insufficient from the foundation of the prison.

The nurses and attendants upon the sick have been most generally Federal prisoners, who in too many cases appear to have been devoid of moral principle, and who not only neglected their duties, but were also engaged in extensive robbing of the sick.

From the want of proper police and hygienic regulations alone it is not wonderful that from February 24 to September 21, 1864, nine thousand four hundred and seventy-nine deaths, nearly one-third the entire number of prisoners, should have been recorded. I found the Stockade and hospital in the following condition during my pathological investigations, instituted in the month of September, 1864:

STOCKADE, CONFEDERATE STATES MILITARY PRISON.

At the time of my visit to Andersonville a large number of Federal prisoners had been removed to Millen, Savannah; Charleston, and other parts of, the Confederacy, in anticipation of an advance of General Sherman's forces from Atlanta, with the design of liberating their captive brethren; however, about fifteen thousand prisoners remained confined within the limits of the Stockade and Confederate States Military Prison Hospital.

In the Stockade, with the exception of the damp lowlands bordering the small stream, the surface was covered with huts, and small ragged tents and parts of blankets and fragments of oil-cloth, coats, and blankets stretched upon stacks. The tents and huts were not arranged according to any order, and there was in most parts of the enclosure scarcely room for two men to walk abreast between the tents and huts.

If one might judge from the large pieces of corn-bread scattered about in every direction on the ground the prisoners were either very lavishly supplied with this article of diet, or else this kind of food was not relished by them.

Each day the dead from the Stockade were carried out by their fellow-prisoners and deposited upon the ground under a bush arbor, just outside of the Southwestern Gate. From thence they were carried in carts to the burying ground, one-quarter of a mile northwest, of the Prison. The dead were buried without coffins, side by side, in trenches four feet deep.

The low grounds bordering the stream were covered with human excrements and filth of all kinds, which in many places appeared to be alive with working maggots. An indescribable sickening stench arose from these fermenting masses of human filth.

There were near five thousand seriously ill Federals in the Stockade and Confederate States Military Prison Hospital, and the deaths exceeded one hundred per day, and large numbers of the prisoners who were walking about, and who had not been entered upon the sick reports, were suffering from severe and incurable diarrhea, dysentery, and scurvy. The sick were attended almost entirely by their fellow-prisoners, appointed as nurses, and as they received but little attention, they were compelled to exert themselves at all times to attend to the calls of nature, and hence they retained the power of moving about to within a comparatively short period of the close of life. Owing to the slow progress of the diseases most prevalent, diarrhea, and chronic dysentery, the corpses were as a general rule emaciated.

I visited two thousand sick within the Stockade, lying under some long sheds which had been built at the northern portion for themselves. At this time only one medical officer was in attendance, whereas at least twenty medical officers should have been employed.

Died in the Stockade from its organization, February 24, 1861 to
September 21 3,254
Died in Hospital during same time 6,225
Total deaths in Hospital and Stockade 9,479

Scurvy, diarrhea, dysentery, and hospital gangrene were the prevailing diseases. I was surprised to find but few cases of malarial fever, and no well-marked cases either of typhus or typhoid fever. The absence of the different forms of malarial fever may be accounted for in the supposition that the artificial atmosphere of the Stockade, crowded densely with human beings and loaded with animal exhalations, was unfavorable to the existence and action of the malarial poison. The absence of typhoid and typhus fevers amongst all the causes which are supposed to generate these diseases, appeared to be due to the fact that the great majority of these prisoners had been in captivity in Virginia, at Belle Island, and in other parts of the Confederacy for months, and even as long as two years, and during this time they had been subjected to the same bad influences, and those who had not had these fevers before either had them during their confinement in Confederate prisons or else their systems, from long exposure, were proof against their action.

The effects of scurvy were manifested on every hand, and in all its various stages, from the muddy, pale complexion, pale gums, feeble, languid muscular motions, lowness of spirits, and fetid breath, to the dusky, dirty, leaden complexion, swollen features, spongy, purple, livid, fungoid, bleeding gums, loose teeth, oedematous limbs, covered with livid vibices, and petechiae spasmodically flexed, painful and hardened extremities, spontaneous hemorrhages from mucous canals, and large, ill-conditioned, spreading ulcers covered with a dark purplish fungus growth. I observed that in some of the cases of scurvy the parotid glands were greatly swollen, and in some instances to such an extent as to preclude entirely the power to articulate. In several cases of dropsy of the abdomen and lower extremities supervening upon scurvy, the patients affirmed that previously to the appearance of the dropsy they had suffered with profuse and obstinate diarrhea, and that when this was checked by a change of diet, from Indian corn-bread baked with the husk, to boiled rice, the dropsy appeared. The severe pains and livid patches were frequently associated with swellings in various parts, and especially in the lower extremities, accompanied with stiffness and contractions of the knee joints and ankles, and often with a brawny feel of the parts, as if lymph had been effused between the integuments and apeneuroses, preventing the motion of the skin over the swollen parts. Many of the prisoners believed that the scurvy was contagious, and I saw men guarding their wells and springs, fearing lest some man suffering with the scurvy might use the water and thus poison them.

I observed also numerous cases of hospital gangrene, and of spreading scorbutic ulcers, which had supervened upon slight injuries. The scorbutic ulcers presented a dark, purple fungoid, elevated surface, with livid swollen edges, and exuded a thin; fetid, sanious fluid, instead of pus. Many ulcers which originated from the scorbutic condition of the system appeared to become truly gangrenous, assuming all the characteristics of hospital gangrene. From the crowded condition, filthy habits, bad diet, and dejected, depressed condition of the prisoners, their systems had become so disordered that the smallest abrasion of the skin, from the rubbing of a shoe, or from the effects of the sun, or from the prick of a splinter, or from scratching, or a musketo bite, in some cases, took on rapid and frightful ulceration and gangrene. The long use of salt meat, ofttimes imperfectly cured, as well as the most total deprivation of vegetables and fruit, appeared to be the chief causes of the scurvy. I carefully examined the bakery and the bread furnished the prisoners, and found that they were supplied almost entirely with corn-bread from which the husk had not been separated. This husk acted as an irritant to the alimentary canal, without adding any nutriment to the bread. As far as my examination extended no fault could be found with the mode in which the bread was baked; the difficulty lay in the failure to separate the husk from the corn-meal. I strongly urged the preparation of large quantities of soup made from the cow and calves' heads with the brains and tongues, to which a liberal supply of sweet potatos and vegetables might have been advantageously added. The material existed in abundance for the preparation of such soup in large quantities with but little additional expense. Such aliment would have been not only highly nutritious, but it would also have acted as an efficient remedial agent for the removal of the scorbutic condition. The sick within the Stockade lay under several long sheds which were originally built for barracks. These sheds covered two floors which were open on all sides. The sick lay upon the bare boards, or upon such ragged blankets as they possessed, without, as far as I observed, any bedding or even straw.

....

The haggard, distressed countenances of these miserable, complaining, dejected, living skeletons, crying for medical aid and food, and cursing their Government for its refusal to exchange prisoners, and the ghastly corpses, with their glazed eye balls staring up into vacant space, with the flies swarming down their open and grinning mouths, and over their ragged clothes, infested with numerous lice, as they lay amongst the sick and dying, formed a picture of helpless, hopeless misery which it would be impossible to portray bywords or by the brush. A feeling of disappointment and even resentment on account of the United States Government upon the subject of the exchange of prisoners, appeared to be widespread, and the apparent hopeless nature of the negotiations for some general exchange of prisoners appeared to be a cause of universal regret and deep and injurious despondency. I heard some of the prisoners go so far as to exonerate the Confederate Government from any charge of intentionally subjecting them to a protracted confinement, with its necessary and unavoidable sufferings, in a country cut off from all intercourse with foreign nations, and sorely pressed on all sides, whilst on the other hand they charged their prolonged captivity upon their own Government, which was attempting to make the negro equal to the white man. Some hundred or more of the prisoners had been released from confinement in the Stockade on parole, and filled various offices as clerks, druggists, and carpenters, etc., in the various departments. These men were well clothed, and presented a stout and healthy appearance, and as a general rule they presented a much more robust and healthy appearance than the Confederate troops guarding the prisoners.

The entire grounds are surrounded by a frail board fence, and are strictly guarded by Confederate soldiers, and no prisoner except the paroled attendants is allowed to leave the grounds except by a special permit from the Commandant of the Interior of the Prison.

The patients and attendants, near two thousand in number, are crowded into this confined space and are but poorly supplied with old and ragged tents. Large numbers of them were without any bunks in the tents, and lay upon the ground, oft-times without even a blanket. No beds or straw appeared to have been furnished. The tents extend to within a few yards of the small stream, the eastern portion of which, as we have before said, is used as a privy and is loaded with excrements; and I observed a large pile of corn-bread, bones, and filth of all kinds, thirty feet in diameter and several feet in hight, swarming with myriads of flies, in a vacant space near the pots used for cooking. Millions of flies swarmed over everything, and covered the faces of the sleeping patients, and crawled down their open mouths, and deposited their maggots in the gangrenous wounds of the living, and in the mouths of the dead. Musketos in great numbers also infested the tents, and many of the patients were so stung by these pestiferous insects, that they resembled those suffering from a slight attack of the measles.

The police and hygiene of the hospital were defective in the extreme; the attendants, who appeared in almost every instance to have been selected from the prisoners, seemed to have in many cases but little interest in the welfare of their fellow-captives. The accusation was made that the nurses in many cases robbed the sick of their clothing, money, and rations, and carried on a clandestine trade with the paroled prisoners and Confederate guards without the hospital enclosure, in the clothing, effects of the sick, dying, and dead Federals. They certainly appeared to neglect the comfort and cleanliness of the sick intrusted to their care in a most shameful manner, even after making due allowances for the difficulties of the situation. Many of the sick were literally encrusted with dirt and filth and covered with vermin. When a gangrenous wound needed washing, the limb was thrust out a little from the blanket, or board, or rags upon which the patient was lying, and water poured over it, and all the putrescent matter allowed to soak into the ground floor of the tent. The supply of rags for dressing wounds was said to be very scant, and I saw the most filthy rags which had been applied several times, and imperfectly washed, used in dressing wounds. Where hospital gangrene was prevailing, it was impossible for any wound to escape contagion under these circumstances. The results of the treatment of wounds in the hospital were of the most unsatisfactory character, from this neglect of cleanliness, in the dressings and wounds themselves, as well as from various other causes which will be more fully considered. I saw several gangrenous wounds filled with maggots. I have frequently seen neglected wounds amongst the Confederate soldiers similarly affected; and as far as my experience extends, these worms destroy only the dead tissues and do not injure specially the well parts. I have even heard surgeons affirm that a gangrenous wound which had been thoroughly cleansed by maggots, healed more rapidly than if it had been left to itself. This want of cleanliness on the part of the nurses appeared to be the result of carelessness and inattention, rather than of malignant design, and the whole trouble can be traced to the want of the proper police and sanitary regulations, and to the absence of intelligent organization and division of labor. The abuses were in a large measure due to the almost total absence of system, government, and rigid, but wholesome sanitary regulations. In extenuation of these abuses it was alleged by the medical officers that the Confederate troops were barely sufficient to guard the prisoners, and that it was impossible to obtain any number of experienced nurses from the Confederate forces. In fact the guard appeared to be too small, even for the regulation of the internal hygiene and police of the hospital.

The manner of disposing of the dead was also calculated to depress the already desponding spirits of these men, many of whom have been confined for months, and even for nearly two years in Richmond and other places, and whose strength had been wasted by bad air, bad food, and neglect of personal cleanliness. The dead-house is merely a frame covered with old tent cloth and a few bushes, situated in the southwestern corner of the hospital grounds. When a patient dies, he is simply laid in the narrow street in front of his tent, until he is removed by Federal negros detailed to carry off the dead; if a patient dies during the night, he lies there until the morning, and during the day even the dead were frequently allowed to remain for hours in these walks. In the dead-house the corpses lie upon the bare ground, and were in most cases covered with filth and vermin.

....

The cooking arrangements are of the most defective character. Five large iron pots similar to those used for boiling sugar cane, appeared to be the only cooking utensils furnished by the hospital for the cooking of nearly two thousand men; and the patients were dependent in great measure upon their own miserable utensils. They were allowed to cook in the tent doors and in the lanes, and this was another source of filth, and another favorable condition for the generation and multiplication of flies and other vermin.

The air of the tents was foul and disagreeable in the extreme, and in fact the entire grounds emitted a most nauseous and disgusting smell. I entered nearly all the tents and carefully examined the cases of interest, and especially the cases of gangrene, upon numerous occasions, during the prosecution of my pathological inquiries at Andersonville, and therefore enjoyed every opportunity to judge correctly of the hygiene and police of the hospital.

There appeared to be almost absolute indifference and neglect on the part of the patients of personal cleanliness; their persons and clothing inmost instances, and especially of those suffering with gangrene and scorbutic ulcers, were filthy in the extreme and covered with vermin. It was too often the case that patients were received from the Stockade in a most deplorable condition. I have seen men brought in from the Stockade in a dying condition, begrimed from head to foot with their own excrements, and so black from smoke and filth that they, resembled negros rather than white men. That this description of the Stockade and hospital has not been overdrawn, will appear from the reports of the surgeons in charge, appended to this report.

....

We will examine first the consolidated report of the sick and wounded Federal prisoners. During six months, from the 1st of March to the 31st of August, forty-two thousand six hundred and eighty-six cases of diseases and wounds were reported. No classified record of the sick in the Stockade was kept after the establishment of the hospital without the Prison. This fact, in conjunction with those already presented relating to the insufficiency of medical officers and the extreme illness and even death of many prisoners in the tents in the Stockade, without any medical attention or record beyond the bare number of the dead, demonstrate that these figures, large as they, appear to be, are far below the truth.

As the number of prisoners varied greatly at different periods, the relations between those reported sick and well, as far as those statistics extend, can best be determined by a comparison of the statistics of each month.

During this period of six months no less than five hundred and sixty-five deaths are recorded under the head of 'morbi vanie.' In other words, those men died without having received sufficient medical attention for the determination of even the name of the disease causing death. During the month of August fifty-three cases and fifty-three deaths are recorded as due to marasmus. Surely this large number of deaths must have been due to some other morbid state than slow wasting. If they were due to improper and insufficient food, they should have been classed accordingly, and if to diarrhea or dysentery or scurvy, the classification should in like manner have been explicit.

We observe a progressive increase of the rate of mortality, from 3.11 per cent. in March to 9.09 per cent. of mean strength, sick and well, in August. The ratio of mortality continued to increase during September, for notwithstanding the removal of one-half of the entire number of prisoners during the early portion of the month, one thousand seven hundred and sixty-seven (1,767) deaths are registered from September 1 to 21, and the largest number of deaths upon any one day occurred during this month, on the 16th, viz. one hundred and nineteen.

The entire number of Federal prisoners confined at Andersonville was about forty thousand six hundred and eleven; and during the period of near seven months, from February 24 to September 21, nine thousand four hundred and seventy-nine (9,479) deaths were recorded; that is, during this period near one-fourth, or more, exactly one in 4.2, or 13.3 per cent., terminated fatally. This increase of mortality was due in great measure to the accumulation of the sources of disease, as the increase of excrements and filth of all kinds, and the concentration of noxious effluvia, and also to the progressive effects of salt diet, crowding, and the hot climate.

CONCLUSIONS.

1st. The great mortality among the Federal prisoners confined in the military prison at Andersonville was not referable to climatic causes, or to the nature of the soil and waters.

2d. The chief causes of death were scurvy and its results and bowel affections-chronic and acute diarrhea and dysentery. The bowel affections appear to have been due to the diet, the habits of the patients, the depressed, dejected state of the nervous system and moral and intellectual powers, and to the effluvia arising from the decomposing animal and vegetable filth. The effects of salt meat, and an unvarying diet of cornmeal, with but few vegetables, and imperfect supplies of vinegar and syrup, were manifested in the great prevalence of scurvy. This disease, without doubt, was also influenced to an important extent in its origin and course by the foul animal emanations.

3d. From the sameness of the food and form, the action of the poisonous gases in the densely crowded and filthy Stockade and hospital, the blood was altered in its constitution, even before the manifestation of actual disease. In both the well and the sick the red corpuscles were diminished; and in all diseases uncomplicated with inflammation, the fibrous element was deficient. In cases of ulceration of the mucous membrane of the intestinal canal, the fibrous element of the blood was increased; while in simple diarrhea, uncomplicated with ulceration, it was either diminished or else remained stationary. Heart clots were very common, if not universally present, in cases of ulceration of the intestinal mucous membrane, while in the uncomplicated cases of diarrhea and scurvy, the blood was fluid and did not coagulate readily, and the heart clots and fibrous concretions were almost universally absent. From the watery condition of the blood, there resulted various serous effusions into the pericardium, ventricles of the brain, and into the abdomen. In almost all the cases which I examined after death, even the most emaciated, there was more or less serous effusion into the abdominal cavity. In cases of hospital gangrene of the extremities, and in cases of gangrene of the intestines, heart clots and fibrous coagula were universally present. The presence of those clots in the cases of hospital gangrene, while they were absent in the cases in which there was no inflammatory symptoms, sustains the conclusion that hospital gangrene is a species of inflammation, imperfect and irregular though it may be in its progress, in which the fibrous element and coagulation of the blood are increased, even in those who are suffering from such a condition of the blood, and from such diseases as are naturally accompanied with a decrease in the fibrous constituent.

4th. The fact that hospital Gangrene appeared in the Stockade first, and originated spontaneously without any previous contagion, and occurred sporadically all over the Stockade and prison hospital, was proof positive that this disease will arise whenever the conditions of crowding, filth, foul air, and bad diet are present. The exhalations from the hospital and Stockade appeared to exert their effects to a considerable distance outside of these localities. The origin of hospital gangrene among these prisoners appeared clearly to depend in great measure upon the state of the general system induced by diet, and various external noxious influences. The rapidity of the appearance and action of the gangrene depended upon the powers and state of the constitution, as well as upon the intensity of the poison in the atmosphere, or upon the direct application of poisonous matter to the wounded surface. This was further illustrated by the important fact that hospital gangrene, or a disease resembling it in all essential respects, attacked the intestinal canal of patients laboring under ulceration of the bowels, although there were no local manifestations of gangrene upon the surface of the body. This mode of termination in cases of dysentery was quite common in the foul atmosphere of the Confederate States Military Hospital, in the depressed, depraved condition of the system of these Federal prisoners.

5th. A scorbutic condition of the system appeared to favor the origin of foul ulcers, which frequently took on true hospital gangrene. Scurvy and hospital gangrene frequently existed in the same individual. In such cases, vegetable diet, with vegetable acids, would remove the scorbutic condition without curing the hospital gangrene. From the results of the existing war for the establishment of the independence of the Confederate States, as well as from the published observations of Dr. Trotter, Sir Gilbert Blane, and others of the English navy and army, it is evident that the scorbutic condition of the system, especially in crowded ships and camps, is most favorable to the origin and spread of foul ulcers and hospital gangrene. As in the present case of Andersonville, so also in past times when medical hygiene was almost entirely neglected, those two diseases were almost universally associated in crowded ships. In many cases it was very difficult to decide at first whether the ulcer was a simple result of scurvy or of the action of the prison or hospital gangrene, for there was great similarity in the appearance of the ulcers in the two diseases. So commonly have those two diseases been combined in their origin and action, that the description of scorbutic ulcers, by many authors, evidently includes also many of the prominent characteristics of hospital gangrene. This will be rendered evident by an examination of the observations of Dr. Lind and Sir Gilbert Blane upon scorbutic ulcers.

6th. Gangrenous spots followed by rapid destruction of tissue appeared in some cases where there had been no known wound. Without such well-established facts, it might be assumed that the disease was propagated from one patient to another. In such a filthy and crowded hospital as that of the Confederate States Military Prison at Andersonville, it was impossible to isolate the wounded from the sources of actual contact of the gangrenous matter. The flies swarming over the wounds and over filth of every kind, the filthy, imperfectly washed and scanty supplies of rags, and the limited supply of washing utensils, the same wash-bowl serving for scores of patients, were sources of such constant circulation of the gangrenous matter that the disease might rapidly spread from a single gangrenous wound. The fact already stated, that a form of moist gangrene, resembling hospital gangrene, was quite common in this foul atmosphere, in cases of dysentery, both with and without the existence of the disease upon the entire surface, not only demonstrates the dependence of the disease upon the state of the constitution, but proves in the clearest manner that neither the contact of the poisonous matter of gangrene, nor the direct action of the poisonous atmosphere upon the ulcerated surfaces is necessary to the development of the disease.

7th. In this foul atmosphere amputation did not arrest hospital gangrene; the disease almost invariably returned. Almost every amputation was followed finally by death, either from the effects of gangrene or from the prevailing diarrhea and dysentery. Nitric acid and escharotics generally in this crowded atmosphere, loaded with noxious effluvia, exerted only temporary effects; after their application to the diseased surfaces, the gangrene would frequently return with redoubled energy; and even after the gangrene had been completely removed by local and constitutional treatment, it would frequently return and destroy the patient. As far as my observation extended, very few of the cases of amputation for gangrene recovered. The progress of these cases was frequently very deceptive. I have observed after death the most extensive disorganization of the structures of the stump, when during life there was but little swelling of the part, and the patient was apparently doing well. I endeavored to impress upon the medical officers the view that in this disease treatment was almost useless, without an abundant supply of pure, fresh air, nutritious food, and tonics and stimulants. Such changes, however, as would allow of the isolation of the cases of hospital gangrene appeared to be out of the power of the medical officers.

8th. The gangrenous mass was without true pus, and consisted chiefly of broken-down, disorganized structures. The reaction of the gangrenous matter in certain stages was alkaline.

9th. The best, and in truth the only means of protecting large armies and navies, as well as prisoners, from the ravages of hospital gangrene, is to furnish liberal supplies of well-cured meat, together with fresh beef and vegetables, and to enforce a rigid system of hygiene.

10th. Finally, this gigantic mass of human misery calls loudly for relief, not only for the sake of suffering humanity, but also on account of our own brave soldiers now captives in the hands of the Federal Government. Strict justice to the gallant men of the Confederate Armies, who have been or who may be, so unfortunate as to be compelled to surrender in battle, demands that the Confederate Government should adopt that course which will best secure their health and comfort in captivity; or at least leave their enemies without a shadow of an excuse for any violation of the rules of civilized warfare in the treatment of prisoners.

[End of the Witness's Testimony.]

The variation—from month to month—of the proportion of deaths to the whole number living is singular and interesting. It supports the theory I have advanced above, as the following facts, taken from the official report, will show:

In April one in every sixteen died.

In May one in every twenty-six died.

In June one in every twenty-two died.

In July one in every eighteen died.

In August one in every eleven died.

In September one in every three died.

In October one in every two died.

In November one in every three died.

Does the reader fully understand that in September one-third of those in the pen died, that in October one-half of the remainder perished, and in November one-third of those who still survived, died? Let him pause for a moment and read this over carefully again; because its startling magnitude will hardly dawn upon him at first reading. It is true that the fearfully disproportionate mortality of those months was largely due to the fact that it was mostly the sick that remained behind, but even this diminishes but little the frightfulness of the showing. Did any one ever hear of an epidemic so fatal that one-third of those attacked by it in one month died; one-half of the remnant the next month, and one-third of the feeble remainder the next month? If he did, his reading has been much more extensive than mine.

The greatest number of deaths in one day is reported to have occurred on the 23d of August, when one hundred and twenty-seven died, or one man every eleven minutes.

The greatest number of prisoners in the Stockade is stated to have been August 8, when there were thirty-three thousand one hundred and fourteen.

I have always imagined both these statements to be short of the truth, because my remembrance is that one day in August I counted over two hundred dead lying in a row. As for the greatest number of prisoners, I remember quite distinctly standing by the ration wagon during the whole time of the delivery of rations, to see how many prisoners there really were inside. That day the One Hundred and Thirty-Third Detachment was called, and its Sergeant came up and drew rations for a full detachment. All the other detachments were habitually kept full by replacing those who died with new comers. As each detachment consisted of two hundred and seventy men, one hundred and thirty-three detachments would make thirty-five thousand nine hundred and ten, exclusive of those in the hospital, and those detailed outside as cooks, clerks, hospital attendants and various other employments—say from one to two thousand more.

CHAPTER XLIII.

DIFFICULTY OF EXERCISING—EMBARRASSMENTS OF A MORNING WALK—THE RIALTO OF THE PRISON—CURSING THE SOUTHERN CONFEDERACY—THE STORY OF THE BATTLE OF SPOTTSYLVANIA COURTHOUSE.

Certainly, in no other great community, that ever existed upon the face of the globe was there so little daily ebb and flow as in this. Dull as an ordinary Town or City may be; however monotonous, eventless, even stupid the lives of its citizens, there is yet, nevertheless, a flow every day of its life-blood—its population towards its heart, and an ebb of the same, every evening towards its extremities. These recurring tides mingle all classes together and promote the general healthfulness, as the constant motion hither and yon of the ocean's waters purify and sweeten them.

The lack of these helped vastly to make the living mass inside the Stockade a human Dead Sea—or rather a Dying Sea—a putrefying, stinking lake, resolving itself into phosphorescent corruption, like those rotting southern seas, whose seething filth burns in hideous reds, and ghastly greens and yellows.

Being little call for motion of any kind, and no room to exercise whatever wish there might be in that direction, very many succumbed unresistingly to the apathy which was so strongly favored by despondency and the weakness induced by continual hunger, and lying supinely on the hot sand, day in and day out, speedily brought themselves into such a condition as invited the attacks of disease.

It required both determination and effort to take a little walking exercise. The ground was so densely crowded with holes and other devices for shelter that it took one at least ten minutes to pick his way through the narrow and tortuous labyrinth which served as paths for communication between different parts of the Camp. Still further, there was nothing to see anywhere or to form sufficient inducement for any one to make so laborious a journey. One simply encountered at every new step the same unwelcome sights that he had just left; there was a monotony in the misery as in everything else, and consequently the temptation to sit or lie still in one's own quarters became very great.

I used to make it a point to go to some of the remoter parts of the Stockade once every day, simply for exercise. One can gain some idea of the crowd, and the difficulty of making one's way through it, when I say that no point in the prison could be more than fifteen hundred feet from where I staid, and, had the way been clear, I could have walked thither and back in at most a half an hour, yet it usually took me from two to three hours to make one of these journeys.

This daily trip, a few visits to the Creek to wash all over, a few games of chess, attendance upon roll call, drawing rations, cooking and eating the same, "lousing" my fragments of clothes, and doing some little duties for my sick and helpless comrades, constituted the daily routine for myself, as for most of the active youths in the prison.

The Creek was the great meeting point for all inside the Stockade. All able to walk were certain to be there at least once during the day, and we made it a rendezvous, a place to exchange gossip, discuss the latest news, canvass the prospects of exchange, and, most of all, to curse the Rebels. Indeed no conversation ever progressed very far without both speaker and listener taking frequent rests to say bitter things as to the Rebels generally, and Wirz, Winder and Davis in particular.

A conversation between two boys—strangers to each other who came to the Creek to wash themselves or their clothes, or for some other purpose, would progress thus:

First Boy—"I belong to the Second Corps,—Hancock's, [the Army of the Potomac boys always mentioned what Corps they belonged to, where the Western boys stated their Regiment.] They got me at Spottsylvania, when they were butting their heads against our breast-works, trying to get even with us for gobbling up Johnson in the morning,"—He stops suddenly and changes tone to say: "I hope to God, that when our folks get Richmond, they will put old Ben Butler in command of it, with orders to limb, skin and jayhawk it worse than he did New Orleans."

Second Boy, (fervently :) "I wish to God he would, and that he'd catch old Jeff., and that grayheaded devil, Winder, and the old Dutch Captain, strip 'em just as we were, put 'em in this pen, with just the rations they are givin' us, and set a guard of plantation niggers over 'em, with orders to blow their whole infernal heads off, if they dared so much as to look at the dead line."

First Boy—(returning to the story of his capture.) "Old Hancock caught the Johnnies that morning the neatest you ever saw anything in your life. After the two armies had murdered each other for four or five days in the Wilderness, by fighting so close together that much of the time you could almost shake hands with the Graybacks, both hauled off a little, and lay and glowered at each other. Each side had lost about twenty thousand men in learning that if it attacked the other it would get mashed fine. So each built a line of works and lay behind them, and tried to nag the other into coming out and attacking. At Spottsylvania our lines and those of the Johnnies weren't twelve hundred yards apart. The ground was clear and clean between them, and any force that attempted to cross it to attack would be cut to pieces, as sure as anything. We laid there three or four days watching each other—just like boys at school, who shake fists and dare each other. At one place the Rebel line ran out towards us like the top of a great letter 'A.' The night of the 11th of May it rained very hard, and then came a fog so thick that you couldn't see the length of a company. Hancock thought he'd take advantage of this. We were all turned out very quietly about four o'clock in the morning. Not a bit of noise was allowed. We even had to take off our canteens and tin cups, that they might not rattle against our bayonets. The ground was so wet that our footsteps couldn't be heard. It was one of those deathly, still movements, when you think your heart is making as much noise as a bass drum.

"The Johnnies didn't seem to have the faintest suspicion of what was coming, though they ought, because we would have expected such an attack from them if we hadn't made it ourselves. Their pickets were out just a little ways from their works, and we were almost on to them before they discovered us. They fired and ran back. At this we raised a yell and dashed forward at a charge. As we poured over the works, the Rebels came double-quicking up to defend them. We flanked Johnson's Division quicker'n you could say 'Jack Robinson,' and had four thousand of 'em in our grip just as nice as you please. We sent them to the rear under guard, and started for the next line of Rebel works about a half a mile away. But we had now waked up the whole of Lee's army, and they all came straight for us, like packs of mad wolves. Ewell struck us in the center; Longstreet let drive at our left flank, and Hill tackled our right. We fell back to the works we had taken, Warren and Wright came up to help us, and we had it hot and heavy for the rest of the day and part of the night. The Johnnies seemed so mad over what we'd done that they were half crazy. They charged us five times, coming up every time just as if they were going to lift us right out of the works with the bayonet. About midnight, after they'd lost over ten thousand men, they seemed to understand that we had pre-empted that piece of real estate, and didn't propose to allow anybody to jump our claim, so they fell back sullen like to their main works. When they came on the last charge, our Brigadier walked behind each of our regiments and said:

"Boys, we'll send 'em back this time for keeps. Give it to 'em by the acre, and when they begin to waver, we'll all jump over the works and go for them with the bayonet.'

"We did it just that way. We poured such a fire on them that the bullets knocked up the ground in front just like you have seen the deep dust in a road in the middle of Summer fly up when the first great big drops of a rain storm strike it. But they came on, yelling and swearing, officers in front waving swords, and shouting—all that business, you know. When they got to about one hundred yards from us, they did not seem to be coming so fast, and there was a good deal of confusion among them. The brigade bugle sounded:

"Stop firing."

"We all ceased instantly. The rebels looked up in astonishment. Our General sang out:

"Fix bayonets!' but we knew what was coming, and were already executing the order. You can imagine the crash that ran down the line, as every fellow snatched his bayonet out and slapped it on the muzzle of his gun. Then the General's voice rang out like a bugle:

"Ready!—FORWARD! CHARGE!'

"We cheered till everything seemed to split, and jumped over the works, almost every man at the same minute. The Johnnies seemed to have been puzzled at the stoppage of our fire. When we all came sailing over the works, with guns brought right, down where they meant business, they were so astonished for a minute that they stood stock still, not knowing whether to come for us, or run. We did not allow them long to debate, but went right towards them on the double quick, with the bayonets looking awful savage and hungry. It was too much for Mr. Johnny Reb's nerves. They all seemed to about face' at once, and they lit out of there as if they had been sent for in a hurry. We chased after 'em as fast as we could, and picked up just lots of 'em. Finally it began to be real funny. A Johnny's wind would begin to give out he'd fall behind his comrades; he'd hear us yell and think that we were right behind him, ready to sink a bayonet through him'; he'd turn around, throw up his hands, and sing out:

"I surrender, mister! I surrender!' and find that we were a hundred feet off, and would have to have a bayonet as long as one of McClellan's general orders to touch him.

"Well, my company was the left of our regiment, and our regiment was the left of the brigade, and we swung out ahead of all the rest of the boys. In our excitement of chasing the Johnnies, we didn't see that we had passed an angle of their works. About thirty of us had become separated from the company and were chasing a squad of about seventy-five or one hundred. We had got up so close to them that we hollered:

"'Halt there, now, or we'll blow your heads off.'

"They turned round with, 'halt yourselves; you —— Yankee —— ——'

"We looked around at this, and saw that we were not one hundred feet away from the angle of the works, which were filled with Rebels waiting for our fellows to get to where they could have a good flank fire upon them. There was nothing to do but to throw down our guns and surrender, and we had hardly gone inside of the works, until the Johnnies opened on our brigade and drove it back. This ended the battle at Spottsylvania Court House."

Second Boy (irrelevantly.) "Some day the underpinning will fly out from under the South, and let it sink right into the middle kittle o' hell."

First Boy (savagely.) "I only wish the whole Southern Confederacy was hanging over hell by a single string, and I had a knife."

CHAPTER XLIV.

REBEL MUSIC—SINGULAR LACK OF THE CREATIVE POWER AMONG THE SOUTHERNERS —CONTRAST WITH SIMILAR PEOPLE ELSEWHERE—THEIR FAVORITE MUSIC, AND WHERE IT WAS BORROWED FROM—A FIFER WITH ONE TUNE.

I have before mentioned as among the things that grew upon one with increasing acquaintance with the Rebels on their native heath, was astonishment at their lack of mechanical skill and at their inability to grapple with numbers and the simpler processes of arithmetic. Another characteristic of the same nature was their wonderful lack of musical ability, or of any kind of tuneful creativeness.

Elsewhere, all over the world, people living under similar conditions to the Southerners are exceedingly musical, and we owe the great majority of the sweetest compositions which delight the ear and subdue the senses to unlettered song-makers of the Swiss mountains, the Tyrolese valleys, the Bavarian Highlands, and the minstrels of Scotland, Ireland and Wales.

The music of English-speaking people is very largely made up of these contributions from the folk-songs of dwellers in the wilder and more mountainous parts of the British Isles. One rarely goes far out of the way in attributing to this source any air that he may hear that captivates him with its seductive opulence of harmony. Exquisite melodies, limpid and unstrained as the carol of a bird in Spring-time, and as plaintive as the cooing of a turtle-dove seems as natural products of the Scottish Highlands as the gorse which blazons on their hillsides in August. Debarred from expressing their aspirations as people of broader culture do—in painting, in sculpture, in poetry and prose, these mountaineers make song the flexible and ready instrument for the communication of every emotion that sweeps across their souls.

Love, hatred, grief, revenge, anger, and especially war seems to tune their minds to harmony, and awake the voice of song in them hearts. The battles which the Scotch and Irish fought to replace the luckless Stuarts upon the British throne—the bloody rebellions of 1715 and 1745, left a rich legacy of sweet song, the outpouring of loving, passionate loyalty to a wretched cause; songs which are today esteemed and sung wherever the English language is spoken, by people who have long since forgotten what burning feelings gave birth to their favorite melodies.

For a century the bones of both the Pretenders have moldered in alien soil; the names of James Edward, and Charles Edward, which were once trumpet blasts to rouse armed men, mean as little to the multitude of today as those of the Saxon Ethelbert, and Danish Hardicanute, yet the world goes on singing—and will probably as long as the English language is spoken—"Wha'll be King but Charlie?" "When Jamie Come Hame," "Over the Water to Charlie," "Charlie is my Darling," "The Bonny Blue Bonnets are Over the Border," "Saddle Your Steeds and Awa," and a myriad others whose infinite tenderness and melody no modern composer can equal.

Yet these same Scotch and Irish, the same Jacobite English, transplanted on account of their chronic rebelliousness to the mountains of Virginia, the Carolinas, and Georgia, seem to have lost their tunefulness, as some fine singing birds do when carried from their native shores. The descendants of those who drew swords for James and Charles at Preston Pans and Culloden dwell to-day in the dales and valleys of the Alleganies, as their fathers did in the dales and valleys of the Grampians, but their voices are mute.

As a rule the Southerners are fond of music. They are fond of singing and listening to old-fashioned ballads, most of which have never been printed, but handed down from one generation to the other, like the 'Volklieder' of Germany. They sing these with the wild, fervid impressiveness characteristic of the ballad singing of unlettered people. Very many play tolerably on the violin and banjo, and occasionally one is found whose instrumentation may be called good. But above this hight they never soar. The only musician produced by the South of whom the rest of the country has ever heard, is Blind Tom, the negro idiot. No composer, no song writer of any kind has appeared within the borders of Dixie.

It was a disappointment to me that even the stress of the war, the passion and fierceness with which the Rebels felt and fought, could not stimulate any adherent of the Stars and Bars into the production of a single lyric worthy in the remotest degree of the magnitude of the struggle, and the depth of the popular feeling. Where two million Scotch, fighting to restore the fallen fortunes of the worse than worthless Stuarts, filled the world with immortal music, eleven million of Southerners, fighting for what they claimed to be individual freedom and national life, did not produce any original verse, or a bar of music that the world could recognize as such. This is the fact; and an undeniable one. Its explanation I must leave to abler analysts than I am.

Searching for peculiar causes we find but two that make the South differ from the ancestral home of these people. These two were Climate and Slavery. Climatic effects will not account for the phenomenon, because we see that the peasantry of the mountains of Spain and the South of France as ignorant as these people, and dwellers in a still more enervating atmosphere-are very fertile in musical composition, and their songs are to the Romanic languages what the Scotch and Irish ballads are to the English.

Then it must be ascribed to the incubus of Slavery upon the intellect, which has repressed this as it has all other healthy growths in the South. Slavery seems to benumb all the faculties except the passions. The fact that the mountaineers had but few or no slaves, does not seem to be of importance in the case. They lived under the deadly shadow of the upas tree, and suffered the consequences of its stunting their development in all directions, as the ague-smitten inhabitant of the Roman Campana finds every sense and every muscle clogged by the filtering in of the insidious miasma. They did not compose songs and music, because they did not have the intellectual energy for that work.

The negros displayed all the musical creativeness of that section. Their wonderful prolificness in wild, rude songs, with strangely melodious airs that burned themselves into the memory, was one of the salient characteristics of that down-trodden race. Like the Russian serfs, and the bondmen of all ages and lands, the songs they made and sang all had an undertone of touching plaintiveness, born of ages of dumb suffering. The themes were exceedingly simple, and the range of subjects limited. The joys, and sorrows, hopes and despairs of love's gratification or disappointment, of struggles for freedom, contests with malign persons and influences, of rage, hatred, jealousy, revenge, such as form the motifs for the majority of the poetry of free and strong races, were wholly absent from their lyrics. Religion, hunger and toil were their main inspiration. They sang of the pleasures of idling in the genial sunshine; the delights of abundance of food; the eternal happiness that awaited them in the heavenly future, where the slave-driver ceased from troubling and the weary were at rest; where Time rolled around in endless cycles of days spent in basking, harp in hand, and silken clad, in golden streets, under the soft effulgence of cloudless skies, glowing with warmth and kindness emanating from the Creator himself. Had their masters condescended to borrow the music of the slaves, they would have found none whose sentiments were suitable for the ode of a people undergoing the pangs of what was hoped to be the birth of a new nation.

The three songs most popular at the South, and generally regarded as distinctively Southern, were "The Bonnie Blue Flag," "Maryland, My Maryland," and "Stonewall Jackson Crossing into Maryland." The first of these was the greatest favorite by long odds. Women sang, men whistled, and the so-called musicians played it wherever we went. While in the field before capture, it was the commonest of experiences to have Rebel women sing it at us tauntingly from the house that we passed or near which we stopped. If ever near enough a Rebel camp, we were sure to hear its wailing crescendo rising upon the air from the lips or instruments of some one more quartered there. At Richmond it rang upon us constantly from some source or another, and the same was true wherever else we went in the so-called Confederacy. I give the air and words below:

All familiar with Scotch songs will readily recognize the name and air as an old friend, and one of the fierce Jacobite melodies that for a long time disturbed the tranquility of the Brunswick family on the English throne. The new words supplied by the Rebels are the merest doggerel, and fit the music as poorly as the unchanged name of the song fitted to its new use. The flag of the Rebellion was not a bonnie blue one; but had quite as much red and white as azure. It did not have a single star, but thirteen.

Near in popularity was "Maryland, My Maryland." The versification of this was of a much higher Order, being fairly respectable. The air is old, and a familiar one to all college students, and belongs to one of the most common of German household songs:

O, Tannenbaum! O, Tannenbaum, wie tru sind deine Blatter!
Da gruenst nicht nur zur Sommerseit,
Nein, auch in Winter, when es Schneit, etc.
which Longfellow has finely translated,
O, hemlock tree! O, hemlock tree! how faithful are thy branches!
Green not alone in Summer time,
But in the Winter's float and rime.
O, hemlock tree O, hemlock tree! How faithful are thy branches. Etc.
The Rebel version ran:
MARYLAND.

The despot's heel is on thy shore,
    Maryland!
His touch is at thy temple door,
    Maryland!
Avenge the patriotic gore
That flecked the streets of Baltimore,
And be the battle queen of yore,
Maryland! My Maryland!

Hark to the wand'ring son's appeal,
    Maryland!
My mother State, to thee I kneel,
    Maryland!
For life and death, for woe and weal,
Thy peerless chivalry reveal,
And gird thy beauteous limbs with steel,
Maryland! My Maryland!

Thou wilt not cower in the duet,
    Maryland!
Thy beaming sword shall never rust
    Maryland!
Remember Carroll's sacred trust,
Remember Howard's warlike thrust—
And all thy slumberers with the just,
Maryland! My Maryland!

Come! 'tis the red dawn of the day,
    Maryland!
Come! with thy panoplied array,
    Maryland!
With Ringgold's spirit for the fray,
With Watson's blood at Monterey,
With fearless Lowe and dashing May,

Maryland! My Maryland!

Comet for thy shield is bright and strong,
    Maryland!
Come! for thy dalliance does thee wrong,
    Maryland!
Come! to thins own heroic throng,
That stalks with Liberty along,
And give a new Key to thy song,
Maryland! My Maryland!

Dear Mother! burst the tyrant's chain,
    Maryland!
Virginia should not call in vain,
    Maryland!
She meets her sisters on the plain—
'Sic semper' 'tis the proud refrain,
That baffles millions back amain,
    Maryland!
Arise, in majesty again,
Maryland! My Maryland!

I see the blush upon thy cheek,
    Maryland!
But thou wast ever bravely meek,
    Maryland!
But lo! there surges forth a shriek
From hill to hill, from creek to creek—
Potomac calls to Chesapeake,
Maryland! My Maryland!

Thou wilt not yield the vandal toll.
    Maryland!
Thou wilt not crook to his control,
    Maryland!
Better the fire upon thee roll,
Better the blade, the shot, the bowl,
Than crucifixion of the soul,
Maryland! My Maryland!

I hear the distant Thunder hem,
    Maryland!
The Old Line's bugle, fife, and drum.
    Maryland!
She is not dead, nor deaf, nor dumb—
Hnzza! she spurns the Northern scum!

She breathes—she burns! she'll come! she'll come!
Maryland! My Maryland!

"Stonewall Jackson Crossing into Maryland," was another travesty, of about the same literary merit, or rather demerit, as "The Bonnie Blue Flag." Its air was that of the well-known and popular negro minstrel song, "Billy Patterson." For all that, it sounded very martial and stirring when played by a brass band.

We heard these songs with tiresome iteration, daily and nightly, during our stay in the Southern Confederacy. Some one of the guards seemed to be perpetually beguiling the weariness of his watch by singing in all keys, in every sort of a voice, and with the wildest latitude as to air and time. They became so terribly irritating to us, that to this day the remembrance of those soul-lacerating lyrics abides with me as one of the chief of the minor torments of our situation. They were, in fact, nearly as bad as the lice.

We revenged ourselves as best we could by constructing fearfully wicked, obscene and insulting parodies on these, and by singing them with irritating effusiveness in the hearing of the guards who were inflicting these nuisances upon us.

Of the same nature was the garrison music. One fife, played by an asthmatic old fellow whose breathings were nearly as audible as his notes, and one rheumatic drummer, constituted the entire band for the post. The fifer actually knew but one tune "The Bonnie Blue Flag" —and did not know that well. But it was all that he had, and he played it with wearisome monotony for every camp call—five or six times a day, and seven days in the week. He called us up in the morning with it for a reveille; he sounded the "roll call" and "drill call," breakfast, dinner and supper with it, and finally sent us to bed, with the same dreary wail that had rung in our ears all day. I never hated any piece of music as I came to hate that threnody of treason. It would have been such a relief if the old asthmatic who played it could have been induced to learn another tune to play on Sundays, and give us one day of rest. He did not, but desecrated the Lord's Day by playing as vilely as on the rest of the week. The Rebels were fully conscious of their musical deficiencies, and made repeated but unsuccessful attempts to induce the musicians among the prisoners to come outside and form a band.

CHAPTER XLV

AUGUST—NEEDLES STUCK IN PUMPKIN SEEDS—SOME PHENOMENA OF STARVATION —RIOTING IN REMEMBERED LUXURIES.

"Illinoy," said tall, gaunt Jack North, of the One Hundred and Fourteenth Illinois, to me, one day, as we sat contemplating our naked, and sadly attenuated underpinning; "what do our legs and feet most look like?"

"Give it up, Jack," said I.

"Why—darning needles stuck in pumpkin seeds, of course." I never heard a better comparison for our wasted limbs.

The effects of the great bodily emaciation were sometimes very startling. Boys of a fleshy habit would change so in a few weeks as to lose all resemblance to their former selves, and comrades who came into prison later would utterly fail to recognize them. Most fat men, as most large men, died in a little while after entering, though there were exceptions. One of these was a boy of my own company, named George Hillicks. George had shot up within a few years to over six feet in hight, and then, as such boys occasionally do, had, after enlisting with us, taken on such a development of flesh that we nicknamed him the "Giant," and he became a pretty good load for even the strongest horse. George held his flesh through Belle Isle, and the earlier weeks in Andersonville, but June, July, and August "fetched him," as the boys said. He seemed to melt away like an icicle on a Spring day, and he grew so thin that his hight seemed preternatural. We called him "Flagstaff," and cracked all sorts of jokes about putting an insulator on his head, and setting him up for a telegraph pole, braiding his legs and using him for a whip lash, letting his hair grow a little longer, and trading him off to the Rebels for a sponge and staff for the artillery, etc. We all expected him to die, and looked continually for the development of the fatal scurvy symptoms, which were to seal his doom. But he worried through, and came out at last in good shape, a happy result due as much as to anything else to his having in Chester Hayward, of Prairie City, Ill.,—one of the most devoted chums I ever knew. Chester nursed and looked out for George with wife-like fidelity, and had his reward in bringing him safe through our lines. There were thousands of instances of this generous devotion to each other by chums in Andersonville, and I know of nothing that reflects any more credit upon our boy soldiers.

There was little chance for any one to accumulate flesh on the rations we were receiving. I say it in all soberness that I do not believe that a healthy hen could have grown fat upon them. I am sure that any good-sized "shanghai" eats more every day than the meager half loaf that we had to maintain life upon. Scanty as this was, and hungry as all were, very many could not eat it. Their stomachs revolted against the trash; it became so nauseous to them that they could not force it down, even when famishing, and they died of starvation with the chunks of the so-called bread under their head. I found myself rapidly approaching this condition. I had been blessed with a good digestion and a talent for sleeping under the most discouraging circumstances. These, I have no doubt, were of the greatest assistance to me in my struggle for existence. But now the rations became fearfully obnoxious to me, and it was only with the greatest effort—pulling the bread into little pieces and swallowing each, of these as one would a pill—that I succeeded in worrying the stuff down. I had not as yet fallen away very much, but as I had never, up, to that time, weighed so much as one hundred and twenty-five pounds, there was no great amount of adipose to lose. It was evident that unless some change occurred my time was near at hand. There was not only hunger for more food, but longing with an intensity beyond expression for alteration of some kind in the rations. The changeless monotony of the miserable saltless bread, or worse mush, for days, weeks and months, became unbearable. If those wretched mule teams had only once a month hauled in something different—if they had come in loaded with sweet potatos, green corn or wheat flour, there would be thousands of men still living who now slumber beneath those melancholy pines. It would have given something to look forward to, and remember when past. But to know each day that the gates would open to admit the same distasteful apologies for food took away the appetite and raised one's gorge, even while famishing for something to eat.

We could for a while forget the stench, the lice, the heat, the maggots, the dead and dying around us, the insulting malignance of our jailors; but it was, very hard work to banish thoughts and longings for food from our minds. Hundreds became actually insane from brooding over it. Crazy men could be found in all parts of the camp. Numbers of them wandered around entirely naked. Their babblings and maunderings about something to eat were painful to hear. I have before mentioned the case of the Plymouth Pilgrim near me, whose insanity took the form of imagining that he was sitting at the table with his family, and who would go through the show of helping them to imaginary viands and delicacies. The cravings for green food of those afflicted with the scurvy were, agonizing. Large numbers of watermelons were brought to the prison, and sold to those who had the money to pay for them at from one to five dollars, greenbacks, apiece. A boy who had means to buy a piece of these would be followed about while eating it by a crowd of perhaps twenty-five or thirty livid-gummed scorbutics, each imploring him for the rind when he was through with it.

We thought of food all day, and were visited with torturing dreams of it at night. One of the pleasant recollections of my pre-military life was a banquet at the "Planter's House," St. Louis, at which I was a boyish guest. It was, doubtless, an ordinary affair, as banquets go, but to me then, with all the keen appreciation of youth and first experience, it was a feast worthy of Lucullus. But now this delightful reminiscence became a torment. Hundreds of times I dreamed I was again at the "Planter's." I saw the wide corridors, with their mosaic pavement; I entered the grand dining-room, keeping timidly near the friend to whose kindness I owed this wonderful favor; I saw again the mirror-lined walls, the evergreen decked ceilings, the festoons and mottos, the tables gleaming with cutglass and silver, the buffets with wines and fruits, the brigade of sleek, black, white-aproned waiters, headed by one who had presence enough for a major General. Again I reveled in all the dainties and dishes on the bill-of-fare; calling for everything that I dared to, just to see what each was like, and to be able to say afterwards that I had partaken of it; all these bewildering delights of the first realization of what a boy has read and wondered much over, and longed for, would dance their rout and reel through my somnolent brain. Then I would awake to find myself a half-naked, half-starved, vermin-eaten wretch, crouching in a hole in the ground, waiting for my keepers to fling me a chunk of corn bread.

Naturally the boys—and especially the country boys and new prisoners —talked much of victuals—what they had had, and what they would have again, when they got out. Take this as a sample of the conversation which might be heard in any group of boys, sitting together on the sand, killin lice and talking of exchange:

Tom—"Well, Bill, when we get back to God's country, you and Jim and John must all come to my house and take dinner with me. I want to give you a square meal. I want to show you just what good livin' is. You know my mother is just the best cook in all that section. When she lays herself out to get up a meal all the other women in the neighborhood just stand back and admire!"

Bill—"O, that's all right; but I'll bet she can't hold a candle to my mother, when it comes to good cooking."

Jim—"No, nor to mine."

John—(with patronizing contempt.) "O, shucks! None of you fellers were ever at our house, even when we had one of our common weekday dinners."

Tom—(unheedful of the counter claims.) I hev teen studyin' up the dinner I'd like, and the bill-of-fare I'd set out for you fellers when you come over to see me. First, of course, we'll lay the foundation like with a nice, juicy loin roast, and some mashed potatos.

Bill—(interrupting.) "Now, do you like mashed potatos with beef? The way may mother does is to pare the potatos, and lay them in the pan along with the beef. Then, you know, they come out just as nice and crisp, and brown; they have soaked up all the beef gravy, and they crinkle between your teeth—"

Jim—"Now, I tell you, mashed Neshannocks with butter on 'em is plenty good enough for me."

John—"If you'd et some of the new kind of peachblows that we raised in the old pasture lot the year before I enlisted, you'd never say another word about your Neshannocks."

Tom—(taking breath and starting in fresh.) "Then we'll hev some fried Spring chickens, of our dominick breed. Them dominicks of ours have the nicest, tenderest meat, better'n quail, a darned sight, and the way my mother can fry Spring chickens——"

Bill—(aside to Jim.) "Every durned woman in the country thinks she can 'spry ching frickens;' but my mother—"

John—"You fellers all know that there's nobody knows half as much about chicken doin's as these 'tinerant Methodis' preachers. They give 'em chicken wherever they go, and folks do say that out in the new settlements they can't get no preachin', no gospel, nor nothin', until the chickens become so plenty that a preacher is reasonably sure of havin' one for his dinner wherever he may go. Now, there's old Peter Cartwright, who has traveled over Illinoy and Indianny since the Year One, and preached more good sermons than any other man who ever set on saddle-bags, and has et more chickens than there are birds in a big pigeon roost. Well, he took dinner at our house when he came up to dedicate the big, white church at Simpkin's Corners, and when he passed up his plate the third time for more chicken, he sez, sez he:—I've et at a great many hundred tables in the fifty years I have labored in the vineyard of the Redeemer, but I must say, Mrs. Kiggins, that your way of frying chickens is a leetle the nicest that I ever knew. I only wish that the sisters generally would get your reseet.' Yes, that's what he said,—'a leetle the nicest.'"

Tom—"An' then, we'll hev biscuits an' butter. I'll just bet five hundred dollars to a cent, and give back the cent if I win, that we have the best butter at our house that there is in Central Illinoy. You can't never hev good butter onless you have a spring house; there's no use of talkin'—all the patent churns that lazy men ever invented—all the fancy milk pans an' coolers, can't make up for a spring house. Locations for a spring house are scarcer than hen's teeth in Illinoy, but we hev one, and there ain't a better one in Orange County, New York. Then you'll see dome of the biscuits my mother makes."

Bill—"Well, now, my mother's a boss biscuit-maker, too."

Jim—"You kin just gamble that mine is."

John—"O, that's the way you fellers ought to think an' talk, but my mother——"

Tom—(coming in again with fresh vigor) "They're jest as light an' fluffy as a dandelion puff, and they melt in your month like a ripe Bartlett pear. You just pull 'em open—Now you know that I think there's nothin' that shows a person's raisin' so well as to see him eat biscuits an' butter. If he's been raised mostly on corn bread, an' common doins,' an' don't know much about good things to eat, he'll most likely cut his biscuit open with a case knife, an' make it fall as flat as one o' yesterday's pancakes. But if he is used to biscuits, has had 'em often at his house, he'll—just pull 'em open, slow an' easy like, then he'll lay a little slice of butter inside, and drop a few drops of clear honey on this, an' stick the two halves back, together again, an—"

"Oh, for God Almighty's sake, stop talking that infernal nonsense," roar out a half dozen of the surrounding crowd, whose mouths have been watering over this unctuous recital of the good things of the table. "You blamed fools, do you want to drive yourselves and everybody else crazy with such stuff as that. Dry up and try to think of something else."

CHAPTER XLVI.

SURLY BRITON—THE STOLID COURAGE THAT MAKES THE ENGLISH FLAG A BANNER OF TRIUMPH—OUR COMPANY BUGLER, HIS CHARACTERISTICS AND HIS DEATH—URGENT DEMAND FOR MECHANICS—NONE WANT TO GO—TREATMENT OF A REBEL SHOEMAKER —ENLARGEMENT OF THE STOCKADE—IT IS BROKEN BY A STORM—THE WONDERFUL SPRING.

Early in August, F. Marriott, our Company Bugler, died. Previous to coming to America he had been for many years an English soldier, and I accepted him as a type of that stolid, doggedly brave class, which forms the bulk of the English armies, and has for centuries carried the British flag with dauntless courage into every land under the sun. Rough, surly and unsocial, he did his duty with the unemotional steadiness of a machine. He knew nothing but to obey orders, and obeyed them under all circumstances promptly, but with stony impassiveness. With the command to move forward into action, he moved forward without a word, and with face as blank as a side of sole leather. He went as far as ordered, halted at the word, and retired at command as phlegmatically as he advanced. If he cared a straw whether he advanced or retreated, if it mattered to the extent of a pinch of salt whether we whipped the Rebels or they defeated us, he kept that feeling so deeply hidden in the recesses of his sturdy bosom that no one ever suspected it. In the excitement of action the rest of the boys shouted, and swore, and expressed their tense feelings in various ways, but Marriott might as well have been a graven image, for all the expression that he suffered to escape. Doubtless, if the Captain had ordered him to shoot one of the company through the heart, he would have executed the command according to the manual of arms, brought his carbine to a "recover," and at the word marched back to his quarters without an inquiry as to the cause of the proceedings. He made no friends, and though his surliness repelled us, he made few enemies. Indeed, he was rather a favorite, since he was a genuine character; his gruffness had no taint of selfish greed in it; he minded his own business strictly, and wanted others to do the same. When he first came into the company, it is true, he gained the enmity of nearly everybody in it, but an incident occurred which turned the tide in his favor. Some annoying little depredations had been practiced on the boys, and it needed but a word of suspicion to inflame all their minds against the surly Englishman as the unknown perpetrator. The feeling intensified, until about half of the company were in a mood to kill the Bugler outright. As we were returning from stable duty one evening, some little occurrence fanned the smoldering anger into a fierce blaze; a couple of the smaller boys began an attack upon him; others hastened to their assistance, and soon half the company were engaged in the assault.

He succeeded in disengaging himself from his assailants, and, squaring himself off, said, defiantly:

"Dom yer cowardly heyes; jest come hat me one hat a time, hand hI'll wollop the 'ole gang uv ye's."

One of our Sergeants styled himself proudly "a Chicago rough," and was as vain of his pugilistic abilities as a small boy is of a father who plays in the band. We all hated him cordially—even more than we did Marriott.

He thought this was a good time to show off, and forcing his way through the crowd, he said, vauntingly:

"Just fall back and form a ring, boys, and see me polish off the—-fool."

The ring was formed, with the Bugler and the Sergeant in the center. Though the latter was the younger and stronger the first round showed him that it would have profited him much more to have let Marriott's challenge pass unheeded. As a rule, it is as well to ignore all invitations of this kind from Englishmen, and especially from those who, like Marriott, have served a term in the army, for they are likely to be so handy with their fists as to make the consequences of an acceptance more lively than desirable.

So the Sergeant found. "Marriott," as one of the spectators expressed it, "went around him like a cooper around a barrel." He planted his blows just where he wished, to the intense delight of the boys, who yelled enthusiastically whenever he got in "a hot one," and their delight at seeing the Sergeant drubbed so thoroughly and artistically, worked an entire revolution in his favor. Thenceforward we viewed his eccentricities with lenient eyes, and became rather proud of his bull-dog stolidity and surliness. The whole battalion soon came to share this feeling, and everybody enjoyed hearing his deep-toned growl, which mischievous boys would incite by some petty annoyances deliberately designed for that purpose. I will mention incidentally, that after his encounter with the Sergeant no one ever again volunteered to "polish" him off.

Andersonville did not improve either his temper or his communicativeness. He seemed to want to get as far away from the rest of us as possible, and took up his quarters in a remote corner of the Stockade, among utter strangers. Those of us who wandered up in his neighborhood occasionally, to see how he was getting along, were received with such scant courtesy, that we did not hasten to repeat the visit. At length, after none of us had seen him for weeks, we thought that comradeship demanded another visit. We found him in the last stages of scurvy and diarrhea. Chunks of uneaten corn bread lay by his head. They were at least a week old. The rations since then had evidently been stolen from the helpless man by those around him. The place where he lay was indescribably filthy, and his body was swarming with vermin. Some good Samaritan had filled his little black oyster can with water, and placed it within his reach. For a week, at least, he had not been able to rise from the ground; he could barely reach for the water near him. He gave us such a glare of recognition as I remembered to have seen light up the fast-darkening eyes of a savage old mastiff, that I and my boyish companions once found dying in the woods of disease and hurts. Had he been able he would have driven us away, or at least assailed us with biting English epithets. Thus he had doubtless driven away all those who had attempted to help him. We did what little we could, and staid with him until the next afternoon, when he died. We prepared his body, in the customary way: folded the hands across his breast, tied the toes together, and carried it outside, not forgetting each of us, to bring back a load of wood.

The scarcity of mechanics of all kinds in the Confederacy, and the urgent needs of the people for many things which the war and the blockade prevented their obtaining, led to continual inducements being offered to the artizans among us to go outside and work at their trade. Shoemakers seemed most in demand; next to these blacksmiths, machinists, molders and metal workers generally. Not a week passed during my imprisonment that I did not see a Rebel emissary of some kind about the prison seeking to engage skilled workmen for some purpose or another. While in Richmond the managers of the Tredegar Iron Works were brazen and persistent in their efforts to seduce what are termed "malleable iron workers," to enter their employ. A boy who was master of any one of the commoner trades had but to make his wishes known, and he would be allowed to go out on parole to work. I was a printer, and I think that at least a dozen times I was approached by Rebel publishers with offers of a parole, and work at good prices. One from Columbia, S. C., offered me two dollars and a half a "thousand" for composition. As the highest price for such work that I had received before enlisting was thirty cents a thousand, this seemed a chance to accumulate untold wealth. Since a man working in day time can set from thirty-five to fifty "thousand" a week, this would make weekly wages run from eighty-seven dollars and fifty cents to one hundred and twenty-five dollars—but it was in Confederate money, then worth from ten to twenty cents on the dollar.

Still better offers were made to iron workers of all kinds, to shoemakers, tanners, weavers, tailors, hatters, engineers, machinists, millers, railroad men, and similar tradesmen. Any of these could have made a handsome thing by accepting the offers made them almost weekly. As nearly all in the prison had useful trades, it would have been of immense benefit to the Confederacy if they could have been induced to work at them. There is no measuring the benefit it would have been to the Southern cause if all the hundreds of tanners and shoemakers in the Stockade could have, been persuaded to go outside and labor in providing leather and shoes for the almost shoeless people and soldiery. The machinists alone could have done more good to the Southern Confederacy than one of our brigades was doing harm, by consenting to go to the railroad shops at Griswoldville and ply their handicraft. The lack of material resources in the South was one of the strongest allies our arms had. This lack of resources was primarily caused by a lack of skilled labor to develop those resources, and nowhere could there be found a finer collection of skilled laborers than in the thirty-three thousand prisoners incarcerated in Andersonville.

All solicitations to accept a parole and go outside to work at one's trade were treated with the scorn they deserved. If any mechanic yielded to them, the fact did not come under my notice. The usual reply to invitations of this kind was:

"No, Sir! By God, I'll stay in here till I rot, and the maggots carry me out through the cracks in the Stockade, before I'll so much as raise my little finger to help the infernal Confederacy, or Rebels, in any shape or form."

In August a Macon shoemaker came in to get some of his trade to go back with him to work in the Confederate shoe factory. He prosecuted his search for these until he reached the center of the camp on the North Side, when some of the shoemakers who had gathered around him, apparently considering his propositions, seized him and threw him into a well. He was kept there a whole day, and only released when Wirz cut off the rations of the prison for that day, and announced that no more would be issued until the man was returned safe and sound to the gate. The terrible crowding was somewhat ameliorated by the opening in July of an addition—six hundred feet long—to the North Side of the Stockade. This increased the room inside to twenty acres, giving about an acre to every one thousand seven hundred men,—a preposterously contracted area still. The new ground was not a hotbed of virulent poison like the olds however, and those who moved on to it had that much in their favor.

The palisades between the new and the old portions of the pen were left standing when the new portion was opened. We were still suffering a great deal of inconvenience from lack of wood. That night the standing timbers were attacked by thousands of prisoners armed with every species of a tool to cut wood, from a case-knife to an ax. They worked the live-long night with such energy that by morning not only every inch of the logs above ground had disappeared, but that below had been dug up, and there was not enough left of the eight hundred foot wall of twenty-five-foot logs to make a box of matches.

One afternoon—early in August—one of the violent rain storms common to that section sprung up, and in a little while the water was falling in torrents. The little creek running through the camp swelled up immensely, and swept out large gaps in the Stockade, both in the west and east sides. The Rebels noticed the breaches as soon as the prisoners. Two guns were fired from the Star Tort, and all the guards rushed out, and formed so as to prevent any egress, if one was attempted. Taken by surprise, we were not in a condition to profit by the opportunity until it was too late.

The storm did one good thing: it swept away a great deal of filth, and left the camp much more wholesome. The foul stench rising from the camp made an excellent electrical conductor, and the lightning struck several times within one hundred feet of the prison.

Toward the end of August there happened what the religously inclined termed a Providential Dispensation. The water in the Creek was indescribably bad. No amount of familiarity with it, no increase of intimacy with our offensive surroundings, could lessen the disgust at the polluted water. As I have said previously, before the stream entered the Stockade, it was rendered too filthy for any use by the contaminations from the camps of the guards, situated about a half-mile above. Immediately on entering the Stockade the contamination became terrible. The oozy seep at the bottom of the hillsides drained directly into it all the mass of filth from a population of thirty-three thousand. Imagine the condition of an open sewer, passing through the heart of a city of that many people, and receiving all the offensive product of so dense a gathering into a shallow, sluggish stream, a yard wide and five inches deep, and heated by the burning rays of the sun in the thirty-second degree of latitude. Imagine, if one can, without becoming sick at the stomach, all of these people having to wash in and drink of this foul flow.

There is not a scintilla of exaggeration in this statement. That it is within the exact truth is demonstrable by the testimony of any man—Rebel or Union—who ever saw the inside of the Stockade at Andersonville. I am quite content to have its truth—as well as that of any other statement made in this book—be determined by the evidence of any one, no matter how bitter his hatred of the Union, who had any personal knowledge of the condition of affairs at Andersonville. No one can successfully deny that there were at least thirty-three thousand prisoners in the Stockade, and that the one shallow, narrow creek, which passed through the prison, was at once their main sewer and their source of supply of water for bathing, drinking and washing. With these main facts admitted, the reader's common sense of natural consequences will furnish the rest of the details.

It is true that some of the more fortunate of us had wells; thanks to our own energy in overcoming extraordinary obstacles; no thanks to our gaolers for making the slightest effort to provide these necessities of life. We dug the wells with case and pocket knives, and half canteens to a depth of from twenty to thirty feet, pulling up the dirt in pantaloons legs, and running continual risk of being smothered to death by the caving in of the unwalled sides. Not only did the Rebels refuse to give us boards with which to wall the wells, and buckets for drawing the water, but they did all in their power to prevent us from digging the wells, and made continual forays to capture the digging tools, because the wells were frequently used as the starting places for tunnels. Professor Jones lays special stress on this tunnel feature in his testimony, which I have introduced in a previous chapter.

The great majority of the prisoners who went to the Creek for water, went as near as possible to the Dead Line on the West Side, where the Creek entered the Stockade, that they might get water with as little filth in it as possible. In the crowds struggling there for their turn to take a dip, some one nearly every day got so close to the Dead Line as to arouse a suspicion in the guard's mind that he was touching it. The suspicion was the unfortunate one's death warrant, and also its execution. As the sluggish brain of the guard conceived it he leveled his gun; the distance to his victim was not over one hundred feet; he never failed his aim; the first warning the wretched prisoner got that he was suspected of transgressing a prison-rule was the charge of "ball-and-buck" that tore through his body. It was lucky if he was, the only one of the group killed. More wicked and unjustifiable murders never were committed than these almost daily assassinations at the Creek.

One morning the camp was astonished beyond measure to discover that during the night a large, bold spring had burst out on the North Side, about midway between the Swamp and the summit of the hill. It poured out its grateful flood of pure, sweet water in an apparently exhaustless quantity. To the many who looked in wonder upon it, it seemed as truly a heaven-wrought miracle as when Moses's enchanted rod smote the parched rock in Sinai's desert waste, and the living waters gushed forth.

The police took charge of the spring, and every one was compelled to take his regular turn in filling his vessel. This was kept up during our whole stay in Andersonville, and every morning, shortly after daybreak, a thousand men could be seen standing in line, waiting their turns to fill their cans and cups with the precious liquid.

I am told by comrades who have revisited the Stockade of recent years, that the spring is yet running as when we left, and is held in most pious veneration by the negros of that vicinity, who still preserve the tradition of its miraculous origin, and ascribe to its water wonderful grace giving and healing properties, similar to those which pious Catholics believe exist in the holy water of the fountain at Lourdes.

I must confess that I do not think they are so very far from right. If I could believe that any water was sacred and thaumaturgic, it would be of that fountain which appeared so opportunely for the benefit of the perishing thousands of Andersonville. And when I hear of people bringing water for baptismal purposes from the Jordan, I say in my heart, "How much more would I value for myself and friends the administration of the chrismal sacrament with the diviner flow from that low sand-hill in Western Georgia."

CHAPTER XLVII.

"SICK CALL," AND THE SCENES THAT ACCOMPANIED IT—MUSTERING THE LAME, HALT AND DISEASED AT THE SOUTH GATE—AN UNUSUALLY BAD CASE—GOING OUT TO THE HOSPITAL—ACCOMMODATION AND TREATMENT OF THE PATIENTS THERE—THE HORRIBLE SUFFERING IN THE GANGRENE WARD—BUNGLING AMPUTATIONS BY BLUNDERING PRACTITIONERS—AFFECTION BETWEEN A SAILOR AND HIS WARD —DEATH OF MY COMRADE.

Every morning after roll-call, thousands of sick gathered at the South Gate, where the doctors made some pretense of affording medical relief. The scene there reminded me of the illustrations in my Sunday-School lessons of that time when "great multitudes came unto Him," by the shores of the Sea of Galilee, "having with them those that were lame, blind, dumb, maimed, and many others." Had the crowds worn the flouting robes of the East, the picture would have lacked nothing but the presence of the Son of Man to make it complete. Here were the burning sands and parching sun; hither came scores of groups of three or four comrades, laboriously staggering under the weight of a blanket in which they had carried a disabled and dying friend from some distant part of the Stockade. Beside them hobbled the scorbutics with swollen and distorted limbs, each more loathsome and nearer death than the lepers whom Christ's divine touch made whole. Dozens, unable to walk, and having no comrades to carry them, crawled painfully along, with frequent stops, on their hands and knees. Every form of intense physical suffering that it is possible for disease to induce in the human frame was visible at these daily parades of the sick of the prison. As over three thousand (three thousand and seventy-six) died in August, there were probably twelve thousand dangerously sick at any given time daring the month; and a large part of these collected at the South Gate every morning.

Measurably-calloused as we had become by the daily sights of horror around us, we encountered spectacles in these gatherings which no amount of visible misery could accustom us to. I remember one especially that burned itself deeply into my memory. It was of a young man not over twenty-five, who a few weeks ago—his clothes looked comparatively new —had evidently been the picture of manly beauty and youthful vigor. He had had a well-knit, lithe form; dark curling hair fell over a forehead which had once been fair, and his eyes still showed that they had gleamed with a bold, adventurous spirit. The red clover leaf on his cap showed that he belonged to the First Division of the Second Corps, the three chevrons on his arm that he was a Sergeant, and the stripe at his cuff that he was a veteran. Some kind-hearted boys had found him in a miserable condition on the North Side, and carried him over in a blanket to where the doctors could see him. He had but little clothing on, save his blouse and cap. Ulcers of some kind had formed in his abdomen, and these were now masses of squirming worms. It was so much worse

than the usual forms of suffering, that quite a little crowd of compassionate spectators gathered around and expressed their pity. The sufferer turned to one who lay beside him with:
"Comrade: If we were only under the old Stars and Stripes, we wouldn't care a G-d d—n for a few worms, would we?"
This was not profane. It was an utterance from the depths of a brave man's heart, couched in the strongest language at his command. It seemed terrible that so gallant a soul should depart from earth in this miserable fashion. Some of us, much moved by the sight, went to the doctors and put the case as strongly as possible, begging them to do something to alleviate his suffering. They declined to see the case, but got rid of us by giving us a bottle of turpentine, with directions to pour it upon the ulcers to kill the maggots. We did so. It must have been cruel torture, and as absurd remedially as cruel, but our hero set his teeth and endured, without a groan. He was then carried out to the hospital to die.

I said the doctors made a pretense of affording medical relief. It was hardly that, since about all the prescription for those inside the Stockade consisted in giving a handful of sumach berries to each of those complaining of scurvy. The berries might have done some good, had there been enough of them, and had their action been assisted by proper food. As it was, they were probably nearly, if not wholly, useless. Nothing was given to arrest the ravages of dysentery.

A limited number of the worst cases were admitted to the Hospital each day. As this only had capacity for about one-quarter of the sick in the Stockade, new patients could only be admitted as others died. It seemed, anyway, like signing a man's death warrant to send him to the Hospital, as three out of every four who went out there died. The following from the official report of the Hospital shows this:

```
Total number admitted .........................................12,900
Died ................................................  8,663
Exchanged ...........................................    828
Took the oath of allegiance .........................     25
Sent elsewhere .....................................  2,889

Total .........................................................12,400
```

Average deaths, 76 per cent.

Early in August I made a successful effort to get out to the Hospital. I had several reasons for this: First, one of my chums, W. W. Watts, of my own company, had been sent out a little whale before very sick with scurvy and pneumonia, and I wanted to see if I could do anything for him, if he still lived: I have mentioned before that for awhile after our entrance into Andersonville five of us slept on one overcoat and covered ourselves with one blanket. Two of these had already died, leaving as possessors of-the blanket and overcoat, W. W. Watts, B. B. Andrews, and myself.

Next, I wanted to go out to see if there was any prospect of escape. I had long since given up hopes of escaping from the Stockade. All our attempts at tunneling had resulted in dead failures, and now, to make us wholly despair of success in that direction, another Stockade was built clear around the prison, at a distance of one hundred and twenty feet from the first palisades. It was manifest that though we might succeed in tunneling past one Stockade, we could not go beyond the second one.

I had the scurvy rather badly, and being naturally slight in frame, I presented a very sick appearance to the physicians, and was passed out to the Hospital.

While this was a wretched affair, it was still a vast improvement on the Stockade. About five acres of ground, a little southeast of the Stockade, and bordering on a creek, were enclosed by a board fence, around which the guard walked, trees shaded the ground tolerably well. There were tents and flies to shelter part of the sick, and in these were beds made of pine leaves. There were regular streets and alleys running through the grounds, and as the management was in the hands of our own men, the place was kept reasonably clean and orderly for Andersonville.

There was also some improvement in the food. Rice in some degree replaced the nauseous and innutritious corn bread, and if served in sufficient quantities, would doubtless have promoted the recovery of many men dying from dysenteric diseases. We also received small quantities of "okra," a plant peculiar to the South, whose pods contained a mucilaginous matter that made a soup very grateful to those suffering from scurvy.

But all these ameliorations of condition were too slight to even arrest the progress of the disease of the thousands of dying men brought out from the Stockade. These still wore the same lice-infested garments as in prison; no baths or even ordinary applications of soap and water cleaned their dirt-grimed skins, to give their pores an opportunity to assist in restoring them to health; even their long, lank and matted hair, swarming with vermin, was not trimmed. The most ordinary and obvious measures for their comfort and care were neglected. If a man recovered he did it almost in spite of fate. The medicines given were scanty and crude. The principal remedial agent—as far as my observation extended—was a rank, fetid species of unrectified spirits, which, I was told, was made from sorgum seed. It had a light-green tinge, and was about as inviting to the taste as spirits of turpentine. It was given to the sick in small quantities mixed with water. I had had some experience with Kentucky "apple-jack," which, it was popularly believed among the boys, would dissolve a piece of the fattest pork thrown into it, but that seemed balmy and oily alongside of this. After tasting some, I ceased to wonder at the atrocities of Wirz and his associates. Nothing would seem too bad to a man who made that his habitual tipple.

[For a more particular description of the Hospital I must refer my reader to the testimony of Professor Jones, in a previous chapter.]

Certainly this continent has never seen—and I fervently trust it will never again see—such a gigantic concentration of misery as that Hospital displayed daily. The official statistics tell the story of this with terrible brevity: There were three thousand seven hundred and nine in the Hospital in August; one thousand four hundred and eighty-nine—nearly every other man died. The rate afterwards became much higher than this.

The most conspicuous suffering was in the gangrene wards. Horrible sores spreading almost visibly from hour to hour, devoured men's limbs and bodies. I remember one ward in which the alterations appeared to be altogether in the back, where they ate out the tissue between the skin and the ribs. The attendants seemed trying to arrest the progress of the sloughing by drenching the sores with a solution of blue vitriol. This was exquisitely painful, and in the morning, when the drenching was going on, the whole hospital rang with the most agonizing screams.

But the gangrene mostly attacked the legs and arms, and the led more than the arms. Sometimes it killed men inside of a week; sometimes they lingered on indefinitely. I remember one man in the Stockade who cut his hand with the sharp corner of a card of corn bread he was lifting from the ration wagon; gangrene set in immediately, and he died four days after.

One form that was quit prevalent was a cancer of the lower one corner of the mouth, and it finally ate the whole side of the face out. Of course the sufferer had the greatest trouble in eating and drinking. For the latter it was customary to whittle out a little wooden tube, and fasten it in a tin cup, through which he could suck up the water. As this mouth cancer seemed contagious, none of us would allow any one afflicted with it to use any of our cooking utensils. The Rebel doctors at the hospital resorted to wholesale amputations to check the progress of the gangrene. They had a two hours session of limb-lopping every morning, each of which resulted in quite a pile of severed members. I presume more bungling operations are rarely seen outside of Russian or Turkish hospitals. Their unskilfulness was apparent even to non-scientific observers like myself. The standard of medical education in the South—as indeed of every other form of education—was quite low. The Chief Surgeon of the prison, Dr. Isaiah White, and perhaps two or three others, seemed to be gentlemen of fair abilities and attainments. The remainder were of that class of illiterate and unlearning quacks who physic and blister the poor whites and negros in the country districts of the South; who believe they can stop bleeding of the nose by repeating a verse from the Bible; who think that if in gathering their favorite remedy of boneset they cut the stem upwards it will purge their patients, and if downward it will vomit them, and who hold that there is nothing so good for "fits" as a black cat, killed in the dark of the moon, cut open, and bound while yet warm, upon the naked chest of the victim of the convulsions.

They had a case of instruments captured from some of our field hospitals, which were dull and fearfully out of order. With poor instruments and unskilled hands the operations became mangling.

In the Hospital I saw an admirable illustration of the affection which a sailor will lavish on a ship's boy, whom he takes a fancy to, and makes his "chicken," as the phrase is. The United States sloop "Water Witch" had recently been captured in Ossabaw Sound, and her crew brought into prison. One of her boys—a bright, handsome little fellow of about fifteen—had lost one of his arms in the fight. He was brought into the Hospital, and the old fellow whose "chicken" he was, was allowed to accompany and nurse him. This "old barnacle-back" was as surly a growler as ever went aloft, but to his "chicken" he was as tender and thoughtful as a woman. They found a shady nook in one corner, and any moment one looked in that direction he could see the old tar hard at work at something for the comfort and pleasure of his pet. Now he was dressing the wound as deftly and gently as a mother caring for a new-born babe; now he was trying to concoct some relish out of the slender materials he could beg or steal from the Quartermaster; now trying to arrange the shade of the bed of pine leaves in a more comfortable manner; now repairing or washing his clothes, and so on.

All the sailors were particularly favored by being allowed to bring their bags in untouched by the guards. This "chicken" had a wonderful supply of clothes, the handiwork of his protector who, like most good sailors, was very skillful with the needle. He had suits of fine white duck, embroidered with blue in a way that would ravish the heart of a fine lady, and blue suits similarly embroidered with white. No belle ever kept her clothes in better order than these were. When the duck came up from the old sailor's patient washing it was as spotless as new-fallen snow.

I found my chum in a very bad condition. His appetite was entirely gone, but he had an inordinate craving for tobacco—for strong, black plug —which he smoked in a pipe. He had already traded off all his brass buttons to the guards for this. I had accumulated a few buttons to bribe the guard to take me out for wood, and I gave these also for tobacco for him. When I awoke one morning the man who laid next to me on the right was dead, having died sometime during the night. I searched his pockets and took what was in them. These were a silk pocket handkerchief, a gutta percha finger-ring, a comb, a pencil, and a leather pocket-book, making in all quite a nice little "find." I hied over to the guard, and succeeded in trading the personal estate which I had inherited from the intestate deceased, for a handful of peaches, a handful of hardly ripe figs, and a long plug of tobacco. I hastened back to Watts, expecting that the figs and peaches would do him a world of good. At first I did not show him the tobacco, as I was strongly opposed to his using it, thinking that it was making him much worse. But he looked at the tempting peaches and figs with lack-luster eyes; he was too far gone to care for them. He pushed them back to me, saying faintly:

"No, you take 'em, Mc; I don't want 'em; I can't eat 'em!"

I then produced the tobacco, and his face lighted up. Concluding that this was all the comfort that he could have, and that I might as well gratify him, I cut up some of the weed, filled his pipe and lighted it. He smoked calmly and almost happily all the afternoon, hardly speaking a word to me. As it grew dark he asked me to bring him a drink. I did so, and as I raised him up he said:

"Mc, this thing's ended. Tell my father that I stood it as long as I could, and——"

The death rattle sounded in his throat, and when I laid him back it was all over. Straightening out his limbs, folding his hands across his breast, and composing his features as best I could, I lay, down beside the body and slept till morning, when I did what little else I could toward preparing for the grave all that was left of my long-suffering little friend.

CHAPTER XLVIII.

DETERMINATION TO ESCAPE—DIFFERENT PLANS AND THEIR MERITS—I PREFER THE APPALACHICOLA ROUTE—PREPARATIONS FOR DEPARTURE—A HOT DAY— THE FENCE PASSED SUCCESSFULLY PURSUED BY THE HOUNDS—CAUGHT — RETURNED TO THE STOCKADE.

After Watt's death, I set earnestly about seeing what could be done in the way of escape. Frank Harvey, of the First West Virginia Cavalry, a boy of about my own age and disposition, joined with me in the scheme. I was still possessed with my original plan of making my way down the creeks to the Flint River, down the Flint River to where it emptied into the Appalachicola River, and down that stream to its debauchure into the bay that connected with the Gulf of Mexico. I was sure of finding my way by this route, because, if nothing else offered, I could get astride of a log and float down the current. The way to Sherman, in the other direction, was long, torturous and difficult, with a fearful gauntlet of blood-hounds, patrols and the scouts of Hood's Army to be run. I had but little difficulty in persuading Harvey into an acceptance of my views, and we began arranging for a solution of the first great problem—how to get outside of the Hospital guards. As I have explained before, the Hospital was surrounded by a board fence, with guards walking their beats on the ground outside. A small creek flowed through the southern end of the grounds, and at its lower end was used as a sink. The boards of the fence came down to the surface of the water, where the Creek passed out, but we found, by careful prodding with a stick, that the hole between the boards and the bottom of the Creek was sufficiently large to allow the passage of our bodies, and there had been no stakes driven or other precautions used to prevent egress by this channel. A guard was posted there, and probably ordered to stand at the edge of the stream, but it smelled so vilely in those scorching days that he had consulted his feelings and probably his health, by retiring to the top of the bank, a rod or more distant. We watched night after night, and at last were gratified to find that none went nearer the Creak than the top of this bank.

Then we waited for the moon to come right, so that the first part of the night should be dark. This took several days, but at last we knew that the next night she would not rise until between 9 and 10 o'clock, which would give us nearly two hours of the dense darkness of a moonless Summer night in the South. We had first thought of saving up some rations for the trip, but then reflected that these would be ruined by the filthy water into which we must sink to go under the fence. It was not difficult to abandon the food idea, since it was very hard to force ourselves to lay by even the smallest portion of our scanty rations.

As the next day wore on, our minds were wrought up into exalted tension by the rapid approach of the supreme moment, with all its chances and consequences. The experience of the past few months was not such as to mentally fit us for such a hazard. It prepared us for sullen, uncomplaining endurance, for calmly contemplating the worst that could come; but it did not strengthen that fiber of mind that leads to venturesome activity and daring exploits. Doubtless the weakness of our bodies reacted upon our spirits. We contemplated all the perils that confronted us; perils that, now looming up with impending nearness, took a clearer and more threatening shape than they had ever done before.

We considered the desperate chances of passing the guard unseen; or, if noticed, of escaping his fire without death or severe wounds. But supposing him fortunately evaded, then came the gauntlet of the hounds and the patrols hunting deserters. After this, a long, weary journey, with bare feet and almost naked bodies, through an unknown country abounding with enemies; the dangers of assassination by the embittered populace; the risks of dying with hunger and fatigue in the gloomy depths of a swamp; the scanty hopes that, if we reached the seashore, we could get to our vessels.

Not one of all these contingencies failed to expand itself to all its alarming proportions, and unite with its fellows to form a dreadful vista, like the valleys filled with demons and genii, dragons and malign enchantments, which confront the heros of the "Arabian Nights," when they set out to perform their exploits.

But behind us lay more miseries and horrors than a riotous imagination could conceive; before us could certainly be nothing worse. We would put life and freedom to the hazard of a touch, and win or lose it all.

The day had been intolerably hot. The sun's rays seemed to sear the earth, like heated irons, and the air that lay on the burning sand was broken by wavy lines, such as one sees indicate the radiation from a hot stove.

Except the wretched chain-gang plodding torturously back and forward on the hillside, not a soul nor an animal could be seen in motion outside the Stockade. The hounds were panting in their kennel; the Rebel officers, half or wholly drunken with villainous sorgum whisky, were stretched at full length in the shade at headquarters; the half-caked gunners crouched under the shadow of the embankments of the forts, the guards hung limply over the Stockade in front of their little perches; the thirty thousand boys inside the Stockade, prone or supine upon the glowing sand, gasped for breath—for one draft of sweet, cool, wholesome air that did not bear on its wings the subtle seeds of rank corruption and death. Everywhere was the prostration of discomfort—the inertia of sluggishness.

Only the sick moved; only the pain-racked cried out; only the dying struggled; only the agonies of dissolution could make life assert itself against the exhaustion of the heat.

Harvey and I, lying in the scanty shade of the trunk of a tall pine, and with hearts filled with solicitude as to the outcome of what the evening would bring us, looked out over the scene as we had done daily for long months, and remained silent for hours, until the sun, as if weary with torturing and slaying, began going down in the blazing West. The groans of the thousands of sick around us, the shrieks of the rotting ones in the gangrene wards rang incessantly in our ears.

As the sun disappeared, and the heat abated, the suspended activity was restored. The Master of the Hounds came out with his yelping pack, and started on his rounds; the Rebel officers aroused themselves from their siesta and went lazily about their duties; the fifer produced his cracked fife and piped forth his unvarying "Bonnie Blue Flag," as a signal for dress parade, and drums beaten by unskilled hands in the camps of the different regiments, repeated the signal. In time Stockade the mass of humanity became full of motion as an ant hill, and resembled it very much from our point of view, with the boys threading their way among the burrows, tents and holes.

It was becoming dark quite rapidly. The moments seemed galloping onward toward the time when we must make the decisive step. We drew from the dirty rag in which it was wrapped the little piece of corn bread that we had saved for our supper, carefully divided it into two equal parts, and each took one and ate it in silence. This done, we held a final consultation as to our plans, and went over each detail carefully, that we might fully understand each other under all possible circumstances, and act in concert. One point we laboriously impressed upon each other, and that was; that under no circumstances were we to allow ourselves to be tempted to leave the Creek until we reached its junction with the Flint River. I then picked up two pine leaves, broke them off to unequal lengths, rolled them in my hands behind my back for a second, and presenting them to Harney with their ends sticking out of my closed hand, said:

"The one that gets the longest one goes first."

Harvey reached forth and drew the longer one.

We made a tour of reconnaissance. Everything seemed as usual, and wonderfully calm compared with the tumult in our minds. The Hospital guards were pacing their beats lazily; those on the Stockade were drawling listlessly the first "call around" of the evening:

"Post numbah foah! Half-past seven o'clock! and a-l-l's we-l-ll!"

Inside the Stockade was a Babel of sounds, above all of which rose the melody of religious and patriotic songs, sung in various parts of the camp. From the headquarters came the shouts and laughter of the Rebel officers having a little "frolic" in the cool of the evening. The groans of the sick around us were gradually hushing, as the abatement of the terrible heat let all but the worst cases sink into a brief slumber, from which they awoke before midnight to renew their outcries. But those in the Gangrene wards seemed to be denied even this scanty blessing. Apparently they never slept, for their shrieks never ceased. A multitude of whip-poor-wills in the woods around us began their usual dismal cry, which had never seemed so unearthly and full of dreadful presages as now.

It was, now quite dark, and we stole noiselessly down to the Creek and reconnoitered. We listened. The guard was not pacing his beat, as we could not hear his footsteps. A large, ill-shapen lump against the trunk of one of the trees on the bank showed that he was leaning there resting himself. We watched him for several minutes, but he did not move, and the thought shot into our minds that he might be asleep; but it seemed impossible: it was too early in the evening. Now, if ever, was the opportunity. Harney squeezed my hand, stepped noiselessly into the Creek, laid himself gently down into the filthy water, and while my heart was beating so that I was certain it could be heard some distance from me, began making toward the fence. He passed under easily, and I raised my eyes toward the guard, while on my strained ear fell the soft plashing made by Harvey as he pulled himself cautiously forward. It seemed as if the sentinel must hear this; he could not help it, and every second I expected to see the black lump address itself to motion, and the musket flash out fiendishly. But he did not; the lump remained motionless; the musket silent.

When I thought that Harvey had gained a sufficient distance I followed. It seemed as if the disgusting water would smother me as I laid myself down into it, and such was my agitation that it appeared almost impossible that I should escape making such a noise as would attract the guard's notice. Catching hold of the roots and limbs at the side of the stream, I pulled myself slowly along, and as noiselessly as possible.

I passed under the fence without difficulty, and was outside, and within fifteen feet of the guard. I had lain down into the creek upon my right side, that my face might be toward the guard, and I could watch him closely all the time.

As I came under the fence he was still leaning motionless against the tree, but to my heated imagination he appeared to have turned and be watching me. I hardly breathed; the filthy water rippling past me seemed to roar to attract the guard's attention; I reached my hand out cautiously to grasp a root to pull myself along by, and caught instead a dry branch, which broke with a loud crack. My heart absolutely stood still. The guard evidently heard the noise. The black lump separated itself from the tree, and a straight line which I knew to be his musket separated itself from the lump. In a brief instant I lived a year of mortal apprehension. So certain was I that he had discovered me, and was leveling his piece to fire, that I could scarcely restrain myself from springing up and dashing away to avoid the shot. Then I heard him take a step, and to my unutterable surprise and relief, he walked off farther from the Creek, evidently to speak to the man whose beat joined his.

I pulled away more swiftly, but still with the greatest caution, until after half-an-hour's painful effort I had gotten fully one hundred and fifty yards away from the Hospital fence, and found Harney crouched on a cypress knee, close to the water's edge, watching for me.

We waited there a few minutes, until I could rest, and calm my perturbed nerves down to something nearer their normal equilibrium, and then started on. We hoped that if we were as lucky in our next step as in the first one we would reach the Flint River by daylight, and have a good long start before the morning roll-call revealed our absence. We could hear the hounds still baying in the distance, but this sound was too customary to give us any uneasiness.

But our progress was terribly slow. Every step hurt fearfully. The Creek bed was full of roots and snags, and briers, and vines trailed across it. These caught and tore our bare feet and legs, rendered abnormally tender by the scurvy. It seemed as if every step was marked with blood. The vines tripped us, and we frequently fell headlong. We struggled on determinedly for nearly an hour, and were perhaps a mile from the Hospital.

The moon came up, and its light showed that the creek continued its course through a dense jungle like that we had been traversing, while on the high ground to our left were the open pine woods I have previously described.

We stopped and debated for a few minutes. We recalled our promise to keep in the Creek, the experience of other boys who had tried to escape and been caught by the hounds. If we staid in the Creek we were sure the hounds would not find our trail, but it was equally certain that at this rate we would be exhausted and starved before we got out of sight of the prison. It seemed that we had gone far enough to be out of reach of the packs patrolling immediately around the Stockade, and there could be but little risk in trying a short walk on the dry ground. We concluded to take the chances, and, ascending the bank, we walked and ran as fast as we could for about two miles further.

All at once it struck me that with all our progress the hounds sounded as near as when we started. I shivered at the thought, and though nearly ready to drop with fatigue, urged myself and Harney on.

An instant later their baying rang out on the still night air right behind us, and with fearful distinctness. There was no mistake now; they had found our trail, and were running us down. The change from fearful apprehension to the crushing reality stopped us stock-still in our tracks. At the next breath the hounds came bursting through the woods in plain sight, and in full cry. We obeyed our first impulse; rushed back into the swamp, forced our way for a few yards through the flesh-tearing impediments, until we gained a large cypress, upon whose great knees we climbed—thoroughly exhausted—just as the yelping pack reached the edge of the water, and stopped there and bayed at us. It was a physical impossibility for us to go another step.

In a moment the low-browed villain who had charge of the hounds came galloping up on his mule, tooting signals to his dogs as he came, on the cow-horn slung from his shoulders. He immediately discovered us, covered us with his revolver, and yelled out:

"Come ashore, there, quick: you—— —— —— ——s!"

There was no help for it. We climbed down off the knees and started towards the land. As we neared it, the hounds became almost frantic, and it seemed as if we would be torn to pieces the moment they could reach us. But the master dismounted and drove them back. He was surly — even savage—to us, but seemed in too much hurry to get back to waste any time annoying us with the dogs. He ordered us to get around in front of the mule, and start back to camp. We moved as rapidly as our fatigue and our lacerated feet would allow, and before midnight were again in the hospital, fatigued, filthy, torn, bruised and wretched beyond description or conception.

The next morning we were turned back into the Stockade as punishment.

CHAPTER XLIX.

AUGUST—GOOD LUCK IN NOT MEETING CAPTAIN WIRZ—THAT WORTHY'S TREATMENT OF RECAPTURED PRISONERS—SECRET SOCIETIES IN PRISON— SINGULAR MEETING AND ITS RESULT—DISCOVERY AND REMOVAL OF THE OFFICERS AMONG THE ENLISTED MEN.

Harney and I were specially fortunate in being turned back into the Stockade without being brought before Captain Wirz.

We subsequently learned that we owed this good luck to Wirz's absence on sick leave—his place being supplied by Lieutenant Davis, a moderate brained Baltimorean, and one of that horde of Marylanders in the Rebel Army, whose principal service to the Confederacy consisted in working themselves into "bomb-proof" places, and forcing those whom they displaced into the field. Winder was the illustrious head of this crowd of bomb-proof Rebels from "Maryland, My Maryland!" whose enthusiasm for the Southern cause and consistency in serving it only in such places as were out of range of the Yankee artillery, was the subject of many bitter jibes by the Rebels—especially by those whose secure berths they possessed themselves of.

Lieutenant Davis went into the war with great brashness. He was one of the mob which attacked the Sixth Massachusetts in its passage through Baltimore, but, like all of that class of roughs, he got his stomach full of war as soon as the real business of fighting began, and he retired to where the chances of attaining a ripe old age were better than in front of the Army of the Potomac's muskets. We shall hear of Davis again.

Encountering Captain Wirz was one of the terrors of an abortive attempt to escape. When recaptured prisoners were brought before him he would frequently give way to paroxysms of screaming rage, so violent as to closely verge on insanity. Brandishing the fearful and wonderful revolver—of which I have spoken in such a manner as to threaten the luckless captives with instant death, he would shriek out imprecations, curses; and foul epithets in French, German and English, until he fairly frothed at the mouth. There were plenty of stories current in camp of his having several times given away to his rage so far as to actually shoot men down in these interviews, and still more of his knocking boys down and jumping upon them, until he inflicted injuries that soon resulted in death. How true these rumors were I am unable to say of my own personal knowledge, since I never saw him kill any one, nor have I talked with any one who did. There were a number of cases of this kind testified to upon his trial, but they all happened among "paroles" outside the Stockade, or among the prisoners inside after we left, so I knew nothing of them.

One of the Old Switzer's favorite ways of ending these seances was to inform the boys that he would have them shot in an hour or so, and bid them prepare for death. After keeping them in fearful suspense for hours he would order them to be punished with the stocks, the ball-and-chain, the chain-gang, or—if his fierce mood had burned itself entirely out —as was quite likely with a man of his shallop' brain and vacillating temper—to be simply returned to the stockade. Nothing, I am sure, since the days of the Inquisition—or still later, since the terrible punishments visited upon the insurgents of 1848 by the Austrian aristocrats—has been so diabolical as the stocks and chain-gangs, as used by Wirz. At one time seven men, sitting in the stocks near the Star Fort—in plain view of the camp—became objects of interest to everybody inside. They were never relieved from their painful position, but were kept there until all of them died. I think it was nearly two weeks before the last one succumbed. What they endured in that time even imagination cannot conceive—I do not think that an Indian tribe ever devised keener torture for its captives.

The chain-gang consisted of a number of men—varying from twelve to twenty-five, all chained to one sixty-four pound ball. They were also stationed near the Star Fort, standing out in the hot sun, without a particle of shade over them. When one moved they all had to move. They were scourged with the dysentery, and the necessities of some one of their number kept them constantly in motion. I can see them distinctly yet, tramping laboriously and painfully back and forward over that burning hillside, every moment of the long, weary Summer days.

A comrade writes to remind me of the beneficent work of the Masonic Order. I mention it most gladly, as it was the sole recognition on the part of any of our foes of our claims to human kinship. The churches of all denominations—except the solitary Catholic priest, Father Hamilton, —ignored us as wholly as if we were dumb beasts. Lay humanitarians were equally indifferent, and the only interest manifested by any Rebel in the welfare of any prisoner was by the Masonic brotherhood. The Rebel Masons interested themselves in securing details outside the Stockade in the cookhouse, the commissary, and elsewhere, for the brethren among the prisoners who would accept such favors. Such as did not feel inclined to go outside on parole received frequent presents in the way of food, and especially of vegetables, which were literally beyond price. Materials were sent inside to build tents for the Masons, and I think such as made themselves known before death, received burial according to the rites of the Order. Doctor White, and perhaps other Surgeons, belonged to the fraternity, and the wearing of a Masonic emblem by a new prisoner was pretty sure to catch their eyes, and be the means of securing for the wearer the tender of their good offices, such as a detail into the Hospital as nurse, ward-master, etc.

I was not fortunate enough to be one of the mystic brethren, and so missed all share in any of these benefits, as well as in any others, and I take special pride in one thing: that during my whole imprisonment I was not beholden to a Rebel for a single favor of any kind. The Rebel does not live who can say that he ever gave me so much as a handful of meal, a spoonful of salt, an inch of thread, or a stick of wood. From first to last I received nothing but my rations, except occasional trifles that I succeeded in stealing from the stupid officers charged with issuing rations. I owe no man in the Southern Confederacy gratitude for anything—not even for a kind word.

Speaking of secret society pins recalls a noteworthy story which has been told me since the war, of boys whom I knew. At the breaking out of hostilities there existed in Toledo a festive little secret society, such as lurking boys frequently organize, with no other object than fun and the usual adolescent love of mystery. There were a dozen or so members in it who called themselves "The Royal Reubens," and were headed by a bookbinder named Ned Hopkins. Some one started a branch of the Order in Napoleon, O., and among the members was Charles E. Reynolds, of that town. The badge of the society was a peculiarly shaped gold pin. Reynolds and Hopkins never met, and had no acquaintance with each other. When the war broke out, Hopkins enlisted in Battery H, First Ohio Artillery, and was sent to the Army of the Potomac, where he was captured, in the Fall of 1863, while scouting, in the neighborhood of Richmond. Reynolds entered the Sixty-Eighth Ohio Volunteer Infantry, and was taken in the neighborhood of Jackson, Miss.,—two thousand miles from the place of Hopkins's capture. At Andersonville Hopkins became one of the officers in charge of the Hospital. One day a Rebel Sergeant, who called the roll in the Stockade, after studying Hopkins's pin a minute, said:

"I seed a Yank in the Stockade to-day a-wearing a pin egzackly like that ere."

This aroused Hopkins's interest, and he went inside in search of the other "feller." Having his squad and detachment there was little difficulty in finding him. He recognized the pin, spoke to its wearer, gave him the "grand hailing sign" of the "Royal Reubens," and it was duly responded to. The upshot of the matter was that he took Reynolds out with him as clerk, and saved his life, as the latter was going down hill very rapidly. Reynolds, in turn, secured the detail of a comrade of the Sixty-Eighth who was failing fast, and succeeded in saving his life—all of which happy results were directly attributable to that insignificant boyish society, and its equally unimportant badge of membership.

Along in the last of August the Rebels learned that there were between two and three hundred Captains and Lieutenants in the Stockade, passing themselves off as enlisted men. The motive of these officers was two-fold: first, a chivalrous wish to share the fortunes and fate of their boys, and second, disinclination to gratify the Rebels by the knowledge of the rank of their captives. The secret was so well kept that none of us suspected it until the fact was announced by the Rebels themselves. They were taken out immediately, and sent to Macon, where the commissioned officers' prison was. It would not do to trust such possible leaders with us another day.

CHAPTER L.

FOOD—THE MEAGERNESS, INFERIOR QUALITY, AND TERRIBLE SAMENESS — REBEL TESTIMONY ON THE SUBJECT—FUTILITY OF SUCCESSFUL EXPLANATION.

I have in other places dwelt upon the insufficiency and the nauseousness of the food. No words that I can use, no insistence upon this theme, can give the reader any idea of its mortal importance to us.

Let the reader consider for a moment the quantity, quality, and variety of food that he now holds to be necessary for the maintenance of life and health. I trust that every one who peruses this book—that every one in fact over whom the Stars and Stripes wave—has his cup of coffee, his biscuits and his beefsteak for breakfast—a substantial dinner of roast or boiled—and a lighter, but still sufficient meal in the evening. In all, certainly not less than fifty different articles are set before him during the day, for his choice as elements of nourishment. Let him scan this extended bill-of-fare, which long custom has made so common-place as to be uninteresting—perhaps even wearisome to think about —and see what he could omit from it, if necessity compelled him. After a reluctant farewell to fish, butter, eggs, milk, sugar, green and preserved fruits, etc., he thinks that perhaps under extraordinary circumstances he might be able to merely sustain life for a limited period on a diet of bread and meat three times a day, washed down with creamless, unsweetened coffee, and varied occasionally with additions of potatos, onions, beans, etc. It would astonish the Innocent to have one of our veterans inform him that this was not even the first stage of destitution; that a soldier who had these was expected to be on the summit level of contentment. Any of the boys who followed Grant to Appomattox Court House, Sherman to the Sea, or "Pap" Thomas till his glorious career culminated with the annihilation of Hood, will tell him of many weeks when a slice of fat pork on a piece of "hard tack" had to do duty for the breakfast of beefsteak and biscuits; when another slice of fat pork and another cracker served for the dinner of roast beef and vegetables, and a third cracker and slice of pork was a substitute for the supper of toast and chops.

I say to these veterans in turn that they did not arrive at the first stages of destitution compared with the depths to which we were dragged. The restriction for a few weeks to a diet of crackers and fat pork was certainly a hardship, but the crackers alone, chemists tell us, contain all the elements necessary to support life, and in our Army they were always well made and very palatable. I believe I risk nothing in saying that one of the ordinary square crackers of our Commissary Department contained much more real nutriment than the whole of our average ration.

I have before compared the size, shape and appearance of the daily half loaf of corn bread issued to us to a half-brick, and I do not yet know of a more fitting comparison. At first we got a small piece of rusty bacon along with this; but the size of this diminished steadily until at last it faded away entirely, and during the last six months of our imprisonment I do not believe that we received rations of meat above a half-dozen times.

To this smallness was added ineffable badness. The meal was ground very coarsely, by dull, weakly propelled stones, that imperfectly crushed the grains, and left the tough, hard coating of the kernels in large, sharp, mica-like scales, which cut and inflamed the stomach and intestines, like handfuls of pounded glass. The alimentary canals of all compelled to eat it were kept in a continual state of irritation that usually terminated in incurable dysentery.

That I have not over-stated this evil can be seen by reference to the testimony of so competent a scientific observer as Professor Jones, and I add to that unimpeachable testimony the following extract from the statement made in an attempted defense of Andersonville by Doctor R. Randolph Stevenson, who styles himself, formerly Surgeon in the Army of the Confederate States of America, Chief Surgeon of the Confederate States Military Prison Hospitals, Andersonville, Ga.:

V. From the sameness of the food, and from the action of the poisonous gases in the densely crowded and filthy Stockade and Hospital, the blood was altered in its constitution, even, before the manifestation of actual disease.

In both the well and the sick, the red corpuscles were diminished; and in all diseases uncomplicated with inflammation, the fibrinous element was deficient. In cases of ulceration of the mucous membrane of the intestinal canal, the fibrinous element of the blood appeared to be increased; while in simple diarrhea, uncomplicated with ulceration, and dependent upon the character of the food and the existence of scurvy, it was either diminished or remained stationary. Heart-clots were very common, if not universally present, in the cases of ulceration of the intestinal mucous membrane; while in the uncomplicated cases of diarrhea and scurvy, the blood was fluid and did not coagulate readily, and the heart-clots and fibrinous concretions were almost universally absent. From the watery condition of the blood there resulted various serous effusions into the pericardium, into the ventricles of the brain, and into the abdominal cavity. In almost all cases which I examined after death, even in the most emaciated, there was more or less serous effusion into the abdominal cavity. In cases of hospital gangrene of the extremities, and in cases of gangrene of the intestines, heart-clots and firm coagula were universally present. The presence of these clots in the cases of hospital gangrene, whilst they were absent in the cases in which there were no inflammatory symptoms, appears to sustain the conclusion that hospital gangrene is a species of inflammation (imperfect and irregular though it may be in its progress), in which the fibrinous element and coagulability of the blood are increased, even in those who are suffering from such a condition of the blood and from such diseases as are naturally accompanied with a decrease in the fibrinous constituent.

VI. The impoverished condition of the blood, which led to serous effusions within the ventricles of the brain, and around the brain and spinal cord, and into the pericardial and abdominal cavities, was gradually induced by the action of several causes, but chiefly by the character of the food.

The Federal prisoners, as a general rule, had been reared upon wheat bread and Irish potatos; and the Indian corn so extensively used at the South, was almost unknown to them as an article of diet previous to their capture. Owing to the impossibility of obtaining the necessary sieves in the Confederacy for the separation of the husk from the corn-meal, the rations of the Confederate soldiers, as well as of the Federal prisoners, consisted of unbolted corn-flour, and meal and grist; this circumstance rendered the corn-bread still more disagreeable and distasteful to the Federal prisoners. While Indian meal, even when prepared with the husk, is one of the most wholesome and nutritious forms of food, as has been already shown by the health and rapid increase of the Southern population, and especially of the negros, previous to the present war, and by the strength, endurance and activity of the Confederate soldiers, who were throughout the war confined to a great extent to unbolted corn-meal; it is nevertheless true that those who have not been reared upon corn-meal, or who have not accustomed themselves to its use gradually, become excessively tired of this kind of diet when suddenly confined to it without a due proportion of wheat bread. Large numbers of the Federal prisoners appeared to be utterly disgusted with Indian corn, and immense piles of corn-bread could be seen in the Stockade and Hospital inclosures. Those who were so disgusted with this form of food that they had no appetite to partake of it, except in quantities insufficient to supply the waste of the tissues, were, of course, in the condition of men slowly starving, notwithstanding that the only farinaceous form of food which the Confederate States produced in sufficient abundance for the maintenance of armies was not withheld from them. In such cases, an urgent feeling of hunger was not a prominent symptom; and even when it existed at first, it soon disappeared, and was succeeded by an actual loathing of food. In this state the muscular strength was rapidly diminished, the tissues wasted, and the thin, skeleton-like forms moved about with the appearance of utter exhaustion and dejection. The mental condition connected with long confinement, with the most miserable surroundings, and with no hope for the future, also depressed all the nervous and vital actions, and was especially active in destroying the appetite. The effects of mental depression, and of defective nutrition, were manifested not only in the slow, feeble motions of the wasted, skeleton-like forms, but also in such lethargy, listlessness, and torpor of the mental faculties as rendered these unfortunate men oblivious and indifferent to their afflicted condition. In many cases, even of the greatest apparent suffering and distress, instead of showing any anxiety to communicate the causes of their distress, or to relate their privations, and their longings for their homes and their friends and relatives, they lay in a listless, lethargic, uncomplaining state, taking no notice either of their own distressed condition, or of the gigantic mass of human misery by which they were surrounded. Nothing appalled and depressed me so much as this silent, uncomplaining misery. It is a fact of great interest, that notwithstanding this defective nutrition in men subjected to crowding and filth, contagious fevers were rare; and typhus fever, which is supposed to be generated in just such a state of things as existed at Andersonville, was unknown. These facts, established by my investigations, stand in striking contrast with such a statement as the following by a recent English writer:

"A deficiency of food, especially of the nitrogenous part, quickly leads to the breaking up of the animal frame. Plague, pestilence and famine are associated with each other in the public mind, and the records of every country show how closely they are related. The medical history of Ireland is remarkable for the illustrations of how much mischief may be occasioned by a general deficiency of food. Always the habitat of fever, it every now and then becomes the very hot-bed of its propagation and development. Let there be but a small failure in the usual imperfect supply of food, and the lurking seeds of pestilence are ready to burst into frightful activity. The famine of the present century is but too forcible and illustrative of this. It fostered epidemics which have not been witnessed in this generation, and gave rise to scenes of devastation and misery which are not surpassed by the most appalling epidemics of the Middle Ages. The principal form of the scourge was known as the contagious famine fever (typhus), and it spread, not merely from end to end of the country in which it had originated, but, breaking through all boundaries, it crossed the broad ocean, and made itself painfully manifest in localities where it was previously unknown. Thousands fell under the virulence of its action, for wherever it came it struck down a seventh of the people, and of those whom it attacked, one out of nine perished. Even those who escaped the fatal influence of it, were left the miserable victims of scurvy and low fever."

While we readily admit that famine induces that state of the system which is the most susceptible to the action of fever poisons, and thus induces the state of the entire population which is most favorable for the rapid and destructive spread of all contagious fevers, at the same time we are forced by the facts established by the present war, as well as by a host of others, both old and new, to admit that we are still ignorant of the causes necessary for the origin of typhus fever. Added to the imperfect nature of the rations issued to the Federal prisoners, the difficulties of their situation were at times greatly increased by the sudden and desolating Federal raids in Virginia, Georgia, and other States, which necessitated the sudden transportation from Richmond and other points threatened of large bodies of prisoners, without the possibility of much previous preparation; and not only did these men suffer in transition upon the dilapidated and overburdened line of railroad communication, but after arriving at Andersonville, the rations were frequently insufficient to supply the sudden addition of several thousand men. And as the Confederacy became more and more pressed, and when powerful hostile armies were plunging through her bosom, the Federal prisoners of Andersonville suffered incredibly during the hasty removal to Millen, Savannah, Charleston, and other points, supposed at the time to be secure from the enemy. Each one of these causes must be weighed when an attempt is made to estimate the unusual mortality among these prisoners of war.

VII. Scurvy, arising from sameness of food and imperfect nutrition, caused, either directly or indirectly, nine-tenths of the deaths among the Federal prisoners at Andersonville.

Not only were the deaths referred to unknown causes, to apoplexy, to anasarca, and to debility, traceable to scurvy and its effects; and not only was the mortality in small-pox, pneumonia, and typhoid fever, and in all acute diseases, more than doubled by the scorbutic taint, but even those all but universal and deadly bowel affections arose from the same causes, and derived their fatal character from the same conditions which produced the scurvy. In truth, these men at Andersonville were in the condition of a crew at sea, confined in a foul ship upon salt meat and unvarying food, and without fresh vegetables. Not only so, but these unfortunate prisoners were men forcibly confined and crowded upon a ship tossed about on a stormy ocean, without a rudder, without a compass, without a guiding-star, and without any apparent boundary or to their voyage; and they reflected in their steadily increasing miseries the distressed condition and waning fortunes of devastated and bleeding country, which was compelled, in justice to her own unfortunate sons, to hold these men in the most distressing captivity.

I saw nothing in the scurvy which prevailed so universally at Andersonville, at all different from this disease as described by various standard writers. The mortality was no greater than that which has afflicted a hundred ships upon long voyages, and it did not exceed the mortality which has, upon me than one occasion, and in a much shorter period of time, annihilated large armies and desolated beleaguered cities. The general results of my investigations upon the chronic diarrhea and dysentery of the Federal prisoners of Andersonville were similar to those of the English surgeons during the war against Russia.

IX. Drugs exercised but little influence over the progress and fatal termination of chronic diarrhea and dysentery in the Military Prison and Hospital at Andersonville, chiefly because the proper form of nourishment (milk, rice, vegetables, anti-scorbutics, and nourishing animal and vegetable soups) was not issued, and could not be procured in sufficient quantities for the sick prisoners.

Opium allayed pain and checked the bowels temporarily, but the frail dam was soon swept away, and the patient appears to be but little better, if not the worse, for this merely palliative treatment. The root of the difficulty could not be reached by drugs; nothing short of the wanting elements of nutrition would have tended in any manner to restore the tone of the digestive system, and of all the wasted and degenerated organs and tissues. My opinion to this effect was expressed most decidedly to the medical officers in charge of these unfortunate men. The correctness of this view was sustained by the healthy and robust condition of the paroled prisoners, who received an extra ration, and who were able to make considerable sums by trading, and who supplied themselves with a liberal and varied diet.

X. The fact that hospital gangrene appeared in the Stockade first, and originated spontaneously, without any previous contagion, and occurred sporadically all over the Stockade and Prison Hospital, was proof positive that this disease will arise whenever the conditions of crowding, filth, foul air, and bad diet are present.

The exhalations from the Hospital and Stockade appeared to exert their effects to a considerable distance outside of these localities. The origin of gangrene among these prisoners appeared clearly to depend in great measure upon the state of the general system, induced by diet, exposure, neglect of personal cleanliness; and by various external noxious influences. The rapidity of the appearance and action of the gangrene depended upon the powers and state of the constitution, as well as upon the intensity of the poison in the atmosphere, or upon the direct application of poisonous matter to the wounded surface. This was further illustrated by the important fact, that hospital gangrene, or a disease resembling this form of gangrene, attacked the intestinal canal of patients laboring under ulceration of the bowels, although there were no local manifestations of gangrene upon the surface of the body. This mode of termination in cases of dysentery was quite common in the foul atmosphere of the Confederate States Military Prison Hospital; and in the depressed, depraved condition of the system of these Federal prisoners, death ensued very rapidly after the gangrenous state of the intestines was established.

XI. A scorbutic condition of the system appeared to favor the origin of foul ulcers, which frequently took on true hospital gangrene.
Scurvy and gangrene frequently existed in the same individual. In such cases, vegetable diet with vegetable acids would remove the scorbutic condition without curing the hospital gangrene. . .
Scurvy consists not only in an alteration in the constitution of the blood, which leads to passive hemorrhages from the bowels, and the effusion into the various tissues of a deeply-colored fibrinous exudation; but, as we have conclusively shown by postmortem examination, this state is attended with consistence of the muscles of the heart, and the mucous membrane of the alimentary canal, and of solid parts generally. We have, according to the extent of the deficiency of certain articles of food, every degree of scorbutic derangement, from the most fearful depravation of the blood and the perversion of every function subserved by the blood to those slight derangements which are scarcely distinguishable from a state of health. We are as yet ignorant of the true nature of the changes of the blood and tissues in scurvy, and wide field for investigation is open for the determination the characteristic changes—physical, chemical, and physiological—of the blood and tissues, and of the secretions and excretions of scurvy. Such inquiries would be of great value in their bearing upon the origin of hospital gangrene. Up to the present war, the results of chemical investigations upon the pathology of the blood in scurvy were not only contradictory, but meager, and wanting in that careful detail of the cases from which the blood was abstracted which would enable us to explain the cause of the apparent discrepancies in different analyses. Thus it is not yet settled whether the fibrin is increased or diminished in this disease; and the differences which exist in the statements of different writers appear to be referable to the neglect of a critical examination and record of all the symptoms of the cases from which the blood was abstracted. The true nature of the changes of the blood in scurvy can be established only by numerous analyses during different stages of the disease, and followed up by carefully performed and recorded postmortem examinations. With such data we could settle such important questions as whether the increase of fibrin in scurvy was invariably dependent upon some local inflammation.
XII. Gangrenous spots, followed by rapid destruction of tissue, appeared in some cases in which there had been no previous or existing wound or abrasion; and without such well established facts, it might be assumed that the disease was propagated from one patient to another in every case, either by exhalations from the gangrenous surface or by direct contact.
In such a filthy and crowded hospital as that of the Confederate, States Military Prison of Camp Sumter, Andersonville, it was impossible to isolate the wounded from the sources of actual contact of the gangrenous matter. The flies swarming over the wounds and over filth of every

description; the filthy, imperfectly washed, and scanty rags; the limited number of sponges and wash-bowls (the same wash-bowl and sponge serving for a score or more of patients), were one and all sources of such constant circulation of the gangrenous matter, that the disease might rapidly be propagated from a single gangrenous wound. While the fact already considered, that a form of moist gangrene, resembling hospital gangrene, was quite common in this foul atmosphere in cases of dysentery, both with and without the existence of hospital gangrene upon the surface, demonstrates the dependence of the disease upon the state of the constitution, and proves in a clear manner that neither the contact of the poisonous matter of gangrene, nor the direct action of the poisoned atmosphere upon the ulcerated surface, is necessary to the development of the disease; on the other hand, it is equally well-established that the disease may be communicated by the various ways just mentioned. It is impossible to determine the length of time which rags and clothing saturated with gangrenous matter will retain the power of reproducing the disease when applied to healthy wounds. Professor Brugmans, as quoted by Guthrie in his commentaries on the surgery of the war in Portugal, Spain, France, and the Netherlands, says that in 1797, in Holland, 'charpie,' composed of linen threads cut of different lengths, which, on inquiry, it was found had been already used in the great hospitals in France, and had been subsequently washed and bleached, caused every ulcer to which it was applied to be affected by hospital gangrene. Guthrie affirms in the same work, that the fact that this disease was readily communicated by the application of instruments, lint, or bandages which had been in contact with infected parts, was too firmly established by the experience of every one in Portugal and Spain to be a matter of doubt. There are facts to show that flies may be the means of communicating malignant pustules. Dr. Wagner, who has related several cases of malignant pustule produced in man and beasts, both by contact and by eating the flesh of diseased animals, which happened in the village of Striessa in Saxony, in 1834, gives two very remarkable cases which occurred eight days after any beast had been affected with the disease. Both were women, one of twenty-six and the other of fifty years, and in them the pustules were well marked, and the general symptoms similar to the other cases. The latter patient said she had been bitten by a fly upon the back d the neck, at which part the carbuncle appeared; and the former, that she had also been bitten upon the right upper arm by a gnat. Upon inquiry, Wagner found that the skin of one of the infected beasts had been hung on a neighboring wall, and thought it very possible that the insects might have been attracted to them by the smell, and had thence conveyed the poison.

[End of Dr. Stevenson's Statement]

....

The old adage says that "Hunger is the best sauce for poor food," but hunger failed to render this detestable stuff palatable, and it became so loathsome that very many actually starved to death because unable to force their organs of deglutition to receive the nauseous dose and pass it to the stomach. I was always much healthier than the average of the boys, and my appetite consequently much better, yet for the last month that I was in Andersonville, it required all my determination to crowd the bread down my throat, and, as I have stated before, I could only do this by breaking off small bits at a time, and forcing each down as I would a pill.

A large part of this repulsiveness was due to the coarseness and foulness of the meal, the wretched cooking, and the lack of salt, but there was a still more potent reason than all these. Nature does not intend that man shall live by bread alone, nor by any one kind of food. She indicates this by the varying tastes and longings that she gives him. If his body needs one kind of constituents, his tastes lead him to desire the food that is richest in those constituents. When he has taken as much as his system requires, the sense of satiety supervenes, and he "becomes tired" of that particular food. If tastes are not perverted, but allowed a free but temperate exercise, they are the surest indicators of the way to preserve health and strength by a judicious selection of alimentation.

In this case Nature was protesting by a rebellion of the tastes against any further use of that species of food. She was saying, as plainly as she ever spoke, that death could only be averted by a change of diet, which would supply our bodies with the constituents they so sadly needed, and which could not be supplied by corn meal.

How needless was this confinement of our rations to corn meal, and especially to such wretchedly prepared meal, is conclusively shown by the Rebel testimony heretofore given. It would have been very little extra trouble to the Rebels to have had our meal sifted; we would gladly have done it ourselves if allowed the utensils and opportunity. It would have been as little trouble to have varied our rations with green corn and sweet potatos, of which the country was then full.

A few wagon loads of roasting ears and sweet potatos would have banished every trace of scurvy from the camp, healed up the wasting dysentery, and saved thousands of lives. Any day that the Rebels had chosen they could have gotten a thousand volunteers who would have given their solemn parole not to escape, and gone any distance into the country, to gather the potatos and corn, and such other vegetables as were readily obtainable, and bring, them into the camp. Whatever else may be said in defense of the Southern management of military prisons, the permitting seven thousand men to die of the scurvy in the Summer time, in the midst of an agricultural region, filled with all manner of green vegetation, must forever remain impossible of explanation.

CHAPTER LI.

SOLICITUDE AS TO THE FATE OF ATLANTA AND SHERMAN'S ARMY—PAUCITY OF NEWS —HOW WE HEARD THAT ATLANTA HAD FALLEN—ANNOUNCEMENT OF A GENERAL EXCHANGE—WE LEAVE ANDERSONVILLE.

We again began to be exceedingly solicitous over the fate of Atlanta and Sherman's Army: we had heard but little directly from that front for several weeks. Few prisoners had come in since those captured in the bloody engagements of the 20th, 22d, and 28th of July. In spite of their confident tones, and our own sanguine hopes, the outlook admitted of very grave doubts. The battles of the last week of July had been looked at it in the best light possible—indecisive. Our men had held their own, it is true, but an invading army can not afford to simply hold its own. Anything short of an absolute success is to it disguised defeat. Then we knew that the cavalry column sent out under Stoneman had been so badly handled by that inefficient commander that it had failed ridiculously in its object, being beaten in detail, and suffering the loss of its commander and a considerable portion of its numbers. This had been followed by a defeat of our infantry at Etowah Creek, and then came a long interval in which we received no news save what the Rebel papers contained, and they pretended no doubt that Sherman's failure was already demonstrated. Next came well-authenticated news that Sherman had raised the siege and fallen back to the Chattahoochee, and we felt something of the bitterness of despair. For days thereafter we heard nothing, though the hot, close Summer air seemed surcharged with the premonitions of a war storm about to burst, even as nature heralds in the same way a concentration of the mighty force of the elements for the grand crash of the thunderstorm. We waited in tense expectancy for the decision of the fates whether final victory or defeat should end the long and arduous campaign.

At night the guards in the perches around the Stockade called out every half hour, so as to show the officers that they were awake and attending to their duty. The formula for this ran thus:

"Post numbah 1; half-past eight o'clock, and a-l-l 's w-e-l-l!"

Post No. 2 repeated this cry, and so it went around.

One evening when our anxiety as to Atlanta was wrought to the highest pitch, one of the guards sang out:

"Post numbah foah—half past eight o'clock—and Atlanta's—gone—t-o —hell."

The heart of every man within hearing leaped to his mouth. We looked toward each other, almost speechless with glad surprise, and then gasped out:

"Did 'you hear THAT?"

The next instant such a ringing cheer burst out as wells spontaneously from the throats and hearts of men, in the first ecstatic moments of victory—a cheer to which our saddened hearts and enfeebled lungs had long been strangers. It was the genuine, honest, manly Northern cheer, as different from the shrill Rebel yell as the honest mastiff's deep-voiced welcome is from the howl of the prowling wolf.

The shout was taken up all over the prison. Even those who had not heard the guard understood that it meant that "Atlanta was ours and fairly won," and they took up the acclamation with as much enthusiasm as we had begun it. All thoughts of sleep were put to flight: we would have a season of rejoicing. Little knots gathered together, debated the news, and indulged in the most sanguine hopes as to the effect upon the Rebels. In some parts of the Stockade stump speeches were made. I believe that Boston Corbett and his party organized a prayer and praise meeting. In our corner we stirred up our tuneful friend "Nosey," who sang again the grand old patriotic hymns that set our thin blood to bounding, and made us remember that we were still Union soldiers, with higher hopes than that of starving and dying in Andersonville. He sang the ever-glorious Star Spangled Banner, as he used to sing it around the camp fire in happier days, when we were in the field. He sang the rousing "Rally Round the Flag," with its wealth of patriotic fire and martial vigor, and we, with throats hoarse from shouting; joined in the chorus until the welkin rang again.

The Rebels became excited, lest our exaltation of spirits would lead to an assault upon the Stockade. They got under arms, and remained so until the enthusiasm became less demonstrative.

A few days later—on the evening of the 6th of September—the Rebel Sergeants who called the roll entered the Stockade, and each assembling his squads, addressed them as follows: "PRISONERS: I am instructed by General Winder to inform you that a general exchange has been agreed upon. Twenty thousand men will be exchanged immediately at Savannah, where your vessels are now waiting for you. Detachments from One to Ten will prepare to leave early to-morrow morning."

The excitement that this news produced was simply indescribable. I have seen men in every possible exigency that can confront men, and a large proportion viewed that which impended over them with at least outward composure. The boys around me had endured all that we suffered with stoical firmness. Groans from pain-racked bodies could not be repressed, and bitter curses and maledictions against the Rebels leaped unbidden to the lips at the slightest occasion, but there was no murmuring or whining. There was not a day—hardly an hour—in which one did not see such exhibitions of manly fortitude as made him proud of belonging to a race of which every individual was a hero.

But the emotion which pain and suffering and danger could not develop, joy could, and boys sang, and shouted and cried, and danced as if in a delirium. "God's country," fairer than the sweet promised land of Canaan appeared to the rapt vision of the Hebrew poet prophet, spread out in glad vista before the mind's eye of every one. It had come—at last it had come that which we had so longed for, wished for, prayed for, dreamed of; schemed, planned, toiled for, and for which went up the last earnest, dying wish of the thousands of our comrades who would now know no exchange save into that eternal "God's country" where

Sickness and sorrow, pain and death
Are felt and feared no more.

Our "preparations," for leaving were few and simple. When the morning came, and shortly after the order to move, Andrews and I picked our well-worn blanket, our tattered overcoat, our rude chessmen, and no less rude board, our little black can, and the spoon made of hoop-iron, and bade farewell to the hole-in-the-ground that had been our home for nearly seven long months. My feet were still in miserable condition from the lacerations received in the attempt to escape, but I took one of our tent poles as a staff and hobbled away. We re-passed the gates which we had entered on that February night, ages since, it seemed, and crawled slowly over to the depot. I had come to regard the Rebels around us as such measureless liars that my first impulse was to believe the reverse of anything they said to us; and even now, while I hoped for the best, my old habit of mind was so strongly upon me that I had some doubts of our going to be exchanged, simply because it was a Rebel who had said so. But in the crowd of Rebels who stood close to the road upon which we were walking was a young Second Lieutenant, who said to a Colonel as I passed:

"Weil, those fellows can sing 'Homeward Bound,' can't they?"

This set my last misgiving at rest. Now I was certain that we were going to be exchanged, and my spirits soared to the skies.

Entering the cars we thumped and pounded toilsomely along, after the manner of Southern railroads, at the rate of six or eight miles an hour. Savannah was two hundred and forty miles away, and to our impatient minds it seemed as if we would never get there. The route lay the whole distance through the cheerless pine barrens which cover the greater part of Georgia. The only considerable town on the way was Macon, which had then a population of five thousand or thereabouts. For scores of miles there would not be a sign of a human habitation, and in the one hundred and eighty miles between Macon and Savannah there were only three insignificant villages. There was a station every ten miles, at which the only building was an open shed, to shelter from sun and rain a casual passenger, or a bit of goods.

The occasional specimens of the poor white "cracker" population that we saw, seemed indigenous products of the starved soil. They suited their poverty-stricken surroundings as well as the gnarled and scrubby vegetation suited the sterile sand. Thin-chested, round-shouldered, scraggy-bearded, dull-eyed and open-mouthed, they all looked alike—all looked as ignorant, as stupid, and as lazy as they were poor and weak. They were "low-downers" in every respect, and made our rough and simple. minded East Tennesseans look like models of elegant and cultured gentlemen in contrast.

We looked on the poverty-stricken land with good-natured contempt, for we thought we were leaving it forever, and would soon be in one which, compared to it, was as the fatness at Egypt to the leanness of the desert of Sinai.

The second day after leaving Andersonville our train struggled across the swamps into Savannah, and rolled slowly down the live oak shaded streets into the center of the City. It seemed like another Deserted Village, so vacant and noiseless the streets, and the buildings everywhere so overgrown with luxuriant vegetation: The limbs of the shade trees crashed along and broke, upon the tops of our cars, as if no train had passed that way for years. Through the interstices between the trees and clumps of foliage could be seen the gleaming white marble of the monuments erected to Greene and Pulaski, looking like giant tombstones in a City of the Dead. The unbroken stillness—so different from what we expected on entering the metropolis of Georgia, and a City that was an important port in Revolutionary days—became absolutely oppressive. We could not understand it, but our thoughts were more intent upon the coming transfer to our flag than upon any speculation as to the cause of the remarkable somnolence of Savannah.

Finally some little boys straggled out to where our car was standing, and we opened up a conversation with them:

"Say, boys, are our vessels down in the harbor yet?"

The reply came in that piercing treble shriek in which a boy of ten or twelve makes even his most confidential communications:

"I don't know."

"Well," (with our confidence in exchange somewhat dashed,) "they intend to exchange us here, don't they?"

Another falsetto scream, "I don't know."

"Well," (with something of a quaver in the questioner's voice,) "what are they going to do, with us, any way?"

"O," (the treble shriek became almost demoniac) "they are fixing up a place over by the old jail for you."

What a sinking of hearts was there then! Andrews and I would not give up hope so speedily as some others did, and resolved to believe, for awhile at least, that we were going to be exchanged. Ordered out of the cars, we were marched along the street. A crowd of small boys, full of the curiosity of the animal, gathered around us as we marched. Suddenly a door in a rather nice house opened; an angry-faced woman appeared on the steps and shouted out:

"Boys! BOYS! What are you doin' there! Come up on the steps immejitely! Come away from them n-a-s-t-y things!"

I will admit that we were not prepossessing in appearance; nor were we as cleanly as young gentlemen should habitually be; in fact, I may as well confess that I would not now, if I could help it, allow a tramp, as dilapidated in raiment, as unwashed, unshorn, uncombed, and populous with insects as we were, to come within several rods of me. Nevertheless, it was not pleasant to hear so accurate a description of our personal appearance sent forth on the wings of the wind by a shrill-voiced Rebel female.

A short march brought us to the place "they were fixing for us by the old jail." It was another pen, with high walls of thick pine plank, which told us only too plainly how vain were our expectations of exchange.

When we were turned inside, and I realized that the gates of another prison had closed upon me, hope forsook me. I flung our odious little possessions-our can, chess-board, overcoat, and blanket-upon the ground, and, sitting down beside them, gave way to the bitterest despair. I wanted to die, O, so badly. Never in all my life had I desired anything in the world so much as I did now to get out of it. Had I had pistol, knife, rope, or poison, I would have ended my prison life then and there, and departed with the unceremoniousness of a French leave. I remembered that I could get a quietus from a guard with very little trouble, but I would not give one of the bitterly hated Rebels the triumph of shooting me. I longed to be another Samson, with the whole Southern Confederacy gathered in another Temple of Dagon, that I might pull down the supporting pillars, and die happy in slaying thousands of my enemies.

While I was thus sinking deeper and deeper in the Slough of Despond, the firing of a musket, and the shriek of the man who was struck, attracted my attention. Looking towards the opposite end of the pen I saw a guard bringing his still smoking musket to a "recover arms," and, not fifteen feet from him, a prisoner lying on the ground in the agonies of death. The latter had a pipe in his mouth when he was shot, and his teeth still clenched its stem. His legs and arms were drawn up convulsively, and he was rocking backward and forward on his back. The charge had struck him just above the hip-bone.

The Rebel officer in command of the guard was sitting on his horse inside the pen at the time, and rode forward to see what the matter was. Lieutenant Davis, who had come with us from Andersonville, was also sitting on a horse inside the prison, and he called out in his usual harsh, disagreeable voice:

"That's all right, Cunnel; the man's done just as I awdahed him to."

I found that lying around inside were a number of bits of plank—each about five feet long, which had been sawed off by the carpenters engaged in building the prison. The ground being a bare common, was destitute of all shelter, and the pieces looked as if they would be quite useful in building a tent. There may have been an order issued forbidding the prisoners to touch them, but if so, I had not heard it, and I imagine the first intimation to the prisoner just killed that the boards were not to be taken was the bullet which penetrated his vitals. Twenty-five cents would be a liberal appraisement of the value of the lumber for which the boy lost his life.

Half an hour afterward we thought we saw all the guards march out of the front gate. There was still another pile of these same kind of pieces of board lying at the further side of the prison. The crowd around me noticed it, and we all made a rush for it. In spite of my lame feet I outstripped the rest, and was just in the act of stooping down to pick the boards up when a loud yell from those behind startled me. Glancing to my left I saw a guard cocking his gun and bringing it up to shoot me. With one frightened spring, as quick as a flash, and before he could cover me, I landed fully a rod back in the crowd, and mixed with it. The fellow tried hard to draw a bead on me, but I was too quick for him, and he finally lowered his gun with an oath expressive of disappointment in not being able to kill a Yankee.

Walking back to my place the full ludicrousness of the thing dawned upon me so forcibly that I forgot all about my excitement and scare, and laughed aloud. Here, not an hour age I was murmuring because I could find no way to die; I sighed for death as a bridegroom for the coming of his bride, an yet, when a Rebel had pointed his gun at me, it had nearly scared me out of a year's growth, and made me jump farther than I could possibly do when my feet were well, and I was in good condition otherwise.

CHAPTER LII.

SAVANNAH—DEVICES TO OBTAIN MATERIALS FOR A TENT—THEIR ULTIMATE SUCCESS —RESUMPTION OF TUNNELING—ESCAPING BY WHOLESALE AND BEING RECAPTURED EN MASSE—THE OBSTACLES THAT LAY BETWEEN US AND OUR LINES.

Andrews and I did not let the fate of the boy who was killed, nor my own narrow escape from losing the top of my head, deter us from farther efforts to secure possession of those coveted boards. My readers remember the story of the boy who, digging vigorously at a hole, replied to the remark of a passing traveler that there was probably no ground-hog there, and, even if there was, "ground-hog was mighty poor eatin', any way," with:

"Mister, there's got to be a ground-hog there; our family's out o' meat!"

That was what actuated us: we were out of material for a tent. Our solitary blanket had rotted and worn full of holes by its long double duty, as bed-clothes and tent at Andersonville, and there was an imperative call for a substitute.

Andrews and I flattered ourselves that when we matched our collective or individual wits against those of a Johnny his defeat was pretty certain, and with this cheerful estimate of our own powers to animate us, we set to work to steal the boards from under the guard's nose. The Johnny had malice in his heart and buck-and-ball in his musket, but his eyes were not sufficiently numerous to adequately discharge all the duties laid upon him. He had too many different things to watch at the same time. I would approach a gap in the fence not yet closed as if I intended making a dash through it for liberty, and when the Johnny had concentrated all his attention on letting me have the contents of his gun just as soon as he could have a reasonable excuse for doing so, Andrews would pick u a couple of boards and slip away with them. Then I would fall back in pretended (and some real) alarm, and—Andrew would come up and draw his attention by a similar feint, while I made off with a couple more pieces. After a few hours c this strategy, we found ourselves the possessors of some dozen planks, with which we made a lean-to, that formed a tolerable shelter for our heads and the upper portion of our bodies. As the boards were not over five feet long, and the slope reduce the sheltered space to about four-and-one-half feet, it left the lower part of our naked feet and legs to project out-of-doors. Andrews used to lament very touchingly the sunburning his toe-nails were receiving. He knew that his complexion was being ruined for life, and all the Balm of a Thousand Flowers in the world would not restore his comely ankles to that condition of pristine loveliness which would admit of their introduction into good society again. Another defect was that, like the fun in a practical joke, it was all on one side; there was not enough of it to go clear round. It was very unpleasant, when a storm came up in a direction different from that we had calculated upon, to be compelled to get out in the midst of it, and build our house over to face the other way.

Still we had a tent, and were that much better off than three-fourths of our comrades who had no shelter at all. We were owners of a brown stone front on Fifth Avenue compared to the other fellows.

Our tent erected, we began a general survey of our new abiding place. The ground was a sandy common in the outskirts of Savannah. The sand was covered with a light sod. The Rebels, who knew nothing of our burrowing propensities, had neglected to make the plank forming the walls of the Prison project any distance below the surface of the ground, and had put up no Dead Line around the inside; so that it looked as if everything was arranged expressly to invite us to tunnel out. We were not the boys to neglect such an invitation. By night about three thousand had been received from Andersonville, and placed inside. When morning came it looked as if a colony of gigantic rats had been at work. There was a tunnel every ten or fifteen feet, and at least twelve hundred of us had gone out through them during the night. I never understood why all in the pen did not follow our example, and leave the guards watching a forsaken Prison. There was nothing to prevent it. An hour's industrious work with a half-canteen would take any one outside, or if a boy was too lazy to dig his own tunnel, he could have the use of one of the hundred others that had been dug.

But escaping was only begun when the Stockade was passed. The site of Savannah is virtually an island. On the north is the Savannah River; to the east, southeast and south, are the two Ogeechee rivers, and a chain of sounds and lagoons connecting with the Atlantic Ocean. To the west is a canal connecting the Savannah and Big Ogeechee Rivers. We found ourselves headed off by water whichever way we went. All the bridges were guarded, and all the boats destroyed. Early in the morning the Rebels discovered our absence, and the whole garrison of Savannah was sent out on patrol after us. They picked up the boys in squads of from ten to thirty, lurking around the shores of the streams waiting for night to come, to get across, or engaged in building rafts for transportation. By evening the whole mob of us were back in the pen again. As nobody was punished for running away, we treated the whole affair as a lark, and those brought back first stood around the gate and yelled derisively as the others came in.

That night big fires were built all around the Stockade, and a line of guards placed on the ground inside of these. In spite of this precaution, quite a number escaped. The next day a Dead Line was put up inside of the Prison, twenty feet from the Stockade. This only increased the labor of burrowing, by making us go farther. Instead of being able to tunnel out in an hour, it now took three or four hours. That night several hundred of us, rested from our previous performance, and hopeful of better luck, brought our faithful half canteens—now scoured very bright by constant use-into requisition again, and before the morning. dawned we had gained the high reeds of the swamps, where we lay concealed until night.

In this way we managed to evade the recapture that came to most of those who went out, but it was a fearful experience. Having been raised in a country where venomous snakes abounded, I had that fear and horror of them that inhabitants of those districts feel, and of which people living in sections free from such a scourge know little. I fancied that the Southern swamps were filled with all forms of loathsome and poisonous reptiles, and it required all my courage to venture into them barefooted. Besides, the snags and roots hurt our feet fearfully. Our hope was to find a boat somewhere, in which we could float out to sea, and trust to being picked up by some of the blockading fleet. But no boat could we find, with all our painful and diligent search. We learned afterward that the Rebels made a practice of breaking up all the boats along the shore to prevent negros and their own deserters from escaping to the blockading fleet. We thought of making a raft of logs, but had we had the strength to do this, we would doubtless have thought it too risky, since we dreaded missing the vessels, and being carried out to sea to perish of hunger. During the night we came to the railroad bridge across the Ogeechee. We had some slender hope that, if we could reach this we might perhaps get across the river, and find better opportunities for escape. But these last expectations were blasted by the discovery that it was guarded. There was a post and a fire on the shore next us, and a single guard with a lantern was stationed on one of the middle spans. Almost famished with hunger, and so weary and footsore that we could scarcely move another step, we went back to a cleared place on the high ground, and laid down to sleep, entirely reckless as to what became of us. Late in the morning we were awakened by the Rebel patrol and taken back to the prison. Lieutenant Davis, disgusted with the perpetual attempts to escape, moved the Dead Line out forty feet from the Stockade; but this restricted our room greatly, since the number of prisoners in the pen had now risen to about six thousand, and, besides, it offered little additional protection against tunneling.

It was not much more difficult to dig fifty feet than it had been to dig thirty feet. Davis soon realized this, and put the Dead Line back to twenty feet. His next device was a much more sensible one. A crowd of one hundred and fifty negros dug a trench twenty feet wide and five feet deep around the whole prison on the outside, and this ditch was filled with water from the City Water Works. No one could cross this without attracting the attention of the guards.

Still we were not discouraged, and Andrews and I joined a crowd that was constructing a large tunnel from near our quarters on the east side of the pen. We finished the burrow to within a few inches of the edge of the ditch, and then ceased operations, to await some stormy night, when we could hope to get across the ditch unnoticed.

Orders were issued to guards to fire without warning on men who were observed to be digging or carrying out dirt after nightfall. They occasionally did so, but the risk did not keep anyone from tunneling. Our tunnel ran directly under a sentry box. When carrying dirt away the bearer of the bucket had to turn his back on the guard and walk directly down the street in front of him, two hundred or three hundred feet, to the center of the camp, where he scattered the sand around—so as to give no indication of where it came from. Though we always waited till the moon went down, it seemed as if, unless the guard were a fool, both by nature and training, he could not help taking notice of what was going on under his eyes. I do not recall any more nervous promenades in my life, than those when, taking my turn, I received my bucket of sand at the mouth of the tunnel, and walked slowly away with it. The most disagreeable part was in turning my back to the guard. Could I have faced him, I had sufficient confidence in my quickness of perception, and talents as a dodger, to imagine that I could make it difficult for him to hit me. But in walling with my back to him I was wholly at his mercy. Fortune, however, favored us, and we were allowed to go on with our work—night after night—without a shot.

In the meanwhile another happy thought slowly gestated in Davis's alleged intellect. How he came to give birth to two ideas with no more than a week between them, puzzled all who knew him, and still more that he survived this extraordinary strain upon the gray matter of the cerebrum. His new idea was to have driven a heavily-laden mule cart around the inside of the Dead Line at least once a day. The wheels or the mule's feet broke through the thin sod covering the tunnels and exposed them. Our tunnel went with the rest, and those of our crowd who wore shoes had humiliation added to sorrow by being compelled to go in and spade the hole full of dirt. This put an end to subterranean engineering.

One day one of the boys watched his opportunity, got under the ration wagon, and clinging close to the coupling pole with hands and feet, was carried outside. He was detected, however, as he came from under the wagon, and brought back.

CHAPTER LIII.

FRANK REVERSTOCK'S ATTEMPT AT ESCAPE—PASSING OFF AS REBEL BOY HE REACHES GRISWOLDVILLE BY RAIL, AND THEN STRIKES ACROSS THE COUNTRY FOR SHERMAN, BUT IS CAUGHT WITHIN TWENTY MILES OF OUR LINES.

One of the shrewdest and nearest successful attempts to escape that came under my notice was that of my friend Sergeant Frank Reverstock, of the Third West Virginia Cavalry, of whom I have before spoken. Frank, who was quite small, with a smooth boyish face, had converted to his own use a citizen's coat, belonging to a young boy, a Sutler's assistant, who had died in Andersonville. He had made himself a pair of bag pantaloons and a shirt from pieces of meal sacks which he had appropriated from day to day. He had also the Sutler's assistant's shoes, and, to crown all, he wore on his head one of those hideous looking hats of quilted calico which the

Rebels had taken to wearing in the lack of felt hats, which they could neither make nor buy. Altogether Frank looked enough like a Rebel to be dangerous to trust near a country store or a stable full of horses. When we first arrived in the prison quite a crowd of the Savannahians rushed in to inspect us. The guards had some difficulty in keeping them and us separate. While perplexed with this annoyance, one of them saw Frank standing in our crowd, and, touching him with his bayonet, said, with some sharpness:

"See heah; you must stand back; you musn't crowd on them prisoners so."

Frank stood back. He did it promptly but calmly, and then, as if his curiosity as to Yankees was fully satisfied, he walked slowly away up the street, deliberating as he went on a plan for getting out of the City. He hit upon an excellent one. Going to the engineer of a freight train making ready to start back to Macon, he told him that his father was working in the Confederate machine shops at Griswoldville, near Macon; that he himself was also one of the machinists employed there, and desired to go thither but lacked the necessary means to pay his passage. If the engineer would let him ride up on the engine he would do work enough to pay the fare. Frank told the story ingeniously, the engineer and firemen were won over, and gave their consent.

No more zealous assistant ever climbed upon a tender than Frank proved to be. He loaded wood with a nervous industry, that stood him in place of great strength. He kept the tender in perfect order, and anticipated, as far as possible, every want of the engineer and his assistant. They were delighted with him, and treated him with the greatest kindness, dividing their food with him, and insisting that he should share their bed when they "laid by" for the night. Frank would have gladly declined this latter kindness with thanks, as he was conscious that the quantity of "graybacks" his clothing contained did not make him a very desirable sleeping companion for any one, but his friends were so pressing that he was compelled to accede.

His greatest trouble was a fear of recognition by some one of the prisoners that were continually passing by the train load, on their way from Andersonville to other prisons. He was one of the best known of the prisoners in Andersonville; bright, active, always cheerful, and forever in motion during waking hours,—every one in the Prison speedily became familiar with him, and all addressed him as "Sergeant Frankie." If any one on the passing trains had caught a glimpse of him, that glimpse would have been followed almost inevitably with a shout of:

"Hello, Sergeant Frankie! What are you doing there?"

Then the whole game would have been up. Frank escaped this by persistent watchfulness, and by busying himself on the opposite side of the engine, with his back turned to the other trains.

At last when nearing Griswoldville, Frank, pointing to a large white house at some distance across the fields, said:

"Now, right over there is where my uncle lives, and I believe I'll just run over and see him, and then walk into Griswoldville."

He thanked his friends fervently for their kindness, promised to call and see them frequently, bade them good by, and jumped off the train.

He walked towards the white house as long as he thought he could be seen, and then entered a large corn field and concealed himself in a thicket in the center of it until dark, when he made his way to the neighboring woods, and began journeying northward as fast as his legs could carry him. When morning broke he had made good progress, but was terribly tired. It was not prudent to travel by daylight, so he gathered himself some ears of corn and some berries, of which he made his breakfast, and finding a suitable thicket he crawled into it, fell asleep, and did not wake up until late in the afternoon.

After another meal of raw corn and berries he resumed his journey, and that night made still better progress.

He repeated this for several days and nights—lying in the woods in the day time, traveling by night through woods, fields, and by-paths avoiding all the fords, bridges and main roads, and living on what he could glean from the fields, that he might not take even so much risk as was involved in going to the negro cabins for food.

But there are always flaws in every man's armor of caution—even in so perfect a one as Frank's. His complete success so far had the natural effect of inducing a growing carelessness, which wrought his ruin. One evening he started off briskly, after a refreshing rest and sleep. He knew that he must be very near Sherman's lines, and hope cheered him up with the belief that his freedom would soon be won.

Descending from the hill, in whose dense brushwood he had made his bed all day, he entered a large field full of standing corn, and made his way between the rows until he reached, on the other side, the fence that separated it from the main road, across which was another corn-field, that Frank intended entering.

But he neglected his usual precautions on approaching a road, and instead of coming up cautiously and carefully reconnoitering in all directions before he left cover, he sprang boldly over the fence and strode out for the other side. As he reached the middle of the road, his ears were assailed with the sharp click of a musket being cocked, and the harsh command:

"Halt! halt, dah, I say!"

Turning with a start to his left he saw not ten feet from him, a mounted patrol, the sound of whose approach had been masked by the deep dust of the road, into which his horse's hoofs sank noiselessly.

Frank, of course, yielded without a word, and when sent to the officer in command he told the old story about his being an employee of the Griswoldville shops, off on a leave of absence to make a visit to sick relatives. But, unfortunately, his captors belonged to that section themselves, and speedily caught him in a maze of cross-questioning from which he could not extricate himself. It also became apparent from his language that he was a Yankee, and it was not far from this to the conclusion that he was a spy—a conclusion to which the proximity of Sherman's lines, then less than twenty miles distant-greatly assisted.

By the next morning this belief had become so firmly fixed in the minds of the Rebels that Frank saw a halter dangling alarmingly near, and he concluded the wisest plan was to confess who he really was.

It was not the smallest of his griefs to realize by how slight a chance he had failed. Had he looked down the road before he climbed the fence, or had he been ten minutes earlier or later, the patrol would not have been there, he could have gained the next field unperceived, and two more nights of successful progress would have taken him into Sherman's lines at Sand Mountain. The patrol which caught him was on the look-out for deserters and shirking conscripts, who had become unusually numerous since the fall of Atlanta.

He was sent back to us at Savannah. As he came into the prison gate Lieutenant Davis was standing near. He looked sternly at Frank and his Rebel garments, and muttering,

"By God, I'll stop this!" caught the coat by the tails, tore it to the collar, and took it and his hat away from Frank.

There was a strange sequel to this episode. A few weeks afterward a special exchange for ten thousand was made, and Frank succeeded in being included in this. He was given the usual furlough from the paroled camp at Annapolis, and went to his home in a little town near Mansfield, O.

One day while on the cars going—I think to Newark, O., he saw Lieutenant Davis on the train, in citizens' clothes. He had been sent by the Rebel Government to Canada with dispatches relating to some of the raids then harassing our Northern borders. Davis was the last man in the world to successfully disguise himself. He had a large, coarse mouth, that made him remembered by all who had ever seen him. Frank recognized him instantly and said:

"You are Lieutenant Davis?"

Davis replied:

"You are totally mistaken, sah, I am ——."

Frank insisted that he was right. Davis fumed and blustered, but though Frank was small, he was as game as a bantam rooster, and he gave Davis to understand that there had been a vast change in their relative positions; that the one, while still the same insolent swaggerer, had not regiments of infantry or batteries of artillery to emphasize his insolence, and the other was no longer embarrassed in the discussion by the immense odds in favor of his jailor opponent.

After a stormy scene Frank called in the assistance of some other soldiers in the car, arrested Davis, and took him to Camp Chase—near Columbus, O.,—where he was fully identified by a number of paroled prisoners. He was searched, and documents showing the nature of his mission beyond a doubt, were found upon his person.

A court martial was immediately convened for his trial.

This found him guilty, and sentenced him to be hanged as a spy.

At the conclusion of the trial Frank stepped up to the prisoner and said:

"Mr. Davis, I believe we're even on that coat, now."

Davis was sent to Johnson's Island for execution, but influences were immediately set at work to secure Executive clemency. What they were I know not, but I am informed by the Rev. Robert McCune, who was then Chaplain of the One Hundred and Twenty-Eighth Ohio Infantry and the Post of Johnson's Island and who was the spiritual adviser appointed to prepare Davis for execution, that the sentence was hardly pronounced before Davis was visited by an emissary, who told him to dismiss his fears, that he should not suffer the punishment.

It is likely that leading Baltimore Unionists were enlisted in his behalf through family connections, and as the Border State Unionists were then potent at Washington, they readily secured a commutation of his sentence to imprisonment during the war.

It seems that the justice of this world is very unevenly dispensed when so much solicitude is shown for the life of such a man, and none at all for the much better men whom he assisted to destroy.

The official notice of the commutation of the sentence was not published until the day set for the execution, but the certain knowledge that it would be forthcoming enabled Davis to display a great deal of bravado on approaching what was supposed to be his end. As the reader can readily imagine, from what I have heretofore said of him, Davis was the man to improve to the utmost every opportunity to strut his little hour, and he did it in this instance. He posed, attitudinized and vapored, so that the camp and the country were filled with stories of the wonderful coolness with which he contemplated his approaching fate.

Among other things he said to his guard, as he washed himself elaborately the night before the day announced for the execution:

"Well, you can be sure of one thing; to-morrow night there will certainly be one clean corpse on this Island."

Unfortunately for his braggadocio, he let it leak out in some way that he had been well aware all the time that he would not be executed.

He was taken to Fort Delaware for confinement, and died there some time after.

Frank Beverstock went back to his regiment, and served with it until the close of the war. He then returned home, and, after awhile became a banker at Bowling Green, O. He was a fine business man and became very prosperous. But though naturally healthy and vigorous, his system carried in it the seeds of death, sown there by the hardships of captivity. He had been one of the victims of the Rebels' vaccination; the virus injected into his blood had caused a large part of his right temple to slough off, and when it healed it left a ghastly cicatrix.

Two years ago he was taken suddenly ill, and died before his friends had any idea that his condition was serious.

CHAPTER LIV.

SAVANNAH PROVES TO BE A CHANGE FOR THE BETTER—ESCAPE FROM THE BRATS OF GUARDS—COMPARISON BETWEEN WIRZ AND DAVIS—A BRIEF INTERVAL OF GOOD RATIONS—WINDER, THE MAN WITH THE EVIL EYE —THE DISLOYAL WORK OF A SHYSTER.

After all Savannah was a wonderful improvement on Andersonville. We got away from the pestilential Swamp and that poisonous ground. Every mouthful of air was not laden with disease germs, nor every cup of water polluted with the seeds of death. The earth did not breed gangrene, nor the atmosphere promote fever. As only the more vigorous had come away, we were freed from the depressing spectacle of every third man dying. The keen disappointment prostrated very many who had been of average health, and I imagine, several hundred died, but there were hospital arrangements of some kind, and the sick were taken away from among us. Those of us who tunneled out had an opportunity of stretching our legs, which we had not had for months in the overcrowded Stockade we had left. The attempts to escape did all engaged in them good, even though they failed, since they aroused new ideas and hopes, set the blood into more rapid circulation, and toned up the mind and system both. I had come away from Andersonville with considerable scurvy manifesting itself in my gums and feet. Soon these signs almost wholly disappeared.

We also got away from those murderous little brats of Reserves, who guarded us at Andersonville, and shot men down as they would stone apples out of a tree. Our guards now were mostly, sailors, from the Rebel fleet in the harbor—Irishmen, Englishmen and Scandinavians, as free hearted and kindly as sailors always are. I do not think they ever fired a shot at one of us. The only trouble we had was with that portion of the guard drawn from the infantry of the garrison. They had the same rattlesnake venom of the Home Guard crowd wherever we met it, and shot us down at the least provocation. Fortunately they only formed a small part of the sentinels.

Best of all, we escaped for a while from the upas-like shadow of Winder and Wirz, in whose presence strong men sickened and died, as when near some malign genii of an Eastern story. The peasantry of Italy believed firmly in the evil eye. Did they ever know any such men as Winder and his satellite, I could comprehend how much foundation they could have for such a belief. Lieutenant Davis had many faults, but there was no comparison between him and the Andersonville commandant. He was a typical young Southern man; ignorant and bumptious as to the most common matters of school-boy knowledge, inordinately vain of himself and his family, coarse in tastes and thoughts, violent in his prejudices, but after all with some streaks of honor and generosity that made the widest possible difference between him and Wirz, who never had any. As one of my chums said to me:

"Wirz is the most even-tempered man I ever knew; he's always foaming mad."

This was nearly the truth. I never saw Wirz when he was not angry; if not violently abusive, he was cynical and sardonic. Never, in my little experience with him did I detect a glint of kindly, generous humanity; if he ever was moved by any sight of suffering its exhibition in his face escaped my eye. If he ever had even a wish to mitigate the pain or hardship of any man the expression of such wish never fell on my ear. How a man could move daily through such misery as he encountered, and never be moved by it except to scorn and mocking is beyond my limited understanding.

Davis vapored a great deal, swearing big round oaths in the broadest of Southern patois; he was perpetually threatening to:

"Open on ye wid de ahtillery," but the only death that I knew him to directly cause or sanction was that I have described in the previous chapter. He would not put himself out of the way to annoy and oppress prisoners, as Wirz would, but frequently showed even a disposition to humor them in some little thing, when it could be done without danger or trouble to himself.

By-and-by, however, he got an idea that there was some money to be made out of the prisoners, and he set his wits to work in this direction. One day, standing at the gate, he gave one of his peculiar yells that he used to attract the attention of the camp with:

"Wh-ah-ye!!"

We all came to "attention," and he announced:

"Yesterday, while I wuz in the camps (a Rebel always says camps,) some of you prisoners picked my pockets of seventy-five dollars in greenbacks. Now, I give you notice that I'll not send in any moah rations till the money's returned to me."

This was a very stupid method of extortion, since no one believed that he had lost the money, and at all events he had no business to have the greenbacks, as the Rebel laws imposed severe penalties upon any citizen, and still more upon any soldier dealing with, or having in his possession any of "the money of the enemy." We did without rations until night, when they were sent in. There was a story that some of the boys in the prison had contributed to make up part of the sum, and Davis took it and was satisfied. I do not know how true the story was. At another time some of the boys stole the bridle and halter off an old horse that was driven in with a cart. The things were worth, at a liberal estimate, one dollar. Davis cut off the rations of the whole six thousand of us for one day for this. We always imagined that the proceeds went into his pocket.

A special exchange was arranged between our Navy Department and that of the Rebels, by which all seamen and marines among us were exchanged. Lists of these were sent to the different prisons and the men called for. About three-fourths of them were dead, but many soldiers divining, the situation of affairs, answered to the dead men's names, went away with the squad and were exchanged. Much of this was through the connivance of the Rebel officers, who favored those who had ingratiated themselves with them. In many instances money was paid to secure this privilege, and I have been informed on good authority that Jack Huckleby, of the Eighth Tennessee, and Ira Beverly, of the One Hundredth Ohio, who kept the big sutler shop on the North Side at Andersonville, paid Davis five hundred dollars each to be allowed to go with the sailors. As for Andrews and me, we had no friends among the Rebels, nor money to bribe with, so we stood no show.

The rations issued to us for some time after our arrival seemed riotous luxury to what we had been getting at Andersonville. Each of us received daily a half-dozen rude and coarse imitations of our fondly-remembered hard tack, and with these a small piece of meat or a few spoonfuls of molasses, and a quart or so of vinegar, and several plugs of tobacco for each "hundred." How exquisite was the taste of the crackers and molasses! It was the first wheat bread I had eaten since my entry into Richmond —nine months before—and molasses had been a stranger to me for years. After the corn bread we had so long lived upon, this was manna. It seems that the Commissary at Savannah labored under the delusion that he must issue to us the same rations as were served out to the Rebel soldiers and sailors. It was some little time before the fearful mistake came to the knowledge of Winder. I fancy that the news almost threw him into an apoplectic fit. Nothing, save his being ordered to the front, could have caused him such poignant sorrow as the information that so much good food had been worse than wasted in undoing his work by building up the bodies of his hated enemies.

Without being told, we knew that he had been heard from when the tobacco, vinegar and molasses failed to come in, and the crackers gave way to corn meal. Still this was a vast improvement on Andersonville, as the meal was fine and sweet, and we each had a spoonful of salt issued to us regularly.

I am quite sure that I cannot make the reader who has not had an experience similar to ours comprehend the wonderful importance to us of that spoonful of salt. Whether or not the appetite for salt be, as some scientists claim, a purely artificial want, one thing is certain, and that is, that either the habit of countless generations or some other cause, has so deeply ingrained it into our common nature, that it has come to be nearly as essential as food itself, and no amount of deprivation can accustom us to its absence. Rather, it seemed that the longer we did without it the more overpowering became our craving. I could get along to-day and to-morrow, perhaps the whole week, without salt in my food, since the lack would be supplied from the excess I had already swallowed, but at the end of that time Nature would begin to demand that I renew the supply of saline constituent of my tissues, and she would become more clamorous with every day that I neglected her bidding, and finally summon Nausea to aid Longing.

The light artillery of the garrison of Savannah—four batteries, twenty-four pieces—was stationed around three sides of the prison, the guns unlimbered, planted at convenient distance, and trained upon us, ready for instant use. We could see all the grinning mouths through the cracks in the fence. There were enough of them to send us as high as the traditional kite flown by Gilderoy. The having at his beck this array of frowning metal lent Lieutenant Davis such an importance in his own eyes that his demeanor swelled to the grandiose. It became very amusing to see him puff up and vaunt over it, as he did on every possible occasion. For instance, finding a crowd of several hundred lounging around the gate, he would throw open the wicket, stalk in with the air of a Jove threatening a rebellious world with the dread thunders of heaven, and shout:

"W-h-a-a y-e-e! Prisoners, I give you jist two minutes to cleah away from this gate, aw I'll open on ye wid de ahtillery!"

One of the buglers of the artillery was a superb musician—evidently some old "regular" whom the Confederacy had seduced into its service, and his instrument was so sweet toned that we imagined that it was made of silver. The calls he played were nearly the same as we used in the cavalry, and for the first few days we became bitterly homesick every time he sent ringing out the old familiar signals, that to us were so closely associated with what now seemed the bright and happy days when we were in the field with our battalion. If we were only back in the valleys of Tennessee with what alacrity we would respond to that "assembly;" no Orderly's patience would be worn out in getting laggards and lazy ones to "fall in for roll-call;" how eagerly we would attend to "stable duty;" how gladly mount our faithful horses and ride away to "water," and what bareback races ride, going and coming. We would be even glad to hear "guard" and "drill" sounded; and there would be music in the disconsolate "surgeon's call:"

"Come-get-your-q-n-i-n-i-n-e; come, get your quinine; It'll make you sad: It'll make you sick. Come, come."

O, if we were only back, what admirable soldiers we would be! One morning, about three or four o'clock, we were awakened by the ground shaking and a series of heavy, dull thumps sounding oft seaward. Our silver-voiced bugler seemed to be awakened, too. He set the echoes ringing with a vigorously played "reveille;" a minute later came an equally earnest "assembly," and when "boots and saddles" followed, we knew that all was not well in Denmark; the thumping and shaking now had a significance. It meant heavy Yankee guns somewhere near. We heard the gunners hitching up; the bugle signal "forward," the wheels roll off, and for a half hour afterwards we caught the receding sound of the bugle commanding "right turn," "left turn," etc., as the batteries marched away. Of course, we became considerably wrought up over the matter, as we fancied that, knowing we were in Savannah, our vessels were trying to pass up to the City and take it. The thumping and shaking continued until late in the afternoon.

We subsequently learned that some of our blockaders, finding time banging heavy upon their hands, had essayed a little diversion by knocking Forts Jackson and Bledsoe—two small forts defending the passage of the Savannah—about their defenders' ears. After capturing the forts our folks desisted and came no farther.

Quite a number of the old Raider crowd had come with us from Andersonville. Among these was the shyster, Peter Bradley. They kept up their old tactics of hanging around the gates, and currying favor with the Rebels in every possible way, in hopes to get paroles outside or other favors. The great mass of the prisoners were so bitter against the Rebels as to feel that they would rather die than ask or accept a favor from their hands, and they had little else than contempt for these trucklers. The raider crowd's favorite theme of conversation with the Rebels was the strong discontent of the boys with the manner of their treatment by our Government. The assertion that there was any such widespread feeling was utterly false. We all had confidence—as we continue to have to this day—that our Government would do everything for us possible, consistent with its honor, and the success of military operations, and outside of the little squad of which I speak, not an admission could be extracted from anybody that blame could be attached to any one, except the Rebels. It was regarded as unmanly and unsoldier-like to the last degree, as well as senseless, to revile our Government for the crimes committed by its foes.

But the Rebels were led to believe that we were ripe for revolt against our flag, and to side with them. Imagine, if possible, the stupidity that would mistake our bitter hatred of those who were our deadly enemies, for any feeling that would lead us to join hands with those enemies. One day we were surprised to see the carpenters erect a rude stand in the center of the camp. When it was finished, Bradley appeared upon it, in company with some Rebel officers and guards. We gathered around in curiosity, and Bradley began making a speech.

He said that it had now become apparent to all of us that our Government had abandoned us; that it cared little or nothing for us, since it could hire as many more quite readily, by offering a bounty equal to the pay which would be due us now; that it cost only a few hundred dollars to bring over a shipload of Irish, "Dutch," and French, who were only too glad to agree to fight or do anything else to get to this country. [The peculiar impudence of this consisted in Bradley himself being a foreigner, and one who had only come out under one of the later calls, and the influence of a big bounty.]

Continuing in this strain he repeated and dwelt upon the old lie, always in the mouths of his crowd, that Secretary Stanton and General Halleck had positively refused to enter upon negotiations for exchange, because those in prison were "only a miserable lot of 'coffee-boilers' and 'blackberry pickers,' whom the Army was better off without."

The terms "coffee-boiler," and "blackberry-pickers" were considered the worst terms of opprobrium we had in prison. They were applied to that class of stragglers and skulkers, who were only too ready to give themselves up to the enemy, and who, on coming in, told some gauzy story about "just having stopped to boil a cup of coffee," or to do something else which they should not have done, when they were gobbled up. It is not risking much to affirm the probability of Bradley and most of his crowd having belonged to this dishonorable class.

The assertion that either the great Chief-of-Staff or the still greater War-Secretary were even capable of applying such epithets to the mass of prisoners is too preposterous to need refutation, or even denial. No person outside the raider crowd ever gave the silly lie a moment's toleration. Bradley concluded his speech in some such language as this:

"And now, fellow prisoners, I propose to you this: that we unite in informing our Government that unless we are exchanged in thirty days, we will be forced by self-preservation to join the Confederate army."

For an instant his hearers seemed stunned at the fellow's audacity, and then there went up such a roar of denunciation and execration that the air trembled. The Rebels thought that the whole camp was going to rush on Bradley and tear him to pieces, and they drew revolvers and leveled muskets to defend him. The uproar only ceased when Bradley was hurried out of the prisons but for hours everybody was savage and sullen, and full of threatenings against him, when opportunity served. We never saw him afterward.

Angry as I was, I could not help being amused at the tempestuous rage of a tall, fine-looking and well educated Irish Sergeant of an Illinois regiment. He poured forth denunciations of the traitor and the Rebels, with the vivid fluency of his Hibernian nature, vowed he'd "give a year of me life, be J——s, to have the handling of the dirty spalpeen for ten minutes; be G-d," and finally in his rage, tore off his own shirt and threw it on the ground and trampled on it.

Imagine my astonishment, some time after getting out of prison, to find the Southern papers publishing as a defense against the charges in regard to Andersonville, the following document, which they claimed to have been adopted by "a mass meeting of the prisoners:"

"At a mass meeting held September 28th, 1864, by the Federal prisoners confined at Savannah, Ga., it was unanimously agreed that the following resolutions be sent to the President of the United States, in the hope that he might thereby take such steps as in his wisdom he may think necessary for our speedy exchange or parole:

"Resolved, That while we would declare our unbounded love for the Union, for the home of our fathers, and for the graves of those we venerate, we would beg most respectfully that our situation as prisoners be diligently inquired into, and every obstacle consistent with the honor and dignity of the Government at once removed.

"Resolved, That while allowing the Confederate authorities all due praise for the attention paid to prisoners, numbers of our men are daily consigned to early graves, in the prime of manhood, far from home and kindred, and this is not caused intentionally by the Confederate Government, but by force of circumstances; the prisoners are forced to go without shelter, and, in a great portion of cases, without medicine.

"Resolved, That, whereas, ten thousand of our brave comrades have descended into an untimely grave within the last six months, and as we believe their death was caused by the difference of climate, the peculiar kind and insufficiency of food, and lack of proper medical treatment; and, whereas, those difficulties still remain, we would declare as our firm belief, that unless we are speedily exchanged, we have no alternative but to share the lamentable fate of our comrades. Must this thing still go on! Is there no hope?

"Resolved, That, whereas, the cold and inclement season of the year is fast approaching, we hold it to be our duty as soldiers and citizens of the United States, to inform our Government that the majority of our prisoners ate without proper clothing, in some cases being almost naked, and are without blankets to protect us from the scorching sun by day or the heavy dews by night, and we would most respectfully request the Government to make some arrangement whereby we can be supplied with these, to us, necessary articles.

"Resolved, That, whereas, the term of service of many of our comrades having expired, they, having served truly and faithfully for the term of their several enlistments, would most respectfully ask their Government, are they to be forgotten? Are past services to be ignored? Not having seen their wives and little ones for over three years, they would most respectfully, but firmly, request the Government to make some arrangements whereby they can be exchanged or paroled.

"Resolved, That, whereas, in the fortune of war, it was our lot to become prisoners, we have suffered patiently, and are still willing to suffer, if by so doing we can benefit the country; but we must most respectfully beg to say, that we are not willing to suffer to further the ends of any party or clique to the detriment of our honor, our families, and our country, and we beg that this affair be explained to us, that we may continue to hold the Government in that respect which is necessary to make a good citizen and soldier.

"P. BRADLEY,
"Chairman of Committee in behalf of Prisoners."

In regard to the above I will simply say this, that while I cannot pretend to know or even much that went on around me, I do not think it was possible for a mass meeting of prisoners to have been held without my knowing it, and its essential features. Still less was it possible for a mass meeting to have been held which would have adopted any such a document as the above, or anything else that a Rebel would have found the least pleasure in republishing. The whole thing is a brazen falsehood.

CHAPTER LV.

WHY WE WERE HURRIED OUT OF ANDERSONVILLE—THE FALL OF ATLANTA — OUR LONGING TO HEAR THE NEWS—ARRIVAL OF SOME FRESH FISH—HOW WE KNEW THEY WERE WESTERN BOYS—DIFFERENCE IN THE APPEARANCE OF THE SOLDIERS OF THE TWO ARMIES.

The reason of our being hurried out of Andersonville under the false pretext of exchange dawned on us before we had been in Savannah long. If the reader will consult the map of Georgia he will understand this, too. Let him remember that several of the railroads which now appear were not built then. The road upon which Andersonville is situated was about one hundred and twenty miles long, reaching from Macon to Americus, Andersonville being about midway between these two. It had no connections anywhere except at Macon, and it was hundreds of miles across the country from Andersonville to any other road. When Atlanta fell it brought our folks to within sixty miles of Macon, and any day they were liable to make a forward movement, which would capture that place, and have us where we could be retaken with ease.

There was nothing left undone to rouse the apprehensions of the Rebels in that direction. The humiliating surrender of General Stoneman at Macon in July, showed them what our folks were thinking of, and awakened their minds to the disastrous consequences of such a movement when executed by a bolder and abler commander. Two days of one of Kilpatrick's swift, silent marches would carry his hard-riding troopers around Hood's right flank, and into the streets of Macon, where a half hour's work with the torch on the bridges across the Ocmulgee and the creeks that enter it at that point, would have cut all of the Confederate Army of the Tennessee's communications. Another day and night of easy marching would bring his guidons fluttering through the woods about the Stockade at Andersonville, and give him a reinforcement of twelve or fifteen thousand able-bodied soldiers, with whom he could have held the whole Valley of the Chattahoochie, and become the nether millstone, against which Sherman could have ground Hood's army to powder.

Such a thing was not only possible, but very probable, and doubtless would have occurred had we remained in Andersonville another week.

Hence the haste to get us away, and hence the lie about exchange, for, had it not been for this, one-quarter at least of those taken on the cars would have succeeded in getting off and attempted to have reached Sherman's lines.

The removal went on with such rapidity that by the end of September only eight thousand two hundred and eighteen remained at Andersonville, and these were mostly too sick to be moved; two thousand seven hundred died in September, fifteen hundred and sixty in October, and four hundred and eighty-five in November, so that at the beginning of December there were only thirteen hundred and fifty-nine remaining. The larger part of those taken out were sent on to Charleston, and subsequently to Florence and Salisbury. About six or seven thousand of us, as near as I remember, were brought to Savannah.

We were all exceedingly anxious to know how the Atlanta campaign had ended. So far our information only comprised the facts that a sharp battle had been fought, and the result was the complete possession of our great objective point. The manner of accomplishing this glorious end, the magnitude of the engagement, the regiments, brigades and corps participating, the loss on both sides, the completeness of the victories, etc., were all matters that we knew nothing of, and thirsted to learn.

The Rebel papers said as little as possible about the capture, and the facts in that little were so largely diluted with fiction as to convey no real information. But few new, prisoners were coming in, and none of these were from Sherman. However, toward the last of September, a handful of "fresh fish" were turned inside, whom our experienced eyes instantly told us were Western boys.

There was never any difficulty in telling, as far as he could be seen, whether a boy belonged to the East or the west. First, no one from the Army of the Potomac was ever without his corps badge worn conspicuously; it was rare to see such a thing on one of Sherman's men. Then there was a dressy air about the Army of the Potomac that was wholly wanting in the soldiers serving west of the Alleghanies.

The Army, of the Potomac was always near to its base of supplies, always had its stores accessible, and the care of the clothing and equipments of the men was an essential part of its discipline. A ragged or shabbily dressed man was a rarity. Dress coats, paper collars, fresh woolen shirts, neat-fitting pantaloons, good comfortable shoes, and trim caps or hats, with all the blazing brass of company letters an inch long, regimental number, bugle and eagle, according to the Regulations, were as common to Eastern boys as they were rare among the Westerners.

The latter usually wore blouses, instead of dress coats, and as a rule their clothing had not been renewed since the opening, of the campaign —and it showed this. Those who wore good boots or shoes generally had to submit to forcible exchanges by their captors, and the same was true of head gear. The Rebels were badly off in regard to hats. They did not have skill and ingenuity enough to make these out of felt or straw, and the make-shifts they contrived of quilted calico and long-leaved pine, were ugly enough to frighten horned cattle.

I never blamed them much for wanting to get rid of these, even if they did have to commit a sort of highway robbery upon defenseless prisoners to do so. To be a traitor in arms was bad certainly, but one never appreciated the entire magnitude of the crime until he saw a Rebel wearing a calico or a pine-leaf hat. Then one felt as if it would be a great mistake to ever show such a man mercy.

The Army of Northern Virginia seemed to have supplied themselves with head-gear of Yankee manufacture of previous years, and they then quit taking the hats of their prisoners. Johnston's Army did not have such good luck, and had to keep plundering to the end of the war.

Another thing about the Army of the Potomac was the variety of the uniforms. There were members of Zouave regiments, wearing baggy breeches of various hues, gaiters, crimson fezes, and profusely braided jackets. I have before mentioned the queer garb of the "Lost Ducks." (Les Enfants Perdu, Forty-eighth New York.)

One of the most striking uniforms was that of the "Fourteenth Brooklyn." They wore scarlet pantaloons, a blue jacket handsomely braided, and a red fez, with a white cloth wrapped around the head, turban-fashion. As a large number of them were captured, they formed quite a picturesque feature of every crowd. They were generally good fellows and gallant soldiers.

Another uniform that attracted much, though not so favorable, attention was that of the Third New Jersey Cavalry, or First New Jersey Hussars, as they preferred to call themselves. The designer of the uniform must have had an interest in a curcuma plantation, or else he was a fanatical Orangeman. Each uniform would furnish occasion enough for a dozen New York riots on the 12th of July. Never was such an eruption of the yellows seen outside of the jaundiced livery of some Eastern potentate. Down each leg of the pantaloons ran a stripe of yellow braid one and one-half inches wide. The jacket had enormous gilt buttons, and was embellished with yellow braid until it was difficult to tell whether it was blue cloth trimmed with yellow, or yellow adorned with blue. From the shoulders swung a little, false hussar jacket, lined with the same flaring yellow. The vizor-less cap was similarly warmed up with the hue of the perfected sunflower. Their saffron magnificence was like the gorgeous gold of the lilies of the field, and Solomon in all his glory could not have beau arrayed like one of them. I hope he was not. I want to retain my respect for him. We dubbed these daffodil cavaliers "Butterflies," and the name stuck to them like a poor relation.

Still another distinction that was always noticeable between the two armies was in the bodily bearing of the men. The Army of the Potomac was drilled more rigidly than the Western men, and had comparatively few long marches. Its members had something of the stiffness and precision of English and German soldiery, while the Western boys had the long, "reachy" stride, and easy swing that made forty miles a day a rather commonplace march for an infantry regiment.

This was why we knew the new prisoners to be Sherman's boys as soon as they came inside, and we started for them to hear the news. Inviting them over to our lean-to, we told them our anxiety for the story of the decisive blow that gave us the Central Gate of the Confederacy, and asked them to give it to us.

CHAPTER LVI.

WHAT CAUSED THE FALL OF ATLANTA—A DISSERTATION UPON AN IMPORTANT PSYCHOLOGICAL PROBLEM—THE BATTLE OF JONESBORO—WHY IT WAS FOUGHT —HOW SHERMAN DECEIVED HOOD—A DESPERATE BAYONET CHARGE, AND THE ONLY SUCCESSFUL ONE IN THE ATLANTA CAMPAIGN—A GALLANT COLONEL AND HOW HE DIED—THE HEROISM OF SOME ENLISTED MEN—GOING CALMLY INTO CERTAIN DEATH.

An intelligent, quick-eyed, sunburned boy, without an ounce of surplus flesh on face or limbs, which had been reduced to gray-hound condition by the labors and anxieties of the months of battling between Chattanooga and Atlanta, seemed to be the accepted talker of the crowd, since all the rest looked at him, as if expecting him to answer for them. He did so:

"You want to know about how we got Atlanta at last, do you? Well, if you don't know, I should think you would want to. If I didn't, I'd want somebody to tell me all about it just as soon as he could get to me, for it was one of the neatest little bits of work that 'old Billy' and his boys ever did, and it got away with Hood so bad that he hardly knew what hurt him.

"Well, first, I'll tell you that we belong to the old Fourteenth Ohio Volunteers, which, if you know anything about the Army of the Cumberland, you'll remember has just about as good a record as any that trains around old Pap Thomas—and he don't 'low no slouches of any kind near him, either—you can bet $500 to a cent on that, and offer to give back the cent if you win. Ours is Jim Steedman's old regiment—you've all heard of old Chickamauga Jim, who slashed his division of 7,000 fresh men into the Rebel flank on the second day at Chickamauga, in a way that made Longstreet wish he'd staid on the Rappahannock, and never tried to get up any little sociable with the Westerners. If I do say it myself, I believe we've got as good a crowd of square, stand-up, trust'em-every-minute-in-your-life boys, as ever thawed hard-tack and sowbelly. We got all the grunters and weak sisters fanned out the first year, and since then we've been on a business basis, all the time. We're in a mighty good brigade, too. Most of the regiments have been with us since we formed the first brigade Pap Thomas ever commanded, and waded with him through the mud of Kentucky, from Wild Cat to Mill Springs, where he gave Zollicoffer just a little the awfulest thrashing that a Rebel General ever got. That, you know, was in January, 1862, and was the first victory gained by the Western Army, and our people felt so rejoiced over it that—"

"Yes, yes; we've read all about that," we broke in, "and we'd like to hear it again, some other time; but tell us now about Atlanta."

"All right. Let's see: where was I? O, yes, talking about our brigade. It is the Third Brigade, of the Third Division, of the Fourteenth Corps, and is made up of the Fourteenth Ohio, Thirty-eighth Ohio, Tenth Kentucky, and Seventy-fourth Indiana. Our old Colonel—George P. Este — commands it. We never liked him very well in camp, but I tell you he's a whole team in a fight, and he'd do so well there that all would take to him again, and he'd be real popular for a while."

"Now, isn't that strange," broke in Andrews, who was given to fits of speculation of psychological phenomena: "None of us yearn to die, but the surest way to gain the affection of the boys is to show zeal in leading them into scrapes where the chances of getting shot are the best. Courage in action, like charity, covers a multitude of sins. I have known it to make the most unpopular man in the battalion, the most popular inside of half an hour. Now, M.(addressing himself to me,) you remember Lieutenant H., of our battalion. You know he was a very fancy young fellow; wore as snipish' clothes as the tailor could make, had gold lace on his jacket wherever the regulations would allow it, decorated his shoulders with the stunningest pair of shoulder knots I ever saw, and so on. Well, he did not stay with us long after we went to the front. He went back on a detail for a court martial, and staid a good while. When he rejoined us, he was not in good odor, at all, and the boys weren't at all careful in saying unpleasant things when he could hear them, A little while after he came back we made that reconnaissance up on the Virginia Road. We stirred up the Johnnies with our skirmish line, and while the firing was going on in front we sat on our horses in line, waiting for the order to move forward and engage. You know how solemn such moments are. I looked down the line and saw Lieutenant H. at the right of Company—, in command of it. I had not seen him since he came back, and I sung out:

"'Hello, Lieutenant, how do you feel?'

"The reply came back, promptly, and with boyish cheerfulness:

"'Bully, by ——; I'm going to lead seventy men of Company into action today!'

"How his boys did cheer him. When the bugle sounded—'forward, trot,' his company sailed in as if they meant it, and swept the Johnnies off in short meter. You never heard anybody say anything against Lieutenant after that."

"You know how it was with Captain G., of our regiment," said one of the Fourteenth to another. "He was promoted from Orderly Sergeant to a Second Lieutenant, and assigned to Company D. All the members of Company D went to headquarters in a body, and protested against his being put in their company, and he was not. Well, he behaved so well at Chickamauga that the boys saw that they had done him a great injustice, and all those that still lived went again to headquarters, and asked to take all back that they had said, and to have him put into the company."

"Well, that was doing the manly thing, sure; but go on about Atlanta."

"I was telling about our brigade," resumed the narrator. "Of course, we think our regiment's the best by long odds in the army—every fellow thinks that of his regiment—but next to it come the other regiments of our brigade. There's not a cent of discount on any of them.

"Sherman had stretched out his right away to the south and west of Atlanta. About the middle of August our corps, commanded by Jefferson C. Davis, was lying in works at Utoy Creek, a couple of miles from Atlanta. We could see the tall steeples and the high buildings of the City quite plainly. Things had gone on dull and quiet like for about ten days. This was longer by a good deal than we had been at rest since we left Resaca in the Spring. We knew that something was brewing, and that it must come to a head soon.

"I belong to Company C. Our little mess—now reduced to three by the loss of two of our best soldiers and cooks, Disbrow and Sulier, killed behind head-logs in front of Atlanta, by sharpshooters—had one fellow that we called 'Observer,' because he had such a faculty of picking up news in his prowling around headquarters. He brought us in so much of this, and it was generally so reliable that we frequently made up his absence from duty by taking his place. He was never away from a fight, though. On the night of the 25th of August, 'Observer' came in with the news that something was in the wind. Sherman was getting awful restless, and we had found out that this always meant lots of trouble to our friends on the other side.

"Sure enough, orders came to get ready to move, and the next night we all moved to the right and rear, out of sight of the Johnnies. Our well built works were left in charge of Garrard's Cavalry, who concealed their horses in the rear, and came up and took our places. The whole army except the Twentieth Corps moved quietly off, and did it so nicely that we were gone some time before the enemy suspected it. Then the Twentieth Corps pulled out towards the North, and fell back to the Chattahoochie, making quite a shove of retreat. The Rebels snapped up the bait greedily. They thought the siege was being raised, and they poured over their works to hurry the Twentieth boys off. The Twentieth fellows let them know that there was lots of sting in them yet, and the Johnnies were not long in discovering that it would have been money in their pockets if they had let that 'moon-and-star' (that's the Twentieth's badge, you know) crowd alone.

"But the Rebs thought the rest of us were gone for good and that Atlanta was saved. Naturally they felt mighty happy over it; and resolved to have a big celebration—a ball, a meeting of jubilee, etc. Extra trains were run in, with girls and women from the surrounding country, and they just had a high old time.

"In the meantime we were going through so many different kinds of tactics that it looked as if Sherman was really crazy this time, sure. Finally we made a grand left wheel, and then went forward a long way in line of battle. It puzzled us a good deal, but we knew that Sherman couldn't get us into any scrape that Pap Thomas couldn't get us out of, and so it was all right.

"Along on the evening of the 31st our right wing seemed to have run against a hornet's nest, and we could hear the musketry and cannon speak out real spiteful, but nothing came down our way. We had struck the railroad leading south from Atlanta to Macon, and began tearing it up. The jollity at Atlanta was stopped right in the middle by the appalling news that the Yankees hadn't retreated worth a cent, but had broken out in a new and much worse spot than ever. Then there was no end of trouble all around, and Hood started part of his army back after us.

"Part of Hardee's and Pat Cleburne's command went into position in front of us. We left them alone till Stanley could come up on our left, and swing around, so as to cut off their retreat, when we would bag every one of them. But Stanley was as slow as he always was, and did not come up until it was too late, and the game was gone.

"The sun was just going down on the evening of the 1st of September, when we began to see we were in for it, sure. The Fourteenth Corps wheeled into position near the railroad, and the sound of musketry and artillery became very loud and clear on our front and left. We turned a little and marched straight toward the racket, becoming more excited every minute. We saw the Carlin's brigade of regulars, who were some distance ahead of us, pile knapsacks, form in line, fix bayonets, and dash off with arousing cheer.

"The Rebel fire beat upon them like a Summer rain-storm, the ground shook with the noise, and just as we reached the edge of the cotton field, we saw the remnant of the brigade come flying back out of the awful, blasting shower of bullets. The whole slope was covered with dead and wounded."

"Yes," interrupts one of the Fourteenth; "and they made that charge right gamely, too, I can tell you. They were good soldiers, and well led. When we went over the works, I remember seeing the body of a little Major of one of the regiments lying right on the top. If he hadn't been killed he'd been inside in a half-a-dozen steps more. There's no mistake about it; those regulars will fight."

"When we saw this," resumed the narrator, "it set our fellows fairly wild; they became just crying mad; I never saw them so before. The order came to strip for the charge, and our knapsacks were piled in half a minute. A Lieutenant of our company, who was then on the staff of Gen. Baird, our division commander, rode slowly down the line and gave us our instructions to load our guns, fix bayonets, and hold fire until we were on top of the Rebel works. Then Colonel Este sang out clear and steady as a bugle signal:

"'Brigade, forward! Guide center! MARCH!!'

"And we started. Heavens, how they did let into us, as we came up into range. They had ten pieces of artillery, and more men behind the breastworks than we had in line, and the fire they poured on us was simply withering. We walked across the hundreds of dead and dying of the regular brigade, and at every step our own men fell down among them. General Baud's horse was shot down, and the General thrown far over his head, but he jumped up and ran alongside of us. Major Wilson, our regimental commander, fell mortally wounded; Lieutenant Kirk was killed, and also Captain Stopfard, Adjutant General of the brigade. Lieutenants Cobb and Mitchell dropped with wounds that proved fatal in a few days. Captain Ugan lost an arm, one-third of the enlisted men fell, but we went straight ahead, the grape and the musketry becoming worse every step, until we gained the edge of the hill, where we were checked a minute by the brush, which the Rebels had fixed up in the shape of abattis. Just then a terrible fire from a new direction, our left, swept down the whole length of our line. The Colonel of the Seventeenth New York—as gallant a man as ever lived saw the new trouble, took his regiment in on the run, and relieved us of this, but he was himself mortally wounded. If our boys were half-crazy before, they were frantic now, and as we got out of the entanglement of the brush, we raised a fearful yell and ran at the works. We climbed the sides, fired right down into the defenders, and then began with the bayonet and sword. For a few minutes it was simply awful. On both sides men acted like infuriated devils. They dashed each other's brains out with clubbed muskets; bayonets were driven into men's bodies up to the muzzle of the gun; officers ran their swords through their opponents, and revolvers, after being emptied into the faces of the Rebels, were thrown with desperate force into the ranks. In our regiment was a stout German butcher named Frank Fleck. He became so excited that he threw down his sword, and rushed among the Rebels with his bare fists, knocking down a swath of them. He yelled to the first Rebel he met:

"Py Gott, I've no patience mit you,' and knocked him sprawling. He caught hold of the commander of the Rebel Brigade, and snatched him back over the works by main strength. Wonderful to say, he escaped unhurt, but the boys will probably not soon let him hear the last of, "Py Gott, I've no patience mit you.'

"The Tenth Kentucky, by the queerest luck in the world, was matched against the Rebel Ninth Kentucky. The commanders of the two regiments were brothers-in-law, and the men relatives, friends, acquaintances and schoolmates. They hated each other accordingly, and the fight between them was more bitter, if possible, than anywhere else on the line. The Thirty-Eighth Ohio and Seventy-fourth Indiana put in some work that was just magnificent. We hadn't time to look at it then, but the dead and wounded piled up after the fight told the story.

"We gradually forced our way over the works, but the Rebels were game to the last, and we had to make them surrender almost one at a time. The artillerymen tried to fire on us when we were so close we could lay our hands on the guns.

"Finally nearly all in the works surrendered, and were disarmed and marched back. Just then an aid came dashing up with the information that we must turn the works, and get ready to receive Hardee, who was advancing to retake the position. We snatched up some shovels lying near, and began work. We had no time to remove the dead and dying Rebels on the works, and the dirt we threw covered them up. It proved a false alarm. Hardee had as much as he could do to save his own hide, and the affair ended about dark.

"When we came to count up what we had gained, we found that we had actually taken more prisoners from behind breastworks than there were in our brigade when we started the charge. We had made the only really successful bayonet charge of the campaign. Every other time since we left Chattanooga the party standing on the defensive had been successful. Here we had taken strong double lines, with ten guns, seven battle flags, and over two thousand prisoners. We had lost terribly—not less than one-third of the brigade, and many of our best men. Our regiment went into the battle with fifteen officers; nine of these were killed or wounded, and seven of the nine lost either their limbs or lives. The Thirty-Eighth Ohio, and the other regiments of the brigade lost equally heavy. We thought Chickamauga awful, but Jonesboro discounted it."

"Do you know," said another of the Fourteenth, "I heard our Surgeon telling about how that Colonel Grower, of the Seventeenth New York, who came in so splendidly on our left, died? They say he was a Wall Street broker, before the war. He was hit shortly after he led his regiment in, and after the fight, was carried back to the hospital. While our Surgeon was going the rounds Colonel Grower called him, and said quietly, 'When you get through with the men, come and see me, please.'

"The Doctor would have attended to him then, but Grower wouldn't let him. After he got through he went back to Grower, examined his wound, and told him that he could only live a few hours. Grower received the news tranquilly, had the Doctor write a letter to his wife, and gave him his things to send her, and then grasping the Doctor's hand, he said:

"Doctor, I've just one more favor to ask; will you grant it?'

"The Doctor said, 'Certainly; what is it?'

"You say I can't live but a few hours?'

"Yes; that is true.' "And that I will likely be in great pain!'

"I am sorry to say so.'

"Well, then, do give me morphia enough to put me to sleep, so that I will wake up only in another world.'

"The Doctor did so; Colonel Grower thanked him; wrung his hand, bade him good-by, and went to sleep to wake no more."

"Do you believe in presentiments and superstitions?" said another of the Fourteenth. There was Fisher Pray, Orderly Sergeant of Company I. He came from Waterville, O., where his folks are now living. The day before we started out he had a presentiment that we were going into a fight, and that he would be killed. He couldn't shake it off. He told the Lieutenant, and some of the boys about it, and they tried to ridicule him out of it, but it was no good. When the sharp firing broke out in front some of the boys said, 'Fisher, I do believe you are right,' and he nodded his head mournfully. When we were piling knapsacks for the charge, the Lieutenant, who was a great friend of Fisher's, said:

"Fisher, you stay here and guard the knapsacks.'

"Fisher's face blazed in an instant.

"No, sir,' said he; I never shirked a fight yet, and I won't begin now.'

"So he went into the fight, and was killed, as he knew he would be. Now, that's what I call nerve."

"The same thing was true of Sergeant Arthur Tarbox, of Company A," said the narrator; "he had a presentiment, too; he knew he was going to be killed, if he went in, and he was offered an honorable chance to stay out, but he would not take it, and went in and was killed."

"Well, we staid there the next day, buried our dead, took care of our wounded, and gathered up the plunder we had taken from the Johnnies. The rest of the army went off, 'hot blocks,' after Hardee and the rest of Hood's army, which it was hoped would be caught outside of entrenchments. But Hood had too much the start, and got into the works at Lovejoy, ahead of our fellows. The night before we heard several very loud explosions up to the north. We guessed what that meant, and so did the Twentieth Corps, who were lying back at the Chattahoochee, and the next morning the General commanding—Slocum—sent out a reconnaissance. It was met by the Mayor of Atlanta, who said that the Rebels had blown up their stores and retreated. The Twentieth Corps then came in and took 'possession of the City, and the next day—the 3d—Sherman came in, and issued an order declaring the campaign at an end, and that we would rest awhile and refit.

"We laid around Atlanta a good while, and things quieted down so that it seemed almost like peace, after the four months of continual fighting we had gone through. We had been under a strain so long that now we boys went in the other direction, and became too careless, and that's how we got picked up. We went out about five miles one night after a lot of nice smoked hams that a nigger told us were stored in an old cotton press, and which we knew would be enough sight better eating for Company C, than the commissary pork we had lived on so long. We found the cotton press, and the hams, just as the nigger told us, and we hitched up a team to take them into camp. As we hadn't seen any Johnny signs anywhere, we set our guns down to help load the meat, and just as we all came stringing out to the wagon with as much meat as we could carry, a company of Ferguson's Cavalry popped out of the woods about one hundred yards in front of us and were on top of us before we could say I scat. You see they'd heard of the meat, too."

CHAPTER LVII.

A FAIR SACRIFICE—THE STORY OF ONE BOY WHO WILLINGLY GAVE HIS YOUNG
LIFE FOR HIS COUNTRY.

Charley Barbour was one of the truest-hearted and best-liked of my school-boy chums and
friends. For several terms we sat together on the same uncompromisingly uncomfortable bench,
worried over the same boy-maddening problems in "Ray's Arithmetic-Part III.," learned the same
jargon of meaningless rules from "Greene's Grammar," pondered over "Mitchell's Geography
and Atlas," and tried in vain to understand why Providence made the surface of one State
obtrusively pink and another ultramarine blue; trod slowly and painfully over the rugged road
"Bullion" points out for beginners in Latin, and began to believe we should hate ourselves and
everybody else, if we were gotten up after the manner shown by "Cutter's Physiology." We were
caught together in the same long series of school-boy scrapes—and were usually ferruled
together by the same strong-armed teacher. We shared nearly everything —our fun and work;
enjoyment and annoyance—all were generally meted out to us together. We read from the same
books the story of the wonderful world we were going to see in that bright future "when we were
men;" we spent our Saturdays and vacations in the miniature explorations of the rocky hills and
caves, and dark cedar woods around our homes, to gather ocular helps to a better comprehension
of that magical land which we were convinced began just beyond our horizon, and had in it,
visible to the eye of him who traveled through its enchanted breadth, all that "Gulliver's Fables,"
the "Arabian Nights," and a hundred books of travel and adventure told of.

We imagined that the only dull and commonplace spot on earth was that where we lived.
Everywhere else life was a grand spectacular drama, full of thrilling effects.

Brave and handsome young men were rescuing distressed damsels, beautiful as they were
wealthy; bloody pirates and swarthy murderers were being foiled by quaint spoken
backwoodsmen, who carried unerring rifles; gallant but blundering Irishmen, speaking the most
delightful brogue, and making the funniest mistakes, were daily thwarting cool and determined
villains; bold tars were encountering fearful sea perils; lionhearted adventurers were cowing and
quelling whole tribes of barbarians; magicians were casting spells, misers hoarding gold,
scientists making astonishing discoveries, poor and unknown boys achieving wealth and fame at
a single bound, hidden mysteries coming to light, and so the world was going on, making reams
of history with each diurnal revolution, and furnishing boundless material for the most delightful
books.

At the age of thirteen a perusal of the lives of Benjamin Franklin and Horace Greeley
precipitated my determination to no longer hesitate in launching my small bark upon the great
ocean. I ran away from home in a truly romantic way, and placed my foot on what I expected to
be the first round of the ladder of fame, by becoming "devil boy" in a printing office in a distant
large City. Charley's attachment to his mother and his home was too strong to permit him to take
this step, and we parted in sorrow, mitigated on my side by roseate dreams of the future.

Six years passed. One hot August morning I met an old acquaintance at the Creek, in

Andersonville. He told me to come there the next morning, after roll-call, and he would take me to see some person who was very anxious to meet me. I was prompt at the rendezvous, and was soon joined by the other party. He threaded his way slowly for over half an hour through the closely-jumbled mass of tents and burrows, and at length stopped in front of a blanket-tent in the northwestern corner. The occupant rose and took my hand. For an instant I was puzzled; then the clear, blue eyes, and well-remembered smile recalled to me my old-time comrade, Charley Barbour. His story was soon told. He was a Sergeant in a Western Virginia cavalry regiment— the Fourth, I think. At the time Hunter was making his retreat from the Valley of Virginia, it was decided to mislead the enemy by sending out a courier with false dispatches to be captured. There was a call for a volunteer for this service. Charley was the first to offer, with that spirit of generous self-sacrifice that was one of his pleasantest traits when a boy. He knew what he had to expect. Capture meant imprisonment at Andersonville; our men had now a pretty clear understanding of what this was. Charley took the dispatches and rode into the enemy's lines. He was taken, and the false information produced the desired effect. On his way to Andersonville he was stripped of all his clothing but his shirt and pantaloons, and turned into the Stockade in this condition. When I saw him he had been in a week or more. He told his story quietly—almost diffidently—not seeming aware that he had done more than his simple duty. I left him with the promise and expectation of returning the next day, but when I attempted to find him again, I was lost in the maze of tents and burrows. I had forgotten to ask the number of his detachment, and after spending several days in hunting for him, I was forced to give the search up. He knew as little of my whereabouts, and though we were all the time within seventeen hundred feet of each other, neither we nor our common acquaintance could ever manage to meet again. This will give the reader an idea of the throng compressed within the narrow limits of the Stockade. After leaving Andersonville, however, I met this man once more, and learned from him that Charley had sickened and died within a month after his entrance to prison.

So ended his day-dream of a career in the busy world.

CHAPTER LVIII.

WE LEAVE SAVANNAH—MORE HOPES OF EXCHANGE—SCENES AT DEPARTURE —"FLANKERS"—ON THE BACK TRACK TOWARD ANDERSONVILLE—ALARM THEREAT —AT THE PARTING OF TWO WAYS—WE FINALLY BRING UP AT CAMP LAWTON.

On the evening of the 11th of October there came an order for one thousand prisoners to fall in and march out, for transfer to some other point.

Of course, Andrews and I "flanked" into this crowd. That was our usual way of doing. Holding that the chances were strongly in favor of every movement of prisoners being to our lines, we never failed to be numbered in the first squad of prisoners that were sent out. The seductive mirage of "exchange" was always luring us on. It must come some time, certainly, and it would be most likely to come to those who were most earnestly searching for it. At all events, we should leave no means untried to avail ourselves of whatever seeming chances there might be. There could be no other motive for this move, we argued, than exchange. The Confederacy was not likely to be at the trouble and expense of hauling us about the country without some good reason—something better than a wish to make us acquainted with Southern scenery and topography. It would hardly take us away from Savannah so soon after bringing us there for any other purpose than delivery to our people.

The Rebels encouraged this belief with direct assertions of its truth. They framed a plausible lie about there having arisen some difficulty concerning the admission of our vessels past the harbor defenses of Savannah, which made it necessary to take us elsewhere—probably to Charleston— for delivery to our men.

Wishes are always the most powerful allies of belief. There is little difficulty in convincing a man of that of which he wants to be convinced. We forgot the lie told us when we were taken from Andersonville, and believed the one which was told us now.

Andrews and I hastily snatched our worldly possessions—our overcoat, blanket, can, spoon, chessboard and men, yelled to some of our neighbors that they could have our hitherto much-treasured house, and running down to the gate, forced ourselves well up to the front of the crowd that was being assembled to go out.

The usual scenes accompanying the departure of first squads were being acted tumultuously. Every one in the camp wanted to be one of the supposed-to-be-favored few, and if not selected at first, tried to "flank in"—that is, slip into the place of some one else who had had better luck. This one naturally resisted displacement, 'vi et armis,' and the fights would become so general as to cause a resemblance to the famed Fair of Donnybrook. The cry would go up:

"Look out for flankers!"

The lines of the selected would dress up compactly, and outsiders trying to force themselves in would get mercilessly pounded.

We finally got out of the pen, and into the cars, which soon rolled away to the westward. We were packed in too densely to be able to lie down. We could hardly sit down. Andrews and I took up our position in one corner, piled our little treasures under us, and trying to lean against each other in such a way as to afford mutual support and rest, dozed fitfully through a long, weary night.

When morning came we found ourselves running northwest through a poor, pine-barren country that strongly resembled that we had traversed in coming to Savannah. The more we looked at it the more familiar it became, and soon there was no doubt we were going back to Andersonville. By noon we had reached Millen—eighty miles from Savannah, and fifty-three from Augusta. It was the junction of the road leading to Macon and that running to Augusta. We halted a little while at the "Y," and to us the minutes were full of anxiety. If we turned off to the left we were going back to Andersonville. If we took the right hand road we were on the way to Charleston or Richmond, with the chances in favor of exchange.

At length we started, and, to our joy, our engine took the right hand track. We stopped again, after a run of five miles, in the midst of one of the open, scattering forests of long leaved pine that I have before described. We were ordered out of the cars, and marching a few rods, came in sight of another of those hateful Stockades, which seemed to be as natural products of the Sterile sand of that dreary land as its desolate woods and its breed of boy murderers and gray-headed assassins.

Again our hearts sank, and death seemed more welcome than incarceration in those gloomy wooden walls. We marched despondently up to the gates of the Prison, and halted while a party of Rebel clerks made a list of our names, rank, companies, and regiments. As they were Rebels it was slow work. Reading and writing never came by nature, as Dogberry would say, to any man fighting for Secession. As a rule, he took to them as reluctantly as if, he thought them cunning inventions of the Northern Abolitionist to perplex and demoralize him. What a half-dozen boys taken out of our own ranks would have done with ease in an hour or so, these Rebels worried over all of the afternoon, and then their register of us was so imperfect, badly written and misspelled, that the Yankee clerks afterwards detailed for the purpose, never could succeed in reducing it to intelligibility.

We learned that the place at which we had arrived was Camp Lawton, but we almost always spoke of it as "Millen," the same as Camp Sumter is universally known as Andersonville.

Shortly after dark we were turned inside the Stockade. Being the first that had entered, there was quite a quantity of wood—the offal from the timber used in constructing the Stockade—lying on the ground. The night was chilly one we soon had a number of fires blazing. Green pitch pine, when burned, gives off a peculiar, pungent odor, which is never forgotten by one who has once smelled it. I first became acquainted with it on entering Andersonville, and to this day it is the most powerful remembrance I can have of the opening of that dreadful Iliad of woes. On my journey to Washington of late years the locomotives are invariably fed with pitch pine as we near the Capital, and as the well-remembered smell reaches me, I grow sick at heart with the flood of saddening recollections indissolubly associated with it.

As our fires blazed up the clinging, penetrating fumes diffused themselves everywhere. The night was as cool as the one when we arrived at Andersonville, the earth, meagerly sodded with sparse, hard, wiry grass, was the same; the same piney breezes blew in from the surrounding trees, the same dismal owls hooted at us; the same mournful whip-poor-will lamented, God knows what, in the gathering twilight. What we both felt in the gloomy recesses of downcast hearts Andrews expressed as he turned to me with:

"My God, Mc, this looks like Andersonville all over again."

A cupful of corn meal was issued to each of us. I hunted up some water. Andrews made a stiff dough, and spread it about half an inch thick on the back of our chessboard. He propped this up before the fire, and when the surface was neatly browned over, slipped it off the board and turned it over to brown the other side similarly. This done, we divided it carefully between us, swallowed it in silence, spread our old overcoat on the ground, tucked chess-board, can, and spoon under far enough to be out of the reach of thieves, adjusted the thin blanket so as to get the most possible warmth out of it, crawled in close together, and went to sleep. This, thank Heaven, we could do; we could still sleep, and Nature had some opportunity to repair the waste of the day. We slept, and forgot where we were.

CHAPTER LIX.

OUR NEW QUARTERS AT CAMP LAWTON—BUILDING A HUT—AN EXCEPTIONAL COMMANDANT—HE IS a GOOD MAN, BUT WILL TAKE BRIBES—RATIONS.

In the morning we took a survey of our new quarters, and found that we were in a Stockade resembling very much in construction and dimensions that at Andersonville. The principal difference was that the upright logs were in their rough state, whereas they were hewed at Andersonville, and the brook running through the camp was not bordered by a swamp, but had clean, firm banks.

Our next move was to make the best of the situation. We were divided into hundreds, each commanded by a Sergeant. Ten hundreds constituted a division, the head of which was also a Sergeant. I was elected by my comrades to the Sergeantcy of the Second Hundred of the First Division. As soon as we were assigned to our ground, we began constructing shelter. For the first and only time in my prison experience, we found a full supply of material for this purpose, and the use we made of it showed how infinitely better we would have fared if in each prison the Rebels had done even so slight a thing as to bring in a few logs from the surrounding woods and distribute them to us. A hundred or so of these would probably have saved thousands of lives at Andersonville and Florence.

A large tree lay on the ground assigned to our hundred. Andrews and I took possession of one side of the ten feet nearest the butt. Other boys occupied the rest in a similar manner. One of our boys had succeeded in smuggling an ax in with him, and we kept it in constant use day and night, each group borrowing it for an hour or so at a time. It was as dull as a hoe, and we were very weak, so that it was slow work "niggering off"—(as the boys termed it) a cut of the log. It seemed as if beavers could have gnawed it off easier and more quickly. We only cut an inch or so at a time, and then passed the ax to the next users. Making little wedges with a dull knife, we drove them into the log with clubs, and split off long, thin strips, like the weatherboards of a house, and by the time we had split off our share of the log in this slow and laborious way, we had a fine lot of these strips. We were lucky enough to find four forked sticks, of which we made the corners of our dwelling, and roofed it carefully with our strips, held in place by sods torn up from the edge of the creek bank. The sides and ends were enclosed; we gathered enough pine tops to cover the ground to a depth of several inches; we banked up the outside, and ditched around it, and then had the most comfortable abode we had during our prison career. It was truly a house builded with our own hands, for we had no tools whatever save the occasional use of the aforementioned dull axe and equally dull knife.

The rude little hut represented as much actual hard, manual labor as would be required to build a comfortable little cottage in the North, but we gladly performed it, as we would have done any other work to better our condition.

For a while wood was quite plentiful, and we had the luxury daily of warm fires, which the increasing coolness of the weather made important accessories to our comfort.

Other prisoners kept coming in. Those we left behind at Savannah followed us, and the prison there was broken up. Quite a number also came in from—Andersonville, so that in a little while we had between six and seven thousand in the Stockade. The last comers found all the material for tents and all the fuel used up, and consequently did not fare so well as the earlier arrivals. The commandant of the prison—one Captain Bowes—was the best of his class it was my fortune to meet. Compared with the senseless brutality of Wirz, the reckless deviltry of Davis, or the stupid malignance of Barrett, at Florence, his administration was mildness and wisdom itself. He enforced discipline better than any of those named, but has what they all lacked—executive ability—and he secured results that they could not possibly attain, and without anything, like the friction that attended their efforts. I do not remember that any one was shot during our six weeks' stay at Millen—a circumstance simply remarkable, since I do not recall a single week passed anywhere else without at least one murder by the guards.

One instance will illustrate the difference of his administration from that of other prison commandants. He came upon the grounds of our division one morning, accompanied by a pleasant-faced, intelligent-appearing lad of about fifteen or sixteen. He said to us:

"Gentlemen: (The only instance during our imprisonment when we received so polite a designation.) This is my son, who will hereafter call your roll. He will treat you as gentlemen, and I know you will do the same to him."

This understanding was observed to the letter on both sides. Young Bowes invariably spoke civilly to us, and we obeyed his orders with a prompt cheerfulness that left him nothing to complain of.

The only charge I have to make against Bowes is made more in detail in another chapter, and that is, that he took money from well prisoners for giving them the first chance to go through on the Sick Exchange. How culpable this was I must leave each reader to decide for himself. I thought it very wrong at the time, but possibly my views might have been colored highly by my not having any money wherewith to procure my own inclusion in the happy lot of the exchanged. Of one thing I am certain: that his acceptance of money to bias his official action was not singular on his part. I am convinced that every commandant we had over us—except Wirz—was habitually in the receipt of bribes from prisoners. I never heard that any one succeeded in bribing Wirz, and this is the sole good thing I can say of that fellow. Against this it may be said, however, that he plundered the boys so effectually on entering the prison as to leave them little of the wherewithal to bribe anybody.

Davis was probably the most unscrupulous bribe-taker of the lot. He actually received money for permitting prisoners to escape to our lines, and got down to as low a figure as one hundred dollars for this sort of service. I never heard that any of the other commandants went this far.

The rations issued to us were somewhat better than those of Andersonville, as the meal was finer and better, though it was absurdedly insufficient in quantity, and we received no salt. On several occasions fresh beef was dealt out to us, and each time the excitement created among those who had not tasted fresh meat for weeks and months was wonderful. On the first occasion the meat was simply the heads of the cattle killed for the use of the guards. Several wagon loads of these were brought in and distributed. We broke them up so that every man got a piece of the bone, which was boiled and reboiled, as long as a single bubble of grease would rise to the surface of the water; every vestige of meat was gnawed and scraped from the surface and then the bone was charred until it crumbled, when it was eaten. No one who has not experienced it can imagine the inordinate hunger for animal food of those who had eaten little else than corn bread for so long. Our exhausted bodies were perishing for lack of proper sustenance. Nature indicated fresh beef as the best medium to repair the great damage already done, and our longing for it became beyond description.

CHAPTER LX

THE RAIDERS REAPPEAR ON THE SCENE—THE ATTEMPT TO ASSASSINATE THOSE WHO WERE CONCERNED IN THE EXECUTION—A COUPLE OF LIVELY FIGHTS, IN WHICH THE RAIDERS ARE DEFEATED—HOLDING AN ELECTION.

Our old antagonists—the Raiders—were present in strong force in Millen. Like ourselves, they had imagined the departure from Andersonville was for exchange, and their relations to the Rebels were such that they were all given a chance to go with the first squads. A number had been allowed to go with the sailors on the Special Naval Exchange from Savannah, in the place of sailors and marines who had died. On the way to Charleston a fight had taken place between them and the real sailors, during which one of their number—a curly-headed Irishman named Dailey, who was in such high favor with the Rebels that he was given the place of driving the ration wagon that came in the North Side at Andersonville —was killed, and thrown under the wheels of the moving train, which passed over him.

After things began to settle into shape at Millen, they seemed to believe that they were in such ascendancy as to numbers and organization that they could put into execution their schemes of vengeance against those of us who had been active participants in the execution of their confederates at Andersonville.

After some little preliminaries they settled upon Corporal "Wat" Payne, of my company, as their first victim. The reader will remember Payne as one of the two Corporals who pulled the trigger to the scaffold at the time of the execution.

Payne was a very good man physically, and was yet in fair condition. The Raiders came up one day with their best man—Pete Donnelly—and provoked a fight, intending, in the course of it, to kill Payne. We, who knew Payee, felt reasonably confident of his ability to handle even so redoubtable a pugilist as Donnelly, and we gathered together a little squad of our friends to see fair play.

The fight began after the usual amount of bad talk on both sides, and we were pleased to see our man slowly get the better of the New York plug-ugly. After several sharp rounds they closed, and still Payne was ahead, but in an evil moment he spied a pine knot at his feet, which he thought he could reach, and end the fight by cracking Donnelly's head with it. Donnelly took instant advantage of the movement to get it, threw Payne heavily, and fell upon him. His crowd rushed in to finish our man by clubbing him over the head. We sailed in to prevent this, and after a rattling exchange of blows all around, succeeded in getting Payne away.

The issue of the fight seemed rather against us, however, and the Raiders were much emboldened. Payne kept close to his crowd after that, and as we had shown such an entire willingness to stand by him, the Raiders —with their accustomed prudence when real fighting was involved—did not attempt to molest him farther, though they talked very savagely.

A few days after this Sergeant Goody and Corporal Ned Carrigan, both of our battalion, came in.

I must ask the reader to again recall the fact that Sergeant Goody was one of the six hangmen who put the meal-sacks over the heads, and the ropes around the necks of the condemned. Corporal Carrigan was the gigantic prize fighter, who was universally acknowledged to be the best man physically among the whole thirty-four thousand in Andersonville. The Raiders knew that Goody had come in before we of his own battalion did. They resolved to kill him then and there, and in broad daylight. He had secured in some way a shelter tent, and was inside of it fixing it up. The Raider crowd, headed by Pete Donnelly, and Dick Allen, went up to his tent and one of them called to him:

"Sergeant, come out; I want to see you."

Goody, supposing it was one of us, came crawling out on his hands and knees. As he did so their heavy clubs crashed down upon his head. He was neither killed nor stunned, as they had reason to expect. He succeeded in rising to his feet, and breaking through the crowd of assassins. He dashed down the side of the hill, hotly pursued by them. Coming to the Creek, he leaped it in his excitement, but his pursuers could not, and were checked. One of our battalion boys, who saw and comprehended the whole affair, ran over to us, shouting:

"Turn out! turn out, for God's sake! the Raiders are killing Goody!"

We snatched up our clubs and started after the Raiders, but before we could reach them, Ned Carrigan, who also comprehended what the trouble was, had run to the side of Goody, armed with a terrible looking club. The sight of Ned, and the demonstration that he was thoroughly aroused, was enough for the Raider crew, and they abandoned the field hastily. We did not feel ourselves strong enough to follow them on to their own dung hill, and try conclusions with them, but we determined to report the matter to the Rebel Commandant, from whom we had reason to believe we could expect assistance. We were right. He sent in a squad of guards, arrested Dick Allen, Pete Donnelly, and several other ringleaders, took them out and put them in the stocks in such a manner that they were compelled to lie upon their stomachs. A shallow tin vessel containing water was placed under their faces to furnish them drink.

They staid there a day and night, and when released, joined the Rebel Army, entering the artillery company that manned the guns in the fort covering the prison. I used to imagine with what zeal they would send us over; a round of shell or grape if they could get anything like an excuse.

This gave us good riddance—of our dangerous enemies, and we had little further trouble with any of them.

The depression in the temperature made me very sensible of the deficiencies in my wardrobe. Unshod feet, a shirt like a fishing net, and pantaloons as well ventilated as a paling fence might do very well for the broiling sun at Andersonville and Savannah, but now, with the thermometer nightly dipping a little nearer the frost line, it became unpleasantly evident that as garments their office was purely perfunctory; one might say ornamental simply, if he wanted to be very sarcastic. They were worn solely to afford convenient quarters for multitudes of lice, and in deference to the prejudice which has existed since the Fall of Man against our mingling with our fellow creatures in the attire provided us by Nature. Had I read Darwin then I should have expected that my long exposure to the weather would start a fine suit of fur, in the effort of Nature to adapt, me to my environment. But no more indications of this appeared than if I had been a hairless dog of Mexico, suddenly transplanted to more northern latitudes. Providence did not seem to be in the tempering-the-wind-to-the-shorn-lamb business, as far as I was concerned. I still retained an almost unconquerable prejudice against stripping the dead to secure clothes, and so unless exchange or death came speedily, I was in a bad fix.

One morning about day break, Andrews, who had started to go to another part of the camp, came slipping back in a state of gleeful excitement. At first I thought he either had found a tunnel or had heard some good news about exchange. It was neither. He opened his jacket and handed me an infantry man's blouse, which he had found in the main street, where it had dropped out of some fellow's bundle. We did not make any extra exertion to find the owner. Andrews was in sore need of clothes himself, but my necessities were so much greater that the generous fellow thought of my wants first. We examined the garment with as much interest as ever a belle bestowed on a new dress from Worth's. It was in fair preservation, but the owner had cut the buttons off to trade to the guard, doubtless for a few sticks of wood, or a spoonful of salt. We supplied the place of these with little wooden pins, and I donned the garment as a shirt and coat and vest, too, for that matter. The best suit I ever put on never gave me a hundredth part the satisfaction that this did. Shortly after, I managed to subdue my aversion so far as to take a good shoe which a one-legged dead man had no farther use for, and a little later a comrade gave me for the other foot a boot bottom from which he had cut the top to make a bucket.

....

The day of the Presidential election of 1864 approached. The Rebels were naturally very much interested in the result, as they believed that the election of McClellan meant compromise and cessation of hostilities, while the re-election of Lincoln meant prosecution of the War to the bitter end. The toadying Raiders, who were perpetually hanging around the gate to get a chance to insinuate themselves into the favor of the Rebel officers, persuaded them that we were all so bitterly hostile to our Government for not exchanging us that if we were allowed to vote we would cast an overwhelming majority in favor of McClellan.

The Rebels thought that this might perhaps be used to advantage as political capital for their friends in the North. They gave orders that we might, if we chose, hold an election on the same day of the Presidential election. They sent in some ballot boxes, and we elected Judges of the Election.

About noon of that day Captain Bowes, and a crowd of tightbooted, broad-hatted Rebel officers, strutted in with the peculiar "Ef-yer-don't-b'lieve—I'm-a-butcher-jest-smell-o'-mebutes" swagger characteristic of the class. They had come in to see us all voting for McClellan. Instead, they found the polls surrounded with ticket pedlers shouting:

"Walk right up here now, and get your Unconditional-Union-Abraham-Lincoln -tickets!"

"Here's your straight-haired prosecution-of-the-war ticket."

"Vote the Lincoln ticket; vote to whip the Rebels, and make peace with them when they've laid down their arms."

"Don't vote a McClellan ticket and gratify Rebels, everywhere," etc.

The Rebel officers did not find the scene what their fancy painted it, and turning around they strutted out.

When the votes came to be counted out there were over seven thousand for Lincoln, and not half that many hundred for McClellan. The latter got very few votes outside the Raider crowd. The same day a similar election was held in Florence, with like result. Of course this did not indicate that there was any such preponderance of Republicans among us. It meant simply that the Democratic boys, little as they might have liked Lincoln, would have voted for him a hundred times rather than do anything to please the Rebels.

I never heard that the Rebels sent the result North.

CHAPTER LXI

THE REBELS FORMALLY PROPOSE TO US TO DESERT TO THEM—CONTUMELIOUS TREATMENT OF THE PROPOSITION—THEIR RAGE—AN EXCITING TIME—AN OUTBREAK THREATENED—DIFFICULTIES ATTENDING DESERTION TO THE REBELS.

One day in November, some little time after the occurrences narrated in the last chapter, orders came in to make out rolls of all those who were born outside of the United States, and whose terms of service had expired.

We held a little council among ourselves as to the meaning of this, and concluded that some partial exchange had been agreed on, and the Rebels were going to send back the class of boys whom they thought would be of least value to the Government. Acting on this conclusion the great majority of us enrolled ourselves as foreigners, and as having served out our terms. I made out the roll of my hundred, and managed to give every man a foreign nativity. Those whose names would bear it were assigned to England, Ireland, Scotland France and Germany, and the balance were distributed through Canada and the West Indies. After finishing the roll and sending it out, I did not wonder that the Rebels believed the battles for the Union were fought by foreign mercenaries. The other rolls were made out in the same way, and I do not suppose that they showed five hundred native Americans in the Stockade.

The next day after sending out the rolls, there came an order that all those whose names appeared thereon should fall in. We did so, promptly, and as nearly every man in camp was included, we fell in as for other purposes, by hundreds and thousands. We were then marched outside, and massed around a stump on which stood a Rebel officer, evidently waiting to make us a speech. We awaited his remarks with the greatest impatience, but He did not begin until the last division had marched out and came to a parade rest close to the stump.

It was the same old story:

"Prisoners, you can no longer have any doubt that your Government has cruelly abandoned you; it makes no efforts to release you, and refuses all our offers of exchange. We are anxious to get our men back, and have made every effort to do so, but it refuses to meet us on any reasonable grounds. Your Secretary of War has said that the Government can get along very well without you, and General Halleck has said that you were nothing but a set of blackberry pickers and coffee boilers anyhow.

"You've already endured much more than it could expect of you; you served it faithfully during the term you enlisted for, and now, when it is through with you, it throws you aside to starve and die. You also can have no doubt that the Southern Confederacy is certain to succeed in securing its independence. It will do this in a few months. It now offers you an opportunity to join its service, and if you serve it faithfully to the end, you will receive the same rewards as the rest of its soldiers. You will be taken out of here, be well clothed and fed, given a good bounty, and, at the conclusion of the War receive a land warrant for a nice farm. If you"—

But we had heard enough. The Sergeant of our division—a man with a stentorian voice sprang out and shouted:

"Attention, first Division!"

We Sergeants of hundreds repeated the command down the line. Shouted he:

"First Division, about—"

Said we:

"First Hundred, about—"

"Second Hundred, about—"

"Third Hundred, about—"

"Fourth Hundred, about—" etc., etc.

Said he:—

"FACE!!"

Ten Sergeants repeated "Face!" one after the other, and each man in the hundreds turned on his heel. Then our leader commanded—

"First Division, forward! MARCH!" and we strode back into the Stockade, followed immediately by all the other divisions, leaving the orator still standing on the stump.

The Rebels were furious at this curt way of replying. We had scarcely reached our quarters when they came in with several companies, with loaded guns and fixed bayonets. They drove us out of our tents and huts, into one corner, under the pretense of hunting axes and spades, but in reality to steal our blankets, and whatever else they could find that they wanted, and to break down and injure our huts, many of which, costing us days of patient labor, they destroyed in pure wantonness.

We were burning with the bitterest indignation. A tall, slender man named Lloyd, a member of the Sixty-First Ohio—a rough, uneducated fellow, but brim full of patriotism and manly common sense, jumped up on a stump and poured out his soul in rude but fiery eloquence:

"Comrades," he said, "do not let the blowing of these Rebel whelps discourage you; pay no attention to the lies they have told you to-day; you know well that our Government is too honorable and just to desert any one who serves it; it has not deserted us; their hell-born Confederacy is not going to succeed. I tell you that as sure as there is a God who reigns and judges in Israel, before the Spring breezes stir the tops of these blasted old pines their Confederacy and all the lousy graybacks who support it will be so deep in hell that nothing but a search warrant from the throne of God Almighty can ever find it again. And the glorious old Stars and Stripes—"

Here we began cheering tremendously. A Rebel Captain came running up, said to the guard, who was leaning on his gun, gazing curiously at Lloyd:

"What in —— are you standing gaping there for? Why don't you shoot the —— —— Yankee son—— — - ——-?" and snatching the gun away from him, cocked and leveled it at Lloyd, but the boys near jerked the speaker down from the stump and saved his life.

We became fearfully, wrought up. Some of the more excitable shouted out to charge on the line of guards, snatch they guns away from them, and force our way through the gate The shouts were taken up by others, and, as if in obedience to the suggestion, we instinctively formed in line-of-battle facing the guards. A glance down the line showed me an array of desperate, tensely drawn faces, such as one sees who looks a men when they are summoning up all their resolution for some deed of great peril. The Rebel officers hastily retreated behind the line of guards, whose faces blanched, but they leveled the muskets and prepared to receive us.

Captain Bowes, who was overlooking the prison from an elevation outside, had, however, divined the trouble at the outset, an was preparing to meet it. The gunners, who had shotted the pieces and trained them upon us when we came out to listen t the speech, had again covered us with them, and were ready to sweep the prison with grape and canister at the instant of command. The long roll was summoning the infantry regiments back into line, and some of the cooler-headed among us pointed these facts out and succeeded in getting the line to dissolve again into groups of muttering, sullen-faced men. When this was done, the guards marched out, by a cautious indirect maneuver, so as not to turn their backs to us.

It was believed that we had some among us who would like to avail themselves of the offer of the Rebels, and that they would try to inform the Rebels of their desires by going to the gate during the night and speaking to the Officer-of-the-Guard. A squad armed themselves with clubs and laid in wait for these. They succeeded in catching several —snatching some of then back even after they had told the guard their wishes in a tone so loud that all near could hear distinctly. The Officer-of-the-Guard rushed in two or three times in a vain attempt to save the would be deserter from the cruel hands that clutched him and bore him away to where he had a lesson in loyalty impressed upon the fleshiest part of his person by a long, flexible strip of pine wielded by very willing hands.

After this was kept up for several nights different ideas began I to prevail. It was felt that if a man wanted to join the Rebels, the best way was to let him go and get rid of him. He was of no benefit to the Government, and would be of none to the Rebels. After this no restriction was put upon any one who desired to go outside and take the oath. But very few did so, however, and these were wholly confined to the Raider crowd.

CHAPTER LXII.

SERGEANT LEROY L. KEY—HIS ADVENTURES SUBSEQUENT TO THE EXECUTIONS —HE GOES OUTSIDE AT ANDERSONVILLE ON PAROLE—LABORS IN THE COOK-HOUSE —ATTEMPTS TO ESCAPE—IS RECAPTURED AND TAKEN TO MACON—ESCAPES FROM THERE, BUT IS COMPELLED TO RETURN—IS FINALLY EXCHANGED AT SAVANNAH.

Leroy L. Key, the heroic Sergeant of Company M, Sixteenth Illinois Cavalry, who organized and led the Regulators at Andersonville in their successful conflict with and defeat of the Raiders, and who presided at the execution of the six condemned men on the 11th of July, furnishes, at the request of the author, the following story of his prison career subsequent to that event:

On the 12th day of July, 1864, the day after the hanging of the six Raiders, by the urgent request of my many friends (of whom you were one), I sought and obtained from Wirz a parole for myself and the six brave men who assisted as executioners of those desperados. It seemed that you were all fearful that we might, after what had been done, be assassinated if we remained in the Stockade; and that we might be overpowered, perhaps, by the friends of the Raiders we had hanged, at a time possibly, when you would not be on hand to give us assistance, and thus lose our lives for rendering the help we did in getting rid of the worst pestilence we had to contend with.

On obtaining my parole I was very careful to have it so arranged and mutually understood, between Wirz and myself, that at any time that my squad (meaning the survivors of my comrades, with whom I was originally captured) was sent away from Andersonville, either to be exchanged or to go to another prison, that I should be allowed to go with them. This was agreed to, and so written in my parole which I carried until it absolutely wore out. I took a position in the cook-house, and the other boys either went to work there, or at the hospital or grave-yard as occasion required. I worked here, and did the best I could for the many starving wretches inside, in the way of preparing their food, until the eighth day of September, at which time, if you remember, quite a train load of men were removed, as many of us thought, for the purpose of exchange; but, as we afterwards discovered, to be taken to another prison. Among the crowd so removed was my squad, or, at least, a portion of them, being my intimate mess-mates while in the Stockade. As soon as I found this to be the case I waited on Wirz at his office, and asked permission to go with them, which he refused, stating that he was compelled to have men at the cookhouse to cook for those in the Stockade until they were all gone or exchanged. I reminded him of the condition in my parole, but this only had the effect of making him mad, and he threatened me with the stocks if I did not go back and resume work. I then and there made up my mind to attempt my escape, considering that the parole had first been broken by the man that granted it.

On inquiry after my return to the cook-house, I found four other boys who were also planning an escape, and who were only too glad to get me to join them and take charge of the affair. Our plans were well laid and well executed, as the sequel will prove, and in this particular my own experience in the endeavor to escape from Andersonville is not entirely dissimilar from yours, though it had different results. I very much regret that in the attempt I lost my penciled memorandum, in which it was my habit to chronicle what went on around me daily, and where I had the names of my brave comrades who made the effort to escape with me. Unfortunately, I cannot now recall to memory the name of one of them or remember to what commands they belonged.

I knew that our greatest risk was run in eluding the guards, and that in the morning we should be compelled to cheat the blood-hounds. The first we managed to do very well, not without many hairbreadth escapes, however; but we did succeed in getting through both lines of guards, and found ourselves in the densest pine forest I ever saw. We traveled, as nearly as we could judge, due north all night until daylight. From our fatigue and bruises, and the long hours that had elapsed since 8 o'clock, the time of our starting, we thought we had come not less than twelve or fifteen miles. Imagine our surprise and mortification, then, when we could plainly hear the reveille, and almost the Sergeant's voice calling the roll, while the answers of "Here!" were perfectly distinct. We could not possibly have been more than a mile, or a mile-and-a-half at the farthest, from the Stockade.

Our anxiety and mortification were doubled when at the usual hour—as we supposed—we heard the well-known and long-familiar sound of the hunter's horn, calling his hounds to their accustomed task of making the circuit of the Stockade, for the purpose of ascertaining whether or not any "Yankee" had had the audacity to attempt an escape. The hounds, anticipating, no doubt, this usual daily work, gave forth glad barks of joy at being thus called forth to duty. We heard them start, as was usual, from about the railroad depot (as we imagined), but the sounds growing fainter and fainter gave us a little hope that our trail had been missed. Only a short time, however, were we allowed this pleasant reflection, for ere long—it could not have been more than an hour—we could plainly see that they were drawing nearer and nearer. They finally appeared so close that I advised the boys to climb a tree or sapling in order to keep the dogs from biting them, and to be ready to surrender when the hunters came up, hoping thus to experience as little misery as possible, and not dreaming but that we were caught. On, on came the hounds, nearer and nearer still, till we imagined that we could see the undergrowth in the forest shaking by coming in contact with their bodies. Plainer and plainer came the sound of the hunter's voice urging them forward. Our hearts were in our throats, and in the terrible excitement we wondered if it could be possible for Providence to so arrange it that the dogs would pass us. This last thought, by some strange fancy, had taken possession of me, and I here frankly acknowledge that I believed it would happen. Why I believed it, God only knows. My excitement was so great, indeed, that I almost lost sight of our danger, and felt like shouting to the dogs myself, while I came near losing my hold on the tree in which I was hidden. By chance I happened to look around at my nearest neighbor in distress. His expression was sufficient to quell any enthusiasm I might have had, and I, too, became despondent. In a very few minutes our suspense was over. The dogs came within not less than three hundred yards of us, and we could even see one of them, God in Heaven can only imagine what great joy was then, brought to our aching hearts, for almost instantly upon coming into sight, the hounds struck off on a different trail, and passed us. Their voices became fainter and fainter, until finally we could hear them no longer. About noon, however, they were called back and taken to camp, but until that time not one of us left our position in the trees.

When we were satisfied that we were safe for the present, we descended to the ground to get what rest we could, in order to be prepared for the night's march, having previously agreed to travel at night and sleep in the day time. "Our Father, who art in Heaven," etc., were the first words that escaped my lips, and the first thoughts that came to my mind as I landed on terra firma. Never before, or since, had I experienced such a profound reverence for Almighty God, for I firmly believe that only through some mighty invisible power were we at that time delivered from untold tortures. Had we been found, we might have been torn and mutilated by the dogs, or, taken back to Andersonville, have suffered for days or perhaps weeks in the stocks or chain gang, as the humor of Wirz might have dictated at the time—either of which would have been almost certain death.

It was very fortunate for us that before our escape from Andersonville we were detailed at the cook-house, for by this means we were enabled to bring away enough food to live for several days without the necessity of theft. Each one of us had our haversacks full of such small delicacies as it was possible for us to get when we started, these consisting of corn bread and fat bacon—nothing less, nothing more. Yet we managed to subsist comfortably until our fourth day out, when we happened to come upon a sweet potato patch, the potatos in which had not been dug. In a very short space of time we were all well supplied with this article, and lived on them raw during that day and the next night.

Just at evening, in going through a field, we suddenly came across three negro men, who at first sight of us showed signs of running, thinking, as they told us afterward, that we were the "patrols." After explaining to them who we were and our condition, they took us to a very quiet retreat in the woods, and two of them went off, stating that they would soon be back. In a very short time they returned laden with well cooked provisions, which not only gave us a good supper, but supplied us for the next day with all that we wanted. They then guided us on our way for several miles, and left us, after having refused compensation for what they had done.

We continued to travel in this way for nine long weary nights, and on the morning of the tenth day, as we were going into the woods to hide as usual, a little before daylight, we came to a small pond at which there was a negro boy watering two mules before hitching them to a cane mill, it then being cane grinding time in Georgia. He saw us at the same time we did him, and being frightened put whip to the animals and ran off. We tried every way to stop him, but it was no use. He had the start of us. We were very fearful of the consequences of this mishap, but had no remedy, and being very tired, could do nothing else but go into the woods, go to sleep and trust to luck.

The next thing I remembered was being punched in the ribs by my comrade nearest to me, and aroused with the remark, "We are gone up." On opening my eyes, I saw four men, in citizens' dress, each of whom had a shot gun ready for use. We were ordered to get up. The first question asked us was:

"Who are you."

This was spoken in so mild a tone as to lead me to believe that we might possibly be in the hands of gentlemen, if not indeed in those of friends. It was some time before any one answered. The boys, by their looks and the expression of their countenances, seemed to appeal to me for a reply to get them out of their present dilemma, if possible. Before I had time to collect my thoughts, we were startled by these words, coming from the same man that had asked the original question: "You had better not hesitate, for we have an idea who you are, and should it prove that we are correct, it will be the worse for you."

"'Who do you think we are?' I inquired."

"'Horse thieves and moss-backs,' was the reply."

I jumped at the conclusion instantly that in order to save our lives, we had better at once own the truth. In a very few words I told them who we were, where we were from, how long we had been on the road, etc. At this they withdrew a short distance from us for consultation, leaving us for the time in terrible suspense as to what our fate might be. Soon, how ever, they returned and informed us that they would be compelled to take us to the County Jail, to await further orders from the Military Commander of the District. While they were talking together, I took a hasty inventory of what valuables we had on hand. I found in the crowd four silver watches, about three hundred dollars in Confederate money, and possibly, about one hundred dollars in greenbacks. Before their return, I told the boys to be sure not to refuse any request I should make. Said I:

"'Gentlemen, we have here four silver watches and several hundred dollars in Confederate money and greenbacks, all of which we now offer you, if you will but allow us to proceed on our journey, we taking our own chances in the future.'"

This proposition, to my great surprise, was refused. I thought then that possibly I had been a little indiscreet in exposing our valuables, but in this I was mistaken, for we had, indeed, fallen into the hands of gentlemen, whose zeal for the Lost Cause was greater than that for obtaining worldly wealth, and who not only refused the bribe, but took us to a well-furnished and well-supplied farm house close by, gave us an excellent breakfast, allowing us to sit at the table in a beautiful dining-room, with a lady at the head, filled our haversacks with good, wholesome food, and allowed us to keep our property, with an admonition to be careful how we showed it again. We were then put into a wagon and taken to Hamilton, a small town, the county seat of Hamilton County, Georgia, and placed in jail, where we remained for two days and nights —fearing, always, that the jail would be burned over our heads, as we heard frequent threats of that nature, by the mob on the streets. But the same kind Providence that had heretofore watched over us, seemed not to have deserted us in this trouble.

One of the days we were confined at this place was Sunday, and some kind-hearted lady or ladies (I only wish I knew their names, as well as those of the gentlemen who had us first in charge, so that I could chronicle them with honor here) taking compassion upon our forlorn condition, sent us a splendid dinner on a very large china platter. Whether it was done intentionally or not, we never learned, but it was a fact, however, that there was not a knife, fork or spoon upon the dish, and no table to set it upon. It was placed on the floor, around which we soon gathered, and, with grateful hearts, we "got away" with it all, in an incredibly short space of time, while many men and boys looked on, enjoying our ludicrous attitudes and manners.

From here we were taken to Columbus, Ga., and again placed in jail, and in the charge of Confederate soldiers. We could easily see that we were gradually getting into hot water again, and that, ere many days, we would have to resume our old habits in prison. Our only hope now was that we would not be returned to Andersonville, knowing well that if we got back into the clutches of Wirz our chances for life would be slim indeed. From Columbus we were sent by rail to Macon, where we were placed in a prison somewhat similar to Andersonville, but of nothing like its pretensions to security. I soon learned that it was only used as a kind of reception place for the prisoners who were captured in small squads, and when they numbered two or three hundred, they would be shipped to Andersonville, or some other place of greater dimensions and strength. What became of the other boys who were with me, after we got to Macon, I do not know, for I lost sight of them there. The very next day after our arrival, there were shipped to Andersonville from this prison between two and three hundred men. I was called on to go with the crowd, but having had a sufficient experience of the hospitality of that hotel, I concluded to play "old soldier," so I became too sick to travel. In this way I escaped being sent off four different times.

Meanwhile, quite a large number of commissioned officers had been sent up from Charleston to be exchanged at Rough and Ready. With them were about forty more than the cartel called for, and they were left at Macon for ten days or two weeks. Among these officers were several of my acquaintance, one being Lieut. Huntly of our regiment (I am not quite sure that I am right in the name of this officer, but I think I am), through whose influence I was allowed to go outside with them on parole. It was while enjoying this parole that I got more familiarly acquainted with Captain Hurtell, or Hurtrell, who was in command of the prison at Macon, and to his honor, I here assert, that he was the only gentleman and the only officer that had the least humane feeling in his breast, who ever had charge of me while a prisoner of war after we were taken out of the hands of our original captors at Jonesville, Va.

It now became very evident that the Rebels were moving the prisoners from Andersonville and elsewhere, so as to place them beyond the reach of Sherman and Stoneman. At my present place of confinement the fear of our recapture had also taken possession of the Rebel authorities, so the prisoners were sent off in much smaller squads than formerly, frequently not more than ten or fifteen in a gang, whereas, before, they never thought of dispatching less than two or three hundred together. I acknowledge that I began to get very uneasy, fearful that the "old soldier" dodge would not be much longer successful, and I would be forced back to my old haunts. It so happened, however, that I managed to make it serve me, by getting detailed in the prison hospital as nurse, so that I was enabled to play another "dodge" upon the Rebel officers. At first, when the Sergeant would come around to find out who were able to walk, with assistance, to the depot, I was shaking with a chill, which, according to my representation, had not abated in the least for several hours. My teeth were actually chattering at the time, for I had learned how to make them do so. I was passed. The next day the orders for removal were more stringent than had yet been issued, stating that all who could stand it to be removed on stretchers must go. I concluded at once that I was gone, so as soon as I learned how matters were, I got out from under my dirty blanket, stood up and found I was able to walk, to my great astonishment, of course. An officer came early in the morning to muster us into ranks preparatory for removal. I fell in with the rest. We were marched out and around to the gate of the prison.

Now, it so happened that just as we neared the gate of the prison, the prisoners were being marched from the Stockade. The officer in charge of us—we numbering possibly about ten—undertook to place us at the head of the column coming out, but the guard in charge of that squad refused to let him do so. We were then ordered to stand at one side with no guard over us but the officer who had brought us from the Hospital.

Taking this in at a glance, I concluded that now was my chance to make my second attempt to escape. I stepped behind the gate office (a small frame building with only one room), which was not more than six feet from me, and as luck (or Providence) would have it, the negro man whose duty it was, as I knew, to wait on and take care of this office, and who had taken quite a liking for me, was standing at the back door. I winked at him and threw him my blanket and the cup, at the same time telling him in a whisper to hide them away for me until he heard from me again. With a grin and a nod, he accepted the trust, and I started down along the walls of the Stockade alone. In order to make this more plain, and to show what a risk I was running at the time, I will state that between the Stockade and a brick wall, fully as high as the Stockade fence that was parallel with it, throughout its entire length on that side, there was a space of not more than thirty feet. On the outside of this Stockade was a platform, built for the guards to walk on, sufficiently clear the top to allow them to look inside with ease, and on this side, on the platform, were three guards. I had traveled about fifty feet only, from the gate office, when I heard the command to "Halt!" I did so, of course.

"Where are you going, you d——d Yank?" said the guard.

"Going after my clothes, that are over there in the wash," pointing to a small cabin just beyond the Stockade, where I happened to know that the officers had their washing done.

"Oh, yes," said he; "you are one of the Yank's that's been on, parole, are you?"

"Yes."

"Well, hurry up, or you will get left."

The other guards heard this conversation and thinking it all right I was allowed to pass without further trouble. I went to the cabin in question—for I saw the last guard on the line watching me, and boldly entered. I made a clear statement to the woman in charge of it about how I had made my escape, and asked her to secrete me in the house until night. I was soon convinced, however, from what she told me, as well as from my own knowledge of how things were managed in the Confederacy, that it would not be right for me to stay there, for if the house was searched and I found in it, it would be the worse for her. Therefore, not wishing to entail misery upon another, I begged her to give me something to eat, and going to the swamp near by, succeeded in getting well without detection.

I lay there all day, and during the time had a very severe chill and afterwards a burning fever, so that when night came, knowing I could not travel, I resolved to return to the cabin and spend the night, and give myself up the next morning. There was no trouble in returning. I learned that my fears of the morning had not been groundless, for the guards had actually searched the house for me. The woman told them that I had got my clothes and left the house shortly after my entrance (which was the truth except the part about the clothes), I thanked her very kindly and begged to be allowed to stay in the cabin till morning, when I would present myself at Captain H.'s office and suffer the consequences. This she allowed me to do. I shall ever feel grateful to this woman for her protection. She was white and her given name was "Sallie," but the other I have forgotten. About daylight I strolled over near the office and looked around there until I saw the Captain take his seat at his desk. I stepped into the door as soon as I saw that he was not occupied and saluted him "a la militaire."

"Who are you?" he asked; "you look like a Yank."

"Yes, sir," said I, "I am called by that name since I was captured in the Federal Army."

"Well, what are you doing here, and what is your name?"

I told him.

"Why didn't you answer to your name when it was called at the gate yesterday, sir?"

"I never heard anyone call my name." Where were you?"

"I ran away down into the swamp."

"Were you re-captured and brought back?"

"No, sir, I came back of my own accord."

"What do you mean by this evasion?"

"I am not trying to evade, sir, or I might not have been here now. The truth is, Captain, I have been in many prisons since my capture, and have been treated very badly in all of them, until I came here."

"I then explained to him freely my escape from Andersonville, and my subsequent re-capture, how it was that I had played 'old soldier'" etc.

"Now," said I, "Captain, as long as I am a prisoner of war, I wish to stay with you, or under your command. This is my reason for running away yesterday, when I felt confident that if I did not do so I would be returned under Wirz's command, and, if I had been so returned, I would have killed myself rather than submit to the untold tortures which he would have put me to, for having the audacity to attempt an escape from him."

The Captain's attention was here called to some other matters in hand, and I was sent back into the Stockade with a command very pleasantly given, that I should stay there until ordered out, which I very gratefully promised to do, and did. This was the last chance I ever had to talk to Captain Hurtrell, to my great sorrow, for I had really formed a liking for the man, notwithstanding the fact that he was a Rebel, and a commander of prisoners.

The next day we all had to leave Macon. Whether we were able or not, the order was imperative. Great was my joy when I learned that we were on the way to Savannah and not to Andersonville. We traveled over the same road, so well described in one of your articles on Andersonville, and arrived in Savannah sometime in the afternoon of the 21st day of November, 1864. Our squad was placed in some barracks and confined there until the next day. I was sick at the time, so sick in fact, that I could hardly hold my head up. Soon after, we were taken to the Florida depot, as they told us, to be shipped to some prison in those dismal swamps. I came near fainting when this was told to us, for I was confident that I could not survive another siege of prison life, if it was anything to compare to-what I had already suffered. When we arrived at the depot, it was raining. The officer in charge of us wanted to know what train to put us on, for there were two, if not three, trains waiting orders to start. He was told to march us on to a certain flat car, near by, but before giving the order he demanded a receipt for us, which the train officer refused. We were accordingly taken back to our quarters, which proved to be a most fortunate circumstance. On the 23d day of November, to our great relief, we were called upon to sign a parole preparatory to being sent down the river on the flat-boat to our exchange ships, then lying in the harbor. When I say we, I mean those of us that had recently come from Macon, and a few others, who had also been fortunate in reaching Savannah in small squads. The other poor fellows, who had already been loaded on the trains, were taken away to Florida, and many of them never lived to return. On the 24th those of us who had been paroled were taken on board our ships, and were once more safely housed under that great, glorious and beautiful Star Spangled Banner. Long may she wave.

CHAPTER LXIII.

DREARY WEATHER—THE COLD RAINS DISTRESS ALL AND KILL HUNDREDS— EXCHANGE OF TEN THOUSAND SICK—CAPTAIN BOWES TURNS A PRETTY, BUT NOT VERY HONEST, PENNY.

As November wore away long-continued, chill, searching rains desolated our days and nights. The great, cold drops pelted down slowly, dismally, and incessantly. Each seemed to beat through our emaciated frames against the very marrow of our bones, and to be battering its way remorselessly into the citadel of life, like the cruel drops that fell from the basin of the inquisitors upon the firmly-fastened head of their victim, until his reason fled, and the death-agony cramped his heart to stillness.

The lagging, leaden hours were inexpressibly dreary. Compared with many others, we were quite comfortable, as our hut protected us from the actual beating of the rain upon our bodies; but we were much more miserable than under the sweltering heat of Andersonville, as we lay almost naked upon our bed of pine leaves, shivering in the raw, rasping air, and looked out over acres of wretches lying dumbly on the sodden sand, receiving the benumbing drench of the sullen skies without a groan or a motion.

It was enough to kill healthy, vigorous men, active and resolute, with bodies well-nourished and well clothed, and with minds vivacious and hopeful, to stand these day-and-night-long solid drenchings. No one can imagine how fatal it was to boys whose vitality was sapped by long months in Andersonville, by coarse, meager, changeless food, by groveling on the bare earth, and by hopelessness as to any improvement of condition.

Fever, rheumatism, throat and lung diseases and despair now came to complete the work begun by scurvy, dysentery and gangrene, in Andersonville.

Hundreds, weary of the long struggle, and of hoping against hope, laid themselves down and yielded to their fate. In the six weeks that we were at Millen, one man in every ten died. The ghostly pines there sigh over the unnoted graves of seven hundred boys, for whom life's morning closed in the gloomiest shadows. As many as would form a splendid regiment—as many as constitute the first born of a populous City—more than three times as many as were slain outright on our side in the bloody battle of Franklin, succumbed to this new hardship. The country for which they died does not even have a record of their names. They were simply blotted out of existence; they became as though they had never been.

About the middle of the month the Rebels yielded to the importunities of our Government so far as to agree to exchange ten thousand sick. The Rebel Surgeons took praiseworthy care that our Government should profit as little as possible by this, by sending every hopeless case, every man whose lease of life was not likely to extend much beyond his reaching the parole boat. If he once reached our receiving officers it was all that was necessary; he counted to them as much as if he had been a Goliath. A very large portion of those sent through died on the way to our lines, or within a few hours after their transports at being once more under the old Stars and Stripes had moderated.

The sending of the sick through gave our commandant—Captain Bowes—a fine opportunity to fill his pockets, by conniving at the passage of well men. There was still considerable money in the hands of a few prisoners. All this, and more, too, were they willing to give for their lives. In the first batch that went away were two of the leading sutlers at Andersonville, who had accumulated perhaps one thousand dollars each by their shrewd and successful bartering. It was generally believed that they gave every cent to Bowes for the privilege of leaving. I know nothing of the truth of this, but I am reasonably certain that they paid him very handsomely. Soon we heard that one hundred and fifty dollars each had been sufficient to buy some men out; then one hundred, seventy-five, fifty, thirty, twenty, ten, and at last five dollars. Whether the upright Bowes drew the line at the latter figure, and refused to sell his honor for less than the ruling rates of a street-walker's virtue, I know not. It was the lowest quotation that came to my knowledge, but he may have gone cheaper. I have always observed that when men or women begin to traffic in themselves, their price falls as rapidly as that of a piece of tainted meat in hot weather. If one could buy them at the rate they wind up with, and sell them at their first price, there would be room for an enormous profit.

The cheapest I ever knew a Rebel officer to be bought was some weeks after this at Florence. The sick exchange was still going on. I have before spoken of the Rebel passion for bright gilt buttons. It used to be a proverbial comment upon the small treasons that were of daily occurrence on both sides, that you could buy the soul of a mean man in our crowd for a pint of corn meal, and the soul of a Rebel guard for a half dozen brass buttons. A boy of the Fifth-fourth Ohio, whose home was at or near Lima, O., wore a blue vest, with the gilt, bright-trimmed buttons of a staff officer. The Rebel Surgeon who was examining the sick for exchange saw the buttons and admired them very much. The boy stepped back, borrowed a knife from a comrade, cut the buttons off, and handed them to the Doctor.

"All right, sir," said he as his itching palm closed over the coveted ornaments; "you can pass," and pass he did to home and friends.

Captain Bowes's merchandizing in the matter of exchange was as open as the issuing of rations. His agent in conducting the bargaining was a Raider—a New York gambler and stool-pigeon—whom we called "Mattie." He dealt quite fairly, for several times when the exchange was interrupted, Bowes sent the money back to those who had paid him, and received it again when the exchange was renewed.

Had it been possible to buy our way out for five cents each Andrews and I would have had to stay back, since we had not had that much money for months, and all our friends were in an equally bad plight. Like almost everybody else we had spent the few dollars we happened to have on entering prison, in a week or so, and since then we had been entirely penniless.

There was no hope left for us but to try to pass the Surgeons as desperately sick, and we expended our energies in simulating this condition. Rheumatism was our forte, and I flatter myself we got up two cases that were apparently bad enough to serve as illustrations for a patent medicine advertisement. But it would not do. Bad as we made our condition appear, there were so many more who were infinitely worse, that we stood no show in the competitive examination. I doubt if we would have been given an average of "50" in a report. We had to stand back, and see about one quarter of our number march out and away home. We could not complain at this—much as we wanted to go ourselves, since there could be no question that these poor fellows deserved the precedence. We did grumble savagely, however, at Captain Bowes's venality, in selling out chances to moneyed men, since these were invariably those who were best prepared to withstand the hardships of imprisonment, as they were mostly new men, and all had good clothes and blankets. We did not blame the men, however, since it was not in human nature to resist an opportunity to get away—at any cost-from that accursed place. "All that a man hath he will give for his life," and I think that if I had owned the City of New York in fee simple, I would have given it away willingly, rather than stand in prison another month.

The sutlers, to whom I have alluded above, had accumulated sufficient to supply themselves with all the necessaries and some of the comforts of life, during any probable term of imprisonment, and still have a snug amount left, but they, would rather give it all up and return to service with their regiments in the field, than take the chances of any longer continuance in prison.

I can only surmise how much Bowes realized out of the prisoners by his venality, but I feel sure that it could not have been less than three thousand dollars, and I would not be astonished to learn that it was ten thousand dollars in green.

CHAPTER LXIV

ANOTHER REMOVAL—SHERMAN'S ADVANCE SCARES THE REBELS INTO RUNNING US AWAY FROM MILLEN—WE ARE TAKEN TO SAVANNAH, AND THENCE DOWN THE ATLANTIC & GULF ROAD TO BLACKSHEAR

One night, toward the last of November, there was a general alarm around the prison. A gun was fired from the Fort, the long-roll was beaten in the various camps of the guards, and the regiments answered by getting under arms in haste, and forming near the prison gates.

The reason for this, which we did not learn until weeks later, was that Sherman, who had cut loose from Atlanta and started on his famous March to the Sea, had taken such a course as rendered it probable that Millen was one of his objective points. It was, therefore, necessary that we should be hurried away with all possible speed. As we had had no news from Sherman since the end of the Atlanta campaign, and were ignorant of his having begun his great raid, we were at an utter loss to account for the commotion among our keepers.

About 3 o'clock in the morning the Rebel Sergeants, who called the roll, came in and ordered us to turn out immediately and get ready to move.

The morning was one of the most cheerless I ever knew. A cold rain poured relentlessly down upon us half-naked, shivering wretches, as we groped around in the darkness for our pitiful little belongings of rags and cooking utensils, and huddled together in groups, urged on continually by the curses and abuse of the Rebel officers sent in to get us ready to move.

Though roused at 3 o'clock, the cars were not ready to receive us till nearly noon. In the meantime we stood in ranks—numb, trembling, and heart-sick. The guards around us crouched over fires, and shielded themselves as best they could with blankets and bits of tent cloth. We had nothing to build fires with, and were not allowed to approach those of the guards.

Around us everywhere was the dull, cold, gray, hopeless desolation of the approach of minter. The hard, wiry grass that thinly covered the once and sand, the occasional stunted weeds, and the sparse foliage of the gnarled and dwarfish undergrowth, all were parched brown and sere by the fiery heat of the long Summer, and now rattled drearily under the pitiless, cold rain, streaming from lowering clouds that seemed to have floated down to us from the cheerless summit of some great iceberg; the tall, naked pines moaned and shivered; dead, sapless leaves fell wearily to the sodden earth, like withered hopes drifting down to deepen some Slough of Despond.

Scores of our crowd found this the culmination of their misery. They laid down upon the ground and yielded to death as s welcome relief, and we left them lying there unburied when we moved to the cars.

As we passed through the Rebel camp at dawn, on our way to the cars, Andrews and I noticed a nest of four large, bright, new tin pans—a rare thing in the Confederacy at that time. We managed to snatch them without the guard's attention being attracted, and in an instant had them wrapped up in our blanket. But the blanket was full of holes, and in spite of all our efforts, it would slip at the most inconvenient times, so as to show a broad glare of the bright metal, just when it seemed it could not help attracting the attention of the guards or their officers. A dozen times at least we were on the imminent brink of detection, but we finally got our treasures safely to the cars, and sat down upon them.

The cars were open flats. The rain still beat down unrelentingly. Andrews and I huddled ourselves together so as to make our bodies afford as much heat as possible, pulled our faithful old overcoat around us as far as it would go, and endured the inclemency as best we could.

Our train headed back to Savannah, and again our hearts warmed up with hopes of exchange. It seemed as if there could be no other purpose of taking us out of a prison so recently established and at such cost as Millen.

As we approached the coast the rain ceased, but a piercing cold wind set in, that threatened to convert our soaked rags into icicles.

Very many died on the way. When we arrived at Savannah almost, if not quite, every car had upon it one whom hunger no longer gnawed or disease wasted; whom cold had pinched for the last time, and for whom the golden portals of the Beyond had opened for an exchange that neither Davis nor his despicable tool, Winder, could control.

We did not sentimentalize over these. We could not mourn; the thousands that we had seen pass away made that emotion hackneyed and wearisome; with the death of some friend and comrade as regularly an event of each day as roll call and drawing rations, the sentiment of grief had become nearly obsolete. We were not hardened; we had simply come to look upon death as commonplace and ordinary. To have had no one dead or dying around us would have been regarded as singular.

Besides, why should we feel any regret at the passing away of those whose condition would probably be bettered thereby! It was difficult to see where we who still lived were any better off than they who were gone before and now "forever at peace, each in his windowless palace of rest." If imprisonment was to continue only another month, we would rather be with them.

Arriving at Savannah, we were ordered off the cars. A squad from each car carried the dead to a designated spot, and land them in a row, composing their limbs as well as possible, but giving no other funeral rites, not even making a record of their names and regiments. Negro laborers came along afterwards, with carts, took the bodies to some vacant ground, and sunk them out of sight in the sand.

We were given a few crackers each—the same rude imitation of "hard tack" that had been served out to us when we arrived at Savannah the first time, and then were marched over and put upon a train on the Atlantic & Gulf Railroad, running from Savannah along the sea coast towards Florida. What this meant we had little conception, but hope, which sprang eternal in the prisoner's breast, whispered that perhaps it was exchange; that there was some difficulty about our vessels coming to Savannah, and we were being taken to some other more convenient sea port; probably to Florida, to deliver us to our folks there. We satisfied ourselves that we were running along the sea coast by tasting the water in the streams we crossed, whenever we could get an opportunity to dip up some. As long as the water tasted salty we knew we were near the sea, and hope burned brightly.

The truth was—as we afterwards learned—the Rebels were terribly puzzled what to do with us. We were brought to Savannah, but that did not solve the problem; and we were sent down the Atlantic & Gulf road as a temporary expedient.

The railroad was the worst of the many bad ones which it was my fortune to ride upon in my excursions while a guest of the Southern Confederacy. It had run down until it had nearly reached the worn-out condition of that Western road, of which an employee of a rival route once said, "that all there was left of it now was two streaks of rust and the right of way." As it was one of the non-essential roads to the Southern Confederacy, it was stripped of the best of its rolling-stock and machinery to supply the other more important lines.

I have before mentioned the scarcity of grease in the South, and the difficulty of supplying the railroads with lubricants. Apparently there had been no oil on the Atlantic & Gulf since the beginning of the war, and the screeches of the dry axles revolving in the worn-out boxes were agonizing. Some thing would break on the cars or blow out on the engine every few miles, necessitating a long stop for repairs. Then there was no supply of fuel along the line. When the engine ran out of wood it would halt, and a couple of negros riding on the tender would assail a panel of fence or a fallen tree with their axes, and after an hour or such matter of hard chopping, would pile sufficient wood upon the tender to enable us to renew our journey.

Frequently the engine stopped as if from sheer fatigue or inanition. The Rebel officers tried to get us to assist it up the grade by dismounting and pushing behind. We respectfully, but firmly, declined. We were gentlemen of leisure, we said, and decidedly averse to manual labor; we had been invited on this excursion by Mr. Jeff. Davis and his friends, who set themselves up as our entertainers, and it would be a gross breach of hospitality to reflect upon our hosts by working our passage. If this was insisted upon, we should certainly not visit them again. Besides, it made no difference to us whether the train got along or not. We were not losing anything by the delay; we were not anxious to go anywhere. One part of the Southern Confederacy was just as good as another to us. So not a finger could they persuade any of us to raise to help along the journey.

The country we were traversing was sterile and poor—worse even than that in the neighborhood of Andersonville. Farms and farmhouses were scarce, and of towns there were none. Not even a collection of houses big enough to justify a blacksmith shop or a store appeared along the whole route. But few fields of any kind were seen, and nowhere was there a farm which gave evidence of a determined effort on the part of its occupants to till the soil and to improve their condition. When the train stopped for wood, or for repairs, or from exhaustion, we were allowed to descend from the cars and stretch our numbed limbs. It did us good in other ways, too. It seemed almost happiness to be outside of those cursed Stockades, to rest our eyes by looking away through the woods, and seeing birds and animals that were free. They must be happy, because to us to be free once more was the summit of earthly happiness.

There was a chance, too, to pick up something green to eat, and we were famishing for this. The scurvy still lingered in our systems, and we were hungry for an antidote. A plant grew rather plentifully along the track that looked very much as I imagine a palm leaf fan does in its green state. The leaf was not so large as an ordinary palm leaf fan, and came directly out of the ground. The natives called it "bull-grass," but anything more unlike grass I never saw, so we rejected that nomenclature, and dubbed them "green fans." They were very hard to pull up, it being usually as much as the strongest of us could do to draw them out of the ground. When pulled up there was found the smallest bit of a stock—not as much as a joint of one's little finger—that was eatable. It had no particular taste, and probably little nutriment, still it was fresh and green, and we strained our weak muscles and enfeebled sinews at every opportunity, endeavoring to pull up a "green fan."

At one place where we stopped there was a makeshift of a garden, one of those sorry "truck patches," which do poor duty about Southern cabins for the kitchen gardens of the Northern, farmers, and produce a few coarse cow peas, a scanty lot of collards (a coarse kind of cabbage, with a stalk about a yard long) and some onions to vary the usual side-meat and corn pone, diet of the Georgia "cracker." Scanning the patch's ruins of vine and stalk, Andrews espied a handful of onions, which had; remained ungathered. They tempted him as the apple did Eve. Without stopping to communicate his intention to me, he sprang from the car, snatched the onions from their bed, pulled up, half a dozen collard stalks and was on his way back before the guard could make up his mind to fire upon him. The swiftness of his motions saved his life, for had he been more deliberate the guard would have concluded he was trying to, escape, and shot him down. As it was he was returning back before the guard could get his gun up. The onions he had, secured were to us more delicious than wine upon the lees. They seemed to find their way into every fiber of our bodies, and invigorate every organ. The collard stalks he had snatched up, in the expectation of finding in them something resembling the nutritious "heart" that we remembered as children, seeking and, finding in the stalks of cabbage. But we were disappointed. The stalks were as dry and rotten as the bones of Southern, society. Even hunger could find no meat in them.

After some days of this leisurely journeying toward the South, we halted permanently about eighty-six miles from Savannah. There was no reason why we should stop there more than any place else where we had been or were likely to go. It seemed as if the Rebels had simply tired of hauling us, and dumped us, off. We had another lot of dead, accumulated since we left Savannah, and the scenes at that place were repeated.

The train returned for another load of prisoners.

CHAPTER LXV.

BLACKSHEAR AND PIERCE COUNTRY—WE TAKE UP NEW QUARTERS, BUT ARE CALLED OUT FOR EXCHANGE—EXCITEMENT OVER SIGNING THE PAROLE—A HAPPY JOURNEY TO SAVANNAH—GRIEVOUS DISAPPOINTMENT

We were informed that the place we were at was Blackshear, and that it was the Court House, i. e., the County seat of Pierce County. Where they kept the Court House, or County seat, is beyond conjecture to me, since I could not see a half dozen houses in the whole clearing, and not one of them was a respectable dwelling, taking even so low a standard for respectable dwellings as that afforded by the majority of Georgia houses.

Pierce County, as I have since learned by the census report, is one of the poorest Counties of a poor section of a very poor State. A population of less than two thousand is thinly scattered over its five hundred square miles of territory, and gain a meager subsistence by a weak simulation of cultivating patches of its sandy dunes and plains in "nubbin" corn and dropsical sweet potatos. A few "razor-back" hogs —a species so gaunt and thin that I heard a man once declare that he had stopped a lot belonging to a neighbor from crawling through the cracks of a tight board fence by simply tying a knot in their tails—roam the woods, and supply all the meat used.

Andrews used to insist that some of the hogs which we saw were so thin that the connection between their fore and hindquarters was only a single thickness of skin, with hair on both sides— but then Andrews sometimes seemed to me to have a tendency to exaggerate.

The swine certainly did have proportions that strongly resembled those of the animals which children cut out of cardboard. They were like the geometrical definition of a superfice—all length and breadth, and no thickness. A ham from them would look like a palm-leaf fan.

I never ceased to marvel at the delicate adjustment of the development of animal life to the soil in these lean sections of Georgia. The poor land would not maintain anything but lank, lazy men, with few wants, and none but lank, lazy men, with few wants, sought a maintenance from it. I may have tangled up cause and effect, in this proposition, but if so, the reader can disentangle them at his leisure.

I was not astonished to learn that it took five hundred square miles of Pierce County land to maintain two thousand "crackers," even as poorly as they lived. I should want fully that much of it to support one fair-sized Northern family as it should be.

After leaving the cars we were marched off into the pine woods, by the side of a considerable stream, and told that this was to be our camp. A heavy guard was placed around us, and a number of pieces of artillery mounted where they would command the camp.

We started in to make ourselves comfortable, as at Millen, by building shanties. The prisoners we left behind followed us, and we soon had our old crowd of five or six thousand, who had been our companions at Savannah and Millers, again with us. The place looked very favorable for escape. We knew we were still near the sea coast—really not more than forty miles away— and we felt that if we could once get there we should be safe. Andrews and I meditated plans of escape, and toiled away at our cabin.

About a week after our arrival we were startled by an order for the one thousand of us who had first arrived to get ready to move out. In a few minutes we were taken outside the guard line, massed close together, and informed in a few words by a Rebel officer that we were about to be taken back to Savannah for exchange.

The announcement took away our breath. For an instant the rush of emotion made us speechless, and when utterance returned, the first use we made of it was to join in one simultaneous outburst of acclamation. Those inside the guard line, understanding what our cheer meant, answered us with a loud shout of congratulation—the first real, genuine, hearty cheering that had been done since receiving the announcement of the exchange at Andersonville, three months before.

As soon as the excitement had subsided somewhat, the Rebel proceeded to explain that we would all be required to sign a parole. This set us to thinking. After our scornful rejection of the proposition to enlist in the Rebel army, the Rebels had felt around among us considerably as to how we were disposed toward taking what was called the "Non-Combatant's Oath;" that is, the swearing not to take up arms against the Southern Confederacy again during the war. To the most of us this seemed only a little less dishonorable than joining the Rebel army. We held that our oaths to our own Government placed us at its disposal until it chose to discharge us, and we could not make any engagements with its enemies that might come in contravention of that duty. In short, it looked very much like desertion, and this we did not feel at liberty to consider.

There were still many among us, who, feeling certain that they could not survive imprisonment much longer, were disposed to look favorably upon the Non-Combatant's Oath, thinking that the circumstances of the case would justify their apparent dereliction from duty. Whether it would or not I must leave to more skilled casuists than myself to decide. It was a matter I believed every man must settle with his own conscience. The opinion that I then held and expressed was, that if a boy, felt that he was hopelessly sick, and that he could not live if he remained in prison, he was justified in taking the Oath. In the absence of our own Surgeons he would have to decide for himself whether he was sick enough to be warranted in resorting to this means of saving his life. If he was in as good health as the majority of us were, with a reasonable prospect of surviving some weeks longer, there was no excuse for taking the Oath, for in that few weeks we might be exchanged, be recaptured, or make our escape. I think this was the general opinion of the prisoners.

While the Rebel was talking about our signing the parole, there flashed upon all of us at the same moment, a suspicion that this was a trap to delude us into signing the Non-Combatant's Oath. Instantly there went up a general shout:

"Read the parole to us."

The Rebel was handed a blank parole by a companion, and he read over the printed condition at the top, which was that those signing agreed not to bear arms against the Confederates in the field, or in garrison, not to man any works, assist in any expedition, do any sort of guard duty, serve in any military constabulary, or perform any kind of military service until properly exchanged.

For a minute this was satisfactory; then their ingrained distrust of any thing a Rebel said or did returned, and they shouted:

"No, no; let some of us read it; let Ilinoy' read it—"

The Rebel looked around in a puzzled manner.

"Who the h—l is 'Illinoy!' Where is he?" said he.

I saluted and said:

"That's a nickname they give me."

"Very well," said he, "get up on this stump and read this parole to these d——d fools that won't believe me."

I mounted the stump, took the blank from his hand and read it over slowly, giving as much emphasis as possible to the all-important clause at the end—"until properly exchanged." I then said:

"Boys, this seems all right to me," and they answered, with almost one voice:
"Yes, that's all right. We'll sign that."

I was never so proud of the American soldier-boy as at that moment. They all felt that signing that paper was to give them freedom and life. They knew too well from sad experience what the alternative was. Many felt that unless released another week would see them in their graves. All knew that every day's stay in Rebel hands greatly lessened their chances of life. Yet in all that thousand there was not one voice in favor of yielding a tittle of honor to save life. They would secure their freedom honorably, or die faithfully. Remember that this was a miscellaneous crowd of boys, gathered from all sections of the country, and from many of whom no exalted conceptions of duty and honor were expected. I wish some one would point out to me, on the brightest pages of knightly record, some deed of fealty and truth that equals the simple fidelity of these unknown heros. I do not think that one of them felt that he was doing anything especially meritorious. He only obeyed the natural promptings of his loyal heart.

The business of signing the paroles was then begun in earnest. We were separated into squads according to the first letters of our names, all those whose name began with A being placed in one squad, those beginning with B, in another, and so on. Blank paroles for each letter were spread out on boxes and planks at different places, and the signing went on under the superintendence of a Rebel Sergeant and one of the prisoners. The squad of M's selected me to superintend the signing for us, and I stood by to direct the boys, and sign for the very few who could not write. After this was done we fell into ranks again, called the roll of the signers, and carefully compared the number of men with the number of signatures so that nobody should pass unparoled. The oath was then administered to us, and two day's rations of corn meal and fresh beef were issued.

This formality removed the last lingering doubt that we had of the exchange being a reality, and we gave way to the happiest emotions. We cheered ourselves hoarse, and the fellows still inside followed our example, as they expected that they would share our good fortune in a day or two. Our next performance was to set to work, cook our two days' rations at once and eat them. This was not very difficult, as the whole supply for two days would hardly make one square meal. That done, many of the boys went to the guard line and threw their blankets, clothing, cooking utensils, etc., to their comrades who were still inside. No one thought they would have any further use for such things.

"To-morrow, at this time, thank Heaven," said a boy near me, as he tossed his blanket and overcoat back to some one inside, "we'll be in God's country, and then I wouldn't touch them d——d lousy old rags with a ten-foot pole."

One of the boys in the M squad was a Maine infantryman, who had been with me in the Pemberton building, in Richmond, and had fashioned himself a little square pan out of a tin plate of a tobacco press, such as I have described in an earlier chapter. He had carried it with him ever since, and it was his sole vessel for all purposes—for cooking, carrying water, drawing rations, etc. He had cherished it as if it were a farm or a good situation. But now, as he turned away from signing his name to the parole, he looked at his faithful servant for a minute in undisguised contempt; on the eve of restoration to happier, better things, it was a reminder of all the petty, inglorious contemptible trials and sorrows he had endured; he actually loathed it for its remembrances, and flinging it upon the ground he crushed it out of all shape and usefulness with his feet, trampling upon it as he would everything connected with his prison life. Months afterward I had to lend this man my little can to cook his rations in.

Andrews and I flung the bright new tin pans we had stolen at Millen inside the line, to be scrambled for. It was hard to tell who were the most surprised at their appearance—the Rebels or our own boys—for few had any idea that there were such things in the whole Confederacy, and certainly none looked for them in the possession of two such poverty-stricken specimens as we were. We thought it best to retain possession of our little can, spoon, chess-board, blanket, and overcoat.

As we marched down and boarded the train, the Rebels confirmed their previous action by taking all the guards from around us. Only some eight or ten were sent to the train, and these quartered themselves in the caboose, and paid us no further attention.

The train rolled away amid cheering by ourselves and those we left behind. One thousand happier boys than we never started on a journey. We were going home. That was enough to wreathe the skies with glory, and fill the world with sweetness and light. The wintry sun had something of geniality and warmth, the landscape lost some of its repulsiveness, the dreary palmettos had less of that hideousness which made us regard them as very fitting emblems of treason. We even began to feel a little good-humored contempt for our hateful little Brats of guards, and to reflect how much vicious education and surroundings were to be held responsible for their misdeeds.

We laughed and sang as we rolled along toward Savannah—going back much faster than the came. We re-told old stories, and repeated old jokes, that had become wearisome months and months ago, but were now freshened up and given their olden pith by the joyousness of the occasion. We revived and talked over old schemes gotten up in the earlier days of prison life, of what "we would do when we got out," but almost forgotten since, in the general uncertainty of ever getting out. We exchanged addresses, and promised faithfully to write to each other and tell how we found everything at home.

So the afternoon and night passed. We were too excited to sleep, and passed the hours watching the scenery, recalling the objects we had passed on the way to Blackshear, and guessing how near we were to Savannah.

Though we were running along within fifteen or twenty miles of the coast, with all our guards asleep in the caboose, no one thought of escape. We could step off the cars and walk over to the seashore as easily as a man steps out of his door and walks to a neighboring town, but why should we? Were we not going directly to our vessels in the harbor of Savannah, and was it not better to do this, than to take the chances of escaping, and encounter the difficulties of reaching our blockaders! We thought so, and we staid on the cars.

A cold, gray Winter morning was just breaking as we reached Savannah. Our train ran down in the City, and then whistled sharply and ran back a mile or so; it repeated this maneuver two or three times, the evident design being to keep us on the cars until the people were ready to receive us. Finally our engine ran with all the speed she was capable of, and as the train dashed into the street we found ourselves between two heavy lines of guards with bayonets fixed.

The whole sickening reality was made apparent by one glance at the guard line. Our parole was a mockery, its only object being to get us to Savannah as easily as possible, and to prevent benefit from our recapture to any of Sherman's Raiders, who might make a dash for the railroad while we were in transit. There had been no intention of exchanging us. There was no exchange going on at Savannah.

After all, I do not think we felt the disappointment as keenly as the first time we were brought to Savannah. Imprisonment had stupefied us; we were duller and more hopeless.

Ordered down out of the cars, we were formed in line in the street.

Said a Rebel officer:

"Now, any of you fellahs that ah too sick to go to Chahlston, step fohwahd one pace."

We looked at each other an instant, and then the whole line stepped forward. We all felt too sick to go to Charleston, or to do anything else in the world.

CHAPTER LXVI.

SPECIMEN CONVERSATION WITH AN AVERAGE NATIVE GEORGIAN—WE LEARN THAT SHERMAN IS HEADING FOR SAVANNAH—THE RESERVES GET A LITTLE SETTLING DOWN.

As the train left the northern suburbs of Savannah we came upon a scene of busy activity, strongly contrasting with the somnolent lethargy that seemed to be the normal condition of the City and its inhabitants. Long lines of earthworks were being constructed, gangs of negros were felling trees, building forts and batteries, making abatis, and toiling with numbers of huge guns which were being moved out and placed in position.

As we had had no new prisoners nor any papers for some weeks—the papers being doubtless designedly kept away from us—we were at a loss to know what this meant. We could not understand this erection of fortifications on that side, because, knowing as we did how well the flanks of the City were protected by the Savannah and Ogeeche Rivers, we could not see how a force from the coast—whence we supposed an attack must come, could hope to reach the City's rear, especially as we had just come up on the right flank of the City, and saw no sign of our folks in that direction.

Our train stopped for a few minutes at the edge of this line of works, and an old citizen who had been surveying the scene with senile interest, tottered over to our car to take a look at us. He was a type of the old man of the South of the scanty middle class, the small farmer. Long white hair and beard, spectacles with great round, staring glasses, a broad-brimmed hat of ante-Revolutionary pattern, clothes that had apparently descended to him from some ancestor who had come over with Oglethorpe, and a two-handed staff with a head of buckhorn, upon which he leaned as old peasants do in plays, formed such an image as recalled to me the picture of the old man in the illustrations in "The Dairyman's Daughter." He was as garrulous as a magpie, and as opinionated as a Southern white always is. Halting in front of our car, he steadied himself by planting his staff, clasping it with both lean and skinny hands, and leaning forward upon it, his jaws then addressed themselves to motion thus:

"Boys, who mout these be that ye got?"

One of the Guards:—"O, these is some Yanks that we've bin hivin' down at Camp Sumter."

"Yes?" (with an upward inflection of the voice, followed by a close scrutiny of us through the goggle-eyed glasses,) "Wall, they're a powerful ornary lookin' lot, I'll declah."

It will be seen that the old, gentleman's perceptive powers were much more highly developed than his politeness.

"Well, they ain't what ye mout call purty, that's a fack," said the guard.

"So yer Yanks, air ye?" said the venerable Goober-Grabber, (the nick-name in the South for Georgians), directing his conversation to me. "Wall, I'm powerful glad to see ye, an' 'specially whar ye can't do no harm; I've wanted to see some Yankees ever sence the beginnin' of the wah, but hev never had no chance. Whah did ye cum from?"

I seemed called upon to answer, and said: "I came from Illinois; most of the boys in this car are from Illinois, Ohio, Indiana, Michigan and Iowa."

"'Deed! All Westerners, air ye? Wall, do ye know I alluz liked the Westerners a heap sight better than them blue-bellied New England Yankees."

No discussion with a Rebel ever proceeded very far without his making an assertion like this. It was a favorite declaration of theirs, but its absurdity was comical, when one remembered that the majority of them could not for their lives tell the names of the New England States, and could no more distinguish a Downeaster from an Illinoisan than they could tell a Saxon from a Bavarian. One day, while I was holding a conversation similar to the above with an old man on guard, another guard, who had been stationed near a squad made up of Germans, that talked altogether in the language of the Fatherland, broke in with:

"Out there by post numbah foahteen, where I wuz yesterday, there's a lot of Yanks who jest jabbered away all the hull time, and I hope I may never see the back of my neck ef I could understand ary word they said, Are them the regular blue-belly kind?"

The old gentleman entered upon the next stage of the invariable routine of discussion with a Rebel:

"Wall, what air you'uns down heah, a-fightin' we'uns foh?"

As I had answered this question several hundred times, I had found the most extinguishing reply to be to ask in return:

"What are you'uns coming up into our country to fight we'uns for?"

Disdaining to notice this return in kind, the old man passed on to the next stage:

"What are you'uns takin' ouah niggahs away from us foh?"

Now, if negros had been as cheap as oreoide watches, it is doubtful whether the speaker had ever had money enough in his possession at one time to buy one, and yet he talked of taking away "ouah niggahs," as if they were as plenty about his place as hills of corn. As a rule, the more abjectly poor a Southerner was, the more readily he worked himself into a rage over the idea of "takin' away ouah niggahs."

I replied in burlesque of his assumption of ownership:

"What are you coming up North to burn my rolling mills and rob my comrade here's bank, and plunder my brother's store, and burn down my uncle's factories?"

No reply, to this counter thrust. The old man passed to the third inevitable proposition:

"What air you'uns puttin' ouah niggahs in the field to fight we'uns foh?"

Then the whole car-load shouted back at him at once:

"What are you'uns putting blood-hounds on our trails to hunt us down, for?"

Old Man—(savagely), "Waal, ye don't think ye kin ever lick us; leastways sich fellers as ye air?"

Myself—"Well, we warmed it to you pretty lively until you caught us. There were none of us but what were doing about as good work as any stock you fellows could turn out. No Rebels in our neighborhood had much to brag on. We are not a drop in the bucket, either. There's millions more better men than we are where we came from, and they are all determined to stamp out your miserable Confederacy. You've got to come to it, sooner or later; you must knock under, sure as white blossoms make little apples. You'd better make up your mind to it."

Old Man—"No, sah, nevah. Ye nevah kin conquer us! We're the bravest people and the best fighters on airth. Ye nevah kin whip any people that's a fightin' fur their liberty an' their right; an' ye nevah can whip the South, sah, any way. We'll fight ye until all the men air killed, and then the wimmen'll fight ye, sah."

Myself—"Well, you may think so, or you may not. From the way our boys are snatching the Confederacy's real estate away, it begins to look as if you'd not have enough to fight anybody on pretty soon. What's the meaning of all this fortifying?"

Old Man—"Why, don't you know? Our folks are fixin' up a place foh Bill Sherman to butt his brains out gain'."

"Bill Sherman!" we all shouted in surprise: "Why he ain't within two hundred miles of this place, is he?"

Old Man—"Yes, but he is, tho'. He thinks he's played a sharp Yankee trick on Hood. He found out he couldn't lick him in a squar' fight, nohow; he'd tried that on too often; so he just sneaked 'round behind him, and made a break for the center of the State, where he thought there was lots of good stealin' to be done. But we'll show him. We'll soon hev him just whar we want him, an' we'll learn him how to go traipesin' 'round the country, stealin' nigahs, burnin' cotton, an' runnin' off folkses' beef critters. He sees now the scrape he's got into, an' he's tryin' to get to the coast, whar the gun-boats'll help 'im out. But he'll nevah git thar, sah; no sah, nevah. He's mouty nigh the end of his rope, sah, and we'll purty' soon hev him jist whar you fellows air, sah."

Myself—"Well, if you fellows intended stopping him, why didn't you do it up about Atlanta? What did you let him come clear through the State, burning and stealing, as you say? It was money in your pockets to head him off as soon as possible."

Old Man—"Oh, we didn't set nothing afore him up thar except Joe Brown's Pets, these sorry little Reserves; they're powerful little account; no stand-up to'em at all; they'd break their necks runnin' away ef ye so much as bust a cap near to 'em."

Our guards, who belonged to these Reserves, instantly felt that the conversation had progressed farther than was profitable and one of them spoke up roughly:

"See heah, old man, you must go off; I can't hev ye talkin' to these prisoners; hits agin my awdahs. Go 'way now!"

The old fellow moved off, but as he did he flung this Parthian arrow:

"When Sherman gits down deep, he'll find somethin' different from the —little snots of Reserves he ran over up about Milledgeville; he'll find he's got to fight real soldiers."

We could not help enjoying the rage of the guards, over the low estimate placed upon the fighting ability of themselves and comrades, and as they raved, around about what they would do if they were only given an opportunity to go into a line of battle against Sherman, we added fuel to the flames of their anger by confiding to each other that we always "knew that little Brats whose highest ambition was to murder a defenseless prisoner, could be nothing else than cowards end skulkers in the field."

"Yaas — sonnies," said Charlie Burroughs, of the Third Michigan, in that nasal Yankee drawl, that he always assumed, when he wanted to say anything very cutting; "you — trundle — bed — soldiers — who've never — seen — a — real — wild — Yankee — don't — know — how — different — they — are — from — the kind — that — are — starved — down — to tameness. They're — jest — as — different — as — a — lion in — a — menagerie — is — from — his — brother — in — the woods — who — has — a — nigger — every day — for-dinner. You — fellows — will — go — into — a — circus — tent — and — throw — tobacco — quids in — the — face — of — the — lion — in — the — cage — when — you — haven't — spunk enough — to — look — a woodchuck — in — the — eye — if — you — met — him — alone. It's — lots — o' — fun — to you — to — shoot — down — a — sick — and — starving-man — in — the — Stockade, but — when — you — see — a — Yank with — a — gun — in — his — hand — your — livers get — so — white — that — chalk — would — make — a — black — mark — on — 'em."

A little later, a paper, which some one had gotten hold of, in some mysterious manner, was secretly passed to me. I read it as I could find opportunity, and communicated its contents to the rest of the boys. The most important of these was a flaming proclamation by Governor Joe Brown, setting forth that General Sherman was now traversing the State, committing all sorts of depredations; that he had prepared the way for his own destruction, and the Governor called upon all good citizens to rise en masse, and assist in crushing the audacious invader. Bridges must be burned before and behind him, roads obstructed, and every inch of soil resolutely disputed.

We enjoyed this. It showed that the Rebels were terribly alarmed, and we began to feel some of that confidence that "Sherman will come out all right," which so marvelously animated all under his command.

CHAPTER LXVII.

OFF TO CHARLESTON—PASSING THROUGH THE RICE SWAMPS—TWO EXTREMES OF SOCIETY—ENTRY INTO CHARLESTON—LEISURELY WARFARE—SHELLING THE CITY AT REGULAR INTERVALS—WE CAMP IN A MASS OF RUINS— DEPARTURE FOR FLORENCE.

The train started in a few minutes after the close of the conversation with the old Georgian, and we soon came to and crossed the Savannah River into South Carolina. The river was wide and apparently deep; the tide was setting back in a swift, muddy current; the crazy old bridge creaked and shook, and the grinding axles shrieked in the dry journals, as we pulled across. It looked very much at times as if we were to all crash down into the turbid flood—and we did not care very much if we did, if we were not going to be exchanged.

The road lay through the tide swamp region of South Carolina, a peculiar and interesting country. Though swamps and fens stretched in all directions as far as the eye could reach, the landscape was more grateful to the eye than the famine-stricken, pine-barrens of Georgia, which had become wearisome to the sight. The soil where it appeared, was rich, vegetation was luxuriant; great clumps of laurel showed glossy richness in the greenness of its verdure, that reminded us of the fresh color of the vegetation of our Northern homes, so different from the parched and impoverished look of Georgian foliage. Immense flocks of wild fowl fluttered around us; the Georgian woods were almost destitute of living creatures; the evergreen live-oak, with its queer festoons of Spanish moss, and the ugly and useless palmettos gave novelty and interest to the view.

The rice swamps through which we were passing were the princely possessions of the few nabobs who before the war stood at the head of South Carolina aristocracy—they were South Carolina, in fact, as absolutely as Louis XIV. was France. In their hands—but a few score in number—was concentrated about all there was of South Carolina education, wealth, culture, and breeding. They represented a pinchbeck imitation of that regime in France which was happily swept out of existence by the Revolution, and the destruction of which more than compensated for every drop of blood shed in those terrible days. Like the provincial 'grandes seigneurs' of Louis XVI's reign, they were gay, dissipated and turbulent; "accomplished" in the superficial acquirements that made the "gentleman" one hundred years ago, but are grotesquely out of place in this sensible, solid age, which demands that a man shall be of use, and not merely for show. They ran horses and fought cocks, dawdled through society when young, and intrigued in politics the rest of their lives, with frequent spice-work of duels. Esteeming personal courage as a supreme human virtue, and never wearying of prating their devotion to the highest standard of intrepidity, they never produced a General who was even mediocre; nor did any one ever hear of a South Carolina regiment gaining distinction. Regarding politics and the art of government as, equally with arms, their natural vocations, they have never given the Nation a statesman, and their greatest politicians achieved eminence by advocating ideas which only attracted attention by their balefulness.

Still further resembling the French 'grandes seigneurs' of the eighteenth century, they rolled in wealth wrung from the laborer by reducing the rewards of his toil to the last fraction that would support his life and strength. The rice culture was immensely profitable, because they had found the secret for raising it more cheaply than even the pauper laborer of the of world could. Their lands had cost them nothing originally, the improvements of dikes and ditches were comparatively, inexpensive, the taxes were nominal, and their slaves were not so expensive to keep as good horses in the North.
Thousands of the acres along the road belonged to the Rhetts, thousands to the Heywards, thousands to the Manigault the Lowndes, the Middletons, the Hugers, the Barnwells, and the

Elliots—all names too well known in the history of our country's sorrows. Occasionally one of their stately mansions could be seen on some distant elevation, surrounded by noble old trees, and superb grounds. Here they lived during the healthy part of the year, but fled thence to summer resort in the highlands as the miasmatic season approached.

The people we saw at the stations along our route were melancholy illustrations of the evils of the rule of such an oligarchy. There was no middle class visible anywhere—nothing but the two extremes. A man was either a "gentleman," and wore white shirt and city-made clothes, or he was a loutish hind, clad in mere apologies for garments. We thought we had found in the Georgia "cracker" the lowest substratum of human society, but he was bright intelligence compared to the South Carolina "clay-eater" and "sand-hiller." The "cracker" always gave hopes to one that if he had the advantage of common schools, and could be made to understand that laziness was dishonorable, he might develop into something. There was little foundation for such hope in the average low South Carolinian. His mind was a shaking quagmire, which did not admit of the erection of any superstructure of education upon it. The South Carolina guards about us did not know the name of the next town, though they had been raised in that section. They did not know how far it was there, or to any place else, and they did not care to learn. They had no conception of what the war was being waged for, and did not want to find out; they did not know where their regiment was going, and did not remember where it had been; they could not tell how long they had been in service, nor the time they had enlisted for. They only remembered that sometimes they had had "sorter good times," and sometimes "they had been powerful bad," and they hoped there would be plenty to eat wherever they went, and not too much hard marching. Then they wondered "whar a feller'd be likely to make a raise of a canteen of good whisky?"

Bad as the whites were, the rice plantation negros were even worse, if that were possible. Brought to the country centuries ago, as brutal savages from Africa, they had learned nothing of Christian civilization, except that it meant endless toil, in malarious swamps, under the lash of the taskmaster. They wore, possibly, a little more clothing than their Senegambian ancestors did; they ate corn meal, yams and rice, instead of bananas, yams and rice, as their forefathers did, and they had learned a bastard, almost unintelligible, English. These were the sole blessings acquired by a transfer from a life of freedom in the jungles of the Gold Coast, to one of slavery in the swamps of the Combahee.

I could not then, nor can I now, regret the downfall of a system of society which bore such fruits. Towards night a distressingly cold breeze, laden with a penetrating mist, set in from the sea, and put an end to future observations by making us too uncomfortable to care for scenery or social conditions. We wanted most to devise a way to keep warm. Andrews and I pulled our overcoat and blanket closely about us, snuggled together so as to make each one's meager body afford the other as much heat as possible—and endured.

We became fearfully hungry. It will be recollected that we ate the whole of the two days' rations issued to us at Blackshear at once, and we had received nothing since. We reached the sullen, fainting stage of great hunger, and for hours nothing was said by any one, except an occasional bitter execration on Rebels and Rebel practices.

It was late at night when we reached Charleston. The lights of the City, and the apparent warmth and comfort there cheered us up somewhat with the hopes that we might have some share in them. Leaving the train, we were marched some distance through well-lighted streets, in which were plenty of people walking to and fro. There were many stores, apparently stocked with goods, and the citizens seemed to be going about their business very much as was the custom up North.

At length our head of column made a "right turn," and we marched away from the lighted portion of the City, to a part which I could see through the shadows was filled with ruins. An almost insupportable odor of gas, escaping I suppose from the ruptured pipes, mingled with the cold, rasping air from the sea, to make every breath intensely disagreeable.

As I saw the ruins, it flashed upon me that this was the burnt district of the city, and they were putting us under the fire of our own guns. At first I felt much alarmed. Little relish as I had on general principles, for being shot I had much less for being killed by our own men. Then I reflected that if they put me there—and kept me—a guard would have to be placed around us, who would necessarily be in as much clanger as we were, and I knew I could stand any fire that a Rebel could.

We were halted in a vacant lot, and sat down, only to jump up the next instant, as some one shouted:

"There comes one of 'em!"

It was a great shell from the Swamp Angel Battery. Starting from a point miles away, where, seemingly, the sky came down to the sea, was a narrow ribbon of fire, which slowly unrolled itself against the star-lit vault over our heads. On, on it came, and was apparently following the sky down to the horizon behind us. As it reached the zenith, there came to our ears a prolonged, but not sharp,

"Whish—ish-ish-ish-ish!"

We watched it breathlessly, and it seemed to be long minutes in running its course; then a thump upon the ground, and a vibration, told that it had struck. For a moment there was a dead silence. Then came a loud roar, and the crash of breaking timber and crushing walls. The shell had bursted.

Ten minutes later another shell followed, with like results. For awhile we forgot all about hunger in the excitement of watching the messengers from "God's country." What happiness to be where those shells came from. Soon a Rebel battery of heavy guns somewhere near and in front of us, waked up, and began answering with dull, slow thumps that made the ground shudder. This continued about an hour, when it quieted down again, but our shells kept coming over at regular intervals with the same slow deliberation, the same prolonged warning, and the same dreadful crash when they struck. They had already gone on this way for over a year, and were to keep it up months longer until the City was captured.

The routine was the same from day to day, month in, and month out, from early in August, 1863, to the middle of April, 1865. Every few minutes during the day our folks would hurl a great shell into the beleaguered City, and twice a day, for perhaps an hour each time, the Rebel batteries would talk back. It must have been a lesson to the Charlestonians of the persistent, methodical spirit of the North. They prided themselves on the length of the time they were holding out against the enemy, and the papers each day had a column headed:

"390th DAY OF THE SIEGE,"

or 391st, 393d, etc., as the number might be since our people opened fire upon the City. The part where we lay was a mass of ruins. Many large buildings had been knocked down; very many more were riddled with shot holes and tottering to their fall. One night a shell passed through a large building about a quarter of a mile from us. It had already been struck several times, and was shaky. The shell went through with a deafening crash. All was still for an instant; then it exploded with a dull roar, followed by more crashing of timber and walls. The sound died away and was succeeded by a moment of silence. Finally the great building fell, a shapeless heap of ruins, with a noise like that of a dozen field pieces. We wanted to cheer but restrained ourselves. This was the nearest to us that any shell came.

There was only one section of the City in reach of our guns and this was nearly destroyed. Fires had come to complete the work begun by the shells. Outside of the boundaries of this region, the people felt themselves as safe as in one of our northern Cities to-day. They had an abiding faith that they were clear out of reach of any artillery that we could mount. I learned afterwards from some of the prisoners, who went into Charleston ahead of us, and were camped on the race course outside of the City, that one day our fellows threw a shell clear over the City to this race course. There was an immediate and terrible panic among the citizens. They thought we had mounted some new guns of increased range, and now the whole city must go. But the next shell fell inside the established limits, and those following were equally well behaved, so that the panic abated. I have never heard any explanation of the matter. It may have been some freak of the gun-squad, trying the effect of an extra charge of powder. Had our people known of its signal effect, they could have depopulated the place in a few hours.

The whole matter impressed me queerly. The only artillery I had ever seen in action were field pieces. They made an earsplitting crash when they were discharged, and there was likely to be oceans of trouble for everybody in that neighborhood about that time. I reasoned from this that bigger guns made a proportionally greater amount of noise, and bred an infinitely larger quantity of trouble. Now I was hearing the giants of the world's ordnance, and they were not so impressive as a lively battery of three-inch rifles. Their reports did not threaten to shatter everything, but had a dull resonance, something like that produced by striking an empty barrel with a wooden maul. Their shells did not come at one in that wildly, ferocious way, with which a missile from a six-pounder convinces every fellow in a long line of battle that he is the identical one it is meant for, but they meandered over in a lazy, leisurely manner, as if time was no object and no person would feel put out at having to wait for them. Then, the idea of firing every quarter of an hour for a year—fixing up a job for a lifetime, as Andrews expressed it,—and of being fired back at for an hour at 9 o'clock every morning and evening; of fifty thousand people going on buying and selling, eating, drinking and sleeping, having dances, drives and balls, marrying and giving in marriage, all within a few hundred yards of where the shells were falling-struck me as a most singular method of conducting warfare.

We received no rations until the day after our arrival, and then they were scanty, though fair in quality. We were by this time so hungry and faint that we could hardly move. We did nothing for hours but lie around on the ground and try to forget how famished we were. At the announcement of rations, many acted as if crazy, and it was all that the Sergeants could do to restrain the impatient mob from tearing the food away and devouring it, when they were trying to divide it out. Very many—perhaps thirty—died during the night and morning. No blame for this is attached to the Charlestonians. They distinguished themselves from the citizens of every other place in the Southern Confederacy where we had been, by making efforts to relieve our condition. They sent quite a quantity of food to us, and the Sisters of Charity came among us, seeking and ministering to the sick. I believe our experience was the usual one. The prisoners who passed through Charleston before us all spoke very highly of the kindness shown them by the citizens there.

We remained in Charleston but a few days. One night we were marched down to a rickety depot, and put aboard a still more rickety train. When morning came we found ourselves running northward through a pine barren country that resembled somewhat that in Georgia, except that the pine was short-leaved, there was more oak and other hard woods, and the vegetation generally assumed a more Northern look. We had been put into close box cars, with guards at the doors and on top. During the night quite a number of the boys, who had fabricated little saws out of case knives and fragments of hoop iron, cut holes through the bottoms of the cars, through which they dropped to the ground and escaped, but were mostly recaptured after several days. There was no hole cut in our car, and so Andrews and I staid in.

Just at dusk we came to the insignificant village of Florence, the junction of the road leading from Charleston to Cheraw with that running from Wilmington to Kingsville. It was about one hundred and twenty miles from Charleston, and the same distance from Wilmington. As our train ran through a cut near the junction a darky stood by the track gazing at us curiously. When the train had nearly passed him he started to run up the bank. In the imperfect light the guards mistook him for one of us who had jumped from the train. They all fired, and the unlucky negro fell, pierced by a score of bullets.

That night we camped in the open field. When morning came we saw, a few hundred yards from us, a Stockade of rough logs, with guards stationed around it. It was another prison pen. They were just bringing the dead out, and two men were tossing the bodies up into the four-horse wagon which hauled them away for burial. The men were going about their business as coolly as if loading slaughtered hogs. One of them would catch the body by the feet, and the other by the arms. They would give it a swing—"One, two, three," and up it would go into the wagon. This filled heaping full with corpses, a negro mounted the wheel horse, grasped the lines, and shouted to his animals:

"Now, walk off on your tails, boys."

The horses strained, the wagon moved, and its load of what were once gallant, devoted soldiers, was carted off to nameless graves. This was a part of the daily morning routine.

As we stood looking at the sickeningly familiar architecture of the prison pen, a Seventh Indianian near me said, in tones of wearisome disgust:

"Well, this Southern Confederacy is the d—-dest country to stand logs on end on God Almighty's footstool."

CHAPTER LXVIII.

FIRST DAYS AT FLORENCE—INTRODUCTION TO LIEUTENANT BARRETT, THE RED-HEADED KEEPER—A BRIEF DESCRIPTION OF OUR NEW QUARTERS—WINDERS MALIGN INFLUENCE MANIFEST.

It did not require a very acute comprehension to understand that the Stockade at which we were gazing was likely to be our abiding place for some indefinite period in the future.

As usual, this discovery was the death-warrant of many whose lives had only been prolonged by the hoping against hope that the movement would terminate inside our lines. When the portentous palisades showed to a fatal certainty that the word of promise had been broken to their hearts, they gave up the struggle wearily, lay back on the frozen ground, and died.

Andrews and I were not in the humor for dying just then. The long imprisonment, the privations of hunger, the scourging by the elements, the death of four out of every five of our number had indeed dulled and stupefied us—bred an indifference to our own suffering and a seeming callosity to that of others, but there still burned in our hearts, and in the hearts of every one about us, a dull, sullen, smoldering fire of hate and defiance toward everything Rebel, and a lust for revenge upon those who had showered woes upon our heads. There was little fear of death; even the King of Terrors loses most of his awful character upon tolerably close acquaintance, and we had been on very intimate terms with him for a year now. He was a constant visitor, who dropped in upon us at all hours of the day and night, and would not be denied to any one.

Since my entry into prison fully fifteen thousand boys had died around me, and in no one of them had I seen the least, dread or reluctance to go. I believe this is generally true of death by disease, everywhere. Our ever kindly mother, Nature, only makes us dread death when she desires us to preserve life. When she summons us hence she tenderly provides that we shall willingly obey the call.

More than for anything else, we wanted to live now to triumph over the Rebels. To simply die would be of little importance, but to die unrevenged would be fearful. If we, the despised, the contemned, the insulted, the starved and maltreated; could live to come back to our oppressors as the armed ministers of retribution, terrible in the remembrance of the wrongs of ourselves and comrade's, irresistible as the agents of heavenly justice, and mete out to them that Biblical return of seven-fold of what they had measured out to us, then we would be content to go to death afterwards. Had the thrice-accursed Confederacy and our malignant gaolers millions of lives, our great revenge would have stomach for them all.

The December morning was gray and leaden; dull, somber, snow-laden clouds swept across the sky before the soughing wind.

The ground, frozen hard and stiff, cut and hurt our bare feet at every step; an icy breeze drove in through the holes in our rags, and smote our bodies like blows from sticks. The trees and shrubbery around were as naked and forlorn as in the North in the days of early Winter before the snow comes.

Over and around us hung like a cold miasma the sickening odor peculiar to Southern forests in Winter time.

Out of the naked, repelling, unlovely earth rose the Stockade, in hideous ugliness. At the gate the two men continued at their monotonous labor of tossing the dead of the previous day into the wagon-heaving into that rude hearse the inanimate remains that had once tempted gallant, manly hearts, glowing with patriotism and devotion to country—piling up listlessly and wearily, in a mass of nameless, emaciated corpses, fluttering with rags, and swarming with vermin, the pride, the joy of a hundred fair Northern homes, whose light had now gone out forever.

Around the prison walls shambled the guards, blanketed like Indians, and with faces and hearts of wolves. Other Rebels—also clad in dingy butternut—slouched around lazily, crouched over diminutive fires, and talked idle gossip in the broadest of "nigger" dialect. Officers swelled and strutted hither and thither, and negro servants loitered around, striving to spread the least amount of work over the greatest amount of time.

While I stood gazing in gloomy silence at the depressing surroundings Andrews, less speculative and more practical, saw a good-sized pine stump near by, which had so much of the earth washed away from it that it looked as if it could be readily pulled up. We had had bitter experience in other prisons as to the value of wood, and Andrews reasoned that as we would be likely to have a repetition of this in the Stockade we were about to enter, we should make an effort to secure the stump. We both attacked it, and after a great deal of hard work, succeeded in uprooting it. It was very lucky that we did, since it was the greatest help in preserving our lives through the three long months that we remained at Florence.

While we were arranging our stump so as to carry it to the best advantage, a vulgar-faced man, with fiery red hair, and wearing on his collar the yellow bars of a Lieutenant, approached. This was Lieutenant Barrett, commandant of the interior of the prison, and a more inhuman wretch even than Captain Wirz, because he had a little more brains than the commandant at Andersonville, and this extra intellect was wholly devoted to cruelty. As he came near he commanded, in loud, brutal tones:

"Attention, Prisoners!"

We all stood up and fell in in two ranks. Said he:

"By companies, right wheel, march!"

This was simply preposterous. As every soldier knows, wheeling by companies is one of the most difficult of manuvers, and requires some preparation of a battalion before attempting to execute it. Our thousand was made up of infantry, cavalry and artillery, representing, perhaps, one hundred different regiments. We had not been divided off into companies, and were encumbered with blankets, tents, cooking utensils, wood, etc., which prevented our moving with such freedom as to make a company wheel, even had we been divided up into companies and drilled for the maneuver. The attempt to obey the command was, of course, a ludicrous failure. The Rebel officers standing near Barrett laughed openly at his stupidity in giving such an order, but he was furious. He hurled at us a torrent of the vilest abuse the corrupt imagination of man can conceive, and swore until he was fairly black in the face. He fired his revolver off over our heads, and shrieked and shouted until he had to stop from sheer exhaustion. Another officer took command then, and marched us into prison.

We found this a small copy of Andersonville. There was a stream running north and south, on either side of which was a swamp. A Stockade of rough logs, with the bark still on, inclosed several acres. The front of the prison was toward the West. A piece of artillery stood before the gate, and a platform at each corner bore a gun, elevated high enough to rake the whole inside of the prison. A man stood behind each of these guns continually, so as to open with them at any moment. The earth was thrown up against the outside of the palisades in a high embankment, along the top of which the guards on duty walked, it being high enough to elevate their head, shoulders and breasts above the tops of the logs. Inside the inevitable dead-line was traced by running a furrow around the prison-twenty feet from the Stockade—with a plow. In one respect it was an improvement on Andersonville: regular streets were laid off, so that motion about the camp was possible, and cleanliness was promoted. Also, the crowd inside was not so dense as at Camp Sumter.

The prisoners were divided into hundreds and thousands, with Sergeants at the heads of the divisions. A very good police force-organized and officered by the prisoners—maintained order and prevented crime. Thefts and other offenses were punished, as at Andersonville, by the Chief of Police sentencing the offenders to be spanked or tied up.

We found very many of our Andersonville acquaintances inside, and for several days comparisons of experience were in order. They had left Andersonville a few days after us, but were taken to Charleston instead of Savannah. The same story of exchange was dinned into their ears until they arrived at Charleston, when the truth was told them, that no exchange was contemplated, and that they had been deceived for the purpose of getting them safely out of reach of Sherman.

Still they were treated well in Charleston—better than they had been anywhere else. Intelligent physicians had visited the sick, prescribed for them, furnished them with proper medicines, and admitted the worst cases to the hospital, where they were given something of the care that one would expect in such an institution. Wheat bread, molasses and rice were issued to them, and also a few spoonfuls of vinegar, daily, which were very grateful to them in their scorbutic condition. The citizens sent in clothing, food and vegetables. The Sisters of Charity were indefatigable in ministering to the sick and dying. Altogether, their recollections of the place were quite pleasant.

Despite the disagreeable prominence which the City had in the Secession movement, there was a very strong Union element there, and many men found opportunity to do favors to the prisoners and reveal to them how much they abhorred Secession.

After they had been in Charleston a fortnight or more, the yellow fever broke out in the City, and soon extended its ravages to the prisoners, quite a number dying from it.

Early in October they had been sent away from the City to their present location, which was then a piece of forest land. There was no stockade or other enclosure about them, and one night they forced the guard-line, about fifteen hundred escaping, under a pretty sharp fire from the guards. After getting out they scattered, each group taking a different route, some seeking Beaufort, and other places along the seaboard, and the rest trying to gain the mountains. The whole State was thrown into the greatest perturbation by the occurrence. The papers magnified the proportion of the outbreak, and lauded fulsomely the gallantry of the guards in endeavoring to withstand the desperate assaults of the frenzied Yankees. The people were wrought up into the highest alarm as to outrages and excesses that these flying desperados might be expected to commit. One would think that another Grecian horse, introduced into the heart of the Confederate Troy, had let out its fatal band of armed men. All good citizens were enjoined to turn out and assist in arresting the runaways. The vigilance of all patrolling was redoubled, and such was the effectiveness of the measures taken that before a month nearly every one of the fugitives had been retaken and sent back to Florence. Few of these complained of any special ill-treatment by their captors, while many reported frequent acts of kindness, especially when their captors belonged to the middle and upper classes. The low-down class—the clay-eaters—on the other hand, almost always abused their prisoners, and sometimes, it is pretty certain, murdered them in cold blood.

About this time Winder came on from Andersonville, and then everything changed immediately to the complexion of that place. He began the erection of the Stockade, and made it very strong. The Dead Line was established, but instead of being a strip of plank upon the top of low posts, as at Andersonville, it was simply a shallow trench, which was sometimes plainly visible, and sometimes not. The guards always resolved matters of doubt against the prisoners, and fired on them when they supposed them too near where the Dead Line ought to be. Fifteen acres of ground were enclosed by the palisades, of which five were taken up by the creek and swamp, and three or four more by the Dead Line; main streets, etc., leaving about seven or eight for the actual use of the prisoners, whose number swelled to fifteen thousand by the arrivals from Andersonville. This made the crowding together nearly as bad as at the latter place, and for awhile the same fatal results followed. The mortality, and the sending away of several thousand on the sick exchange, reduced the aggregate number at the time of our arrival to about eleven thousand, which gave more room to all, but was still not one-twentieth of the space which that number of men should have had.

No shelter, nor material for constructing any, was furnished. The ground was rather thickly wooded, and covered with undergrowth, when the Stockade was built, and certainly no bit of soil was ever so thoroughly cleared as this was. The trees and brush were cut down and worked up into hut building materials by the same slow and laborious process that I have described as employed in building our huts at Millen.

Then the stumps were attacked for fuel, and with such persistent thoroughness that after some weeks there was certainly not enough woody material left in that whole fifteen acres of ground to kindle a small kitchen fire. The men would begin work on the stump of a good sized tree, and chip and split it off painfully and slowly until they had followed it to the extremity of the tap root ten or fifteen feet below the surface. The lateral roots would be followed with equal determination, and trenches thirty feet long, and two or three feet deep were dug with case-knives and half-canteens, to get a root as thick as one's wrist. The roots of shrubs and vines were followed up and gathered with similar industry. The cold weather and the scanty issues of wood forced men to do this.

The huts constructed were as various as the materials and the tastes of the builders. Those who were fortunate enough to get plenty of timber built such cabins as I have described at Millen. Those who had less eked out their materials in various ways. Most frequently all that a squad of three or four could get would be a few slender poles and some brush. They would dig a hole in the ground two feet deep and large enough for them all to lie in. Then putting up a stick at each end and laying a ridge pole across, they, would adjust the rest of their material so as to form sloping sides capable of supporting earth enough to make a water-tight roof. The great majority were not so well off as these, and had absolutely, nothing of which to build. They had recourse to the clay of the swamp, from which they fashioned rude sun-dried bricks, and made adobe houses, shaped like a bee hive, which lasted very well until a hard rain came, when they dissolved into red mire about the bodies of their miserable inmates.

Remember that all these makeshifts were practiced within a half-a-mile of an almost boundless forest, from which in a day's time the camp could have been supplied with material enough to give every man a comfortable hut.

CHAPTER LXIX.

BARRETT'S INSANE CRUELTY—HOW HE PUNISHED THOSE ALLEGED TO BE ENGAGED IN TUNNELING—THE MISERY IN THE STOCKADE—MEN'S LIMBS ROTTING OFF WITH DRY GANGRENE.

Winder had found in Barrett even a better tool for his cruel purposes than Wirz. The two resembled each other in many respects. Both were absolutely destitute of any talent for commanding men, and could no more handle even one thousand men properly than a cabin boy could navigate a great ocean steamer. Both were given to the same senseless fits of insane rage, coming and going without apparent cause, during which they fired revolvers and guns or threw clubs into crowds of prisoners, or knocked down such as were within reach of their fists. These exhibitions were such as an overgrown child might be expected to make. They did not secure any result except to increase the prisoners' wonder that such ill-tempered fools could be given any position of responsibility.

A short time previous to our entry Barrett thought he had reason to suspect a tunnel. He immediately announced that no more rations should be issued until its whereabouts was revealed and the ringleaders in the attempt to escape delivered up to him. The rations at that time were very scanty, so that the first day they were cut off the sufferings were fearful. The boys thought he would surely relent the next day, but they did not know their man. He was not suffering any, why should he relax his severity? He strolled leisurely out from his dinner table, picking his teeth with his penknife in the comfortable, self-satisfied way of a coarse man who has just filled his stomach to his entire content—an attitude and an air that was simply maddening to the famishing wretches, of whom he inquired tantalizingly:

"Air ye're hungry enough to give up them G-d d d s—s of b——s yet?"

That night thirteen thousand men, crazy, fainting with hunger, walked hither and thither, until exhaustion forced them to become quiet, sat on the ground and pressed their bowels in by leaning against sticks of wood laid across their thighs; trooped to the Creek and drank water until their gorges rose and they could swallow no more—did everything in fact that imagination could suggest—to assuage the pangs of the deadly gnawing that was consuming their vitals. All the cruelties of the terrible Spanish Inquisition, if heaped together, would not sum up a greater aggregate of anguish than was endured by them. The third day came, and still no signs of yielding by Barrett. The Sergeants counseled together. Something must be done. The fellow would starve the whole camp to death with as little compunction as one drowns blind puppies. It was necessary to get up a tunnel to show Barrett, and to get boys who would confess to being leaders in the work. A number of gallant fellows volunteered to brave his wrath, and save the rest of their comrades. It required high courage to do this, as there was no question but that the punishment meted out would be as fearful as the cruel mind of the fellow could conceive. The Sergeants decided that four would be sufficient to answer the purpose; they selected these by lot, marched them to the gate and delivered them over to Barrett, who thereupon ordered the rations to be sent in. He was considerate enough, too, to feed the men he was going to torture.

The starving men in the Stockade could not wait after the rations were issued to cook them, but in many instances mixed the meal up with water, and swallowed it raw. Frequently their stomachs, irritated by the long fast, rejected the mess; any very many had reached the stage where they loathed food; a burning fever was consuming them, and seething their brains with delirium. Hundreds died within a few days, and hundreds more were so debilitated by the terrible strain that they did not linger long afterward.

The boys who had offered themselves as a sacrifice for the rest were put into a guard house, and kept over night that Barrett might make a day of the amusement of torturing them. After he had laid in a hearty breakfast, and doubtless fortified himself with some of the villainous sorgum whisky, which the Rebels were now reduced to drinking, he set about his entertainment.

The devoted four were brought out—one by one—and their hands tied together behind their backs. Then a noose of a slender, strong hemp rope was slipped over the first one's thumbs and drawn tight, after which the rope was thrown over a log projecting from the roof of the guard house, and two or three Rebels hauled upon it until the miserable Yankee was lifted from the ground, and hung suspended by the thumbs, while his weight seemed tearing his limbs from his shoulder blades. The other three were treated in the same manner.

The agony was simply excruciating. The boys were brave, and had resolved to stand their punishment without a groan, but this was too much for human endurance. Their will was strong, but Nature could not be denied, and they shrieked aloud so pitifully that a young Reserve standing near fainted. Each one screamed:

"For God's sake, kill me! kill me! Shoot me if—you want to, but let me down from here!" The only effect of this upon Barrett was to light up his brutal face with a leer of fiendish satisfaction. He said to the guards with a gleeful wink:

"By God, I'll learn these Yanks to be more afeard of me than of the old devil himself. They'll soon understand that I'm not the man to fool with. I'm old pizen, I am, when I git started. Jest hear 'em squeal, won't yer?"

Then walking from one prisoner to another, he said:

"D—n yer skins, ye'll dig tunnels, will ye? Ye'll try to git out, and run through the country stealin' and carryin' off niggers, and makin' more trouble than yer d——d necks are worth. I'll learn ye all about that. If I ketch ye at this sort of work again, d——d ef I don't kill ye ez soon ez I ketch ye."

And so on, ad infinitum. How long the boys were kept up there undergoing this torture can not be said. Perhaps it was an hour or more. To the locker-on it seemed long hours, to the poor fellows themselves it was ages. When they were let down at last, all fainted, and were carried away to the hospital, where they were weeks in recovering from the effects. Some of them were crippled for life.

When we came into the prison there were about eleven thousand there. More uniformly wretched creatures I had never before seen. Up to the time of our departure from Andersonville the constant influx of new prisoners had prevented the misery and wasting away of life from becoming fully realized. Though thousands were continually dying, thousands more of healthy, clean, well-clothed men were as continually coming in from the front, so that a large portion of those inside looked in fairly good condition. Put now no new prisoners had come in for months; the money which made such a show about the sutler shops of Andersonville had been spent; and there was in every face the same look of ghastly emaciation, the same shrunken muscles and feeble limbs, the same lack-luster eyes and hopeless countenances.

One of the commonest sights was to see men whose hands and feet were simply rotting off. The nights were frequently so cold that ice a quarter of an inch thick formed on the water. The naked frames of starving men were poorly calculated to withstand this frosty rigor, and thousands had their extremities so badly frozen as to destroy the life in those parts, and induce a rotting of the tissues by a dry gangrene. The rotted flesh frequently remained in its place for a long time —a loathsome but painless mass, that gradually sloughed off, leaving the sinews that passed through it to stand out like shining, white cords.

While this was in some respects less terrible than the hospital gangrene at Andersonville, it was more generally diffused, and dreadful to the last degree. The Rebel Surgeons at Florence did not follow the habit of those at Andersonville, and try to check the disease by wholesale amputation, but simply let it run its course, and thousands finally carried their putrefied limbs through our lines, when the Confederacy broke up in the Spring, to be treated by our Surgeons.

I had been in prison but a little while when a voice called out from a hole in the ground, as I was passing:

"S-a-y, Sergeant! Won't you please take these shears and cut my toes off?"

"What?" said I, in amazement, stopping in front of the dugout.

"Just take these shears, won't you, and cut my toes off?" answered the inmate, an Indiana infantryman—holding up a pair of dull shears in his hand, and elevating a foot for me to look at. I examined the latter carefully. All the flesh of the toes, except little pads at the ends, had rotted off, leaving the bones as clean as if scraped. The little tendons still remained, and held the bones to their places, but this seemed to hurt the rest of the feet and annoy the man.

"You'd better let one of the Rebel doctors see this," I said, after finishing my survey, "before you conclude to have them off. May be they can be saved."

"No; d——d if I'm going to have any of them Rebel butchers fooling around me. I'd die first, and then I wouldn't," was the reply. "You can do it better than they can. It's just a little snip. Just try it."

"I don't like to," I replied. "I might lame you for life, and make you lots of trouble."

"O, bother! what business is that of yours? They're my toes, and I want 'em off. They hurt me so I can't sleep. Come, now, take the shears and cut 'em off."

I yielded, and taking the shears, snipped one tendon after another, close to the feet, and in a few seconds had the whole ten toes lying in a heap at the bottom of the dug-out. I picked them up and handed them to their owner, who gazed at them, complacently, and remarked:

"Well, I'm darned glad they're off. I won't be bothered with corns any more, I flatter myself."

CHAPTER LXX

HOUSE AND CLOTHES—EFFORTS TO ERECT A SUITABLE RESIDENCE—
DIFFICULTIES ATTENDING THIS—VARIETIES OF FLORENTINE ARCHITECTURE—
WAITING FOR DEAD MEN'S CLOTHES—CRAVING FOR TOBACCO.

We were put into the old squads to fill the places of those who had recently died, being assigned to these vacancies according to the initials of our surnames, the same rolls being used that we had signed as paroles. This separated Andrews and me, for the "A's" were taken to fill up the first hundreds of the First Thousand, while the "M's," to which I belonged, went into the next Thousand.

I was put into the Second Hundred of the Second Thousand, and its Sergeant dying shortly after, I was given his place, and commanded the hundred, drew its rations, made out its rolls, and looked out for its sick during the rest of our stay there.

Andrews and I got together again, and began fixing up what little we could to protect ourselves against the weather. Cold as this was we decided that it was safer to endure it and risk frost-biting every night than to build one of the mud-walled and mud-covered holes that so many, lived in. These were much warmer than lying out on the frozen ground, but we believed that they were very unhealthy, and that no one lived long who inhabited them.

So we set about repairing our faithful old blanket—now full of great holes. We watched the dead men to get pieces of cloth from their garments to make patches, which we sewed on with yarn raveled from other fragments of woolen cloth. Some of our company, whom we found in the prison, donated us the three sticks necessary to make tent-poles —wonderful generosity when the preciousness of firewood is remembered. We hoisted our blanket upon these; built a wall of mud bricks at one end, and in it a little fireplace to economize our scanty fuel to the last degree, and were once more at home, and much better off than most of our neighbors.

One of these, the proprietor of a hole in the ground covered with an arch of adobe bricks, had absolutely no bed-clothes except a couple of short pieces of board—and very little other clothing. He dug a trench in the bottom of what was by courtesy called his tent, sufficiently large to contain his body below his neck. At nightfall he would crawl into this, put his two bits of board so that they joined over his breast, and then say: "Now, boys, cover me over;" whereupon his friends would cover him up with dry sand from the sides of his domicile, in which he would slumber quietly till morning, when he would rise, shake the sand from his garments, and declare that he felt as well refreshed as if he had slept on a spring mattress.

There has been much talk of earth baths of late years in scientific and medical circles. I have been sorry that our Florence comrade if he still lives—did not contribute the results of his experience.

The pinching cold cured me of my repugnance to wearing dead men's clothes, or rather it made my nakedness so painful that I was glad to cover it as best I could, and I began foraging among the corpses for garments. For awhile my efforts to set myself up in the mortuary second-hand clothing business were not all successful. I found that dying men with good clothes were as carefully watched over by sets of fellows who constituted themselves their residuary legatees as if they were men of fortune dying in the midst of a circle of expectant nephews and nieces. Before one was fairly cold his clothes would be appropriated and divided, and I have seen many sharp fights between contesting claimants.

I soon perceived that my best chance was to get up very early in the morning, and do my hunting. The nights were so cold that many could not sleep, and they would walk up and down the streets, trying to keep warm by exercise. Towards morning, becoming exhausted, they would lie down on the ground almost anywhere, and die. I have frequently seen so many as fifty of these. My first "find" of any importance was a young Pennsylvania Zouave, who was lying dead near the bridge that crossed the Creek. His clothes were all badly worn, except his baggy, dark trousers, which were nearly new. I removed these, scraped out from each of the dozens of great folds in the legs about a half pint of lice, and drew the garments over my own half-frozen limbs, the first real covering those members had had for four or five months. The pantaloons only came down about half-way between my knees and feet, but still they were wonderfully comfortable to what I had been—or rather not been—wearing. I had picked up a pair of boot bottoms, which answered me for shoes, and now I began a hunt for socks. This took several morning expeditions, but on one of them I was rewarded with finding a corpse with a good brown one — army make—and a few days later I got another, a good, thick genuine one, knit at home, of blue yarn, by some patient, careful housewife. Almost the next morning I had the good fortune to find a dead man with a warm, whole, infantry dress-coat, a most serviceable garment. As I still had for a shirt the blouse Andrews had given me at Millen, I now considered my wardrobe complete, and left the rest of the clothes to those who were more needy than I.

Those who used tobacco seemed to suffer more from a deprivation of the weed than from lack of food. There were no sacrifices they would not make to obtain it, and it was no uncommon thing for boys to trade off half their rations for a chew of "navy plug." As long as one had anything—especially buttons—to trade, tobacco could be procured from the guards, who were plentifully supplied with it. When means of barter were gone, chewers frequently became so desperate as to beg the guards to throw them a bit of the precious nicotine. Shortly after our arrival at Florence, a prisoner on the East Side approached one of the Reserves with the request:

"Say, Guard, can't you give a fellow a chew of tobacco?"

To which the guard replied:

"Yes; come right across the line there and I'll drop you down a bit."

The unsuspecting prisoner stepped across the Dead Line, and the guard—a boy of sixteen—raised his gun and killed him.

At the North Side of the prison, the path down to the Creek lay right along side of the Dead Line, which was a mere furrow in the ground.

At night the guards, in their zeal to kill somebody, were very likely to imagine that any one going along the path for water was across the Dead Line, and fire upon him. It was as bad as going upon the skirmish line to go for water after nightfall. Yet every night a group of boys would be found standing at the head of the path crying out:

"Fill your buckets for a chew of tobacco."

That is, they were willing to take all the risk of running that gauntlet for this moderate compensation.

CHAPTER LXXI.

DECEMBER—RATIONS OF WOOD AND FOOD GROW LESS DAILY—UNCERTAINTY AS TO THE MORTALITY AT FLORENCE—EVEN THE GOVERNMENT'S STATISTICS ARE VERY DEFICIENT—CARE FOB THE SICK.

The rations of wood grew smaller as the weather grew colder, until at last they settled down to a piece about the size of a kitchen rolling-pin per day for each man. This had to serve for all purposes—cooking, as well as warming. We split the rations up into slips about the size of a carpenter's lead pencil, and used them parsimoniously, never building a fire so big that it could not be covered with a half-peck measure. We hovered closely over this—covering it, in fact, with our hands and bodies, so that not a particle of heat was lost. Remembering the Indian's sage remark, "That the white man built a big fire and sat away off from it; the Indian made a little fire and got up close to it," we let nothing in the way of caloric be wasted by distance. The pitch-pine produced great quantities of soot, which, in cold and rainy days, when we hung over the fires all the time, blackened our faces until we were beyond the recognition of intimate friends.

There was the same economy of fuel in cooking. Less than half as much as is contained in a penny bunch of kindling was made to suffice in preparing our daily meal. If we cooked mush we elevated our little can an inch from the ground upon a chunk of clay, and piled the little sticks around it so carefully that none should burn without yielding all its heat to the vessel, and not one more was burned than absolutely necessary. If we baked bread we spread the dough upon our chessboard, and propped it up before the little fire-place, and used every particle of heat evolved. We had to pinch and starve ourselves thus, while within five minutes' walk from the prison-gate stood enough timber to build a great city.

The stump Andrews and I had the foresight to save now did us excellent service. It was pitch pine, very fat with resin, and a little piece split off each day added much to our fires and our comfort.

One morning, upon examining the pockets of an infantryman of my hundred who had just died, I had the wonderful luck to find a silver quarter. I hurried off to tell Andrews of our unexpected good fortune. By an effort he succeeded in calming himself to the point of receiving the news with philosophic coolness, and we went into Committee of the Whole Upon the State of Our Stomachs, to consider how the money could be spent to the best advantage. At the south side of the Stockade on the outside of the timbers, was a sutler shop, kept by a Rebel, and communicating with the prison by a hole two or three feet square, cut through the logs. The Dead Line was broken at this point, so as to permit prisoners to come up to the hole to trade. The articles for sale were corn meal and bread, flour and wheat bread, meat, beaus, molasses, honey, sweet potatos, etc. I went down to the place, carefully inspected the stock, priced everything there, and studied the relative food value of each. I came back, reported my observations and conclusions to Andrews, and then staid at the tent while he went on a similar errand. The consideration of the matter was continued during the day and night, and the next morning we determined upon investing our twenty-five cents in sweet potatos, as we could get nearly a half-bushel of them, which was "more fillin' at the price," to use the words of Dickens's Fat Boy, than anything else offered us. We bought the potatos, carried them home in our blanket, buried them in the bottom of our tent, to keep them from being stolen, and restricted ourselves to two per day until we had eaten them all.

The Rebels did something more towards properly caring for the sick than at Andersonville. A hospital was established in the northwestern corner of the Stockade, and separated from the rest of the camp by a line of police, composed of our own men. In this space several large sheds were erected, of that rude architecture common to the coarser sort of buildings in the South. There was not a nail or a bolt used in their entire construction. Forked posts at the ends and sides supported poles upon which were laid the long "shakes," or split shingles, forming the roofs, and which were held in place by other poles laid upon them. The sides and ends were enclosed by similar "shakes," and altogether they formed quite a fair protection against the weather. Beds of pine leaves were provided for the sick, and some coverlets, which our Sanitary Commission had been allowed to send through. But nothing was done to bathe or cleanse them, or to exchange their lice-infested garments for others less full of torture. The long tangled hair and whiskers were not cut, nor indeed were any of the commonest suggestions for the improvement of the condition of the sick put into execution. Men who had laid in their mud hovels until they had become helpless and hopeless, were admitted to the hospital, usually only to die.

The diseases were different in character from those which swept off the prisoners at Andersonville. There they were mostly of the digestive organs; here of the respiratory. The filthy, putrid, speedily fatal gangrene of Andersonville became here a dry, slow wasting away of the parts, which continued for weeks, even months, without being necessarily fatal. Men's feet and legs, and less frequently their hands and arms, decayed and sloughed off. The parts became so dead that a knife could be run through them without causing a particle of pain. The dead flesh hung on to the bones and tendons long after the nerves and veins had ceased to perform their functions, and sometimes startled one by dropping off in a lump, without causing pain or hemorrhage.

The appearance of these was, of course, frightful, or would have been, had we not become accustomed to them. The spectacle of men with their feet and legs a mass of dry ulceration, which had reduced the flesh to putrescent deadness, and left the tendons standing out like cords, was too common to excite remark or even attention. Unless the victim was a comrade, no one specially heeded his condition. Lung diseases and low fevers ravaged the camp, existing all the time in a more or less virulent condition, according to the changes of the weather, and occasionally ragging in destructive epidemics. I am unable to speak with any degree of definiteness as to the death rate, since I had ceased to interest myself about the number dying each day. I had now been a prisoner a year, and had become so torpid and stupefied, mentally and physically, that I cared comparatively little for anything save the rations of food and of fuel. The difference of a few spoonfuls of meal, or a large splinter of wood in the daily issues to me, were of more actual importance than the increase or decrease of the death rate by a half a score or more. At Andersonville I frequently took the trouble to count the number of dead and living, but all curiosity of this kind had now died out.

Nor can I find that anybody else is in possession of much more than my own information on the subject. Inquiry at the War Department has elicited the following letters:

I.

The prison records of Florence, S. C., have never come to light, and therefore the number of prisoners confined there could not be ascertained from the records on file in this office; nor do I think that any statement purporting to show that number has ever been made.

In the report to Congress of March 1, 1869, it was shown from records as follows:

Escaped, fifty-eight; paroled, one; died, two thousand seven hundred and ninety-three. Total, two thousand eight hundred and fifty-two.

Since date of said report there have been added to the records as follows:

Died, two hundred and twelve; enlisted in Rebel army, three hundred and twenty-six. Total, five hundred and thirty-eight.

Making a total disposed of from there, as shown by records on file, of three thousand three hundred and ninety.

This, no doubt, is a small proportion of the number actually confined there.

The hospital register on file contains that part only of the alphabet subsequent to, and including part of the letter S, but from this register, it is shown that the prisoners were arranged in hundreds and thousands, and the hundred and thousand to which he belonged is recorded opposite each man's name on said register. Thus:

"John Jones, 11th thousand, 10th hundred."

Eleven thousand being the highest number thus recorded, it is fair to presume that not less than that number were confined there on a certain date, and that more than that number were confined there during the time it was continued as a prison.

II.

Statement showing the whole number of Federals and Confederates captured, (less the number paroled on the field), the number who died while prisoners, and the percentage of deaths, 1861-1865

FEDERALS

Captured 187,818
Died, (as shown by prison and hospital records on file).... 30,674
Percentage of deaths 16.375

CONFEDERATES

Captured 227,570
Died 26,774
Percentage of deaths 11.768

In the detailed statement prepared for Congress dated March 1, 1869, the whole number of deaths given as shown by Prisoner of War records was twenty-six thousand three hundred and twenty-eight, but since that date evidence of three thousand six hundred and twenty-eight additional deaths has been obtained from the captured Confederate records, making a total of twenty-nine thousand nine hundred and fifty-six as above shown. This is believed to be many thousands less than the actual number of Federal prisoners who died in Confederate prisons, as we have no records from those at Montgomery Ala., Mobile, Ala., Millen, Ga., Marietta, Ga., Atlanta, Ga., Charleston, S. C., and others. The records of Florence, S. C., and Salisbury, N. C., are very incomplete. It also appears from Confederate inspection reports of Confederate prisons, that large percentage of the deaths occurred in prison quarter without the care or knowledge of the Surgeon. For the month of December, 1864 alone, the Confederate "burial report"; Salisbury, N. C., show that out, of eleven hundred and fifty deaths, two hundred and twenty-three, or twenty per cent., died in prison quarters and are not accounted for in the report of the Surgeon, and therefore not taken into consideration in the above report, as the only records of said prisons on file (with one exception) are the Hospital records. Calculating the percentage of deaths on this basis would give the number of deaths at thirty-seven thousand four hundred and forty-five and percentage of deaths at 20.023.

[End of the Letters from the War Department.]

If we assume that the Government's records of Florence as correct, it will be apparent that one man in every three die there, since, while there might have been as high as fifty thousand at one time in the prison, during the last three months of its existence I am quite sure that the number did not exceed seven thousand. This would make the mortality much greater than at Andersonville, which it undoubtedly was, since the physical condition of the prisoners confined there had been greatly depressed by their long confinement, while the bulk c the prisoners at Andersonville were those who had been brought thither directly from the field. I think also that all who experienced confinement in the two places are united in pronouncing Florence to be, on the whole, much the worse place and more fatal to life.

The medicines furnished the sick were quite simple in nature and mainly composed of indigenous substances. For diarrhea red pepper and decoctions of blackberry root and of pine leave were given. For coughs and lung diseases, a decoction of wild cherry bark was administered. Chills and fever were treated with decoctions of dogwood bark, and fever patients who craved something sour, were given a weak acid drink, made by fermenting a small quantity of meal in a barrel of water. All these remedies were quite good in their way, and would have benefitted the patients had they been accompanied by proper shelter, food and clothing. But it was idle to attempt to arrest with blackberry root the diarrhea, or with wild cherry bark the consumption of a man lying in a cold, damp, mud hovel, devoured by vermin, and struggling to maintain life upon less than a pint of unsalted corn meal per diem.

Finding that the doctors issued red pepper for diarrhea, and an imitation of sweet oil made from peanuts, for the gangrenous sores above described, I reported to them an imaginary comrade in my tent, whose symptoms indicated those remedies, and succeeded in drawing a small quantity of each, two or three times a week. The red pepper I used to warm up our bread and mush, and give some different taste to the corn meal, which had now become so loathsome to us. The peanut oil served to give a hint of the animal food we hungered for. It was greasy, and as we did not have any meat for three months, even this flimsy substitute was inexpressibly grateful to palate and stomach. But one morning the Hospital Steward made a mistake, and gave me castor oil instead, and the consequences were unpleasant.

A more agreeable remembrance is that of two small apples, about the size of walnuts, given me by a boy named Henry Clay Montague Porter, of the Sixteenth Connecticut. He had relatives living in North Carolina, who sent him a small packs of eatables, out of which, in the fulness of his generous heart he gave me this share—enough to make me always remember him with kindness.

Speaking of eatables reminds me of an incident. Joe Darling, of the First Maine, our Chief of Police, had a sister living at Augusta, Ga., who occasionally came to Florence with basket of food and other necessaries for her brother. On one of these journeys, while sitting in Colonel Iverson's tent, waiting for her brother to be brought out of prison, she picked out of her basket a nicely browned doughnut and handed it to the guard pacing in front of the tent, with:

"Here, guard, wouldn't you like a genuine Yankee doughnut?"

The guard-a lank, loose-jointed Georgia cracker—who in all his life seen very little more inviting food than the his hominy and molasses, upon which he had been raised, took the cake, turned it over and inspected it curiously for some time without apparently getting the least idea of what it was for, and then handed it back to the donor, saying:

"Really, mum, I don't believe I've got any use for it"

CHAPTER LXXII.

DULL WINTER DAYS—TOO WEAK AND TOO STUPID To AMUSE OURSELVES— ATTEMPTS OF THE REBELS TO RECRUIT US INTO THEIR ARMY—THE CLASS OF MEN THEY OBTAINED —VENGEANCE ON "THE GALVANIZED"—A SINGULAR

EXPERIENCE—RARE GLIMPSES OF FUN—INABILITY OF THE REBELS TO COUNT.
The Rebels continued their efforts to induce prisoners to enlist in their army, and with much better success than at any previous time. Many men had become so desperate that they were reckless as to what they did. Home, relatives, friends, happiness—all they had remembered or looked forward to, all that had nerved them up to endure the present and brave the future—now seemed separated from them forever by a yawning and impassable chasm. For many weeks no new prisoners had come in to rouse their drooping courage with news of the progress of our arms towards final victory, or refresh their remembrances of home, and the gladsomeness of "God's Country." Before them they saw nothing but weeks of slow and painful progress towards bitter death. The other alternative was enlistment in the Rebel army.

Another class went out and joined, with no other intention than to escape at the first opportunity. They justified their bad faith to the Rebels by recalling the numberless instances of the Rebels' bad faith to us, and usually closed their arguments in defense of their course with:

"No oath administered by a Rebel can have any binding obligation. These men are outlaws who have not only broken their oaths to the Government, but who have deserted from its service, and turned its arms against it. They are perjurers and traitors, and in addition, the oath they administer to us is under compulsion and for that reason is of no account."

Still another class, mostly made up from the old Raider crowd, enlisted from natural depravity. They went out more than for anything else because their hearts were prone to evil and they did that which was wrong in preference to what was right. By far the largest portion of those the Rebels obtained were of this class, and a more worthless crowd of soldiers has not been seen since Falstaff mustered his famous recruits.

After all, however, the number who deserted their flag was astonishingly small, considering all the circumstances. The official report says three hundred and twenty-six, but I imaging this is under the truth, since quite a number were turned back in after their utter uselessness had been demonstrated. I suppose that five hundred "galvanized," as we termed it, but this was very few when the hopelessness of exchange, the despair of life, and the wretchedness of the condition of the eleven or twelve thousand inside the Stockade is remembered.

The motives actuating men to desert were not closely analyzed by us, but we held all who did so as despicable scoundrels, too vile to be adequately described in words. It was not safe for a man to announce his intention of "galvanizing," for he incurred much danger of being beaten until he was physically unable to reach the gate. Those who went over to the enemy had to use great discretion in letting the Rebel officer, know so much of their wishes as would secure their being taker outside. Men were frequently knocked down and dragged away while telling the officers they wanted to go out.

On one occasion one hundred or more of the raider crowd who had galvanized, were stopped for a few hours in some little Town, on their way to the front. They lost no time in stealing everything they could lay their hands upon, and the disgusted Rebel commander ordered them to be returned to the Stockade. They came in in the evening, all well rigged out in Rebel uniforms, and carrying blankets. We chose to consider their good clothes and equipments an aggravation of their offense and an insult to ourselves. We had at that time quite a squad of negro soldiers inside with us. Among them was a gigantic fellow with a fist like a wooden beetle. Some of the white boys resolved to use these to wreak the camp's displeasure on the Galvanized. The plan was carried out capitally. The big darky, followed by a crowd of smaller and nimbler "shades," would approach one of the leaders among them with:

"Is you a Galvanized?"

The surly reply would be,

"Yes, you —— black ——. What the business is that of yours?"

At that instant the bony fist of the darky, descending like a pile-driver, would catch the recreant under the ear, and lift him about a rod. As he fell, the smaller darkies would pounce upon him, and in an instant despoil him of his blanket and perhaps the larger portion of his warm clothing. The operation was repeated with a dozen or more. The whole camp enjoyed it as rare fun, and it was the only time that I saw nearly every body at Florence laugh.

A few prisoners were brought in in December, who had been taken in Foster's attempt to cut the Charleston & Savannah Railroad at Pocataligo. Among them we were astonished to find Charley Hirsch, a member of Company I's of our battalion. He had had a strange experience. He was originally a member of a Texas regiment and was captured at Arkansas Post. He then took the oath of allegiance and enlisted with us. While we were at Savannah he approached a guard one day to trade for tobacco. The moment he spoke to the man he recognized him as a former comrade in the Texas regiment. The latter knew him also, and sang out,

"I know you; you're Charley Hirsch, that used to be in my company."

Charley backed into the crowd as quickly as possible; to elude the fellow's eyes, but the latter called for the Corporal of the Guard, had himself relieved, and in a few minutes came in with an officer in search of the deserter. He found him with little difficulty, and took him out. The luckless Charley was tried by court martial, found, guilty, sentenced to be shot, and while waiting execution was confined in the jail. Before the sentence could be carried into effect Sherman came so close to the City that it was thought best to remove the prisoners. In the confusion Charley managed to make his escape, and at the moment the battle of Pocataligo opened, was lying concealed between the two lines of battle, without knowing, of course, that he was in such a dangerous locality. After the firing opened, he thought it better to lie still than run the risk from the fire of both sides, especially as he momentarily expected our folks to advance and drive the Rebels away. But the reverse happened; the Johnnies drove our fellows, and, finding Charley in his place of concealment, took him for one of Foster's men, and sent him to Florence, where he staid until we went through to our lines.

Our days went by as stupidly and eventless as can be conceived. We had grown too spiritless and lethargic to dig tunnels or plan escapes. We had nothing to read, nothing to make or destroy, nothing to work with, nothing to play with, and even no desire to contrive anything for amusement. All the cards in the prison were worn out long ago. Some of the boys had made dominos from bones, and Andrews and I still had our chessmen, but we were too listless to play. The mind, enfeebled by the long disuse of it except in a few limited channels, was unfitted for even so much effort as was involved in a game for pastime.

Nor were there any physical exercises, such as that crowd of young men would have delighted in under other circumstances. There was no running, boxing, jumping, wrestling, leaping, etc. All were too weak and hungry to make any exertion beyond that absolutely necessary. On cold days everybody seemed totally benumbed. The camp would be silent and still. Little groups everywhere hovered for hours, moody and sullen, over diminutive, flickering fires, made with one poor handful of splinters. When the sun shone, more activity was visible. Boys wandered around, hunted up their friends, and saw what gaps death—always busiest during the cold spells—had made in the ranks of their acquaintances. During the warmest part of the day everybody disrobed, and spent an hour or more killing the lice that had waxed and multiplied to grievous proportions during the few days of comparative immunity.

Besides the whipping of the Galvanized by the darkies, I remember but two other bits of amusement we had while at Florence. One of these was in hearing the colored soldiers sing patriotic songs, which they did with great gusto when the weather became mild. The other was the antics of a circus clown—a member, I believe, of a Connecticut or a New York regiment, who, on the rare occasions when we were feeling not exactly well so much as simply better than we had been, would give us an hour or two of recitations of the drolleries with which he was wont to set the crowded canvas in a roar. One of his happiest efforts, I remember, was a stilted paraphrase of "Old Uncle Ned" a song very popular a quarter of a century ago, and which ran something like this:

There was an old darky, an' his name was Uncle Ned,
But he died long ago, long ago
He had no wool on de top of his head,
De place whar de wool ought to grouw.

CHORUS

Den lay down de shubel an' de hoe,
Den hang up de fiddle an' de bow;
For dere's no more hard work for poor Uncle Ned
He's gone whar de good niggahs go.

His fingers war long, like de cane in de brake,
And his eyes war too dim for to see;
He had no teeth to eat de corn cake,
So he had to let de corn cake be.

CHORUS.

His legs were so bowed dat he couldn't lie still.
An' he had no nails on his toes;

His neck was so crooked dot he couldn't take a pill,
So he had to take a pill through his nose.

CHORUS.

One cold frosty morning old Uncle Ned died,
An' de tears ran down massa's cheek like rain,
For he knew when Uncle Ned was laid in de groun',
He would never see poor Uncle Ned again,

In the hands of this artist the song became—
CHORUS.

There was an aged and indigent African whose cognomen was Uncle Edward,
But he is deceased since a remote period, a very remote period;
He possessed no capillary substance on the summit of his cranium,
The place designated by kind Nature for the capillary substance to vegetate.

CHORUS.

Then let the agricultural implements rest recumbent upon the ground;
And suspend the musical instruments in peace neon the wall,
For there's no more physical energy to be displayed by our Indigent Uncle Edward
He has departed to that place set apart by a beneficent Providence for the
Reception of the better class of Africans.

And so on. These rare flashes of fun only served to throw the underlying misery out in greater relief. It was like lightning playing across the surface of a dreary morass.

I have before alluded several times to the general inability of Rebels to count accurately, even in low numbers. One continually met phases of this that seemed simply incomprehensible to us, who had taken in the multiplication table almost with our mother's milk, and knew the Rule of Three as well as a Presbyterian boy does the Shorter Catechism. A cadet—an undergraduate of the South Carolina Military Institute —called our roll at Florence, and though an inborn young aristocrat, who believed himself made of finer clay than most mortals, he was not a bad fellow at all. He thought South Carolina aristocracy the finest gentry, and the South Carolina Military Institute the greatest institution of learning in the world; but that is common with all South Carolinians.

One day he came in so full of some matter of rare importance that we became somewhat excited as to its nature. Dismissing our hundred after roll-call, he unburdened his mind:

"Now you fellers are all so d——-d peart on mathematics, and such things, that you want to snap me up on every opportunity, but I guess I've got something this time that'll settle you. Its something that a fellow gave out yesterday, and Colonel Iverson, and all the officers out there have been figuring on it ever since, and none have got the right answer, and I'm powerful sure that none of you, smart as you think you are, can do it."

"Heavens, and earth, let's hear this wonderful problem," said we all.

"Well," said he, "what is the length of a pole standing in a river, one-fifth of which is in the mud, two-thirds in the water, and one-eighth above the water, while one foot and three inches of the top is broken off?"

In a minute a dozen answered, "One hundred and fifty feet."

The cadet could only look his amazement at the possession of such an amount of learning by a crowd of mudsills, and one of our fellows said contemptuously:

"Why, if you South Carolina Institute fellows couldn't answer such questions as that they wouldn't allow you in the infant class up North."

Lieutenant Barrett, our red-headed tormentor, could not, for the life of him, count those inside in hundreds and thousands in such a manner as to be reasonably certain of correctness. As it would have cankered his soul to feel that he was being beaten out of a half-dozen rations by the superior cunning of the Yankees, he adopted a plan which he must have learned at some period of his life when he was a hog or sheep drover. Every Sunday morning all in the camp were driven across the Creek to the East Side, and then made to file slowly back—one at a time—between two guards stationed on the little bridge that spanned the Creek. By this means, if he was able to count up to one hundred, he could get our number correctly.

The first time this was done after our arrival he gave us a display of his wanton malevolence. We were nearly all assembled on the East Side, and were standing in ranks, at the edge of the swamp, facing the west. Barrett was walking along the opposite edge of the swamp, and, coming to a little gully jumped, it. He was very awkward, and came near falling into the mud. We all yelled derisively. He turned toward us in a fury, shook his fist, and shouted curses and imprecations. We yelled still louder. He snatched out his revolver, and began firing at our line. The distance was considerable—say four or five hundred feet—and the bullets struck in the mud in advance of the line. We still yelled. Then he jerked a gun from a guard and fired, but his aim was still bad, and the bullet sang over our heads, striking in the bank above us. He posted of to get another gun, but his fit subsided before he obtained it.

CHAPTER LXXIII.

CHRISTMAS—AND THE WAY THE WAS PASSED—THE DAILY ROUTINE OF RATION DRAWING—SOME PECULIARITIES OF LIVING AND DYING.

Christmas, with its swelling flood of happy memories,—memories now bitter because they marked the high tide whence our fortunes had receded to this despicable state—came, but brought no change to mark its coming. It is true that we had expected no change; we had not looked forward to the day, and hardly knew when it arrived, so indifferent were we to the lapse of time.

When reminded that the day was one that in all Christendom was sacred to good cheer and joyful meetings; that wherever the upraised cross proclaimed followers of Him who preached "Peace on Earth and good will to men," parents and children, brothers and sisters, long-time friends, and all congenial spirits were gathering around hospitable boards to delight in each other's society, and strengthen the bonds of unity between them, we listened as to a tale told of some foreign land from which we had parted forever more.

It seemed years since we had known anything of the kind. The experience we had had of it belonged to the dim and irrevocable past. It could not come to us again, nor we go to it. Squalor, hunger, cold and wasting disease had become the ordinary conditions of existence, from which there was little hope that we would ever be exempt.

Perhaps it was well, to a certain degree, that we felt so. It softened the poignancy of our reflections over the difference in the condition of ourselves and our happier comrades who were elsewhere.

The weather was in harmony with our feelings. The dull, gray, leaden sky was as sharp a contrast with the crisp, bracing sharpness of a Northern Christmas morning, as our beggarly little ration of saltless corn meal was to the sumptuous cheer that loaded the dinner-tables of our Northern homes.

We turned out languidly in the morning to roll-call, endured silently the raving abuse of the cowardly brute Barrett, hung stupidly over the flickering little fires, until the gates opened to admit the rations. For an hour there was bustle and animation. All stood around and counted each sack of meal, to get an idea of the rations we were likely to receive.

This was a daily custom. The number intended for the day's issue were all brought in and piled up in the street. Then there was a division of the sacks to the thousands, the Sergeant of each being called up in turn, and allowed to pick out and carry away one, until all were taken. When we entered the prison each thousand received, on an average, ten or eleven sacks a day. Every week saw a reduction in the number, until by midwinter the daily issue to a thousand averaged four sacks. Let us say that one of these sacks held two bushels, or the four, eight bushels. As there are thirty-two quarts in a bushel, one thousand men received two hundred and fifty-six quarts, or less than a half pint each.

We thought we had sounded the depths of misery at Andersonville, but Florence showed us a much lower depth. Bad as was parching under the burning sun whose fiery rays bred miasma and putrefaction, it was still not so bad as having one's life chilled out by exposure in nakedness upon the frozen ground to biting winds and freezing sleet. Wretched as the rusty bacon and coarse, maggot-filled bread of Andersonville was, it would still go much farther towards supporting life than the handful of saltless meal at Florence.

While I believe it possible for any young man, with the forces of life strong within him, and healthy in every way, to survive, by taking due precautions, such treatment as we received in Andersonville, I cannot understand how anybody could live through a month of Florence. That many did live is only an astonishing illustration of the tenacity of life in some individuals.

Let the reader imagine—anywhere he likes—a fifteen-acre field, with a stream running through the center. Let him imagine this inclosed by a Stockade eighteen feet high, made by standing logs on end. Let him conceive of ten thousand feeble men, debilitated by months of imprisonment, turned inside this inclosure, without a yard of covering given them, and told to make their homes there. One quarter of them—two thousand five hundred—pick up brush, pieces of rail, splits from logs, etc., sufficient to make huts that will turn the rain tolerably. The huts are in no case as good shelter as an ordinarily careful farmer provides for his swine. Half of the prisoners—five thousand—who cannot do so well, work the mud up into rude bricks, with which they build shelters that wash down at every hard rain. The remaining two thousand five hundred do not do even this, but lie around on the ground, on old blankets and overcoats, and in day-time prop these up on sticks, as shelter from the rain and wind. Let them be given not to exceed a pint of corn meal a day, and a piece of wood about the size of an ordinary stick for a cooking stove to cook it with. Then let such weather prevail as we ordinarily have in the North in November—freezing cold rains, with frequent days and nights when the ice forms as thick as a pane of glass. How long does he think men could live through that? He will probably say that a week, or at most a fortnight, would see the last and strongest of these ten thousand lying dead in the frozen mire where he wallowed. He will be astonished to learn that probably not more than four or five thousand of those who underwent this in Florence died there. How many died after release—in Washington, on the vessels coming to Annapolis, in hospital and camp at Annapolis, or after they reached home, none but the Recording Angel can tell. All that I know is we left a trail of dead behind us, wherever we moved, so long as I was with the doleful caravan.

Looking back, after these lapse of years, the most salient characteristic seems to be the ease with which men died. There, was little of the violence of dissolution so common at Andersonville. The machinery of life in all of us, was running slowly and feebly; it would simply grow still slower and feebler in some, and then stop without a jar, without a sensation to manifest it. Nightly one of two or three comrades sleeping together would die. The survivors would not know it until they tried to get him to "spoon" over, when they would find him rigid and motionless. As they could not spare even so little heat as was still contained in his body, they would not remove this, but lie up the closer to it until morning. Such a thing as a boy making an outcry when he discovered his comrade dead, or manifesting any, desire to get away from the corpse, was unknown.

I remember one who, as Charles II. said of himself, was —"an unconscionable long time in dying." His name was Bickford; he belonged to the Twenty-First Ohio Volunteer Infantry, lived, I think, near Findlay, O., and was in my hundred. His partner and he were both in a very bad condition, and I was not surprised, on making my rounds, one morning, to find them apparently quite dead. I called help, and took his partner away to the gate. When we picked up Bickford we found he still lived, and had strength enough to gasp out:

"You fellers had better let me alone." We laid him back to die, as we supposed, in an hour or so. When the Rebel Surgeon came in on his rounds, I showed him Bickford, lying there with his eyes closed, and limbs motionless. The Surgeon said:

"O, that man's dead; why don't you have him taken out?"

I replied: "No, he isn't. Just see." Stooping, I shook the boy sharply, and said:

"Bickford! Bickford!! How do you feel?"

The eyes did not unclose, but the lips opened slowly, and said with a painful effort:

"F-i-r-s-t R-a-t-e!"

This scene was repeated every morning for over a week. Every day the Rebel Surgeon would insist that the man should betaken out, and every morning Bickford would gasp out with troublesome exertion that he felt:

"F-i-r-s-t R-a-t-e!"

It ended one morning by his inability, to make his usual answer, and then he was carried out to join the two score others being loaded into the wagon.

CHAPTER LXXIV.

NEW YEAR'S DAY—DEATH OF JOHN H. WINDER—HE DIES ON HIS WAY TO A DINNER —SOMETHING AS TO CHARACTER AND CAREER—ONE OF THE WORST MEN THAT EVER LIVED.

On New Year's Day we were startled by the information that our old-time enemy—General John H. Winder—was dead. It seemed that the Rebel Sutler of the Post had prepared in his tent a grand New Year's dinner to which all the officers were invited. Just as Winder bent his head to enter the tent he fell, and expired shortly after. The boys said it was a clear case of Death by

Visitation of the Devil, and it was always insisted that his last words were:
"My faith is in Christ; I expect to be saved. Be sure and cut down the prisoners' rations."
Thus passed away the chief evil genius of the Prisoners-of-War. American history has no other character approaching his in vileness. I doubt if the history of the world can show another man, so insignificant in abilities and position, at whose door can be laid such a terrible load of human misery. There have been many great conquerors and warriors who have
Waded through slaughter to a throne,
And shut the gates of mercy on mankind,

but they were great men, with great objects, with grand plans to carry out, whose benefits they thought would be more than an equivalent for the suffering they caused. The misery they inflicted was not the motive of their schemes, but an unpleasant incident, and usually the sufferers were men of other races and religions, for whom sympathy had been dulled by long antagonism.
But Winder was an obscure, dull old man—the commonplace descendant of a pseudo-aristocrat whose cowardly incompetence had once cost us the loss of our National Capital. More prudent than his runaway father, he held himself aloof from the field; his father had lost reputation and almost his commission, by coming into contact with the enemy; he would take no such foolish risks, and he did not. When false expectations of the ultimate triumph of Secession led him to cast his lot with the Southern Confederacy, he did not solicit a command in the field, but took up his quarters in Richmond, to become a sort of Informer-General, High-Inquisitor and Chief Eavesdropper for his intimate friend, Jefferson Davis. He pried and spied around into every man's bedroom and family circle, to discover traces of Union sentiment. The wildest tales malice and vindictiveness could concoct found welcome reception in his ears. He was only too willing to believe, that he might find excuse for harrying and persecuting. He arrested, insulted, imprisoned, banished, and shot people, until the patience even of the citizens of Richmond gave way, and pressure was brought upon Jefferson Davis to secure the suppression of his satellite. For a long while Davis resisted, but at last yielded, and transferred Winder to the office of Commissary General of Prisoners. The delight of the Richmond people was great. One of the papers expressed it in an article, the key note of which was:
"Thank God that Richmond is at last rid of old Winder. God have mercy upon those to whom he has been sent."
Remorseless and cruel as his conduct of the office of Provost Marshal General was, it gave little hint of the extent to which he would go in that of Commissary General of Prisoners. Before, he was restrained somewhat by public opinion and the laws of the land. These no longer deterred him. From the time he assumed command of all the Prisons east of the Mississippi—some time in the Fall of 1863—until death removed him, January 1, 1865—certainly not less than twenty-five thousand incarcerated men died in the most horrible manner that the mind can conceive. He cannot be accused of exaggeration, when, surveying the thousands of new graves at Andersonville, he could say with a quiet chuckle that he was "doing more to kill off the Yankees than twenty regiments at the front." No twenty regiments in the Rebel Army ever succeeded in slaying anything like thirteen thousand Yankees in six months, or any other time. His cold blooded cruelty was such as to disgust even the Rebel officers. Colonel D. T. Chandler, of the Rebel War Department, sent on a tour of inspection to Andersonville, reported back, under date of August 5, 1864:
"My duty requires me respectfully to recommend a change in the officer in command of the post,

Brigadier General John H. Winder, and the substitution in his place of some one who unites both energy and good judgment with some feelings of humanity and consideration for the welfare and comfort, as far as is consistent with their safe keeping, of the vast number of unfortunates placed under his control; some one who, at least, will not advocate deliberately, and in cold blood, the propriety of leaving them in their present condition until their number is sufficiently reduced by death to make the present arrangements suffice for their accommodation, and who will not consider it a matter of self-laudation and boasting that he has never been inside of the Stockade —a place the horrors of which it is difficult to describe, and which is a disgrace to civilization— the condition of which he might, by the exercise of a little energy and judgment, even with the limited means at his command, have considerably improved."

In his examination touching this report, Colonel Chandler says:

"I noticed that General Winder seemed very indifferent to the welfare of the prisoners, indisposed to do anything, or to do as much as I thought he ought to do, to alleviate their sufferings. I remonstrated with him as well as I could, and he used that language which I reported to the Department with reference to it—the language stated in the report. When I spoke of the great mortality existing among the prisoners, and pointed out to him that the sickly season was coming on, and that it must necessarily increase unless something was done for their relief— the swamp, for instance, drained, proper food furnished, and in better quantity, and other sanitary suggestions which I made to him—he replied to me that he thought it was better to see half of them die than to take care of the men."

It was he who could issue such an order as this, when it was supposed that General Stoneman was approaching Andersonville:

HEADQUARTERS MILITARY PRISON,
ANDERSONVILLE, Ga., July 27, 1864.

The officers on duty and in charge of the Battery of Florida Artillery at the time will, upon receiving notice that the enemy has approached within seven miles of this post, open upon the Stockade with grapeshot, without reference to the situation beyond these lines of defense.
JOHN H. WINDER,
Brigadier General Commanding.

This man was not only unpunished, but the Government is to-day supporting his children in luxury by the rent it pays for the use of his property —the well-known Winder building, which is occupied by one of the Departments at Washington.

I confess that all my attempts to satisfactorily analyze Winder's character and discover a sufficient motive for his monstrous conduct have been futile. Even if we imagine him inspired by a hatred of the people of the North that rose to fiendishness, we can not understand him. It seems impossible for the mind of any man to cherish so deep and insatiable an enmity against his fellow-creatures that it could not be quenched and turned to pity by the sight of even one day's misery at Andersonville or Florence. No one man could possess such a grievous sense of private or national wrongs as to be proof against the daily spectacle of thousands of his own fellow citizens, inhabitants of the same country, associates in the same institutions, educated in the same principles, speaking the same language—thousands of his brethren in race, creed, and all that unite men into great communities, starving, rotting and freezing to death.

There is many a man who has a hatred so intense that nothing but the death of the detested one will satisfy it. A still fewer number thirst for a more comprehensive retribution; they would slay perhaps a half-dozen persons; and there may be such gluttons of revenge as would not be satisfied with the sacrifice of less than a score or two, but such would be monsters of whom there have been very few, even in fiction. How must they all bow their diminished heads before a man who fed his animosity fat with tens of thousands of lives.

But, what also militates greatly against the presumption that either revenge or an abnormal predisposition to cruelty could have animated Winder, is that the possession of any two such mental traits so strongly marked would presuppose a corresponding activity of other intellectual faculties, which was not true of him, as from all I can learn of him his mind was in no respect extraordinary.

It does not seem possible that he had either the brain to conceive, or the firmness of purpose to carry out so gigantic and long-enduring a career of cruelty, because that would imply superhuman qualities in a man who had previously held his own very poorly in the competition with other men.

The probability is that neither Winder nor his direct superiors—Howell Cobb and Jefferson Davis—conceived in all its proportions the gigantic engine of torture and death they were organizing; nor did they comprehend the enormity of the crime they were committing. But they were willing to do much wrong to gain their end; and the smaller crimes of to-day prepared them for greater ones to-morrow, and still greater ones the day following. Killing ten men a day on Belle Isle in January, by starvation and hardship, led very easily to killing one hundred men a day in Andersonville, in July, August and September. Probably at the beginning of the war they would have felt uneasy at slaying one man per day by such means, but as retribution came not, and as their appetite for slaughter grew with feeding, and as their sympathy with human misery atrophied from long suppression, they ventured upon ever widening ranges of destructiveness. Had the war lasted another year, and they lived, five hundred deaths a day would doubtless have been insufficient to disturb them.

Winder doubtless went about his part of the task of slaughter coolly, leisurely, almost perfunctorily. His training in the Regular Army was against the likelihood of his displaying zeal in anything. He instituted certain measures, and let things take their course. That course was a rapid transition from bad to worse, but it was still in the direction of his wishes, and, what little of his own energy was infused into it was in the direction of impetus,-not of controlling or improving the course. To have done things better would have involved soma personal discomfort. He was not likely to incur personal discomfort to mitigate evils that were only afflicting someone else. By an effort of one hour a day for two weeks he could have had every man in Andersonville and Florence given good shelter through his own exertions. He was not only too indifferent and too lazy to do this, but he was too malignant; and this neglect to allow— simply allow, remember—the prisoners to protect their lives by providing their own shelter, gives the key to his whole disposition, and would stamp his memory with infamy, even if there were no other charges against him.

CHAPTER LXXV.

ONE INSTANCE OF A SUCCESSFUL ESCAPE—THE ADVENTURES OF SERGEANT

WALTER HARTSOUGH, OF COMPANY K, SIXTEENTH ILLINOIS CAVALRY—HE GETS AWAY FROM THE REBELS AT THOMASVILLE, AND AFTER A TOILSOME AND DANGEROUS JOURNEY OF SEVERAL HUNDRED MILES, REACHES OUR LINES IN FLORIDA.

While I was at Savannah I got hold of a primary geography in possession of one of the prisoners, and securing a fragment of a lead pencil from one comrade, and a sheet of note paper from another, I made a copy of the South Carolina and Georgia sea coast, for the use of Andrews and myself in attempting to escape. The reader remembers the ill success of all our efforts in that direction. When we were at Blackshear we still had the map, and intended to make another effort, "as soon as the sign got right." One day while we were waiting for this, Walter Hartsough, a Sergeant of Company g, of our battalion, came to me and said:

"Mc., I wish you'd lend me your map a little while. I want to make a copy."

I handed it over to him, and never saw him more, as almost immediately after we were taken out "on parole" and sent to Florence. I heard from other comrades of the battalion that he had succeeded in getting past the guard line and into the Woods, which was the last they ever heard of him. Whether starved to death in some swamp, whether torn to pieces by dogs, or killed by the rifles of his pursuers, they knew not. The reader can judge of my astonishment as well as pleasure, at receiving among the dozens of letters which came to me every day while this account was appearing in the BLADE, one signed "Walter Hartsough, late of Co. K, Sixteenth Illinois Cavalry." It was like one returned from the grave, and the next mail took a letter to him, inquiring eagerly of his adventures after we separated. I take pleasure in presenting the reader with his reply, which was only intended as a private communication to myself. The first part of the letter I omit, as it contains only gossip about our old comrades, which, however interesting to myself, would hardly be so to the general reader.

GENOA, WAYNE COUNTY, IA.,
May 27, 1879.
Dear Comrade Mc.:

....

I have been living in this town for ten years, running a general store, under the firm name of Hartsough & Martin, and have been more successful than I anticipated.

I made my escape from Thomasville, Ga., Dec. 7, 1864, by running the guards, in company with Frank Hommat, of Company M, and a man by the name of Clipson, of the Twenty-First Illinois Infantry. I had heard the officers in charge of us say that they intended to march us across to the other road, and take us back to Andersonville. We concluded we would take a heavy risk on our lives rather than return there. By stinting ourselves we had got a little meal ahead, which we thought we would bake up for the journey, but our appetites got the better of us, and we ate it all up before starting. We were camped in the woods then, with no Stockade—only a line of guards around us. We thought that by a little strategy and boldness we could pass these. We determined to try. Clipson was to go to the right, Hommat in the center, and myself to the left. We all slipped through, without a shot. Our rendezvous was to be the center of a small swamp, through which flowed a small stream that supplied the prisoners with water. Hommat and I got together soon after passing the guard lines, and we began signaling for Clipson. We laid down by a large log that lay across the stream, and submerged our limbs and part of our bodies in the water, the better to screen ourselves from observation. Pretty soon a Johnny came along with a bunch of turnip tops, that he was taking up to the camp to trade to the prisoners. As he passed over the log I could have caught him by the leg, which I intended to do if he saw us, but he passed along, heedless of those concealed under his very feet, which saved him a ducking at least, for we were resolved to drown him if he discovered us. Waiting here a little longer we left our lurking place and made a circuit of the edge of the swamp, still signaling for Clipson. But we could find nothing of him, and at last had to give him up.

We were now between Thomasville and the camp, and as Thomasville was the end of the railroad, the woods were full of Rebels waiting transportation, and we approached the road carefully, supposing that it was guarded to keep their own men from going to town. We crawled up to the road, but seeing no one, started across it. At that moment a guard about thirty yards to our left, who evidently supposed that we were Rebels, sang out:

"Whar ye gwine to thar boys?"

I answered:

"Jest a-gwine out here a little ways."

Frank whispered me to run, but I said, "No; wait till he halts us, and then run." He walked up to where we had crossed his beat—looked after us a few minutes, and then, to our great relief, walked back to his post. After much trouble we succeeded in getting through all the troops, and started fairly on our way. We tried to shape our course toward Florida. The country was very swampy, the night rainy and dark, no stars were out to guide us, and we made such poor progress that when daylight came we were only eight miles from our starting place, and close to a road leading from Thomasville to Monticello. Finding a large turnip patch, we filled our pockets, and then hunted a place to lie concealed in during the day. We selected a thicket in the center of a large pasture. We crawled into this and laid down. Some negros passed close to us, going to their work in an adjoining field. They had a bucket of victuals with them for dinner, which they hung on the fence in such a way that we could have easily stolen it without detection. The temptation to hungry men was very great, but we concluded that it was best and safest to let it alone.

As the negros returned from work in the evening they separated, one old man passing on the opposite side of the thicket from the rest. We halted him and told him that we were Rebs, who had taken a French leave of Thomasville; that we were tired of guarding Yanks, and were going home; and further, that we were hungry, and wanted something to eat. He told us that he was the boss on the plantation. His master lived in Thomasville. He, himself, did not have much to eat, but he would show us where to stay, and when the folks went to bed he would bring us some food. Passing up close to the negro quarters we got over the fence and lay down behind it, to wait for our supper.

We had been there but a short time when a young negro came out, and passing close by us, went into a fence corner a few panels distant and, kneeling down, began praying aloud, and very, earnestly, and stranger still, the burden of his supplication was for the success of our armies. I thought it the best prayer I ever listened to. Finishing his devotions he returned to the house, and shortly after the old man came with a good supper of corn bread, molasses and milk. He said that he had no meat, and that he had done the best he could for us. After we had eaten, he said that as the young people had gone to bed, we had better come into his cabin and rest awhile, which we did.

Hommat had a full suit of Rebel clothes, and I had stolen sacks enough at Andersonville, when they were issuing rations, to make me a shirt and pantaloons, which a sailor fabricated for me. I wore these over what was left of my blue clothes. The old negro lady treated us very coolly. In a few minutes a young negro came in, whom the old gentleman introduced as his son, and whom I immediately recognized as our friend of the prayerful proclivities. He said that he had been a body servant to his young master, who was an officer in the Rebel army.

"Golly!" says he, "if you 'uns had stood a little longer at Stone River, our men would have run."
I turned to him sharply with the question of what he meant by calling us "You 'uns," and asked
him if he believed we were Yankees. He surveyed us carefully for a few seconds, and then said:
"Yes; I bleav you is Yankees."

He paused a second, and added:

"Yes, I know you is."

I asked him how he knew it, and he said that we neither looked nor talked like their men. I then
acknowledged that we were Yankee prisoners, trying to make our escape to our lines. This
announcement put new life into the old lady, and, after satisfying herself that we were really
Yankees, she got up from her seat, shook hands with us, and declared we must have a better
supper than we had had. She set immediately about preparing it for us. Taking up a plank in the
floor, she pulled out a nice flitch of bacon, from which she cut as much as we could eat, and gave
us some to carry with us. She got up a real substantial supper, to which we did full justice, in
spite of the meal we had already eaten.

They gave us a quantity of victuals to take with us, and instructed us as well as possible as to our
road. They warned us to keep away from the young negros, but trust the old ones implicitly.
Thanking them over and over for their exceeding kindness, we bade them good-by, and started
again on our journey. Our supplies lasted two days, during which time we made good progress,
keeping away from the roads, and flanking the towns, which were few and insignificant. We
occasionally came across negros, of whom we cautiously inquired as to the route and towns, and
by the assistance of our map and the stars, got along very well indeed, until we came to the
Suwanee River. We had intended to cross this at Columbus or Alligator. When within six miles
of the river we stopped at some negro huts to get some food. The lady who owned the negros
was a widow, who was born and raised in Massachusetts. Her husband had died before the war
began. An old negro woman told her mistress that we were at the quarters, and she sent for us to
come to the house. She was a very nice-looking lady, about thirty-five years of age, and treated
us with great kindness. Hommat being barefooted, she pulled off her own shoes and stockings
and gave them to him, saying that she would go to Town the next day and get herself another
pair. She told us not to try to cross the river near Columbus, as their troops had been deserting in
great numbers, and the river was closely picketed to catch the runaways. She gave us directions
how to go so as to cross the river about fifty miles below Columbus. We struck the river again
the next night, and I wanted to swim it, but Hommat was afraid of alligators, and I could not
induce him to venture into the water.

We traveled down the river until we came to Moseley's Ferry, where we stole an old boat about a
third full of water, and paddled across. There was quite a little town at that place, but we walked
right down the main street without meeting any one. Six miles from the river we saw an old
negro woman roasting sweet potatos in the back yard of a house. We were very hungry, and
thought we would risk something to get food. Hommat went around near her, and asked her for
something to eat. She told him to go and ask the white folks. This was the answer she made to
every question. He wound up by asking her how far it was to Mossley's Ferry, saying that he
wanted to go there, and get something to eat. She at last ran into the house, and we ran away as
fast as we could. We had gone but a short distance when we heard a horn, and soon-the-cursed
hounds began bellowing. We did our best running, but the hounds circled around the house a few
times and then took our trail. For a little while it seemed all up with us, as the sound of the
baying came closer and closer. But our inquiry about the distance to Moseley's Ferry seems to

have saved us. They soon called the hounds in, and started them on the track we had come, instead of that upon which we were going. The baying shortly died away in the distance. We did not waste any time congratulating ourselves over our marvelous escape, but paced on as fast as we could for about eight miles farther. On the way we passed over the battle ground of Oolustee, or Ocean Pond.

Coming near to Lake City we fell in with some negros who had been brought from Maryland. We stopped over one day with them, to rest, and two of them concluded to go with us. We were furnished with a lot of cooked provisions, and starting one night made forty-two miles before morning. We kept the negros in advance. I told Hommat that it was a poor command that could not afford an advance guard. After traveling two nights with the negros, we came near Baldwin. Here I was very much afraid of recapture, and I did not want the negros with us, if we were, lest we should be shot for slave-stealing. About daylight of the second morning we gave them the slip.

We had to skirt Baldwin closely, to head the St. Mary's River, or cross it where that was easiest. After crossing the river we came to a very large swamp, in the edge of which we lay all day. Before nightfall we started to go through it, as there was no fear of detection in these swamps. We got through before it was very dark, and as we emerged from it we discovered a dense cloud of smoke to our right and quite close. We decided this was a camp, and while we were talking the band began to play. This made us think that probably our forces had come out from Fernandina, and taken the place. I proposed to Hommat that we go forward and reconnoiter. He refused, and leaving him alone, I started forward. I had gone but a short distance when a soldier came out from the camp with a bucket. He began singing, and the song he sang convinced me that he was a Rebel. Rejoining Hommat, we held a consultation and decided to stay where we were until it became darker, before trying to get out. It was the night of the 22d of December, and very cold for that country. The camp guard had small fires built, which we could see quite plainly. After starting we saw that the pickets also had fires, and that we were between the two lines. This discovery saved us from capture, and keeping about an equal distance between the two, we undertook to work our way out.

We first crossed a line of breastworks, then in succession the Fernandina Railroad, the Jacksonville Railroad, and pike, moving all the time nearly parallel with the picket line. Here we had to halt. Hommat was suffering greatly with his feet. The shoes that had been given him by the widow lady were worn out, and his feet were much torn and cut by the terribly rough road we had traveled through swamps, etc. We sat down on a log, and I, pulling off the remains of my army shirt, tore it into pieces, and Hommat wrapped his feet up in them. A part I reserved and tore into strips, to tie up the rents in our pantaloons. Going through the swamps and briers had torn them into tatters, from waistband to hem, leaving our skins bare to be served in the same way.

We started again, moving slowly and bearing towards the picket fires, which we could see for a distance on our left. After traveling some little time the lights on our left ended, which puzzled us for a while, until we came to a fearful big swamp, that explained it all, as this, considered impassable, protected the right of the camp. We had an awful time in getting through. In many places we had to lie down and crawl long distances through the paths made in the brakes by hogs and other animals. As we at length came out, Hommat turned to me and whispered that in the morning we would have some Lincoln coffee. He seemed to think this must certainly end our troubles.

We were now between the Jacksonville Railroad and the St. John's River. We kept about four miles from the railroad, for fear of running into the Rebel outposts. We had traveled but a few miles when Hommat said he could go no farther, as his feet and legs were so swelled and numb that he could not tell when he set them upon the ground. I had some matches that a negro had given me, and gathering together a few pine knots we made a fire—the first that we had lighted on the trip—and laid down with it between us. We had slept but a few minutes when I awoke and found Hommat's clothes on fire. Rousing him we put out the flames before he was badly burned, but the thing had excited him so as to give him new life, and be proposed to start on again.

By sunrise we were within eight miles of our lines, and concluding that it would be safe to travel in the daytime, we went ahead, walking along the railroad. The excitement being over, Hommat began to move very slowly again. His feet and legs were so swollen that he could scarcely walk, and it took us a long while to pass over those eight miles.

At last we came in sight of our pickets. They were negros. They halted us, and Hommat went forward to speak to them. They called for the Officer of the Guard, who came, passed us inside, and shook hands cordially with us. His first inquiry was if we knew Charley Marseilles, whom you remember ran that little bakery at Andersonville.

We were treated very kindly at Jacksonville. General Scammon was in command of the post, and had only been released but a short time from prison, so he knew how it was himself. I never expect to enjoy as happy a moment on earth as I did when I again got under the protection of the old flag. Hommat went to the hospital a few days, and was then sent around to New York by sea. Oh, it was a fearful trip through those Florida swamps. We would very often have to try a swamp in three or four different places before we could get through. Some nights we could not travel on account of its being cloudy and raining. There is not money enough in the United States to induce me to undertake the trip again under the same circumstances. Our friend Clipson, that made his escape when we did, got very nearly through to our lines, but was taken sick, and had to give himself up. He was taken back to Andersonville and kept until the next Spring, when he came through all right. There were sixty-one of Company K captured at Jonesville, and I think there was only seventeen lived through those horrible prisons.

You have given the best description of prison life that I have ever seen written. The only trouble is that it cannot be portrayed so that persons can realize the suffering and abuse that our soldiers endured in those prison hells. Your statements are all correct in regard to the treatment that we received, and all those scenes you have depicted are as vivid in my mind today as if they had only occurred yesterday. Please let me hear from you again. Wishing you success in all your undertakings, I remain your friend,

WALTER, HARTSOUGH,

Late of K Company, Sixteenth Illinois Volunteer of Infantry.

CHAPTER LXXVI.

THE PECULIAR TYPE OF INSANITY PREVALENT AT FLORENCE—BARRETT'S WANTONNESS OF CRUELTY—WE LEARN OF SHERMAN'S ADVANCE INTO SOUTH CAROLINA—THE REBELS BEGIN MOVING THE PRISONERS AWAY—ANDREWS AND I CHANGE OUR TACTICS, AND STAY BEHIND—ARRIVAL OF FIVE PRISONERS

One terrible phase of existence at Florence was the vast increase of insanity. We had many insane men at Andersonville, but the type of the derangement was different, partaking more of what the doctors term melancholia. Prisoners coming in from the front were struck aghast by the horrors they saw everywhere. Men dying of painful and repulsive diseases lined every step of whatever path they trod; the rations given them were repugnant to taste and stomach; shelter from the fiery sun there was none, and scarcely room enough for them to lie down upon. Under these discouraging circumstances, home-loving, kindly-hearted men, especially those who had passed out of the first flush of youth, and had left wife and children behind when they entered the service, were speedily overcome with despair of surviving until released; their hopelessness fed on the same germs which gave it birth, until it became senseless, vacant-eyed, unreasoning, incurable melancholy, when the victim would lie for hours, without speaking a word, except to babble of home, or would wander aimlessly about the camp—frequently stark naked—until he died or was shot for coming too near the Dead Line. Soldiers must not suppose that this was the same class of weaklings who usually pine themselves into the Hospital within three months after their regiment enters the field. They were as a rule, made up of seasoned soldiery, who had become inured to the dangers and hardships of active service, and were not likely to sink down under any ordinary trials.

The insane of Florence were of a different class; they were the boys who had laughed at such a yielding to adversity in Andersonville, and felt a lofty pity for the misfortunes of those who succumbed so. But now the long strain of hardship, privation and exposure had done for them what discouragement had done for those of less fortitude in Andersonville. The faculties shrank under disuse and misfortune, until they forgot their regiments, companies, places and date of capture, and finally, even their names. I should think that by the middle of January, at least one in every ten had sunk to this imbecile condition. It was not insanity so much as mental atrophy— not so much aberration of the mind, as a paralysis of mental action. The sufferers became apathetic idiots, with no desire or wish to do or be anything. If they walked around at all they had to be watched closely, to prevent their straying over the Dead Line, and giving the young brats of guards the coveted opportunity of killing them. Very many of such were killed, and one of my Midwinter memories of Florence was that of seeing one of these unfortunate imbeciles wandering witlessly up to the Dead Line from the Swamp, while the guard—a boy of seventeen—stood with gun in hand, in the attitude of a man expecting a covey to be flushed, waiting for the poor devil to come so near the Dead Line as to afford an excuse for killing him. Two sane prisoners, comprehending the situation, rushed up to the lunatic, at the risk of their own lives, caught him by the arms, and drew him back to safety.

The brutal Barrett seemed to delight in maltreating these demented unfortunates. He either could not be made to understand their condition, or willfully disregarded it, for it was one of the commonest sights to see him knock down, beat, kick or otherwise abuse them for not instantly obeying orders which their dazed senses could not comprehend, or their feeble limbs execute, even if comprehended.

In my life I have seen many wantonly cruel men. I have known numbers of mates of Mississippi river steamers—a class which seems carefully selected from ruffians most proficient in profanity, obscenity and swift-handed violence; I have seen negro-drivers in the slave marts of St. Louis, Memphis and New Orleans, and overseers on the plantations of Mississippi and Louisiana; as a police reporter in one of the largest cities in America, I have come in contact with thousands of the brutalized scoundrels—the thugs of the brothel, bar-room and alley—who form the dangerous classes of a metropolis. I knew Captain Wirz. But in all this exceptionally extensive and varied experience, I never met a man who seemed to love cruelty for its own sake as well as Lieutenant Barrett. He took such pleasure in inflicting pain as those Indians who slice off their prisoners' eyelids, ears, noses and hands, before burning them at the stake.

That a thing hurt some one else was always ample reason for his doing it. The starving, freezing prisoners used to collect in considerable numbers before the gate, and stand there for hours gazing vacantly at it. There was no special object in doing this, only that it was a central point, the rations came in there, and occasionally an officer would enter, and it was the only place where anything was likely to occur to vary the dreary monotony of the day, and the boys went there because there was nothing else to offer any occupation to their minds. It became a favorite practical joke of Barrett's to slip up to the gate with an armful of clubs, and suddenly opening the wicket, fling them one after another, into the crowd, with all the force he possessed. Many were knocked down, and many received hurts which resulted in fatal gangrene. If he had left the clubs lying where thrown, there would have been some compensation for his meanness, but he always came in and carefully gathered up such as he could get, as ammunition for another time.

I have heard men speak of receiving justice—even favors from Wirz. I never heard any one saying that much of Barrett. Like Winder, if he had a redeeming quality it was carefully obscured from the view of all that I ever met who knew him.

Where the fellow came from, what State was entitled to the discredit of producing and raising him, what he was before the War, what became of him after he left us, are matters of which I never heard even a rumor, except a very vague one that he had been killed by our cavalry, some returned prisoner having recognized and shot him.

Colonel Iverson, of the Fifth Georgia, was the Post Commander. He was a man of some education, but had a violent, ungovernable temper, during fits of which he did very brutal things. At other times he would show a disposition towards fairness and justice. The worst point in my indictment against him is that he suffered Barrett to do as he did.

Let the reader understand that I have no personal reasons for my opinion of these men. They never did anything to me, save what they did to all of my companions. I held myself aloof from them, and shunned intercourse so effectually that during my whole imprisonment I did not speak as many words to Rebel officers as are in this and the above paragraphs, and most of those were spoken to the Surgeon who visited my hundred. I do not usually seek conversation with people I do not like, and certainly did not with persons for whom I had so little love as I had for Turner, Ross, Winder, Wirz, Davis, Iverson, Barrett, et al. Possibly they felt badly over my distance and reserve, but I must confess that they never showed it very palpably.

As January dragged slowly away into February, rumors of the astonishing success of Sherman began to be so definite and well authenticated as to induce belief. We knew that the Western Chieftain had marched almost unresisted through Georgia, and captured Savannah with comparatively little difficulty. We did not understand it, nor did the Rebels around us, for neither of us comprehended the Confederacy's near approach to dissolution, and we could not explain why a desperate attempt was not made somewhere to arrest the onward sweep of the conquering armies of the West. It seemed that if there was any vitality left in Rebeldom it would deal a blow that would at least cause the presumptuous invader to pause. As we knew nothing of the battles of Franklin and Nashville, we were ignorant of the destruction of Hood's army, and were at a loss to account for its failure to contest Sherman's progress. The last we had heard of Hood, he had been flanked out of Atlanta, but we did not understand that the strength or morale of his force had been seriously reduced in consequence.

Soon it drifted in to us that Sherman had cut loose from Savannah, as from Atlanta, and entered South Carolina, to repeat there the march through her sister State. Our sources of information now were confined to the gossip which our men—working outside on parole,—could overhear from the Rebels, and communicate to us as occasion served. These occasions were not frequent, as the men outside were not allowed to come in except rarely, or stay long then. Still we managed to know reasonably, soon that Sherman was sweeping resistlessly across the State, with Hardee, Dick Taylor, Beauregard, and others, vainly trying to make head against him. It seemed impossible to us that they should not stop him soon, for if each of all these leaders had any command worthy the name the aggregate must make an army that, standing on the defensive, would give Sherman a great deal of trouble. That he would be able to penetrate into the State as far as we were never entered into our minds.

By and by we were astonished at the number of the trains that we could hear passing north on the Charleston & Cheraw Railroad. Day and night for two weeks there did not seem to be more than half an hour's interval at any time between the rumble and whistles of the trains as they passed Florence Junction, and sped away towards Cheraw, thirty-five miles north of us. We at length discovered that Sherman had reached Branchville, and was singing around toward Columbia, and other important points to the north; that Charleston was being evacuated, and its garrison, munitions and stores were being removed to Cheraw, which the Rebel Generals intended to make their new base. As this news was so well confirmed as to leave no doubt of it, it began to wake up and encourage all the more hopeful of us. We thought we could see some premonitions of the glorious end, and that we were getting vicarious satisfaction at the hands of our friends under the command of Uncle Billy.

One morning orders came for one thousand men to get ready to move. Andrews and I held a council of war on the situation, the question before the house being whether we would go with that crowd, or stay behind. The conclusion we came to was thus stated by Andrews:

"Now, Mc., we've flanked ahead every time, and see how we've come out. We flanked into the first squad that left Richmond, and we were consequently in the first that got into Andersonville. May be if we'd staid back we'd got into that squad that was exchanged. We were in the first squad that left Andersonville. We were the first to leave Savannah and enter Millen. May be if we'd staid back, we'd got exchanged with the ten thousand sick. We were the first to leave Millen and the first to reach Blackshear. We were again the first to leave Blackshear. Perhaps those fellows we left behind then are exchanged. Now, as we've played ahead every time, with such infernal luck, let's play backward this time, and try what that brings us."

"But, Lale," (Andrews's nickname—his proper name being Bezaleel), said I, "we made something by going ahead every time—that is, if we were not going to be exchanged. By getting into those places first we picked out the best spots to stay, and got tent-building stuff that those who came after us could not. And certainly we can never again get into as bad a place as this is. The chances are that if this does not mean exchange, it means transfer to a better prison."

But we concluded, as I said above, to reverse our usual order of procedure and flank back, in hopes that something would favor our escape to Sherman. Accordingly, we let the first squad go off without us, and the next, and the next, and so on, till there were only eleven hundred — mostly those sick in the Hospital—remaining behind. Those who went away—we afterwards learned, were run down on the cars to Wilmington, and afterwards up to Goldsboro, N. C.

For a week or more we eleven hundred tenanted the Stockade, and by burning up the tents of those who had gone had the only decent, comfortable fires we had while in Florence. In hunting around through the tents for fuel we found many bodies of those who had died as their comrades were leaving. As the larger portion of us could barely walk, the Rebels paroled us to remain inside of the Stockade or within a few hundred yards of the front of it, and took the guards off. While these were marching down, a dozen or more of us, exulting in even so much freedom as we had obtained, climbed on the Hospital shed to see what the outlook was, and perched ourselves on the ridgepole. Lieutenant Barrett came along, at a distance of two hundred yards, with a squad of guards. Observing us, he halted his men, faced them toward us, and they leveled their guns as if to fire. He expected to see us tumble down in ludicrous alarm, to avoid the bullets. But we hated him and them so bad, that we could not give them the poor satisfaction of scaring us. Only one of our party attempted to slide down, but the moment we swore at him he came back and took his seat with folded arms alongside of us. Barrett gave the order to fire, and the bullets shrieked aver our heads, fortunately not hitting anybody. We responded with yells of derision, and the worst abuse we could think of.

Coming down after awhile, I walked to the now open gate, and looped through it over the barren fields to the dense woods a mile away, and a wild desire to run off took possession of me. It seemed as if I could not resist it. The woods appeared full of enticing shapes, beckoning me to come to them, and the winds whispered in my ears:

"Run! Run! Run!"

But the words of my parole were still fresh in my mind, and I stilled my frenzy to escape by turning back into the Stockade and looking away from the tempting view.

Once five new prisoners, the first we had seen in a long time, were brought in from Sherman's army. They were plump, well-conditioned, well-dressed, healthy, devil-may-care young fellows, whose confidence in themselves and in Sherman was simply limitless, and their contempt for all Rebels and especially those who terrorized over us, enormous.

"Come up here to headquarters," said one of the Rebel officers to them as they stood talking to us; "and we'll parole you."

"O go to h—— with your parole," said the spokesman of the crowd, with nonchalant contempt; "we don't want none of your paroles. Old Billy'll parole us before Saturday."

To us they said:

"Now, you boys want to cheer right up; keep a stiff upper lip. This thing's workin' all right. Their old Confederacy's goin' to pieces like a house afire. Sherman's promenadin' through it just as it suits him, and he's liable to pay a visit at any hour. We're expectin' him all the time, because it was generally understood all through the Army that we were to take the prison pen here in on our way."

I mentioned my distrust of the concentration of Rebels at Cheraw, and their faces took on a look of supreme disdain.

"Now, don't let that worry you a minute," said the confident spokesman. "All the Rebels between here and Lee's Army can't prevent Sherman from going just where he pleases. Why, we've quit fightin' 'em except with the Bummers advance. We haven't had to go into regular line of battle against them for I don't know how long. Sherman would like anything better than to have 'em make a stand somewhere so that he could get a good fair whack at 'em."

No one can imagine the effect of all this upon us. It was better than a carload of medicines and a train load of provisions would have been. From the depths of despondency we sprang at once to tip-toe on the mountain-tops of expectation. We did little day and night but listen for the sound of Sherman's guns and discuss what we would do when he came. We planned schemes of terrible vengeance on Barrett and Iverson, but these worthies had mysteriously disappeared—whither no one knew. There was hardly an hour of any night passed without some one of us fancying that he heard the welcome sound of distant firing. As everybody knows, by listening intently at night, one can hear just exactly what he is intent upon hearing, and so was with us. In the middle of the night boys listening awake with strained ears, would say:

"Now, if ever I heard musketry firing in my life, that's a heavy skirmish line at work, and sharply too, and not more than three miles away, neither."

Then another would say:

"I don't want to ever get out of here if that don't sound just as the skirmishing at Chancellorsville did the first day to us. We were lying down about four miles off, when it began pattering just as that is doing now."

And so on.

One night about nine or ten, there came two short, sharp peals of thunder, that sounded precisely like the reports of rifled field pieces. We sprang up in a frenzy of excitement, and shouted as if our throats would split. But the next peal went off in the usual rumble, and our excitement had to subside.

CHAPTER LXXVII

FRUITLESS WAITING FOR SHERMAN—WE LEAVE FLORENCE—INTELLIGENCE OF THE FALL OF WILMINGTON COMMUNICATED TO US BY A SLAVE—THE TURPENTINE REGION OF NORTH CAROLINA—WE COME UPON A REBEL LINE OF BATTLE—YANKEES AT BOTH ENDS OF THE ROAD.

Things had gone on in the way described in the previous chapter until past the middle of February. For more than a week every waking hour was spent in anxious expectancy of Sherman—listening for the far-off rattle of his guns—straining our ears to catch the sullen boom of his artillery—scanning the distant woods to see the Rebels falling back in hopeless confusion before the pursuit of his dashing advance. Though we became as impatient as those ancient sentinels who for ten long years stood upon the Grecian hills to catch the first glimpse of the flames of burning Troy, Sherman came not. We afterwards learned that two expeditions were sent down towards us from Cheraw, but they met with unexpected resistance, and were turned back.

It was now plain to us that the Confederacy was tottering to its fall, and we were only troubled by occasional misgivings that we might in some way be caught and crushed under the toppling ruins. It did not seem possible that with the cruel tenacity with which the Rebels had clung to us they would be willing to let us go free at last, but would be tempted in the rage of their final defeat to commit some unparalleled atrocity upon us.

One day all of us who were able to walk were made to fall in and march over to the railroad, where we were loaded into boxcars. The sick —except those who were manifestly dying—were loaded into wagons and hauled over. The dying were left to their fate, without any companions or nurses.

The train started off in a northeasterly direction, and as we went through Florence the skies were crimson with great fires, burning in all directions. We were told these were cotton and military stores being destroyed in anticipation of a visit from, a part of Sherman's forces.

When morning came we were still running in the same direction that we started. In the confusion of loading us upon the cars the previous evening, I had been allowed to approach too near a Rebel officer's stock of rations, and the result was his being the loser and myself the gainer of a canteen filled with fairly good molasses. Andrews and I had some corn bread, and we, breakfasted sumptuously upon it and the molasses, which was certainly none-the-less sweet from having been stolen.

Our meal over, we began reconnoitering, as much for employment as anything else. We were in the front end of a box car. With a saw made on the back of a case-knife we cut a hole through the boards big enough to permit us to pass out, and perhaps escape. We found that we were on the foremost box car of the train—the next vehicle to us being a passenger coach, in which were the Rebel officers. On the rear platform of this car was seated one of their servants—a trusty old slave, well dressed, for a negro, and as respectful as his class usually was. Said I to him:

"Well, uncle, where are they taking us?"

He replied:

"Well, sah, I couldn't rightly say."

"But you could guess, if you tried, couldn't you?"

"Yes sah."

He gave a quick look around to see if the door behind him was so securely shut that he could not be overheard by the Rebels inside the car, his dull, stolid face lighted up as a negro's always does in the excitement of doing something cunning, and he said in a loud whisper:

"Dey's a-gwine to take you to Wilmington—ef dey kin get you dar!"

"Can get us there!" said I in astonishment. "Is there anything to prevent them taking us there?"

The dark face filled with inexpressible meaning. I asked:

"It isn't possible that there are any Yankees down there to interfere, is it?"

The great eyes flamed up with intelligence to tell me that I guessed aright; again he glanced nervously around to assure himself that no one was eavesdropping, and then he said in a whisper, just loud enough to be heard above the noise of the moving train:

"De Yankees took Wilmington yesterday mawning."

The news startled me, but it was true, our troops having driven out the Rebel troops, and entered Wilmington, on the preceding day—the 22d of February, 1865, as I learned afterwards. How this negro came to know more of what was going on than his masters puzzled me much. That he did know more was beyond question, since if the Rebels in whose charge we were had known of Wilmington's fall, they would not have gone to the trouble of loading us upon the cars and hauling us one, hundred miles in the direction of a City which had come into the hands of our men.

It has been asserted by many writers that the negros had some occult means of diffusing important news among the mass of their people, probably by relays of swift runners who traveled at night, going twenty-five or thirty miles and back before morning. Very astonishing stories are told of things communicated in this way across the length or breadth of the Confederacy. It is said that our officers in the blockading fleet in the Gulf heard from the negros in advance of the publication in the Rebel papers of the issuance of the Proclamation of Emancipation, and of several of our most important Victories. The incident given above prepares me to believe all that has been told of the perfection to which the negros had brought their "grapevine telegraph," as it was jocularly termed.

The Rebels believed something of it, too. In spite of their rigorous patrol, an institution dating long before the war, and the severe punishments visited upon negros found off their master's premises without a pass, none of them entertained a doubt that the young negro men were in the habit of making long, mysterious journeys at night, which had other motives than love-making or chicken-stealing. Occasionally a young man would get caught fifty or seventy-five miles from his "quarters," while on some errand of his own, the nature of which no punishment could make him divulge. His master would be satisfied that he did not intend running away, because he was likely going in the wrong direction, but beyond this nothing could be ascertained. It was a common belief among overseers, when they saw an active, healthy young "buck" sleepy and languid about his work, that he had spent the night on one of these excursions.

The country we were running through—if such straining, toilsome progress as our engine was making could be called running—was a rich turpentine district. We passed by forests where all the trees were marked with long scores through the bark, and extended up to a hight of twenty feet or more. Into these, the turpentine and rosin, running down, were caught, and conveyed by negros to stills near by, where it was prepared for market. The stills were as rude as the mills we had seen in Eastern Tennessee and Kentucky, and were as liable to fiery destruction as a powder-house. Every few miles a wide space of ground, burned clean of trees and underbrush, and yet marked by a portion of the stones which had formed the furnace, showed where a turpentine still, managed by careless and ignorant blacks, had been licked up by the breath of flame. They never seemed to re-build on these spots—whether from superstition or other reasons, I know not. Occasionally we came to great piles of barrels of turpentine, rosin and tar, some of which had laid there since the blockade had cut off communication with the outer world. Many of the barrels of rosin had burst, and their contents melted in the heat of the sun, had run over the ground like streams of lava, covering it to a depth of many inches. At the enormous price rosin, tar and turpentine were commanding in the markets of the world, each of these piles represented a superb fortune. Any one of them, if lying upon the docks of New York, would have yielded enough to make every one of us upon the train comfortable for life. But a few months after the blockade was raised, and they sank to one-thirtieth of their present value.

These terebinthine stores were the property of the plantation lords of the lowlands of North Carolina, who correspond to the pinchbeck barons of the rice districts of South Carolina. As there, the whites and negros we saw were of the lowest, most squalid type of humanity. The people of the middle and upland districts of North Carolina are a much superior race to the same class in South Carolina. They are mostly of Scotch-Irish descent, with a strong infusion of English-Quaker blood, and resemble much the best of the Virginians. They make an effort to diffuse education, and have many of the virtues of a simple, non-progressive, tolerably industrious middle class. It was here that the strong Union sentiment of North Carolina numbered most of its adherents. The people of the lowlands were as different as if belonging to another race. The enormous mass of ignorance—the three hundred and fifty thousand men and women who could not read or write—were mostly black and white serfs of the great landholders, whose plantations lie within one hundred miles of the Atlantic coast.

As we approached the coast the country became swampier, and our old acquaintances, the cypress, with their malformed "knees," became more and more numerous.

About the middle of the afternoon our train suddenly stopped. Looking out to ascertain the cause, we were electrified to see a Rebel line of battle stretched across the track, about a half mile ahead of the engine, and with its rear toward us. It was as real a line as was ever seen on any field. The double ranks of "Butternuts," with arms gleaming in the afternoon sun, stretched away out through the open pine woods, farther than we could see. Close behind the motionless line stood the company officers, leaning on their drawn swords. Behind these still, were the regimental officers on their horses. On a slight rise of the ground, a group of horsemen, to whom other horsemen momentarily dashed up to or sped away from, showed the station of the General in command. On another knoll, at a little distance, were several-field pieces, standing "in battery," the cannoneers at the guns, the postillions dismounted and holding their horses by the bits, the caisson men standing in readiness to serve out ammunition. Our men were evidently close at hand in strong force, and the engagement was likely to open at any instant.

For a minute we were speechless with astonishment. Then came a surge of excitement. What should we do? What could we do? Obviously nothing. Eleven hundred, sick, enfeebled prisoners could not even overpower their guards, let alone make such a diversion in the rear of a line-of-battle as would assist our folks to gain a victory. But while we debated the engine whistled sharply—a frightened shriek it sounded to us—and began pushing our train rapidly backward over the rough and wretched track. Back, back we went, as fast as rosin and pine knots could force the engine to move us. The cars swayed continually back and forth, momentarily threatening to fly the crazy roadway, and roll over the embankment or into one of the adjacent swamps. We would have hailed such a catastrophe, as it would have probably killed more of the guards than of us, and the confusion would have given many of the survivors opportunity to escape. But no such accident happened, and towards midnight we reached the bridge across the Great Pedee River, where our train was stopped by a squad of Rebel cavalrymen, who brought the intelligence that as Kilpatrick was expected into Florence every hour, it would not do to take us there.

We were ordered off the cars, and laid down on the banks of the Great Pedee, our guards and the cavalry forming a line around us, and taking precautions to defend the bridge against Kilpatrick, should he find out our whereabouts and come after us.

"Well, Mc," said Andrews, as we adjusted our old overcoat and blanket on the ground for a bed; "I guess we needn't care whether school keeps or not. Our fellows have evidently got both ends of the road, and are coming towards us from each way. There's no road—not even a wagon road —for the Johnnies to run us off on, and I guess all we've got to do is to stand still and see the salvation of the Lord. Bad as these hounds are, I don't believe they will shoot us down rather than let our folks retake us. At least they won't since old Winder's dead. If he was alive, he'd order our throats cut—one by one—with the guards' pocket knives, rather than give us up. I'm only afraid we'll be allowed to starve before our folks reach us."

I concurred in this view.

CHAPTER LXXVIII.

RETURN TO FLORENCE AND A SHORT SOJOURN THERE—OFF TOWARDS WILMINGTON AGAIN—CRUISING A REBEL OFFICER'S LUNCH—SIGNS OF APPROACHING OUR LINES —TERROR OF OUR RASCALLY GUARDS—ENTRANCE INTO GOD'S COUNTRY AT LAST.

But Kilpatrick, like Sherman, came not. Perhaps he knew that all the prisoners had been removed from the Stockade; perhaps he had other business of more importance on hand; probably his movement was only a feint. At all events it was definitely known the next day that he had withdrawn so far as to render it wholly unlikely that he intended attacking Florence, so we were brought back and returned to our old quarters. For a week or more we loitered about the now nearly-abandoned prison; skulked and crawled around the dismal mud-tents like the ghostly denizens of some Potter's Field, who, for some reason had been allowed to return to earth, and for awhile creep painfully around the little hillocks beneath which they had been entombed. A few score, whose vital powers were strained to the last degree of tension, gave up the ghost, and sank to dreamless rest. It mattered now little to these when Sherman came, or when Kilpatrick's guidons should flutter through the forest of sighing pines, heralds of life, happiness, and home—

After life's fitful fever they slept well
Treason had done its worst. Nor steel nor poison:
Malice domestic, foreign levy, nothing
Could touch them farther.

One day another order came for us to be loaded on the cars, and over to the railroad we went again in the same fashion as before. The comparatively few of us who were still able to walk at all well, loaded ourselves down with the bundles and blankets of our less fortunate companions, who hobbled and limped—many even crawling on their hands and knees—over the hard, frozen ground, by our sides.

Those not able to crawl even, were taken in wagons, for the orders were imperative not to leave a living prisoner behind.

At the railroad we found two trains awaiting us. On the front of each engine were two rude white flags, made by fastening the halves of meal sacks to short sticks. The sight of these gave us some hope, but our belief that Rebels were constitutional liars and deceivers was so firm and fixed, that we persuaded ourselves that the flags meant nothing more than some wilful delusion for us. Again we started off in the direction of Wilmington, and traversed the same country described in the previous chapter. Again Andrews and I found ourselves in the next box car to the passenger coach containing the Rebel officers. Again we cut a hole through the end, with our saw, and again found a darky servant sitting on the rear platform. Andrews went out and sat down alongside of him, and found that he was seated upon a large gunny-bag sack containing the cooked rations of the Rebel officers.

The intelligence that there was something there worth taking Andrews communicated to me by an expressive signal, of which soldiers campaigning together as long as he and I had, always have an extensive and well understood code.

I took a seat in the hole we had made in the end of the car, in reach of Andrews. Andrews called the attention of the negro to some feature of the country near by, and asked him a question in regard to it. As he looked in the direction indicated, Andrews slipped his hand into the mouth of the bag, and pulled out a small sack of wheat biscuits, which he passed to me and I concealed. The darky turned and told Andrews all about the matter in regard to which the interrogation had been made. Andrews became so much interested in what was being told him, that he sat up closer and closer to the darky, who in turn moved farther away from the sack.

Next we ran through a turpentine plantation, and as the darky was pointing out where the still, the master's place, the "quarters," etc., were, Andrews managed to fish out of that bag and pass to me three roasted chickens. Then a great swamp called for description, and before we were through with it, I had about a peck of boiled sweet potatos.

Andrews emptied the bag as the darky was showing him a great peanut plantation, taking from it a small frying-pan, a canteen of molasses, and a half-gallon tin bucket, which had been used to make coffee in. We divided up our wealth of eatables with the rest of the boys in the car, not forgetting to keep enough to give ourselves a magnificent meal.

As we ran along we searched carefully for the place where we had seen the line-of-battle, expecting that it would now be marked with signs of a terrible conflict, but we could see nothing. We could not even fix the locality where the line stood.

As it became apparent that we were going directly toward Wilmington, as fast as our engines could pull us, the excitement rose. We had many misgivings as to whether our folks still retained possession of Wilmington, and whether, if they did, the Rebels could not stop at a point outside of our lines, and transfer us to some other road.

For hours we had seen nobody in the country through which we were passing. What few houses were visible were apparently deserted, and there were no Towns or stations anywhere. We were very anxious to see some one, in hopes of getting a hint of what the state of affairs was in the direction we were going. At length we saw a young man—apparently a scout—on horseback, but his clothes were equally divided between the blue and the butternut, as to give no clue to which side he belonged.

An hour later we saw two infantrymen, who were evidently out foraging. They had sacks of something on their backs, and wore blue clothes. This was a very hopeful sign of a near approach to our lines, but bitter experience in the past warned us against being too sanguine.

About 4 o'clock P. M., the trains stopped and whistled long and loud. Looking out I could see—perhaps half-a-mile away—a line of rifle pits running at right angles with the track. Guards, whose guns flashed as they turned, were pacing up and down, but they were too far away for me to distinguish their uniforms.

The suspense became fearful.

But I received much encouragement from the singular conduct of our guards. First I noticed a Captain, who had been especially mean to us while at Florence.

He was walking on the ground by the train. His face was pale, his teeth set, and his eyes shone with excitement. He called out in a strange, forced voice to his men and boys on the roof of the cars:

"Here, you fellers git down off'en thar and form a line."

The fellows did so, in a slow, constrained, frightened ways and huddled together, in the most unsoldierly manner.

The whole thing reminded me of a scene I once saw in our line, where a weak-kneed Captain was ordered to take a party of rather chicken-hearted recruits out on the skirmish-line.

We immediately divined what was the matter. The lines in front of us were really those of our people, and the idiots of guards, not knowing of their entire safety when protected by a flag of truce, were scared half out of their small wits at approaching so near to armed Yankees.

We showered taunts and jeers upon them. An Irishman in my car yelled out:

"Och, ye dirty spalpeens; it's not shootin' prisoners ye are now; it's cumin' where the Yankee b'ys hev the gun; and the minnit ye say thim yer white livers show themselves in yer pale faces. Bad luck to the blatherin' bastards that yez are, and to the mothers that bore ye."

At length our train moved up so near to the line that I could see it was the grand, old loyal blue that clothed the forms of the men who were pacing up and down.

And certainly the world does not hold as superb looking men as these appeared to me. Finely formed, stalwart, full-fed and well clothed, they formed the most delightful contrast with the scrawny, shambling, villain-visaged little clay-eaters and white trash who had looked down upon us from the sentry boxes for many long months.

I sprang out of the cars and began washing my face and hands in the ditch at the side of the road. The Rebel Captain, noticing me, said, in the old, hateful, brutal, imperious tone:

"Git back in dat cah, dah."

An hour before I would have scrambled back as quickly as possible, knowing that an instant's hesitation would be followed by a bullet. Now, I looked him in the face, and said as irritatingly as possible:

"O, you go to ——, you Rebel. I'm going into Uncle Sam's lines with as little Rebel filth on me as possible."

He passed me without replying.

His day of shooting was past.

Descending from the cars, we passed through the guards into our lines, a Rebel and a Union clerk checking us off as we passed. By the time it was dark we were all under our flag again. The place where we came through was several miles west of Wilmington, where the railroad crossed a branch of the Cape Fear River. The point was held by a brigade of Schofield's army— the Twenty-Third Army Corps.

The boys lavished unstinted kindness upon us. All of the brigade off duty crowded around, offering us blankets, shirts shoes, pantaloons and other articles of clothing and similar things that we were obviously in the greatest need of. The sick were carried, by hundreds of willing hands, to a sheltered spot, and laid upon good, comfortable beds improvised with leaves and blankets. A great line of huge, generous fires was built, that every one of us could have plenty of place around them.

By and by a line of wagons came over from Wilmington laden with rations, and they were dispensed to us with what seemed reckless prodigality. The lid of a box of hard tack would be knocked off, and the contents handed to us as we filed past, with absolute disregard as to quantity. If a prisoner looked wistful after receiving one handful of crackers, another was handed to him; if his long-famished eyes still lingered as if enchained by the rare display of food, the men who were issuing said:

"Here, old fellow, there's plenty of it: take just as much as you can carry in your arms."

So it was also with the pickled pork, the coffee, the sugar, etc. We had been stinted and starved so long that we could not comprehend that there was anywhere actually enough of anything.

The kind-hearted boys who were acting as our hosts began preparing food for the sick, but the Surgeons, who had arrived in the meanwhile, were compelled to repress them, as it was plain that while it was a dangerous experiment to give any of us all we could or would eat, it would never do to give the sick such a temptation to kill themselves, and only a limited amount of food was allowed to be given those who were unable to walk.

Andrews and I hungered for coffee, the delightful fumes of which filled the air and intoxicated our senses. We procured enough to make our half-gallon bucket full and very strong.

We drank so much of this that Andrews became positively drunk, and fell helplessly into some brush. I pulled him out and dragged him away to a place where we had made our rude bed.

I was dazed. I could not comprehend that the long-looked for, often-despaired-of event had actually happened. I feared that it was one of those tantalizing dreams that had so often haunted my sleep, only to be followed by a wretched awakening. Then I became seized with a sudden fear lest the Rebel attempt to retake me. The line of guards around us seemed very slight. It might be forced in the night, and all of us recaptured. Shivering at this thought, absurd though it was, I arose from our bed, and taking Andrews with me, crawled two or three hundred yards into a dense undergrowth, where in the event of our lines being forced, we would be overlooked.

CHAPTER LXXIX.

GETTING USED TO FREEDOM—DELIGHTS OF A LAND WHERE THERE IS ENOUGH OF EVERYTHING—FIRST GLIMPSE OF THE OLD FLAG—WILMINGTON AND ITS HISTORY —LIEUTENANT CUSHING—FIRST ACQUAINTANCE WITH THE COLORED TROOPS—LEAVING FOR HOME—DESTRUCTION OF THE "THORN" BY A TORPEDO—THE MOCK MONITOR'S ACHIEVEMENT.

After a sound sleep, Andrews and I awoke to the enjoyment of our first day of freedom and existence in God's country. The sun had already risen, bright and warm, consonant with the happiness of the new life now opening up for us.

But to nearly a score of our party his beams brought no awakening gladness. They fell upon stony, staring eyes, from out of which the light of life had now faded, as the light of hope had done long ago. The dead lay there upon the rude beds of fallen leaves, scraped together by thoughtful comrades the night before, their clenched teeth showing through parted lips, faces fleshless and pinched, long, unkempt and ragged hair and whiskers just stirred by the lazy breeze, the rotting feet and limbs drawn up, and skinny hands clenched in the last agonies. Their fate seemed harder than that of any who had died before them. It was doubtful if many of them knew that they were at last inside of our own lines.

Again the kind-hearted boys of the brigade crowded around us with proffers of service. Of an Ohio boy who directed his kind tenders to Andrews and me, we procured a chunk of coarse rosin soap about as big as a pack of cards, and a towel. Never was there as great a quantity of solid comfort got out of that much soap as we obtained. It was the first that we had since that which I stole in Wirz's headquarters, in June —nine months before. We felt that the dirt which had accumulated upon us since then would subject us to assessment as real estate if we were in the North.

Hurrying off to a little creek we began our ablutions, and it was not long until Andrews declared that there was a perceptible sand-bar forming in the stream, from what we washed off. Dirt deposits of the Pliocene era rolled off feet and legs. Eocene incrustations let loose reluctantly from neck and ears; the hair was a mass of tangled locks matted with nine months' accumulation of pitch pine tar, rosin soot, and South Carolina sand, that we did not think we had better start in upon it until we either had the shock cut off, or had a whole ocean and a vat of soap to wash it out with.

After scrubbing until we were exhausted we got off the first few outer layers—the post tertiary formation, a geologist would term it—and the smell of many breakfasts cooking, coming down over the hill, set our stomachs in a mutiny against any longer fasting.

We went back, rosy, panting, glowing, but happy, to get our selves some breakfast.

Should Providence, for some inscrutable reason, vouchsafe me the years of Methuselah, one of the pleasantest recollections that will abide with me to the close of the nine hundredth and sixty-ninth year, will be of that delightful odor of cooking food which regaled our senses as we came back. From the boiling coffee and the meat frying in the pan rose an incense sweeter to the senses a thousand times than all the perfumes of far Arabia. It differed from the loathsome odor of cooking corn meal as much as it did from the effluvia of a sewer.

Our noses were the first of our senses to bear testimony that we had passed from the land of starvation to that of plenty. Andrews and I hastened off to get our own breakfast, and soon had a half-gallon of strong coffee, and a frying-pan full, of meat cooking over the fire—not one of the beggarly skimped little fires we had crouched over during our months of imprisonment, but a royal, generous fire, fed with logs instead of shavings and splinters, and giving out heat enough to warm a regiment.

Having eaten positively all that we could swallow, those of us who could walk were ordered to fall in and march over to Wilmington. We crossed the branch of the river on a pontoon bridge, and took the road that led across the narrow sandy island between the two branches, Wilmington being situated on the opposite bank of the farther one.

When about half way a shout from some one in advance caused us to look up, and then we saw, flying from a tall steeple in Wilmington, the glorious old Stars and Stripes, resplendent in the morning sun, and more beautiful than the most gorgeous web from Tyrian looms. We stopped with one accord, and shouted and cheered and cried until every throat was sore and every eye red and blood-shot. It seemed as if our cup of happiness would certainly run over if any more additions were made to it.

When we arrived at the bank of the river opposite Wilmington, a whole world of new and interesting sights opened up before us. Wilmington, during the last year-and-a-half of the war, was, next to Richmond, the most important place in the Southern Confederacy. It was the only port to which blockade running was at all safe enough to be lucrative. The Rebels held the strong forts of Caswell and Fisher, at the mouth of Cape Fear River, and outside, the Frying Pan Shoals, which extended along the coast forty or fifty miles, kept our blockading fleet so far off, and made the line so weak and scattered, that there was comparatively little risk to the small, swift-sailing vessels employed by the blockade runners in running through it. The only way that blockade running could be stopped was by the reduction of Forts Caswell and Fisher, and it was not stopped until this was done.

Before the war Wilmington was a dull, sleepy North Carolina Town, with as little animation of any kind as a Breton Pillage. The only business was the handling of the tar, turpentine, rosin, and peanuts produced in the surrounding country, a business never lively enough to excite more than a lazy ripple in the sluggish lagoons of trade. But very new wine was put into this old bottle when blockade running began to develop in importance. Then this Sleepy hollow of a place took on the appearance of San Francisco in the hight of the gold fever. The English houses engaged in blockade running established branches there conducted by young men who lived like princes. All the best houses in the City were leased by them and fitted up in the most gorgeous style. They literally clothed themselves in purple and fine linen and fared sumptuously every day, with their fine wines and imported delicacies and retinue of servants to wait upon them. Fast young Rebel officers, eager for a season of dissipation, could imagine nothing better than a leave of absence to go to Wilmington. Money flowed like water. The common sailors—the scum of all foreign ports—who manned the blockade runners, received as high as one hundred dollars in gold per month, and a bounty of fifty dollars for every successful trip, which from Nassau could be easily made in seven days. Other people were paid in proportion, and as the old proverb says, "What comes over the Devil's back is spent under his breast," the money so obtained was squandered recklessly, and all sorts of debauchery ran riot.

On the ground where we were standing had been erected several large steam cotton presses, built to compress cotton for the blockade runners. Around them were stored immense quantities of cotton, and near by were nearly as great stores of turpentine, rosin and tar. A little farther down the river was navy yard with docks, etc., for the accommodation, building and repair of blockade runners. At the time our folks took Fort Fisher and advanced on Wilmington the docks were filled with vessels. The retreating Rebels set fire to everything—cotton, cotton presses, turpentine, rosin, tar, navy yard, naval stores, timber, docks, and vessels, and the fire made clean work. Our people arrived too late to save anything, and when we came in the smoke from the burned cotton, turpentine, etc., still filled the woods. It was a signal illustration of the ravages of war. Here had been destroyed, in a few hours, more property than a half-million industrious men would accumulate in their lives.

Almost as gratifying as the sight of the old flag flying in triumph, was the exhibition of our naval power in the river before us. The larger part of the great North Atlantic squadron, which had done such excellent service in the reduction of the defenses of Wilmington, was lying at anchor, with their hundreds of huge guns yawning as if ardent for more great forts to beat down, more vessels to sink, more heavy artillery to crush, more Rebels to conquer. It seemed as if there were cannon enough there to blow the whole Confederacy into kingdom-come. All was life and animation around the fleet. On the decks the officers were pacing up and down. One on each vessel carried a long telescope, with which he almost constantly swept the horizon. Numberless small boats, each rowed by neatly-uniformed men, and carrying a flag in the stern, darted hither and thither, carrying officers on errands of duty or pleasure. It was such a scene as enabled me to realize in a measure, the descriptions I had read of the pomp and circumstance of naval warfare. While we were standing, contemplating all the interesting sights within view, a small steamer, about the size of a canal-boat, and carrying several bright brass guns, ran swiftly and noiselessly up to the dock near by, and a young, pale-faced officer, slender in build and nervous in manner, stepped ashore. Some of the blue jackets who were talking to us looked at him and the vessel with the greatest expression of interest, and said:

"Hello! there's the 'Monticello' and Lieutenant Cushing."

This, then, was the naval boy hero, with whose exploits the whole country was ringing. Our sailor friends proceeded to tell us of his achievements, of which they were justly proud. They told us of his perilous scouts and his hairbreadth escapes, of his wonderful audacity and still more wonderful success—of his capture of Towns with a handful of sailors, and the destruction of valuable stores, etc. I felt very sorry that the man was not a cavalry commander. There he would have had full scope for his peculiar genius. He had come prominently into notice in the preceding Autumn, when he had, by one of the most daring performances narrated in naval history, destroyed the formidable ram "Albermarle." This vessel had been constructed by the Rebels on the Roanoke River, and had done them very good service, first by assisting to reduce the forts and capture the garrison at Plymouth, N. C., and afterward in some minor engagements. In October, 1864, she was lying at Plymouth. Around her was a boom of logs to prevent sudden approaches of boats or vessels from our fleet. Cushing, who was then barely twenty-one, resolved to attempt her destruction. He fitted up a steam launch with a long spar to which he attached a torpedo. On the night of October 27th, with thirteen companions, he ran quietly up the Sound and was not discovered until his boat struck the boom, when a terrific fire was opened upon him. Backing a short distance, he ran at the boom with such velocity that his boat leaped across it into the water beyond. In an instant more his torpedo struck the side of the "Albemarle" and exploded, tearing a great hole in her hull, which sank her in a few minutes. At the moment the torpedo went off the "Albermarle" fired one of her great guns directly into the launch, tearing it completely to pieces. Lieutenant Cushing and one comrade rose to the surface of the seething water and, swimming ashore, escaped. What became of the rest is not known, but their fate can hardly be a matter of doubt.

We were ferried across the river into Wilmington, and marched up the streets to some vacant ground near the railroad depot, where we found most of our old Florence comrades already assembled. When they left us in the middle of February they were taken to Wilmington, and thence to Goldsboro, N. C., where they were kept until the rapid closing in of our Armies made it impracticable to hold them any longer, when they were sent back to Wilmington and given up to our forces as we had been.

It was now nearly noon, and we were ordered to fall in and draw rations, a bewildering order to us, who had been so long in the habit of drawing food but once a day. We fell in in single rank, and marched up, one at a time, past where a group of employees of the Commissary Department dealt out the food. One handed each prisoner as he passed a large slice of meat; another gave him a handful of ground coffee; a third a handful of sugar; a fourth gave him a pickle, while a fifth and sixth handed him an onion and a loaf of fresh bread. This filled the horn of our plenty full. To have all these in one day—meat, coffee, sugar, onions and soft bread—was simply to riot in undreamed-of luxury. Many of the boys—poor fellows—could not yet realize that there was enough for all, or they could not give up their old "flanking" tricks, and they stole around, and falling into the rear, came up again for' another share. We laughed at them, as did the Commissary men, who, nevertheless, duplicated the rations already received, and sent them away happy and content.

What a glorious dinner Andrews and I had, with our half gallon of strong coffee, our soft bread, and a pan full of fried pork and onions! Such an enjoyable feast will never be, eaten again by us. Here we saw negro troops under arms for the first time—the most of the organization of colored soldiers having been, done since our capture. It was startling at first to see a stalwart, coal-black negro stalking along with a Sergeant's chevrons on his arm, or to gaze on a regimental line of dusky faces on dress parade, but we soon got used to it. The first strong peculiarity of the negro soldier that impressed itself, upon us was his literal obedience of orders. A white soldier usually allows himself considerable discretion in obeying orders—he aims more at the spirit, while the negro adheres to the strict letter of the command.

For instance, the second day after our arrival a line of guards were placed around us, with orders not to allow any of us to go up town without a pass. The reason of this was that many weak— even dying-men would persist in wandering about, and would be found exhausted, frequently dead, in various parts of the City. Andrews and I concluded to go up town. Approaching a negro sentinel he warned us back with,

"Stand back, dah; don't come any furder; it's agin de awdahs; you can't pass."

He would not allow us to argue the case, but brought his gun to such a threatening position that we fell back. Going down the line a little farther, we came to a white sentinel, to whom I said: "Comrade, what are your orders:"

He replied:

"My orders are not to let any of you fellows pass, but my beat only extends to that out-house there."

Acting on this plain hint, we walked around the house and went up-town. The guard simply construed his orders in a liberal spirit. He reasoned that they hardly applied to us, since we were evidently able to take care of ourselves.

Later we had another illustration of this dog like fidelity of the colored sentinel. A number of us were quartered in a large and empty warehouse. On the same floor, and close to us, were a couple of very fine horses belonging to some officer. We had not been in the warehouse very long until we concluded that the straw with which the horses were bedded would be better used in making couches for ourselves, and this suggestion was instantly acted upon, and so thoroughly that there was not a straw left between the animals and the bare boards. Presently the owner of the horses came in, and he was greatly incensed at what had been done. He relieved his mind of a few sulphurous oaths, and going out, came back soon with a man with more straw, and a colored soldier whom he stationed by the horses, saying:

"Now, look here. You musn't let anybody take anything sway from these stalls; d'you understand me?—not a thing."

He then went out. Andrews and I had just finished cooking dinner, and were sitting down to eat it. Wishing to lend our frying-pan to another mess, I looked around for something to lay our meat upon. Near the horses I saw a book cover, which would answer the purpose admirably. Springing up, I skipped across to where it was, snatched it up, and ran back to my place. As I reached it a yell from the boys made me look around. The darky was coming at me "full tilt," with his gun at a "charge bayonets." As I turned he said:

"Put dat right back dah!"

I said:

"Why, this don't amount to anything, this is only an old book cover. It hasn't anything in the world to do with the horses."

He only replied:

"Put dat right back dah!"

I tried another appeal:

"Now, you woolly-headed son of thunder, haven't you got sense enough to know that the officer who posted you didn't mean such a thing as this! He only meant that we should not be allowed to take any of the horses' bedding or equipments; don't you see?"

I might as well have reasoned with a cigar store Indian. He set his teeth, his eyes showed a dangerous amount of white, and foreshortening his musket for a lunge, he hissed out again "Put dat right back dah, I tell you!"

I looked at the bayonet; it was very long, very bright, and very sharp. It gleamed cold and chilly like, as if it had not run through a man for a long time, and yearned for another opportunity. Nothing but the whites of the darky's eyes could now be seen. I did not want to perish there in the fresh bloom of my youth and loveliness; it seemed to me as if it was my duty to reserve myself for fields of future usefulness, so I walked back and laid the book cover precisely on the spot whence I had obtained it, while the thousand boys in the house set up a yell of sarcastic laughter.

We staid in Wilmington a few days, days of almost purely animal enjoyment—the joy of having just as much to eat as we could possibly swallow, and no one to molest or make us afraid in any way. How we did eat and fill up. The wrinkles in our skin smoothed out under the stretching, and we began to feel as if we were returning to our old plumpness, though so far the plumpness was wholly abdominal.

One morning we were told that the transports would begin going back with us that afternoon, the first that left taking the sick. Andrews and I, true to our old prison practices, resolved to be among those on the first boat. We slipped through the guards and going up town, went straight to Major General Schofield's headquarters and solicited a pass to go on the first boat—the steamer "Thorn." General Schofield treated us very kindly; but declined to let anybody but the helplessly sick go on the "Thorn." Defeated here we went down to where the vessel was lying at the dock, and tried to smuggle ourselves aboard, but the guard was too strong and too vigilant, and we were driven away. Going along the dock, angry and discouraged by our failure, we saw a Surgeon, at a little distance, who was examining and sending the sick who could walk aboard another vessel—the "General Lyon." We took our cue, and a little shamming secured from him tickets which permitted us to take our passage in her. The larger portion of those on board were in the hold, and a few were on deck. Andrews and I found a snug place under the forecastle, by the anchor chains.

Both vessels speedily received their complement, and leaving their docks, started down the river. The "Thorn" steamed ahead of us, and disappeared. Shortly after we got under way, the Colonel who was put in command of the boat—himself a released prisoner—came around on a tour of inspection. He found about one thousand of us aboard, and singling me out made me the non-commissioned officer in command. I was put in charge, of issuing the rations and of a barrel of milk punch which the Sanitary Commission had sent down to be dealt out on the voyage to such as needed it. I went to work and arranged the boys in the best way I could, and returned to the deck to view the scenery.

Wilmington is thirty-four miles from the sea, and the river for that distance is a calm, broad estuary. At this time the resources of Rebel engineering were exhausted in defense against its passage by a hostile fleet, and undoubtedly the best work of the kind in the Southern Confederacy was done upon it. At its mouth were Forts Fisher and Caswell, the strongest sea coast forts in the Confederacy. Fort Caswell was an old United States fort, much enlarged and strengthened. Fort Fisher was a new work, begun immediately after the beginning of the war, and labored at incessantly until captured. Behind these every one of the thirty-four miles to Wilmington was covered with the fire of the best guns the English arsenals could produce, mounted on forts built at every advantageous spot. Lines of piles running out into the water, forced incoming vessels to wind back and forth across the stream under the point-blank range of massive Armstrong rifles. As if this were not sufficient, the channel was thickly studded with torpedoes that would explode at the touch of the keel of a passing vessel. These abundant precautions, and the telegram from General Lee, found in Fort Fisher, stating that unless that stronghold and Fort Caswell were held he could not hold Richmond, give some idea of the importance of the place to the Rebels.

We passed groups of hundreds of sailors fishing for torpedos, and saw many of these dangerous monsters, which they had hauled up out of the water. We caught up with the "Thorn," when about half way to the sea, passed her, to our great delight, and soon left a gap between us of nearly half-a-mile. We ran through an opening in the piling, holding up close to the left side, and she apparently followed our course exactly. Suddenly there was a dull roar; a column of water, bearing with it fragments of timbers, planking and human bodies, rose up through one side of the vessel, and, as it fell, she lurched forward and sank. She had struck a torpedo. I never learned the number lost, but it must have been very great.

Some little time after this happened we approached Fort Anderson, the most powerful of the works between Wilmington and the forts at the mouth of the sea. It was built on the ruins of the little Town of Brunswick, destroyed by Cornwallis during the Revolutionary War. We saw a monitor lying near it, and sought good positions to view this specimen of the redoubtable ironclads of which we had heard and read so much. It looked precisely as it did in pictures, as black, as grim, and as uncompromising as the impregnable floating fortress which had brought the "Merrimac" to terms.

But as we approached closely we noticed a limpness about the smoke stack that seemed very inconsistent with the customary rigidity of cylindrical iron. Then the escape pipe seemed scarcely able to maintain itself upright. A few minutes later we discovered that our terrible Cyclops of the sea was a flimsy humbug, a theatrical imitation, made by stretching blackened canvas over a wooden frame.

One of the officers on board told us its story. After the fall of Fort Fisher the Rebels retired to Fort Anderson, and offered a desperate resistance to our army and fleet. Owing to the shallowness of the water the latter could not come into close enough range to do effective work. Then the happy idea of this sham monitor suggested itself to some one. It was prepared, and one morning before daybreak it was sent floating in on the tide. The other monitors opened up a heavy fire from their position. The Rebels manned their guns and replied vigorously, by concentrating a terrible cannonade on the sham monitor, which sailed grandly on, undisturbed by the heavy rifled bolts tearing through her canvas turret. Almost frantic with apprehension of the result if she could not be checked, every gun that would bear was turned upon her, and torpedos were exploded in her pathway by electricity. All these she treated with the silent contempt they merited from so invulnerable a monster. At length, as she reached a good easy range of the fort, her bow struck something, and she swung around as if to open fire. That was enough for the Rebels. With Schofield's army reaching out to cut off their retreat, and this dreadful thing about to tear the insides out of their fort with four-hundred-pound shot at quarter-mile range, there was nothing for them to do but consult their own safety, which they did with such haste that they did not spike a gun, or destroy a pound of stores.

CHAPTER LXXX.

VISIT TO FORT FISHER, AND INSPECTION OF THAT STRONGHOLD—THE WAY IT WAS CAPTURED—OUT ON THE OCEAN SAILING—TERRIBLY SEASICK—RAPID RECOVERY —ARRIVAL AT ANNAPOLIS—WASHED, CLOTHED AND FED— UNBOUNDED LUXURY, AND DAYS OF UNADULTERATED HAPPINESS.

When we reached the mouth of Cape Fear River the wind was blowing so hard that our Captain did not think it best to venture out, so he cast anchor. The cabin of the vessel was filled with officers who had been released from prison about the same time we were. I was also given a berth in the cabin, in consideration of my being the non-commissioned officer in charge of the men, and I found the associations quite pleasant. A party was made up, which included me, to visit Fort Fisher, and we spent the larger part of a day very agreeably in wandering over that great stronghold. We found it wonderful in its strength, and were prepared to accept the statement of those who had seen foreign defensive works, that it was much more powerful than the famous Malakoff, which so long defied the besiegers of Sebastopol.

The situation of the fort was on a narrow and low spit of ground between Cape Fear River and the ocean. On this the Rebels had erected, with prodigious labor, an embankment over a mile in length, twenty-five feet thick and twenty feet high. About two-thirds of this bank faced the sea; the other third ran across the spit of land to protect the fort against an attack from the land side. Still stronger than the bank forming the front of the fort were the traverses, which prevented an enfilading fire These were regular hills, twenty-five to forty feet high, and broad and long in proportion. There were fifteen or twenty of them along the face of the fort. Inside of them were capacious bomb proofs, sufficiently large to shelter the whole garrison. It seemed as if a whole Township had been dug up, carted down there and set on edge. In front of the works was a strong palisade. Between each pair of traverses were one or two enormous guns, none less than one-hundred-and-fifty pounders. Among these we saw a great Armstrong gun, which had been presented to the Southern Confederacy by its manufacturer, Sir William Armstrong, who, like the majority of the English nobility, was a warm admirer of the Jeff. Davis crowd. It was the finest piece of ordnance ever seen in this country. The carriage was rosewood, and the mountings gilt brass. The breech of the gun had five reinforcements.

To attack this place our Government assembled the most powerful fleet ever sent on such an expedition. Over seventy-five men-of-war, including six monitors, and carrying six hundred guns, assailed it with a storm of shot and shell that averaged four projectiles per second for several hours; the parapet was battered, and the large guns crushed as one smashes a bottle with a stone. The garrison fled into the bomb-proofs for protection. The troops, who had landed above the fort, moved up to assail the land face, while a brigade of sailors and marines attacked the sea face.

As the fleet had to cease firing to allow the charge, the Rebels ran out of their casemates and, manning the parapet, opened such a fire of musketry that the brigade from the fleet was driven back, but the soldiers made a lodgment on the land face. Then began some beautiful cooperative tactics between the Army and Navy, communication being kept up with signal flags. Our men were on one side of the parapets and the Rebels on the other, with the fighting almost hand-to-hand. The vessels ranged out to where their guns would rake the Rebel line, and as their shot tore down its length, the Rebels gave way, and falling back to the next traverse, renewed the conflict there. Guided by the signals our vessels changed their positions, so as to rake this line also, and so the fight went on until twelve traverses had been carried, one after the other, when the rebels surrendered.

The next day the Rebels abandoned Fort Caswell and other fortifications in the immediate neighborhood, surrendered two gunboats, and fell back to the lines at Fort Anderson. After Fort Fisher fell, several blockade-runners were lured inside and captured.

Never before had there been such a demonstration of the power of heavy artillery. Huge cannon were pounded into fragments, hills of sand ripped open, deep crevasses blown in the ground by exploding shells, wooden buildings reduced to kindling-wood, etc. The ground was literally paved with fragments of shot and shell, which, now red with rust from the corroding salt air, made the interior of the fort resemble what one of our party likened it to "an old brickyard." Whichever way we looked along the shores we saw abundant evidence of the greatness of the business which gave the place its importance. In all directions, as far as the eye could reach, the beach was dotted with the bleaching skeletons of blockade-runners—some run ashore by their mistaking the channel, more beached to escape the hot pursuit of our blockaders.

Directly in front of the sea face of the fort, and not four hundred yards from the savage mouths of the huge guns, the blackened timbers of a burned blockade-runner showed above the water at low tide. Coming in from Nassau with a cargo of priceless value to the gasping Confederacy, she was observed and chased by one of our vessels, a swifter sailer, even, than herself. The war ship closed rapidly upon her. She sought the protection of the guns of Fort Fisher, which opened venomously on the chaser. They did not stop her, though they were less than half a mile away. In another minute she would have sent the Rebel vessel to the bottom of the sea, by a broadside from her heavy guns, but the Captain of the latter turned her suddenly, and ran her high up on the beach, wrecking his vessel, but saving the much more valuable cargo. Our vessel then hauled off, and as night fell, quiet was restored. At midnight two boat-loads of determined men, rowing with muffled oars moved silently out from the blockader towards the beached vessel. In their boats they had some cans of turpentine, and several large shells. When they reached the blockade-runner they found all her crew gone ashore, save one watchman, whom they overpowered before he could give the alarm. They cautiously felt their way around, with the aid of a dark lantern, secured the ship's chronometer, her papers and some other desired objects. They then saturated with the turpentine piles of combustible material, placed about the vessel to the best advantage, and finished by depositing the shells where their explosion would ruin the machinery. All this was done so near to the fort that the sentinels on the parapets could be heard with the greatest distinctness as they repeated their half-hourly cry of "All's well." Their preparations completed, the daring fellows touched matches to the doomed vessel in a dozen places at once, and sprang into their boats. The flames instantly enveloped the ship, and showed the gunners the incendiaries rowing rapidly away. A hail of shot beat the water into a foam around the boats, but their good fortune still attended them, and they got back without losing a man.

The wind at length calmed sufficiently to encourage our Captain to venture out, and we were soon battling with the rolling waves, far out of sight of land. For awhile the novelty of the scene fascinated me. I was at last on the ocean, of which I had heard, read and imagined so much. The creaking cordage, the straining engine, the plunging ship, the wild waste of tumbling billows, everyone apparently racing to where our tossing bark was struggling to maintain herself, all had an entrancing interest for me, and I tried to recall Byron's sublime apostrophe to the ocean:

Thou glorious mirror, where the Almighty's form
Classes itself in tempest: in all time,
Calm or convulsed-in breeze, or gale, or storm,
Icing the pole, or in the torrid clime
Dark-heaving—boundless, endless, and sublime—
The image of eternity—the throne
Of the invisible; even from out thy slime
The monsters of the deep are made; each zone
Obey thee: thou goest forth, dread, fathomless, alone,

Just then, my reverie was broken by the strong hand of the gruff Captain of, the vessel descending upon my shoulder, and he said:

"See, here, youngster! Ain't you the fellow that was put in command of these men?"

I acknowledged such to be the case.

"Well," said the Captain; "I want you to 'tend to your business and straighten them around, so that we can clean off the decks."

I turned from the bulwark over which I had been contemplating the vasty deep, and saw the sorriest, most woe-begone lot that the imagination can conceive. Every mother's son was wretchedly sea-sick. They were paying the penalty of their overfeeding in Wilmington; and every face looked as if its owner was discovering for the first time what the real lower depths of human misery was. They all seemed afraid they would not die; as if they were praying for death, but feeling certain that he was going back on them in a most shameful way.

We straightened them around a little, washed them and the decks off with a hose, and then I started down in the hold to see how matters were with the six hundred down there. The boys there were much sicker than those on deck. As I lifted the hatch there rose an odor which appeared strong enough to raise the plank itself. Every onion that had been issued to us in Wilmington seemed to lie down there in the last stages of decomposition. All of the seventy distinct smells which Coleridge counted at Cologne might have been counted in any given cubic foot of atmosphere, while the next foot would have an entirely different and equally demonstrative "bouquet."

I recoiled, and leaned against the bulwark, but soon summoned up courage enough to go half-way down the ladder, and shout out in as stern a tone as I could command:

"Here, now! I want you fellows to straighten around there, right off, and help clean up!"

They were as angry and cross as they were sick. They wanted nothing in the world so much as the opportunity I had given them to swear at and abuse somebody. Every one of them raised on his elbow, and shaking his fist at me yelled out:

"O, you go to ——, you —— —— ——. Just come down another step, and I'll knock the whole head off 'en you."

I did not go down any farther.

Coming back on the deck my stomach began to feel qualmish. Some wretched idiot, whose grandfather's grave I hope the jackasses have defiled, as the Turks would say, told me that the best preventive of sea-sickness was to drink as much of the milk punch as I could swallow. Like another idiot, I did so.

I went again to the side of the vessel, but now the fascination of the scene had all faded out. The restless billows were dreary, savage, hungry and dizzying; they seemed to claw at, and tear, and wrench the struggling ship as a group of huge lions would tease and worry a captive dog. They distressed her and all on board by dealing a blow which would send her reeling in one direction, but before she had swung the full length that impulse would have sent her, catching her on the opposite side with a stunning shock that sent her another way, only to meet another rude buffet from still another side.

I thought we could all have stood it if the motion had been like that of a swing-backward and forward—or even if the to and fro motion had been complicated with a side-wise swing, but to be put through every possible bewildering motion in the briefest space of time was more than heads of iron and stomachs of brass could stand.

Mine were not made of such perdurable stuff.

They commenced mutinous demonstrations in regard to the milk punch.

I began wondering whether the milk was not the horrible beer swill, stump-tail kind of which I had heard so much.

And the whisky in it; to use a vigorous Westernism, descriptive of mean whisky, it seemed to me that I could smell the boy's feet who plowed the corn from which it was distilled.

Then the onions I had eaten in Wilmington began to rebel, and incite the bread, meat and coffee to gastric insurrection, and I became so utterly wretched that life had no farther attractions.

While I was leaning over the bulwark, musing on the complete hollowness of all earthly things, the Captain of the vessel caught hold of me roughly, and said:

"Look here, you're just playin' the very devil a-commandin' these here men. Why in —— don't you stiffen up, and hump yourself around, and make these men mind, or else belt them over the head with a capstan bar! Now I want you to 'tend to your business. D'you understand me?"

I turned a pair of weary and hopeless eyes upon him, and started to say that a man who would talk to one in my forlorn condition of "stiffening up," and "belting other fellows over the head with a capstan bar," would insult a woman dying with consumption, but I suddenly became too full for utterance.

The milk punch, the onions, the bread, and meat and coffee tired of fighting it out in the narrow quarters where I had stowed them, had started upwards tumultuously.

I turned my head again to the sea, and looking down into its smaragdine depths, let go of the victualistic store which I had been industriously accumulating ever since I had come through the lines.

I vomited until I felt as empty and hollow as a stove pipe. There was a vacuum that extended clear to my toe-nails. I feared that every retching struggle would dent me in, all over, as one sees tin preserving cans crushed in by outside pressure, and I apprehended that if I kept on much longer my shoe-soles would come up after the rest.

I will mention, parenthetically, that, to this day I abhor milk punch, and also onions.

Unutterably miserable as I was I could not refrain from a ghost of a smile, when a poor country boy near me sang out in an interval between vomiting spells:

"O, Captain, for God's sake, stop the boat and lem'me go ashore, and I swear I'll walk every step of the way home."

He was like old Gonzalo in the 'Tempest:'

Now world I give a thousand furlongs of sea for an acre of barren ground; long heath; brown furze; anything. The wills above be done!

but I would fain die a dry death.

After this misery had lasted about two days we got past Cape Hatteras, and out of reach of its malign influence, and recovered as rapidly as we had been prostrated.

We regained spirits and appetites with amazing swiftness; the sun came out warm and cheerful, we cleaned up our quarters and ourselves as best we could, and during the remainder of the voyage were as blithe and cheerful as so many crickets.

The fun in the cabin was rollicking. The officers had been as sick as the men, but were wonderfully vivacious when the 'mal du mer' passed off. In the party was a fine glee club, which had been organized at "Camp Sorgum," the officers' prison at Columbia. Its leader was a Major of the Fifth Iowa Cavalry, who possessed a marvelously sweet tenor voice, and well developed musical powers. While we were at Wilmington he sang "When Sherman Marched Down to the Sea," to an audience of soldiers that packed the Opera House densely.

The enthusiasm he aroused was simply indescribable; men shouted, and the tears ran down their faces. He was recalled time and again, each time with an increase in the furore. The audience would have staid there all night to listen to him sing that one song. Poor fellow, he only went home to die. An attack of pneumonia carried him off within a fortnight after we separated at Annapolis.

The Glee Club had several songs which they rendered in regular negro minstrel style, and in a way that was irresistibly ludicrous. One of their favorites was "Billy Patterson." All standing up in a ring, the tenors would lead off:

"I saw an old man go riding by,"

and the baritones, flinging themselves around with the looseness of Christy's Minstrels, in a "break down," would reply:

"Don't tell me! Don't tell me!"

Then the tenors would resume:

"Says I, Ole man, your horse'll die."

Then the baritones, with an air of exaggerated interest;

"A-ha-a-a, Billy Patterson!"

Tenors:

"For. It he dies, I'll tan his skin;
An' if he lives I'll ride him agin,"

All-together, with a furious "break down" at the close:

"Then I'll lay five dollars down,
And count them one by one;
Then I'll lay five dollars down,
If anybody will show me the man
That struck Billy Patterson."

And so on. It used to upset my gravity entirely to see a crowd of grave and dignified Captains, Majors and Colonels going through this nonsensical drollery with all the abandon of professional burnt-cork artists.

As we were nearing the entrance to Chesapeake Bay we passed a great monitor, who was exercising her crew at the guns. She fired directly across our course, the huge four hundred pound balls shipping along the water, about a mile ahead of us, as we boys used to make the flat stones skip in the play of "Ducks and Drakes." One or two of the shots came so. close that I feared she might be mistaking us for a Rebel ship intent on some raid up the Bay, and I looked up anxiously to see that the flag should float out so conspicuously that she could not help seeing it.

The next day our vessel ran alongside of the dock at the Naval Academy at Annapolis, that institution now being used as a hospital for paroled prisoners. The musicians of the Post band came down with stretchers to carry the sick to the Hospital, while those of us who were able to walk were ordered to fall in and march up. The distance was but a few hundred yards. On reaching the building we marched up on a little balcony, and as we did so each one of us was seized by a hospital attendant, who, with the quick dexterity attained by long practice, snatched every one of our filthy, lousy rags off in the twinkling of an eye, and flung them over the railing to the ground, where a man loaded them into a wagon with a pitchfork.

With them went our faithful little black can, our hoop-iron spoon, and our chessboard and men. Thus entirely denuded, each boy was given a shove which sent him into a little room, where a barber pressed him down upon a stool, and almost before he understood what was being done, had his hair and beard cut off as close as shears would do it. Another tap on the back sent the shorn lamb into a room furnished with great tubs of water and with about six inches of soap suds on the zinc-covered floor.

In another minute two men with sponges had removed every trace of prison grime from his body, and passed him on to two more men, who wiped him dry, and moved him on to where a man handed him a new shirt, a pair of drawers, pair of socks, pair of pantaloons, pair of slippers, and a hospital gown, and motioned him to go on into the large room, and array himself in his new garments. Like everything else about the Hospital this performance was reduced to a perfect system. Not a word was spoken by anybody, not a moment's time lost, and it seemed to me that it was not ten minutes after I marched up on the balcony, covered with dirt, rags, vermin, and a matted shock of hair, until I marched out of the room, clean and well clothed. Now I began to feel as if I was really a man again.

The next thing done was to register our names, rank, regiment, when and where captured, when and where released. After this we were shown to our rooms. And such rooms as they were. All the old maids in the country could not have improved their spick-span neatness. The floors were as white as pine plank could be scoured; the sheets and bedding as clean as cotton and linen and woolen could be washed. Nothing in any home in the land was any more daintily, wholesomely, unqualifiedly clean than were these little chambers, each containing two beds, one for each man assigned to their occupancy.

Andrews doubted if we could stand all this radical change in our habits. He feared that it was rushing things too fast. We might have had our hair cut one week, and taken a bath all over a week later, and so progress down to sleeping between white sheets in the course of six months, but to do it all in one day seemed like tempting fate.

Every turn showed us some new feature of the marvelous order of this wonderful institution. Shortly after we were sent to our rooms, a Surgeon entered with a Clerk. After answering the usual questions as to name, rank, company and regiment, the Surgeon examined our tongues, eyes, limbs and general appearance, and communicated his conclusions to the Clerk, who filled out a blank card. This card was stuck into a little tin holder at the head of my bed. Andrews's card was the same, except the name. The Surgeon was followed by a Sergeant, who was Chief of the Dining-Room, and the Clerk, who made a minute of the diet ordered for us, and moved off. Andrews and I immediately became very solicitous to know what species of diet No. 1 was. After the seasickness left us our appetites became as ravenous as a buzz-saw, and unless Diet No. 1 was more than No. 1 in name, it would not fill the bill. We had not long to remain in suspense, for soon another non-commissioned officer passed through at the head of a train of attendants, bearing trays. Consulting the list in his hand, he said to one of his followers, "Two No. 1's," and that satellite set down two large plates, upon each of which were a cup of coffee, a shred of meat, two boiled eggs and a couple of rolls.

"Well," said Andrews, as the procession moved away, "I want to know where this thing's going to stop. I am trying hard to get used to wearing a shirt without any lice in it, and to sitting down on a chair, and to sleeping in a clean bed, but when it comes to having my meals sent to my room, I'm afraid I'll degenerate into a pampered child of luxury. They are really piling it on too strong. Let us see, Mc.; how long's it been since we were sitting on the sand there in Florence, boiling our pint of meal in that old can?"

"It seems many years, Lale," I said; "but for heaven's sake let us try to forget it as soon as possible. We will always remember too much of it."

And we did try hard to make the miserable recollections fade out of our minds. When we were stripped on the balcony we threw away every visible token that could remind us of the hateful experience we had passed through. We did not retain a scrap of paper or a relic to recall the unhappy past. We loathed everything connected with it.

The days that followed were very happy ones. The Paymaster came around and paid us each two months' pay and twenty-five cents a day "ration money" for every day we had been in prison. This gave Andrews and I about one hundred and sixty-five dollars apiece—an abundance of spending money. Uncle Sam was very kind and considerate to his soldier nephews, and the Hospital authorities neglected nothing that would add to our comfort. The superbly-kept grounds of the Naval Academy were renewing the freshness of their loveliness under the tender wooing of the advancing Spring, and every step one sauntered through them was a new delight. A magnificent band gave us sweet music morning and evening. Every dispatch from the South told of the victorious progress of our arms, and the rapid approach of the close of the struggle. All we had to do was to enjoy the goods the gods were showering upon us, and we did so with appreciative, thankful hearts. After awhile all able to travel were given furloughs of thirty days to visit their homes, with instructions to report at the expiration of their leaves of absence to the camps of rendezvous nearest their homes, and we separated, nearly every man going in a different direction.

[CHAPTER LXXXI. Written by a Rev. Sheppard and omitted in this edition.]

CHAPTER LXXXII.

CAPTAIN WIRZ THE ONLY ONE OF THE PRISON-KEEPERS PUNISHED—HIS ARREST, TRIAL AND EXECUTION.

Of all those more or less concerned in the barbarities practiced upon our prisoners, but one—Captain Henry Wirz—was punished. The Turners, at Richmond; Lieutenant Boisseux, of Belle Isle; Major Gee, of Salisbury; Colonel Iverson and Lieutenant Barrett, of Florence; and the many brutal miscreants about Andersonville, escaped scot free. What became of them no one knows; they were never heard of after the close of the war. They had sense enough to retire into obscurity, and stay there, and this saved their lives, for each one of them had made deadly enemies among those whom they had maltreated, who, had they known where they were, would have walked every step of the way thither to kill them.

When the Confederacy went to pieces in April, 1865, Wirz was still at Andersonville. General Wilson, commanding our cavalry forces, and who had established his headquarters at Macon, Ga., learned of this, and sent one of his staff—Captain H. E. Noyes, of the Fourth Regular Cavalry —with a squad. of men, to arrest him. This was done on the 7th of May. Wirz protested against his arrest, claiming that he was protected by the terms of Johnson's surrender, and, addressed the following letter to General Wilson:

ANDERSONVILLE, GA., May 7, 1865.

GENERAL:—It is with great reluctance that I address you these lines, being fully aware how little time is left you to attend to such matters as I now have the honor to lay before you, and if I could see any other way to accomplish my object I would not intrude upon you. I am a native of Switzerland, and was before the war a citizen of Louisiana, and by profession a physician. Like hundreds and thousands of others, I was carried away by the maelstrom of excitement and joined the Southern army. I was very severely wounded at the battle of "Seven Pines," near Richmond, Va., and have nearly lost the use of my right arm. Unfit for field duty, I was ordered to report to Brevet Major General John H. Winder, in charge of the Federal prisoners of war, who ordered me to take charge of a prison in Tuscaloosa, Ala. My health failing me, I applied for a furlough and went to Europe, from whence I returned in February, 1864. I was then ordered to report to the commandant of the military prison at Andersonville, Ga., who assigned me to the command of the interior of the prison. The duties I had to perform were arduous and unpleasant, and I am satisfied that no man can or will justly blame me for things that happened here, and which were beyond my power to control. I do not think that I ought to be held responsible for the shortness of rations, for the overcrowded state of the prison, (which was of itself a prolific source of fearful mortality), for the inadequate supply of clothing, want of shelter, etc., etc. Still I now bear the odium, and men who were prisoners have seemed disposed to wreak their vengeance upon me for what they have suffered—I, who was only the medium, or, I may better say, the tool in the hands of my superiors. This is my condition. I am a man with a family. I lost all my property when the Federal army besieged Vicksburg. I have no money at present to go to any place, and, even if I had, I know of no place where I can go. My life is in danger, and I most respectfully ask of you help and relief. If you will be so generous as to give me some sort of a safe conduct, or, what I should greatly prefer, a guard to protect myself and family against violence, I should be thankful to you, and you may rest assured that your protection will not be given to one who is unworthy of it. My intention is to return with my family to Europe, as soon as I can make the arrangements. In the meantime I have the honor General, to remain, very respectfully, your obedient servant,

Hy. WIRZ, Captain C. S. A.
Major General T. H. WILSON,
Commanding, Macon. Ga.

He was kept at Macon, under guard, until May 20, when Captain Noyes was ordered to take him, and the hospital records of Andersonville, to Washington. Between Macon and Cincinnati the journey was a perfect gauntlet.

Our men were stationed all along the road, and among them everywhere were ex-prisoners, who recognized Wirz, and made such determined efforts to kill him that it was all that Captain Noyes, backed by a strong guard, could do to frustrate them. At Chattanooga and Nashville the struggle between his guards and his would-be slayers, was quite sharp.

At Louisville, Noyes had Wirz clean-shaved, and dressed in a complete suit of black, with a beaver hat, which so altered his appearance that no one recognized him after that, and the rest of the journey was made unmolested.

The authorities at Washington ordered that he be tried immediately, by a court martial composed of Generals Lewis Wallace, Mott, Geary, L. Thomas, Fessenden, Bragg and Baller, Colonel Allcock, and Lieutenant-Colonel Stibbs. Colonel Chipman was Judge Advocate, and the trial began August 23.

The prisoner was arraigned on a formidable list of charges and specifications, which accused him of "combining, confederating, and conspiring together with John H. Winder, Richard B. Winder, Isaiah II. White, W. S. Winder, R. R. Stevenson and others unknown, to injure the health and destroy the lives of soldiers in the military service of the United States, there held, and being prisoners of war within the lines of the so-called Confederate States, and in the military prisons thereof, to the end that the armies of the United States might be weakened and impaired, in violation of the laws and customs of war." The main facts of the dense over-crowding, the lack of sufficient shelter, the hideous mortality were cited, and to these added a long list of specific acts of brutality, such as hunting men down with hounds, tearing them with dogs, robbing them, confining them in the stocks, cruelly beating and murdering them, of which Wirz was personally guilty.

When the defendant was called upon to plead he claimed that his case was covered by the terms of Johnston's surrender, and furthermore, that the country now being at peace, he could not be lawfully tried by a court-martial. These objections being overruled, he entered a plea of not guilty to all the charges and specifications. He had two lawyers for counsel.

The prosecution called Captain Noyes first, who detailed the circumstances of Wirz's arrest, and denied that he had given any promises of protection.

The next witness was Colonel George C. Gibbs, who commanded the troops of the post at Andersonville. He testified that Wirz was the commandant of the prison, and had sole authority under Winder over all the prisoners; that there was a Dead Line there, and orders to shoot any one who crossed it; that dogs were kept to hunt down escaping prisoners; the dogs were the ordinary plantation dogs, mixture of hound and cur.

Dr. J. C. Bates, who was a Surgeon of the Prison Hospital, (a Rebel), testified that the condition of things in his division was horrible. Nearly naked men, covered with lice, were dying on all sides. Many were lying in the filthy sand and mud.

He went on and described the terrible condition of men—dying from scurvy, diarrhea, gangrenous sores, and lice. He wanted to carry in fresh vegetables for the sick, but did not dare, the orders being very strict against such thing. He thought the prison authorities might easily have sent in enough green corn to have stopped the scurvy; the miasmatic effluvia from the prison was exceedingly offensive and poisonous, so much so that when the surgeons received a slight scratch on their persons, they carefully covered it up with court plaster, before venturing near the prison.

A number of other Rebel Surgeons testified to substantially the same facts. Several residents of that section of the State testified to the plentifulness of the crops there in 1864.

In addition to these, about one hundred and fifty Union prisoners were examined, who testified to all manner of barbarities which had come under their personal observation. They had all seen Wirz shoot men, had seen him knock sick and crippled men down and stamp upon them, had been run down by him with hounds, etc. Their testimony occupies about two thousand pages of manuscript, and is, without doubt, the most, terrible record of crime ever laid to the account of any man.

The taking of this testimony occupied until October 18, when the Government decided to close the case, as any further evidence would be simply cumulative.

The prisoner presented a statement in which he denied that there had been an accomplice in a conspiracy of John H. Winder and others, to destroy the lives of United States soldiers; he also denied that there had been such a conspiracy, but made the pertinent inquiry why he alone, of all those who were charged with the conspiracy, was brought to trial. He said that Winder has gone to the great judgment seat, to answer for all his thoughts, words and deeds, "and surely I am not to be held culpable for them. General Howell Cobb has received the pardon of the President of the United States." He further claimed that there was no principle of law which would sanction the holding of him—a mere subordinate —guilty, for simply obeying, as literally as possible, the orders of his superiors.

He denied all the specific acts of cruelty alleged against him, such as maltreating and killing prisoners with his own hands. The prisoners killed for crossing the Dead Line, he claimed, should not be charged against him, since they were simply punished for the violation of a known order which formed part of the discipline, he believed, of all military prisons. The statement that soldiers were given a furlough for killing a Yankee prisoner, was declared to be "a mere idle, absurd camp rumor." As to the lack of shelter, room and rations for so many prisoners, he claimed that the sole responsibility rested upon the Confederate Government. There never were but two prisoners whipped by his order, and these were for sufficient cause. He asked the Court to consider favorably two important items in his defense: first, that he had of his own accord taken the drummer boys from the Stockade, and placed them where they could get purer air and better food. Second, that no property taken from prisoners was retained by him, but was turned over to the Prison Quartermaster.

The Court, after due deliberation, declared the prisoner guilty on all the charges and specifications save two unimportant ones, and sentenced him to be hanged by the neck until dead, at such time and place as the President of the United States should direct.

November 3 President Johnson approved of the sentence, and ordered Major General C. C. Augur to carry the same into effect on Friday, November 10, which was done. The prisoner made frantic appeals against the sentence; he wrote imploring letters to President Johnson, and lying ones to the New York News, a Rebel paper. It is said that his wife attempted to convey poison to him, that he might commit suicide and avoid the ignomy of being hanged. When all hope was gone he nerved himself up to meet his fate, and died, as thousands of other scoundrels have, with calmness. His body was buried in the grounds of the Old Capitol Prison, alongside of that of Azterodt, one of the accomplices in the assassination of President Lincoln.

CHAPTER LXXXIII.

THE RESPONSIBILITY—WHO WAS TO BLAME FOR ALL THE MISERY—AN EXAMINATION OF THE FLIMSY EXCUSES MADE FOR THE REBELS—ONE DOCUMENT THAT CONVICTS THEM—WHAT IS DESIRED.

I have endeavored to tell the foregoing story as calmly, as dispassionately, as free from vituperation and prejudice as possible. How well I have succeeded the reader must judge. How difficult this moderation has been at times only those know who, like myself, have seen, from day to day, the treason-sharpened fangs of Starvation and Disease gnaw nearer and nearer to the hearts of well-beloved friends and comrades. Of the sixty-three of my company comrades who entered prison with me, but eleven, or at most thirteen, emerged alive, and several of these have since died from the effects of what they suffered. The mortality in the other companies of our battalion was equally great, as it was also with the prisoners generally. Not less than twenty-five thousand gallant, noble-hearted boys died around me between the dates of my capture and release. Nobler men than they never died for any cause. For the most part they were simple-minded, honest-hearted boys; the sterling products of our Northern home-life, and Northern Common Schools, and that grand stalwart Northern blood, the yeoman blood of sturdy middle class freemen—the blood of the race which has conquered on every field since the Roman Empire went down under its sinewy blows. They prated little of honor, and knew nothing of "chivalry" except in its repulsive travesty in the South. As citizens at home, no honest labor had been regarded by them as too humble to be followed with manly pride in its success; as soldiers in the field, they did their duty with a calm defiance of danger and death, that the world has not seen equaled in the six thousand years that men have followed the trade of war. In the prison their conduct was marked by the same unostentatious but unflinching heroism. Death stared them in the face constantly. They could read their own fate in that of the loathsome, unburied dead all around them. Insolent enemies mocked their sufferings, and sneered at their devotion to a Government which they asserted had abandoned them, but the simple faith, the ingrained honesty of these plain-mannered, plain-spoken boys rose superior to every trial. Brutus, the noblest Roman of them all, says in his grandest flight:

> Set honor in one eye and death in the other,
> And I will look on both indifferently.

They did not say this: they did it. They never questioned their duty; no repinings, no murmurings against their Government escaped their lips, they took the dread fortunes brought to them as calmly, as unshrinkingly as they had those in the field; they quailed not, nor wavered in their faith before the worst the Rebels could do. The finest epitaph ever inscribed above a soldier's grave was that graven on the stone which marked the resting-place of the deathless three hundred who fell at Thermopylae:

> Go, stranger, to Lacedaemon,—
> And tell Sparta that we lie here in obedience to her laws.

They who lie in the shallow graves of Andersonville, Belle Isle, Florence and Salisbury, lie there in obedience to the precepts and maxims inculcated into their minds in the churches and Common Schools of the North; precepts which impressed upon them the duty of manliness and honor in all the relations and exigencies of life; not the "chivalric" prate of their enemies, but the calm steadfastness which endureth to the end. The highest tribute that can be paid them is to say they did full credit to their teachings, and they died as every American should when duty bids him. No richer heritage was ever bequeathed to posterity.

It was in the year 1864, and the first three months of 1865 that these twenty-five thousand youths mere cruelly and needlessly done to death. In these fatal fifteen months more young men than to-day form the pride, the hope, and the vigor of any one of our leading Cities, more than at the beginning of the war were found in either of several States in the Nation, were sent to their graves, "unknelled, uncoffined, and unknown," victims of the most barbarous and unnecessary cruelty recorded since the Dark Ages. Barbarous, because the wit of man has not yet devised a more savage method of destroying fellow-beings than by exposure and starvation; unnecessary, because the destruction of these had not, and could not have the slightest effect upon the result of the struggle. The Rebel leaders have acknowledged that they knew the fate of the Confederacy was sealed when the campaign of 1864 opened with the North displaying an unflinching determination to prosecute the war to a successful conclusion. All that they could hope for after that was some fortuitous accident, or unexpected foreign recognition that would give them peace with victory. The prisoners were non-important factors in the military problem. Had they all been turned loose as soon as captured, their efforts would not have hastened the Confederacy's fate a single day.

As to the responsibility for this monstrous cataclysm of human misery and death: That the great mass of the Southern people approved of these outrages, or even knew of them, I do not, for an instant, believe. They are as little capable of countenancing such a thing as any people in the world. But the crowning blemish of Southern society has ever been the dumb acquiescence of the many respectable, well-disposed, right-thinking people in the acts of the turbulent and unscrupulous few. From this direful spring has flowed an Iliad of unnumbered woes, not only to that section but to our common country. It was this that kept the South vibrating between patriotism and treason during the revolution, so that it cost more lives and treasure to maintain the struggle there than in all the rest of the country. It was this that threatened the dismemberment of the Union in 1832. It was this that aggravated and envenomed every wrong growing out of Slavery; that outraged liberty, debauched citizenship, plundered the mails, gagged the press, stiffled speech, made opinion a crime, polluted the free soil of God with the unwilling step of the bondman, and at last crowned three-quarters of a century of this unparalleled iniquity by dragging eleven millions of people into a war from which their souls revolted, and against which they had declared by overwhelming majorities in every State except South Carolina, where the people had no voice. It may puzzle some to understand how a relatively small band of political desperados in each State could accomplish such a momentous wrong; that they did do it, no one conversant with our history will deny, and that they— insignificant as they were in numbers, in abilities, in character, in everything save capacity and indomitable energy in mischief—could achieve such gigantic wrongs in direct opposition to the better sense of their communities is a fearful demonstration of the defects of the constitution of Southern society.

Men capable of doing all that the Secession leaders were guilty of—both before and during the war—were quite capable of revengefully destroying twenty-five thousand of their enemies by the most hideous means at their command. That they did so set about destroying their enemies, wilfully, maliciously, and with malice prepense and aforethought, is susceptible of proof as conclusive as that which in a criminal court sends murderers to the gallows.

Let us examine some of these proofs:

1. The terrible mortality at Andersonville and elsewhere was a matter of as much notoriety throughout the Southern Confederacy as the military operations of Lee and Johnson. No intelligent man—much less the Rebel leaders—was ignorant of it nor of its calamitous proportions.

2. Had the Rebel leaders within a reasonable time after this matter became notorious made some show of inquiring into and alleviating the deadly misery, there might be some excuse for them on the ground of lack of information, and the plea that they did as well as they could would have some validity. But this state of affairs was allowed to continue over a year—in fact until the downfall of the Confederacy—without a hand being raised to mitigate the horrors of those places—without even an inquiry being made as to whether they were mitigable or not. Still worse: every month saw the horrors thicken, and the condition of the prisoners become more wretched.

The suffering in May, 1864, was more terrible than in April; June showed a frightful increase over May, while words fail to paint the horrors of July and August, and so the wretchedness waxed until the end, in April, 1865.

3. The main causes of suffering and death were so obviously preventible that the Rebel leaders could not have been ignorant of the ease with which a remedy could be applied. These main causes were three in number:

    a. Improper and insufficient food.
    b. Unheard-of crowding together.
    c. Utter lack of shelter.

It is difficult to say which of these three was the most deadly. Let us admit, for the sake of argument, that it was impossible for the Rebels to supply sufficient and proper food. This admission, I know, will not stand for an instant in the face of the revelations made by Sherman's

March to the Sea; and through the Carolinas, but let that pass, that we may consider more easily demonstrable facts connected with the next two propositions, the first of which is as to the crowding together. Was land so scarce in the Southern Confederacy that no more than sixteen acres could be spared for the use of thirty-five thousand prisoners? The State of Georgia has a population of less than one-sixth that of New York, scattered over a territory one-quarter greater than that State's, and yet a pitiful little tract—less than the corn-patch "clearing" of the laziest "cracker" in the State—was all that could be allotted to the use of three-and-a-half times ten thousand young men! The average population of the State does not exceed sixteen to the square mile, yet Andersonville was peopled at the rate of one million four hundred thousand to the square mile. With millions of acres of unsettled, useless, worthless pine barrens all around them, the prisoners were wedged together so closely that there was scarcely room to lie down at night, and a few had space enough to have served as a grave. This, too, in a country where the land was of so little worth that much of it had never been entered from the Government.

Then, as to shelter and fire: Each of the prisons was situated in the heart of a primeval forest, from which the first trees that had ever been cut were those used in building the pens. Within a gun-shot of the perishing men was an abundance of lumber and wood to have built every man in prison a warm, comfortable hut, and enough fuel to supply all his wants. Supposing even, that the Rebels did not have the labor at hand to convert these forests into building material and fuel, the prisoners themselves would have gladly undertaken the work, as a means of promoting their own comfort, and for occupation and exercise. No tools would have been too poor and clumsy for them to work with. When logs were occasionally found or brought into prison, men tore them to pieces almost with their naked fingers. Every prisoner will bear me out in the assertion that there was probably not a root as large as a bit of clothes-line in all the ground covered by the prisons, that eluded the faithfully eager search of freezing men for fuel. What else than deliberate design can account for this systematic withholding from the prisoners of that which was so essential to their existence, and which it was so easy to give them?

This much for the circumstantial evidence connecting the Rebel authorities with the premeditated plan for destroying the prisoners. Let us examine the direct evidence:

The first feature is the assignment to the command of the prisons of "General" John H. Winder, the confidential friend of Mr. Jefferson Davis, and a man so unscrupulous, cruel and bloody-thirsty that at the time of his appointment he was the most hated and feared man in the Southern Confederacy. His odious administration of the odious office of Provost Marshal General showed him to be fittest of tools for their purpose. Their selection—considering the end in view, was eminently wise. Baron Haynau was made eternally infamous by a fraction of the wanton cruelties which load the memory of Winder. But it can be said in extenuation of Haynau's offenses that he was a brave, skilful and energetic soldier, who overthrew on the field the enemies he maltreated. If Winder, at any time during the war, was nearer the front than Richmond, history does not mention it. Haynau was the bastard son of a German Elector and of the daughter of a village, druggist. Winder was the son of a sham aristocrat, whose cowardice and incompetence in the war of 1812 gave Washington into the hands of the British ravagers. It is sufficient indication of this man's character that he could look unmoved upon the terrible suffering that prevailed in Andersonville in June, July, and August; that he could see three thousand men die each month in the most horrible manner, without lifting a finger in any way to assist them; that he could call attention in a self-boastful way to the fact that "I am killing off more Yankees than twenty regiments in Lee's Army," and that he could respond to the suggestions of the horror-struck visiting Inspector that the prisoners be given at least more room, with the assertion that he intended to leave matters just as they were—the operations of death would soon thin out the crowd so that the survivors would have sufficient room.

It was Winder who issued this order to the Commander of the Artillery:

ORDER No. 13.

    HEADQUARTERS MILITARY PRISON,
    ANDERSONVILLE, Ga., July 27, 1864.

The officers on duty and in charge of the Battery of Florida Artillery at the time will, upon receiving notice that the enemy has approached within seven miles of this post, open upon the Stockade with grapeshot, without reference to the situation beyond these lines of defense.

    JOHN H. WINDER,
    Brigadier General Commanding.

Diabolical is the only word that will come at all near fitly characterizing such an infamous order. What must have been the nature of a man who would calmly order twenty-five guns to be opened with grape and canister at two hundred yards range, upon a mass of thirty thousand prisoners, mostly sick and dying! All this, rather than suffer them to be rescued by their friends. Can there be any terms of reprobation sufficiently strong to properly denounce so malignant a monster? History has no parallel to him, save among the blood-reveling kings of Dahomey, or those sanguinary Asiatic chieftains who built pyramids of human skulls, and paved roads with men's bones. How a man bred an American came to display such a Timour-like thirst for human life, such an Oriental contempt for the sufferings of others, is one of the mysteries that perplexes me the more I study it.

If the Rebel leaders who appointed this man, to whom he reported direct, without intervention of superior officers, and who were fully informed of all his acts through other sources than himself, were not responsible for him, who in Heaven's name was? How can there be a possibility that they were not cognizant and approving of his acts?

The Rebels have attempted but one defense to the terrible charges against them, and that is, that our Government persistently refused to exchange, preferring to let its men rot in prison, to yielding up the Rebels it held. This is so utterly false as to be absurd. Our Government made overture after overture for exchange to the Rebels, and offered to yield many of the points of difference. But it could not, with the least consideration for its own honor, yield up the negro soldiers and their officers to the unrestrained brutality of the Rebel authorities, nor could it, consistent with military prudence, parole the one hundred thousand well-fed, well-clothed, able-bodied Rebels held by it as prisoners, and let them appear inside of a week in front of Grant or Sherman. Until it would agree to do this the Rebels would not agree to exchange, and the only motive—save revenge—which could have inspired the Rebel maltreatment of the prisoners, was the expectation of raising such a clamor in the North as would force the Government to consent to a disadvantageous exchange, and to give back to the Confederacy, at its most critical period one hundred thousand fresh, able-bodied soldiers. It was for this purpose, probably, that our Government and the Sanitary Commission were refused all permission to send us food and clothing. For my part, and I know I echo the feelings of ninety-nine out of every hundred of my comrades, I would rather have staid in prison till I rotted, than that our Government should have yielded to the degrading demands of insolent Rebels.

There is one document in the possession of the Government which seems to me to be unanswerable proof, both of the settled policy of the Richmond Government towards the Union prisoners, and of the relative merits of Northern and Southern treatment of captives. The document is a letter reading as follows:

CITY POINT, Va., March 17, 1863.

SIR:—A flag-of-truce boat has arrived with three hundred and fifty political prisoners, General Barrow and several other prominent men among them.

I wish you to send me on four o'clock Wednesday morning, all the military prisoners (except officers), and all the political prisoners you have. If any of the political prisoners have on hand proof enough to convict them of being spies, or of having committed other offenses which should subject them to punishment, so state opposite their names. Also, state whether you think, under all the circumstances, they should be released. The arrangement I have made works largely in our favor. WE GET RID OF A SET OF MISERABLE WRETCHES, AND RECEIVE SOME OF THE BEST MATERIAL I EVER SAW.

Tell Captain Turner to put down on the list of political prisoners the names of Edward P. Eggling, and Eugenia Hammermister. The President is anxious that they should get off. They are here now. This, of course, is between ourselves. If you have any political prisoners whom you can send off safely to keep her company, I would like you to send her.

Two hundred and odd more political prisoners are on their way.

I would be more full in my communication if I had time. Yours truly,

ROBERT OULD, Commissioner of Exchange.

To Brigadier general John H. Winder.

But, supposing that our Government, for good military reasons, or for no reason at all, declined to exchange prisoners, what possible excuse is that for slaughtering them by exquisite tortures? Every Government has ap unquestioned right to decline exchanging when its military policy suggests such a course; and such declination conveys no right whatever to the enemy to slay those prisoners, either outright with the edge of the sword, or more slowly by inhuman treatment. The Rebels' attempts to justify their conduct, by the claim that our Government refused to accede to their wishes in a certain respect, is too preposterous to be made or listened to by intelligent men.

The whole affair is simply inexcusable, and stands out a foul blot on the memory of every Rebel in high place in the Confederate Government.

"Vengeance is mine," saith the Lord, and by Him must this great crime be avenged, if it ever is avenged. It certainly transcends all human power. I have seen little indication of any Divine interposition to mete out, at least on this earth, adequate punishment to those who were the principal agents in that iniquity. Howell Cobb died as peacefully in his bed as any Christian in the land, and with as few apparent twinges of remorse as if he had spent his life in good deeds and prayer. The arch-fiend Winder died in equal tranquility, murmuring some cheerful hope as to his soul's future. Not one of the ghosts of his hunger-slain hovered around to embitter his dying moments, as he had theirs. Jefferson Davis "still lives, a prosperous gentleman," the idol of a large circle of adherents, the recipient of real estate favors from elderly females of morbid sympathies, and a man whose mouth is full of plaints of his wrongs, and misappreciation. The rest of the leading conspirators have either departed this life in the odor of sanctity, surrounded by sorrowing friends, or are gliding serenely down the mellow autumnal vale of a benign old age.

Only Wirz—small, insignificant, miserable Wirz, the underling, the tool, the servile, brainless, little fetcher-and-carrier of these men, was punished—was hanged, and upon the narrow shoulders of this pitiful scapegoat was packed the entire sin of Jefferson Davis and his crew. What a farce!

A petty little Captain made to expiate the crimes of Generals, Cabinet Officers, and a President. How absurd!

But I do not ask for vengeance. I do not ask for retribution for one of those thousands of dead comrades, the glitter of whose sightless eyes will follow me through life. I do not desire even justice on the still living authors and accomplices in the deep damnation of their taking off. I simply ask that the great sacrifices of my dead comrades shall not be suffered to pass unregarded to irrevocable oblivion; that the example of their heroic self-abnegation shall not be lost, but the lesson it teaches be preserved and inculcated into the minds of their fellow-countrymen, that future generations may profit by it, and others be as ready to die for right and honor and good government as they were. And it seems to me that if we are to appreciate their virtues, we must loathe and hold up to opprobrium those evil men whose malignity made all their sacrifices necessary. I cannot understand what good self-sacrifice and heroic example are to serve in this world, if they are to be followed by such a maudlin confusion of ideas as now threatens to obliterate all distinction between the men who fought and died for the Right and those who resisted them for the Wrong.